OXFORD MEDIEVAL TEXTS

General Editors

D. E. GREENWAY   B. F. HARVEY

M. LAPIDGE

THREE ELEVENTH-CENTURY ANGLO-LATIN SAINTS' LIVES

THREE ELEVENTH-CENTURY ANGLO-LATIN SAINTS' LIVES

Vita S. Birini,
Vita et miracula S. Kenelmi and
Vita S. Rumwoldi

EDITED AND TRANSLATED BY

ROSALIND C. LOVE

CLARENDON PRESS · OXFORD
1996

Oxford University Press, Walton Street, Oxford OX2 6DP

Oxford New York
Athens Auckland Bangkok Bombay
Calcutta Cape Town Dar es Salaam Delhi
Florence Hong Kong Istanbul Karachi
Kuala Lumpur Madras Madrid Melbourne
Mexico City Nairobi Paris Singapore
Taipei Tokyo Toronto
and associated companies in
Berlin Ibadan

Oxford is trade mark of Oxford University Press

Published in the United States
by Oxford University Press Inc., New York

British Library Cataloguing in Publication Data
Data available

Library of Congress Cataloging in Publication Data
Data applied for
ISBN 0-19-820524-4

1 3 5 7 9 10 8 6 4 2

Typeset by Joshua Associates Ltd, Oxford
Printed in Great Britain
on acid-free paper by
Biddles Ltd, Guildford and King's Lynn

PREFACE

THIS book began as a dissertation submitted for the degree of Doctor of Philosophy at Cambridge in January 1993. Since then, with the help of a year's position as Borsista at the Fondazione Ezio Franceschini in Florence, and now a British Academy Post-doctoral Research Fellowship and a Research Fellowship at Robinson College, Cambridge, I have been able to chew over the material again, revise some of my earlier opinions, and make many corrections and additions. In this I have been helped very much by the comments and criticisms of the examiners of my dissertation, Dr Diana Greenway and Dr Andy Orchard, to whom I must express my warm thanks. Without my research supervisor, Michael Lapidge, under whose aegis I first became acquainted with Anglo-Latin and with hagiography, I should never have been able to embark upon this project, let alone manage to bring it to this point. It is to him, for unfailing support and generosity, and martyr-like fortitude in the face of my endless vacillations, that I owe my greatest debt of gratitude.

In the preface to the aforementioned dissertation, there was a substantial list of persons to whom I expressed thanks which I should like here to recapitulate: to the many libraries which have permitted me to consult the manuscripts upon which the present editions are based, to Neil Wright for inspecting my Latin texts and pointing out some sources which I had overlooked, to Christopher Hohler for an epistolary shower of interesting suggestions concerning St Rumwold, to Paul Hayward for supplying me with a copy of his MA dissertation on the cult of St Kenelm, and for many hours of stimulating debate about saints, and to David Dumville and Patrick Sims-Williams for help and advice on several occasions. In addition to them, I should now like to thank Alicia Corrêa for furnishing me with information about liturgical documents in Sweden, and Philip Hall for helping me to curb the worst vices of my Anglicity. The technological side to the production of the typescript for this book has been made considerably less painful than it might have been by the generous assistance of Philip Jones, and

I am indebted to him. Graeme, and many kind friends in Cambridge, have long indulged and sustained me with the very patience of the saints themselves, for which I shall remain ever grateful. Last to be mentioned, but first in my thoughts of thankfulness, are my parents, Pamela and John Love, to whom this book is affectionately dedicated.

R.C.L.

June, 1994

CONTENTS

4. ST RUMWOLD OF BUCKINGHAM AND *VITA SANCTI RVMWOLDI*

ABBREVIATIONS

ActaS	[Bollandists] *Acta sanctorum* (Brussels, 1643–)
AB	*Analecta Bollandiana*
AH	*Analecta Hymnica Medii Aevi*, ed. G. M. Dreves and C. Blume, 55 vols. (Leipzig, 1886–1922)
ASC	*The Anglo-Saxon Chronicle*
ASE	*Anglo-Saxon England*
BCS	*Cartularium Saxonicum*, ed. W. de G. Birch, 3 vols. and index (London, 1885–99)
Bede, *HE*	*Bede's Ecclesiastical History of the English People*, ed. B. Colgrave and R. A. B. Mynors, OMT (Oxford, 1969)
BHL	[Bollandists], *Bibliotheca Hagiographica Latina, antiquae et mediae aetatis*, 2 vols. (Brussels, 1899–1901), with supplement by H. Fros (1986)
BL	British Library
BofE	The Buildings of England, general ed. N. Pevsner (Harmondsworth)
BN	Bibliothèque Nationale (Paris)
CCCC	Cambridge, Corpus Christi College
CCCM	*Corpus Christianorum Continuatio Medievalis* (Turnhout)
CCSL	*Corpus Christianorum Series Latina* (Turnhout)
CSEL	*Corpus Scriptorum Ecclesiasticorum Latinorum* (Vienna)
DACL	*Dictionnaire d'archéologie chrétienne et de liturgie*, ed. F. Cabrol and H. Leclercq, 15 vols. in 30 (Paris, 1907–53)
DB	*The Domesday Book*, general ed. J. Morris, 34 vols. in 40 parts (Chichester, 1974–86)
DMLBS	*Dictionary of Medieval Latin from British Sources*, ed. R. E. Latham and D. R. Howlett (London, 1975–)
EETS	Early English Text Society (London)
os	Original Series
ss	Supplementary Series
EHD	*English Historical Documents, I: c.500–1042*, ed. D. Whitelock, 2nd edn. (London, 1979)

EPNS	English Place-Name Society (Cambridge)
Gneuss, 'List'	H. Gneuss, 'A preliminary list of manuscripts written or owned in England up to 1100', *ASE* ix (1981), 1–60
Hardy, *Catalogue*	T. D. Hardy, *Descriptive Catalogue of Materials Relating to the History of Great Britain and Ireland*, 3 vols. in 4, RS xxvi (1862–71)
HBC	*A Handbook of British Chronology*, ed. E. B. Fryde, D. E. Greenway, S. Porter, and I. Roy, Royal Historical Society, 3rd edn. (London, 1986)
HBS	Henry Bradshaw Society Publications (London)
Heads	*The Heads of Religious Houses, England and Wales, 940–1216*, ed. D. Knowles, C. N. L. Brooke, and V. C. M. London (Cambridge, 1972)
Latham, *Word-List*	R. E. Latham, *Revised Medieval Latin Word-List from British and Irish Sources* (Oxford, 1965)
MGH	*Monumenta Germaniae Historica*
AA	Auctores antiquissimi
SRM	Scriptores rerum Merovingicarum
NLA	*Nova Legenda Angliae*, ed. C. Horstman, 2 vols. (Oxford, 1901)
NMT	Nelson's Medieval Texts (London)
OLD	*Oxford Latin Dictionary* (Oxford, 1968–82)
OMT	Oxford Medieval Texts (Oxford)
PL	*Patrologia Latina*, ed. J.-P. Migne, 221 vols. (Paris, 1844–64)
Raine, *HCY*	*The Historians of the Church of York and its Archbishops*, ed. J. Raine, 3 vols., RS lxxi (1879–94)
RS	Rolls Series (London)
S	P. H. Sawyer, *Anglo-Saxon Charters. An Annotated List and Bibliography* (London, 1968)
SC	*A Summary Catalogue of Western Manuscripts in the Bodleian Library at Oxford*, 7 vols. (Oxford, 1895–1953)
TLL	*Thesaurus Linguae Latinae* (Leipzig, 1900–)
UL	University Library
VCH	*Victoria History of the Counties of England*, general ed. W. Page

1. ELEVENTH-CENTURY ANGLO-LATIN HAGIOGRAPHY AND THE RISE OF THE LEGENDARY

(i) *Introduction*

THE cult of the saints was a fundamental aspect of the religion of the Middle Ages; saints' relics were significant in some way to members of every class in society, and objects of intense and universal veneration. Consequently, hagiography, the written expression of that veneration, was among the most common forms of literature in the medieval period—by the fifteenth century literally thousands of texts had been produced. Many Lives survive in countless copies widely dispersed.[1] Certain periods were marked by particularly intensive hagiographical activity, one of which seems to have been the eleventh century, not only in England, but also on the Continent.[2] The many saints' Lives produced in eleventh-century England have hitherto received comparatively little attention as a group, to be studied for their own sake, rather than merely as treacherous repositories of historical data. Several remain as yet unpublished, available only in manuscript and thus relatively inaccessible, while others are to be found in nineteenth-century editions which are inaccurate or incomplete. As a small contribution towards the remedying of this situation, three critical editions, of *Vita S. Birini* (*BHL* 1361), *Vita et miracula S. Kenelmi* (*BHL* 4641n–4641t) and *Vita S. Rumwoldi* (*BHL* 7385) are offered here.[3]

---

[1] The indispensable tool with which such a vast body of material may be controlled is the Bollandists' *Bibliotheca Hagiographica Latina*, 2 vols. (Brussels, 1899–1901) with a *Supplementum* by H. Fros (Brussels, 1986). There, the number of texts cited exceeds 9,000.

[2] For hagiography on the Continent in the 11th cent. see, for example, B. de Gaiffier, 'L'Hagiographie dans le Marquisat de Flandre et le Duché de Basse-Lotharingie au XIe siècle', in *Études critiques d'hagiographie et d'iconologie*, Subsidia Hagiographica, xliii (Brussels, 1967), pp. 415–507; and T. Head, *Hagiography and the Cult of Saints: The Diocese of Orleans, 800–1200*, Cambridge Studies in Medieval Life and Thought, 4th series, xiv (Cambridge, 1990).

[3] When this project was first undertaken, *Vita S. Birini* had never been edited, although subsequently an edition has been published; see below, p. lxxxviii. *Vita S. Rumwoldi* was last printed in *ActaS* in 1887, since which time additional material has

These three texts offer an insight into the geographically wide-spread and diverse nature of the proliferation of hagiography in later eleventh-century England, and the different ways in which the commemoration of a long-dead saint could be approached, in the face of a varying amount of pre-existing documentation. *Vita S. Birini*, an account (over 4,500 words long) of the mission of the apostle of Wessex, was written at Winchester, a prominent administrative, ecclesiastical, and literary centre, as part of a wider hagiographical scheme, which included the Life and posthumous miracles of St Swithun. At the other end of the scale (in more than one respect), *Vita S. Rumwoldi* (about 2,340 words), seemingly produced at, or for, Buckingham church, presses the claim to sanctity of a highly improbable three-day-old saint, who seems to have enjoyed surprisingly wide popularity. In view of how little is known about the practicalities of the rite of Christian initiation in the medieval period, the description of the arrangements for the baptism of the infant saint, and of the hollowed-out stone used as a font, is of especial interest. *Vita S. Kenelmi* was composed, quite possibly by Goscelin of Saint-Bertin, for Winchcombe Abbey, Gloucestershire, to promote the cult of a royal boy-martyr at his supposed place of burial. The text is just one example of a distinct group of saints' Lives written mostly in the eleventh century, each of which describes the murder of a member (or members) of some royal house. The principal claim to sanctity of these royal personages lay precisely in the fact that they had been murdered unjustly.[4]

The intention of this first section is broadly to describe the intellectual context for the composition of the three Lives edited here, but also, first of all, to examine something of the physical context for their dissemination. All three of the texts with which we are concerned are preserved in at least one large collection of saints' Lives, or legendary. Legendaries are substantial manuscript compilations of hagiographical texts which became increasingly popular, and compendious, from the later eleventh century onwards. Their significance lies in the fact that they were the principal vehicles for the transmission of many saints' Lives, both in

come to light. *Vita et miracula S. Kenelmi* has only been edited once before, as part of an unpublished German doctoral dissertation in 1965; see p. cxxxix below.

[4] The group of cults in question has been described by D. W. Rollason, 'The cults of murdered royal saints in Anglo-Saxon England', *ASE* xi (1983), 1–22.

England and on the Continent.[5] These often vast collections of texts have a particular internal group-dynamic, as it were, which needs to be borne in mind when a single text is plucked from their midst. As the surviving examples compiled in England have not been studied extensively, some preliminary observations are offered here.[6]

(ii) *Hagiographical Manuscripts*

It is important to be clear first of all about the variety of ways in which hagiographical texts have been transmitted. From early in the medieval period, Lives seem to have circulated separately,[7] in a codicologically independent unit generally known as a *libellus*.[8] The most celebrated *libellus* is that containing Sulpicius Severus's works on St Martin, often known as the *Martinellus* or *Martinulus*.[9] These originally separate documents seem often to have been subsequently bound together with other smaller groups of texts. Several *libelli* survive from Anglo-Saxon England;[10] one of the earliest examples may be represented by the fragments of Felix's Life of Guthlac, datable to the late eighth or early ninth century, found in London, BL, Royal 4. A. xiv (fos. 107–8), perhaps written at Winchester.[11] It is perhaps permissible to include in this class of document also those copies of saints' Lives which occur together

---

[5] See the detailed study of Continental legendaries by G. Philippart, *Les Légendiers latins et autres manuscrits hagiographiques*, Typologie des sources du moyen âge occidental (Turnhout, 1977), and *Les Légendiers latins: Mise à jour* (Turnhout, 1985); cf. F. Dolbeau, 'Notes sur l'organisation interne des légendiers latins', in *Hagiographie: Cultures et Sociétés, IVe–XIIe siècles* (Paris, 1981), pp. 11–31.

[6] As mentioned at the outset, medieval hagiography is a vast genre, so that what follows can only really be a general survey of the available materials, highlighting the areas which require further, and more detailed, research and analysis.

[7] I am here using 'Lives' as a general term, embracing both *Passiones* (recording the afflictions of the martyrs) and *Vitae* (describing persons who displayed the glory of God rather than in the pattern of their life than in the means of their death).

[8] Early examples of *libelli* are listed by Philippart, *Légendiers*, pp. 99–100. See also Dolbeau, in *Hagiographie*, p. 12.

[9] See W. Levison, 'Conspectus codicum hagiographicorum', *MGH*, SRM vii (Hanover and Leipzig, 1920), pp. 529–706, at 529–30.

[10] See the recent discussion by D. N. Dumville, *Liturgy and the Ecclesiastical History of Late Anglo-Saxon England: Four Studies*, Studies in Anglo-Saxon History, v (Woodbridge, 1992), pp. 108–10; he reckons to have counted about forty examples (p. 140).

[11] E. A. Lowe, *Codices Latini Antiquiores*, 11 vols. and suppl. (Oxford, 1934–71; 2nd edn. of vol. ii, 1972), ii. 216; Gneuss, 'List', no. 456.

with other materials relating to the cult of the saint in question, such as homilies, or even mass-sets.[12]

Evidence indicates that, by the middle of the eighth century, individual Lives (initially perhaps only *passiones*) had also begun to be collected together, at first in relatively small groups, and in no particular order, but later in ever-increasing numbers, and often with the texts arranged in calendrical order according to the feast day of each saint, or occasionally, on the principle of ecclesiastical hierarchy (martyrs, confessors; or bishops, monks, virgins).[13] These collections are known as passionals or legendaries. The earliest extant passional from the Continent is preserved in Munich, Bayerische Staatsbibliothek, clm. 3514 (the 'Codex Velseri'), which contains twenty-four *passiones*, and one *vita* (in no particular order) and was written in the mid-eighth century, possibly at Soissons.[14]

Paris, BN, lat. 10861, written in the early part of the ninth century, quite possibly in Canterbury, may be the earliest surviving passional from Anglo-Saxon England.[15] Like the Codex Velseri, this manuscript contains only a small selection of texts—just eighteen *passiones*, mostly of third- and fourth-century martyrs, and of the two apostles Philip and James the Great. The texts were not organized according to the feast-days of the saints, but according to a roughly hierarchical scheme, by which the two apostles come first, then other males (except Cecilia, the account of whose Life is combined with that of three male martyrs), and finally six female saints. Such an arrangement may indicate that the collection was intended for devotional use rather than for liturgical purposes.

By means of evidence other than that of surviving manuscripts, it may be possible to demonstrate that some form of passional was

---

[12] Examples are a 10th-cent. copy of Bili's *Vita S. Machuti* and a homily for the feast of the same saint, now forming part 2 of London, BL, Royal 13. A. x (see p. clxxv below), and perhaps also a late 11th-cent. group of materials—lections drawn from Bede *HE*, a homily, two mass-sets and, originally, a hymn, relating to the cult of St Birinus, preserved in Oxford, Bodleian Library, Digby 39 (see below, pp. lxvi–lxx). Cf. Dumville, *Liturgy*, p. 110.

[13] This development is described by Philippart, *Légendiers*, pp. 21–5; see also W. Berschin, *Biographie und Epochenstil im lateinischen Mittelalter*, 3 vols. (Stuttgart, 1986– ; in progress), i. 5–7.

[14] Early passionals are listed by Philippart, *Légendiers*, p. 31.

[15] M. P. Brown, 'Paris, Bibliothèque Nationale, lat. 10861 and the Scriptorium of Christ Church, Canterbury', *ASE* xv (1986), 119–37.

available in England even earlier than the ninth century. For example, Aldhelm, when composing his prose and verse *De uirginitate* at some time in the last quarter of the seventh century, or very early in the eighth,[16] apparently had access to the Lives of several virgins.[17] Although only four of the Lives Aldhelm used are found also in Paris, BN, lat. 10861, he may nevertheless have had before him a similar compilation of texts, rather than a very extensive library of *libelli*, which may account for the sometimes surprising choice of virgins referred to in *De uirginitate*.[18]

Likewise, at much the same time, Bede may have been able to use a passional of some sort when compiling his martyrology.[19] He drew on over forty different saints' Lives (almost all martyrs), of which twelve are also found in Paris, BN, lat. 10861. It is interesting to note that one particular text included in that passional, *Passio S. Felicis episcopi Tubzacensis* (*BHL* 2895b), is the only surviving copy of a distinctive interpolated recension, and seems to be the form of that Life which was used by Bede.[20]

Another prominent figure of eighth-century England, Wynfrith/ Boniface, would also evidently have made use of a passional if he had been able to. Among the surviving correspondence of that missionary saint, is a letter from the nun Bugga, in which she referred to one of Boniface's many requests for books:[21] 'Simulque sciat caritas tua, quod passiones martyrum, quas petisti tibi transmitti, adhuc minime potui impetrare. Sed, dum ualeam, faciam.' The 'passiones martyrum' might well have been a particular collection of Lives, similar to Paris, BN, lat. 10861 or the Codex Velseri, known to Boniface. He could have used such a passional before he left England, or had heard of its existence. Unfortunately,

---

[16] The prose *De uirginitate* was edited by R. Ehwald, *MGH*, AA xv (Berlin, 1919), pp. 228–323, Eng. trans. M. Lapidge and M. Herren, *Aldhelm: The Prose Works* (Cambridge, 1979), pp. 59–132. The *Carmen de uirginitate* was edited by Ehwald, op. cit., pp. 350–471, trans. M. Lapidge and J. L. Rosier, *Aldhelm: The Poetic Works* (Cambridge, 1985), pp. 102–67. For a discussion of the difficulty of dating *De uirginitate*, see Lapidge and Herren, *Prose Works*, pp. 14–15.

[17] See Appendix III of Lapidge and Herren, *Prose Works*, pp. 176–8, where the sources for these virgins are listed.

[18] Cf. Lapidge and Herren, *Prose Works*, p. 57.

[19] See H. Quentin, *Les Martyrologes du Moyen Age*, 2nd edn. (Paris, 1908), pp. 16–119. The sources are listed pp. 56–112.

[20] See Brown, 'Paris, BN, lat. 10861', p. 124; and Quentin, *Martyrologes*, p. 74 n. 1, and pp. 526–9.

[21] M. Tangl (ed.), *Die Briefe des Heiligen Bonifatius und Lullus*, *MGH*, Epistolae Selectae i (Berlin, 1916), pp. 26–8, no. 15.

neither the letter of request, nor any record of whether Bugga succeeded in her search, has survived, nor is it possible to detect in Boniface's surviving works any clear indication that he received the material he wanted.

A place where we might find signs that a passional or legendary of some sort was available in England by the ninth century is the Old English Martyrology.[22] The oldest surviving manuscript, now only fragments of the text, is datable to the latter part of the ninth century (part of London, BL, Addit. 23211), and a date during that century is likely for the composition of the text.[23] The compiler, probably working at some Mercian centre, drew partly upon Bede's martyrology, but may also have had in his hands some other Latin martyrology which he translated directly, or even a legendary, from which he took excerpts to translate and include in his work.[24]

From tenth- and early eleventh-century England there are just a few surviving collections of saints' Lives which could be described as legendaries or passionals.[25] One interesting example is a small group of *passiones*, now bound with a *libellus* of Benedict Biscop, in London, BL, Harley 3020, fos. 36–132, apparently written at Canterbury in the early eleventh century.[26] Another is the collection of *passiones* and visions in the first part of the now-fragmentary London, BL, Cotton Otho A. XIII, also datable to the early eleventh century.[27] Evidence is available for the presence in England of other, conceivably more substantial legendaries at about this time. In a study of Ælfric's Old English Lives of the saints,[28] and his *Catholic Homilies*,[29] Patrick Zettel showed that not

---

[22] Ed. G. Kotzor, *Das altenglische Martyrologium*, 2 vols., Bayerische Akademie der Wissenschaften phil.-hist. Klasse, lxxxviii (Munich, 1981).

[23] Ibid. i. 443–54 for the dating and localization.

[24] Cf. Kotzor's discussion of the Old English martyrologist's dependence upon a hagiographical compilation of some sort, i. 275–8. Cf. J. E. Cross, 'On the library of the Old English martyrologist', in *Learning and Literature in Anglo-Saxon England*, ed. M. Lapidge and H. Gneuss (Cambridge, 1985), pp. 91–141.

[25] Cf. the list of MSS in Dumville, *Liturgy*, pp. 139–40, some of which only contain two or three texts.

[26] Some eight *passiones*; almost all of which are included also in the 'Cotton-Corpus legendary'. Cf. Dumville, *Liturgy*, p. 110 n. 92.

[27] See T. Smith, *Catalogus Librorum Manuscriptorum Bibliothecae Cottonianae* (Oxford, 1696), repr. and ed. C. G. C. Tite (Woodbridge, 1984), p. 67.

[28] Ed. W. W. Skeat, *Ælfric's Lives of Saints*, 2 vols., EETS, os lxxvi, lxxxii, xciv, cxiv (1881–1900).

[29] Ed. B. Thorpe, *The Homilies of the Anglo-Saxon Church: The first part, containing the sermons catholici or homilies of Ælfric*, 2 vols. (London, 1844–6), and M. Godden, *Ælfric's Catholic Homilies. The Second Series: Text*, EETS, ss v (1979).

only the selection of saints represented there, but also the particular versions of the Lives, are in many cases strikingly similar to those included in the so-called 'Cotton-Corpus legendary' (as preserved in manuscripts of the mid-eleventh century), which will be discussed in more detail in the next section.[30] He concluded that an early form of that collection may have served as Ælfric's chief source.[31] More recent studies seem to suggest that in some cases, recensions of Latin saints' Lives distinct from those of the 'Cotton-Corpus legendary', and preserved in legendaries of Continental origin, are in fact closer to Ælfric's Old English translations.[32] Hence, it cannot be proved by reference to Ælfric alone that the 'Cotton-Corpus legendary' came to England much before the mid-eleventh century; though it is possible that other, not dissimilar collections of saints' Lives (perhaps on a slightly more modest scale) had already been introduced from the Continent at the end of the previous century.

With time, passionals and legendaries steadily grew in number and size, towards a peak in production during the twelfth century.[33] Strictly speaking, the term 'passional' should be restricted to collections of *passiones* only, but such rigid terminology does not seem to have been observed in the Middle Ages. In many cases 'passional' or 'passionarius' signified a mixed collection, perhaps

---

[30] P. Zettel, 'Saints' Lives in Old English: Latin Manuscripts and Vernacular Accounts: Ælfric', *Peritia*, i (1982), 17–37, an article which was drawn from the more detailed account in his doctoral thesis, 'Ælfric's hagiographic sources and the Latin legendary preserved in BL MS. Cotton Nero E. 1 + CCCC MS. 9 and other manuscripts', D.Phil. thesis (Oxford, 1979).

[31] Ælfric was active at the end of the 10th cent. and the early years of the 11th (d. c. 1010). On the dating of the Catholic Homilies and the Lives of Saints see Godden, *Ælfric's Catholic Homilies*, pp. xci–xciv; and P. Clemoes, 'The Chronology of Ælfric's Works', in *The Anglo-Saxons, Studies in Aspects of their History and Culture presented to Bruce Dickins*, ed. P. Clemoes (London, 1959), pp. 212–47, at 243–4.

[32] See e.g. C. Morini, 'Le fonti della *Passio S. Agathae* di Ælfric', *AIUON, Filologia Germanica* xxx–xxxi (1987–8), 83–94; and id., 'Pascasio, il fidanzato di Lucia: il riflesso di una "varia lectio" nella S. Lucia di Ælfric', *Le forme e la storia: Rivista di filologia moderna*, NS ii (2) (1990), 315–23. Cf. the comments by H. Magennis, 'On the sources of non-Ælfrician Lives in the Old English *Lives of Saints*, with reference to the Cotton-Corpus Legendary', *Notes and Queries*, NS xxxii (1985), 292–9 at p. 295, and id., 'The Anonymous Old English *Legend of the Seven Sleepers* and its Latin Source', *Leeds Studies in English*, NS xxii (1991), 43–56, esp. pp. 45–6.

[33] Philippart, *Légendiers*, pp. 38–9, shows, in tabular form, both the increase, century by century, in the physical format of the Continental legendaries, and also the 'ampleur du sanctoral'. A similar table, for the smaller number of surviving English legendaries, would follow a comparable pattern.

because *passiones* were usually in the majority.[34] Although the surviving Continental legendaries and passionals have been the
subject of some detailed examination by Guy Philippart and
others, the same kind of attention has not yet been paid to their
English counterparts of the eleventh century and later. What
follows is a preliminary survey.

(iii)   *The 'Cotton-Corpus Legendary' and its Dissemination*

The oldest legendary of any size surviving from England is the so-
called 'Cotton-Corpus legendary',[35] named after the earliest
manuscripts in which it is preserved, London, BL, Cotton Nero E.
1, part 1, fos. 55–208, part 2, fos. 1–155 and 166–80, and CCCC 9,
pp. 61–458. This earliest copy, originally a two-volume legendary
with over 150 texts covering the entire liturgical year, was written
in Worcester in the third quarter of the eleventh century.[36] Before
proceeding any further with this discussion it is important to be
clear about a point of terminology which may otherwise lead to
misunderstanding. Somewhat confusingly, Patrick Zettel used the
names of the two manuscripts making up the aforementioned
legendary to refer, not to that particular Worcester production, but
to the international collection of Lives contained in it (and in
other, later, manuscripts).[37] To avoid ambiguity, the term 'Cotton-
Corpus legendary' will here be used strictly according to Zettel's
definition, and the earliest copy of that compilation, preserved in
Nero E. 1 and CCCC 9, will be referred to as 'the Worcester
legendary'.

It is probable, to judge from its contents, that the 'Cotton-
Corpus legendary' was originally compiled on the Continent. The
great majority of the Lives included are those of the Apostles, the

---

[34] Philippart, *Légendiers*, p. 30. See also the comments of H. Gneuss on the Anglo-
Saxon terminology for legendaries, 'Liturgical books in Anglo-Saxon England and their
Old-English terminology', in *Learning*, ed. Lapidge and Gneuss, pp. 91–141, at 125–6.

[35] This title was coined by Zettel in his doctoral dissertation and in the article,
'Saints' Lives in Old English'. A published list of the contents of the earliest MS of the
collection is to be found in P. Jackson and M. Lapidge, 'The Contents of the Cotton-
Corpus Legendary' (forthcoming).

[36] The scattered parts of the legendary were 'reconstituted' by N. R. Ker, 'Membra
disiecta, second series', *British Museum Quarterly*, xiv (1939–40), 79–86, at pp. 82–3. See
also id., *Catalogue of Manuscripts containing Anglo-Saxon* (Oxford, 1957), p. 217 (no. 166),
and *English Manuscripts in the Century after the Norman Conquest* (Oxford, 1960), pp. 49, 53
and pl. 26.

[37] Zettel, 'Saints' Lives', p. 18 n. 1.

Roman martyrs from the first to early fourth centuries (105 out of 165 items), or of saints whose Lives were already widely popular by the ninth century, such as the Latin translation of the Life of St Mary of Egypt (made in 875 by Paul of Naples) and Cogitosus's *Vita S. Brigidae*, none of which provides any clue to the origin of the collection in terms of a localized cult. However, there are some eighteen or so texts which relate to saints whose principal cult-centres lie in Northern France or Flanders.[38] At present it does not seem possible more precisely to pin-point the centre at which the 'Cotton-Corpus legendary' was assembled. Some advance might be made by examining the textual transmission of the more widely disseminated Lives in the 'Cotton-Corpus legendary', identifying groups of closely-related witnesses and tracing their presence in surviving legendaries from the Continent.[39] If it is permissible to conjecture that the 'Cotton-Corpus legendary' derived from a single Continental compilation, then the *terminus post quem* for such a compilation is provided by the latest datable text in the collection, namely *Vita S. Remigii*, composed by Hincmar of Rheims in 877 or 878.[40]

The second oldest copy of the 'Cotton-Corpus legendary', written at Salisbury in the late eleventh century, is preserved in Salisbury, Cathedral Library 221 and 222 (formerly Oxford, Bodleian Library, Fell 4 and 1, *SC* 8689 and 8688), and contains a series of Lives virtually identical with that found in the Worcester legendary, although a portion has been lost from the end of the second volume.[41] However, a complete contents-list does survive for this second volume, and provides some indication of the texts now missing. There is a strong probability that the Worcester and

[38] These are listed in Jackson and Lapidge, 'Cotton-Corpus Legendary'.

[39] In this endeavour, the editions of saints' Lives which are included in the volumes of *MGH*, Scriptores Rerum Merovingicarum (and Levison's 'Conspectus'), are especially helpful, since the witnesses are usually listed and drawn up into groups. For an example of this kind of enquiry, see my unpublished Ph.D. dissertation, 'The Texts, Transmission and Circulation of some Eleventh-century Anglo-Latin Saints' Lives' (Cambridge, 1993), pp. 28–9.

[40] See Berschin, *Biographie*, iii. 365–71.

[41] The last text is now Alcuin's *Vita S. Richarii*, for 9 Oct. The contents of the Salisbury legendary are listed in N. R. Ker, *Medieval Manuscripts in British Libraries*, vols. i–iii, and with A. J. Piper, vol. iv (Oxford, 1969–92), iv. 257–62. Cf. N. R. Ker, 'Salisbury Cathedral manuscripts and Patrick Young's catalogue', *Wiltshire Archaeological and Natural History Magazine*, liii (1949), 153–83, at p. 178. See also the discussion of this MS in T. Webber, *Scribes and Scholars at Salisbury c.1075–c.1125* (Oxford, 1992), p. 40, with a contents list, according to scribal stint at pp. 154–7 and 169–70.

Salisbury legendaries were copied from the same immediate exemplar, to judge from the arrangement and form of the constituent texts.[42] A small portion (9 October onwards) of another strikingly similar collection (with just a few substitutions) is to be found in Oxford, Bodleian Library, Bodley 354 (*SC* 2432), a manuscript of the second half of the twelfth century, from an unknown English scriptorium possibly located in the West Country. The exact relationship of this legendary to the other two has yet to be established, but its value lies in the fact that it preserves precisely the same Lives as those now missing from the end of the Salisbury legendary.

It is possible, by a careful comparison of the three above-named, and closely similar, copies of the 'Cotton-Corpus legendary', to go some way towards establishing the form and order of the original compilation which served as the exemplar (at least for the two oldest copies), and to distinguish the earliest layers of accretion. Useful evidence is supplied by the lists of contents (contemporary with the rest of the text) which are to be found at the beginning of both of the volumes of the Worcester legendary, as originally constituted, and at the beginning of the second volume of the Salisbury legendary.[43] The items in these lists were numbered,[44] as were the majority of the texts included in the legendaries (in the running titles at the top of each page). Especially in the Worcester legendary, not every item found in the manuscripts is included in the corresponding contents-list. Furthermore, some of the items in the Worcester legendary have also been marked in the margin with numbers which bear no relation to those of the contents-list. Those extra numbers are not consecutive, and thus may reproduce the numbering-system of the conjectured exemplar.[45] The Worces-

[42] See Zettel, 'Saints' Lives', p. 19, and the comments of Webber, *Scribes*, pp. 69–70. The relationship of individual texts was established by M. Esposito, 'On the earliest Latin life of St Brigid of Kildare', *Proceedings of the Royal Irish Academy* (*C*), xxx (1912), 307–26, at p. 310; and L. Bieler, *Libri epistolarum S. Patricii episcopi*, 2 vols., Irish Manuscripts Commission (Dublin, 1952), i. 13. Evidence is also supplied by two large lacunae found in the text of Possidius' *Vita S. Augustini ep.* as supplied by both Nero E. I, pt. 2 (fos. 95ᵛ–105ᵛ, where gaps were filled by a later scribe), and Salisbury Cathedral 222 (fos. 91ʳ–110ᵛ).

[43] Cotton Nero E. I, pt. I, fo. 55ʳ⁻ᵛ; CCCC 9, p. 61; Salisbury Cathedral 222, fo. 184ʳ.

[44] The numerals are contemporary with the copying of the lists.

[45] The contents-list in CCCC 9 is numbered 'I–XLI', and the numbers match with those of the running titles at the top of each page. The corresponding list in Salisbury Cathedral 222 is numbered 'CXII–CLXI', and just occasionally the texts in CCCC 9 have been supplied in the margin (by the main scribe) with an extra number which matches

ter legendary alone contains various sermons relating to feasts of the Blessed Virgin Mary, as well as Felix's *Vita S. Guthlaci*, all of which are included neither in the table of contents, nor in the Salisbury legendary (nor in Bodley 354), and thus may be regarded as independent additions to the common exemplar. It may be possible to identify a yet earlier layer of accretion. Bodley 354, and the contents-list in the Salisbury legendary (in lieu of the portion of that manuscript now missing) place two texts at the end of the collection, out of calendrical order, whereas the scribe of the Worcester legendary copied them into the correct position.[46] Quite possibly those two texts were early additions to the exemplar-legendary, tagged on at the end of the original collection of Lives after its completion.

Before going on to describe the other copies of the 'Cotton-Corpus legendary' made in England, it seems appropriate at this juncture to consider the present constitution of the parts of the Worcester legendary, as a good example of the way in which the later and larger legendaries evolved. The earliest additions to the 'Cotton-Corpus' collection, made by the scribe of the Worcester legendary, have just been mentioned. Very shortly (a quarter of a century at the most) after the two-volume copy of the 'core' collection of some 150 Lives had been finished by one scribe, other texts were bound in at the beginning and end of each of the two volumes.

Three Anglo-Latin saints' Lives, composed in the tenth or early eleventh century, were added to the beginning of Nero E. i, part 1:[47] Byrhtferth's *Vita S. Oswaldi* (fos. 3ʳ–23ᵛ) and *Vita S. Ecgwini* (fos. 24ʳ–34ᵛ), and Lantfred's *Translatio et miracula S. Swithuni* (fos.

that of the *Salisbury* list. An example may be found at p. 261 of CCCC 9—*Passio Beatorum martyrum Simproniani, Claudii, Nicostrati, Castorii et Simplicii* was numbered 'cxxvii', and at p. 268, *Passio S. Theodori* = 'cxxviii', and the next text, *Passio Beati Menne* = 'cxxx'; in other words 'cxxix' is missing. In the table of contents for the Salisbury legendary, and in Bodley 354, *Vita S. Martini* comes between those of Theodore and Mennas. Thus the evidence seems to suggest that the compiler of the Worcester legendary (or its antecedent) was rearranging the material he found in his exemplar. This whole issue requires further examination. It may also be noteworthy that several of the Lives of the apostles found in the Worcester and Salisbury legendaries are not listed in the tables of contents.

[46] The texts in question are *Vita S. Wandregisilus* (Nero E. i, pt. 2, fos. 44ʳ–48ᵛ; Bodley 354, fos. 254ʳ–265ʳ) and Paschasius Radbertus, *Cogitis me*, on the Assumption of the Virgin, Nero E. i, pt. 2, fos. 79ʳ–86ᵛ; Bodley 354, fos. 274ᵛ–287ᵛ.

[47] Nero E. i was evidently deemed at some point, probably fairly early on, to have grown too large a codex to be manageable, and was split into two parts with some loss of text at the divide.

35^r–52^v), as well as a hymn to St Swithun (fos. 52^v–53^r). These texts are only the earliest of several layers of accretion, which include various saints' Lives written in a hand of the second quarter of the twelfth century.[48] Four texts, *Vita S. Saluii*,[49] *Vita et Miracula S. Nicholai*,[50] *Vita S. Rumwoldi* and *Passio SS. Cirici et Iulitte matris eius*,[51] were added, by various later eleventh-century hands, to the beginning of CCCC 9.[52]

The 'Cotton-Corpus legendary', as it stands, contains no English saints.[53] Already we have noted that the Worcester scribe inserted the Life of Guthlac among the texts he drew from his exemplar. Four of the seven texts appended at an early stage to the Worcester legendary pertain to English saints—Oswald, Ecgwine, Swithun and Rumwold. The cult of St Nicholas (and presumably the texts relating to it) was apparently introduced into England from Normandy during the second half of the eleventh century and became widely popular.[54] A relic of a St Salvius of Valenciennes was given to Canterbury by William the Conqueror in about 1085.[55] That donation may have promoted an increased interest in the cult of Salvius, although his feast is already to be found at 26 June in some pre-Conquest calendars.[56] It is less easy to explain the addition of the Life of Cyriacus and Julitta—the presence of this text in CCCC 9 may be due partly to association of ideas, since St Cyriacus was supposedly an infant martyr just 3 years old, who nevertheless professed his faith to his persecutor, and thus may be compared with the 3-day-old confessor, Rumwold.[57] It should be noted also that the feasts of both Nicholas and Rumwold occur as late eleventh-century

[48] Cf. Jackson and Lapidge, 'Cotton-Corpus Legendary'. Subsequently, the last remnants of a once substantial 13th-cent. legendary were bound in at the end of Nero E. 1, part 2, on which see M. Lapidge and M. Winterbottom, *Wulfstan of Winchester: The Life of St Æthelwold*, OMT (1991), pp. clxxv–clxxvii.

[49] *BHL* 7472 = Salvius of Valenciennes.   [50] *BHL* 6104–6, 6169.

[51] Similar to *BHL* 1804–6.   [52] See p. clxxiv below.

[53] In the view of M. Brett, 'The use of universal chronicle at Worcester', in *L'Historiographie médiévale en Europe. Actes du colloque organisé par la Fondation Européenne de la Science au Centre de Recherches Historiques et Juridiques de l'Université Paris I du 29 mars au 1er avril 1989*, ed. J.-P. Genet (Paris, 1991), pp. 277–85, this fact may be taken as a sign that the legendary had only reached England shortly before the making of the Worcester copy (p. 283 n. 28).

[54] See K. Meisen, *Nikolauskult und Nikolausbrauch im Abendlande. Eine Kultgeographische-volkskundliche Untersuchung* (Mainz, 1981), p. 513.

[55] An account (never printed) of the translation to Canterbury of the relics of Salvius is to be found in London, Lambeth Palace Library, 159, fos. 111^v–112 (s. xvi).

[56] See F. Wormald, *English Kalendars Before A.D. 1100*, HBS lxxii (1934, repr. Woodbridge, 1988), nos. 2, 3, 5, and 13.

[57] Cf. pp. clxxi–clxxii below.

additions to the calendar (datable to the second quarter of the same century) included at the front of CCCC 9.[58] The addition of these texts can be regarded as the earliest stage in the gradual modernization and anglicization of the originally Continental (possibly Flemish) 'Cotton-Corpus legendary'.

(iv) *The English Legendaries*

Although the focus here is mainly upon the hagiography of the eleventh century, it is worthwhile considering legendaries written in England during the following century or so, since they almost certainly incorporate texts and groups of texts which had been in circulation for some time. It is unlikely that the compilers of later legendaries started, as it were, *ex nihilo*, with a vast selection of separate *libelli*, but rather with pre-existing collections of Lives, which they rearranged and amplified.[59] The core material of the 'Cotton-Corpus legendary' (and other collections like it) seems to have been copied and recopied, through the century or so following its introduction into England, gathering to itself more and more new and indigenously produced Lives, and occasionally shedding a text here and there. The end result of such a process is exemplified by the massive legendary (possibly from Winchester), of which London, BL, Arundel 169 (see below) is all that remains— the mere tip of an enormous iceberg.[60] In the following account of

---

[58] The feasts of Cyriacus and Julitta and of Nicholas were added in the 12th cent. to the later 11th-cent. Worcester calendar preserved in CCCC 391 (Wormald, *English Kalendars*, no. 17), while that of Rumwold was one of the very few additions made to the Worcester calendar (of the third quarter of the 11th cent.) in Oxford, Bodleian Library, Hatton 113 (ibid., no. 16).

[59] Cf. Philippart, *Légendiers*, p. 101, 'la plupart des éditeurs n'ont pas travaillé *ab ovo*, pratiquement n'ont pas réuni leur collection uniquement à partir de petits *libelli*, mais ont procédé presque toujours à partir d'œuvres déjà organisés de leurs devanciers, qu'ils ont enrichies, restructurées ou remaniées à leur gré ... "comme la boule de neige".'

[60] The one problem with the large compilations of the 12th cent. and later, is determining the extent to which sheer acquisitiveness—the desire to accumulate as many texts as possible for the sake of comprehensiveness—takes over from a real interest in the cult of saints commemorated by those texts; cf. the comments by G. Philippart in 'Hagiographies Locale, Régionale, Diocésaine, Universelle. Les hagiographies du saint patron dans l'aire belge du Xe siècle', in *Lateinische Kultur im X. Jahrhundert. Akten des I. Internationalen Mittellateinerkongresses, Heidelberg, 12.–15.IX.1988*, ed. W. Berschin, *Mittellateinisches Jahrbuch* xxiv–xxv (1991), 355–67, at p. 360. It is necessary to control analysis of the contents of a legendary by comparing them, where possible, with other more obviously liturgical documents belonging to the same centre.

the other surviving English legendaries, the stages of this evolution will be described.

Two similar, but both now incomplete, copies of a large collection of saints' Lives survive from early twelfth-century Canterbury. From Christ Church, we have the scattered fragments of a seven-volume legendary,[61] written in the first quarter of the twelfth century, now Canterbury, Dean and Chapter Library Lit. E. 42, fos. 1–68, 75–81 + Maidstone, Kent County Archives Office, S/Rm Fae. 2[62] + London, BL, Cotton Nero C. vii, fos. 29–79 + Harley 315, fos. 1–39 + Harley 624, fos. 84–143.[63] A reasonably precise date is potentially obtainable for this legendary: Harley 315 (fos. 16^r–39^v) contains a copy of Eadmer's *Vita S. Anselmi* which cannot have been written much after 1123.[64] On the other hand, Canterbury, E. 42 contains a copy of Eadmer's account of the miracles of St Audoen (Ouen), to which a different hand added a supplement which is datable from its inclusion of a miracle to which Elmer (prior of Christ Church, 1128–37) was said to be a witness.[65] This may imply that the legendary had been completed before 1128, the earliest date at which the additional material could have been composed, but after 1123. Caution is, however, necessary here: because of the fragmentary state of the Christ Church legendary, and the fact that the surviving portions show the work of several different scribes, it is difficult to distinguish the stages by which the compilation reached its present form. Southern suggested that the production of this great legendary may be connected with, indeed may have been supervised by, Eadmer, the English hagiographer who was precentor at Christ Church from about 1121.[66]

[61] The volumes of this legendary are listed as 'Passionalia' in the early 15th-cent. catalogue of Christ Church, printed by M. R. James, *The Ancient Libraries of Canterbury and Dover* (Cambridge, 1903), p. 52, nos. 359, 361–6. Nothing has survived of vols. iv and vii of the collection, but there is a second copy of vol. ii, of slightly later date, but also apparently from Christ Church, listed in the catalogue (no. 360), now London, BL, Cotton Otho D. viii, fos. 8–173 + Cambridge, Trinity College 1155 (2 flyleaves).

[62] Ker, *Medieval Manuscripts*, ii. 289–96.

[63] N. R. Ker, *Medieval Libraries of Great Britain*, 2nd edn. (London, 1964), p. 36. On this legendary, see also Ker, 'Membra disiecta', pp. 83–5.

[64] See *The Life of St Anselm Archbishop of Canterbury*, ed. and trans. R. W. Southern, OMT (repr. with corrections, 1972), p. xxiii.

[65] See A. Wilmart, 'Les Reliques de S. Ouen à Cantorbéry', *AB* li (1933), 285–92; id., 'Edmeri Cantuariensis Cantoris Noua Opuscula de Sanctorum ueneratione et obsecratione', *Revue des Sciences Religieuses*, xv (1935), 184–219, 364–79, at pp. 185–6; and N. R. Ker, 'Un nouveau fragment des Miracles de S. Ouen à Cantorbéry', *AB* lxiv (1946), 50–3.

[66] R. W. Southern, *Saint Anselm and his Biographer* (Cambridge, 1963), p. 238.

Part of an almost identical collection of Lives is to be found in London, BL, Arundel 91 and Oxford, Bodleian Library, Fell 2 (*SC* 8690), which were consecutive volumes (probably the last two of the set) of a legendary copied at St Augustine's, Canterbury, early in the second quarter of the twelfth century.[67] There is a strong possibility that this St Augustine's legendary was copied directly from the Christ Church legendary, or at the very least, made from the same exemplar—apart from the very close similarity of content, textual evidence points in this direction.[68] A single leaf, Oxford, Worcester College 273, datable to the early twelfth century, now survives from what may have been the penultimate volume of a legendary closely related to the two from Canterbury, and belonging to Rochester Cathedral Priory.[69]

The Canterbury legendaries contain a large proportion of the texts integral to the 'Cotton-Corpus legendary'. It is likely that a copy of that collection, very similar to those surviving from Worcester and Salisbury, had reached Canterbury, either St Augustine's or Christ Church, by the late eleventh century, but soon came to be regarded as out-of-date, or not sufficiently representative of the observances of those houses. As a consequence of this realization, a new legendary could have been compiled, based on the old core of material, but omitting some texts, and adding many more which pertained both to English saints and to others whose *vitae* were available to the compiler. Furthermore, it is possible that additions continued to be made after the completion of this new legendary (rather in the way that the Worcester legendary progressively acquired accretions). To consider only specifically English saints, for example, the Christ Church legendary includes Bede's prose Life of St Cuthbert, Willibald's Life of St Boniface,[70] excerpts from Bede, *HE* (iii. 12–13) concerning St Oswald the martyr, Osbern's Life of St Ælfheah and his account of that saint's translation,[71] both Adelard's and Osbern's Lives of St Dunstan,[72] Miracles of St Audouen performed at Canterbury,[73] Eadmer's Life of St Oda, archbishop of Canterbury,[74] and his Life

---

[67] Zettel, 'Saints' Lives', p. 19, discards the St Augustine's legendary as containing 'substantial variations in content, arrangement and textual tradition not relevant to our purpose'. There is no indication that he was aware of the existence of the part of the St Augustine's legendary preserved in the British Library.

[68] This evidence is discussed below, pp. clxxxiii–clxxxiv.

[69] See pp. clxxvii–clxxviii below.

[70] *BHL* 1400.

[71] *BHL* 2518 and 2519. Written *c.*1090.

[72] *BHL* 2343 and 2344–5.

[73] *BHL* 758.

[74] *BHL* 6289.

of St Anselm.[75] The remaining portion of the St Augustine's legendary includes Eadmer's Life of Wilfrid,[76] Alcuin's Life of Willibrord,[77] Abbo's *passio* of Edmund, king and martyr,[78] and an abbreviated copy of *Vita S. Birini*. Eadmer's Life of Peter, the first abbot of St Augustine's, was added to the end of Fell 2 (pp. 460–4) in a slightly later hand.[79] Both of the Canterbury legendaries include the *Vita S. Rumwoldi*.[80]

The range of saints contained in the Canterbury legendaries could be compared with the surviving liturgical calendars from the two Canterbury houses. For example, the name of Archbishop Oda was added in the twelfth century to the early eleventh-century calendar preserved in London, BL, Arundel 155, fos. 2–7ᵛ, at 2 June (fo. 4ᵛ), as was also the feast of the Translation of St Ælfheah on 8 June.[81] Such a correspondence between a legendary written at Christ Church, Canterbury and a calendar probably from the same house is hardly a surprise. In a sense, negative evidence may also be correlated with the observations made above about the texts included in these legendaries. For example, *Vita S. Birini* is only present in Fell 2 in a very heavily abbreviated form, as if it were considered to be sufficient only to preserve the bare bones of his story, nothing more, because he was not especially venerated at Canterbury. The liturgical evidence reflects this attitude, since although both Birinus's feasts are marked in the pre-Conquest Christ Church calendar in Arundel 155,[82] he is not to be found in any surviving post-Conquest Canterbury calendar, nor is the saint commemorated in the late eleventh-century sacramentary from St Augustine's, CCCC 270.[83]

We should also consider another, slightly closer, relative of the Worcester and Salisbury legendaries. Lives for November and December are to be found in a mid-twelfth-century manuscript possibly written at Hereford, now Hereford Cathedral Library

---

[75] *BHL* 526.   [76] *BHL* 8893.

[77] *BHL* 8935.   [78] *BHL* 2392.

[79] *BHL* 6702m; ed. Wilmart, 'Noua Opuscula', pp. 354–61. The Life was probably composed between 1124 and 1130; see Southern, *St Anselm*, p. 371.

[80] One of the few pre-Conquest liturgical calendars which mark the feast of Rumwold on 3 Nov. is that found in the Bosworth Psalter, written at Canterbury in the later 10th cent.

[81] See Wormald, *English Kalendars*, pp. 169–81 (no. 13), at p. 175.

[82] Wormald, *English Kalendars*, no. 13.

[83] Ed. M. Rule, *The Missal of St Augustine's Abbey, Canterbury* (Cambridge, 1896).

P. VII. 6.[84] This manuscript is only the final volume of an extensive collection, which represents a modernization of the 'Cotton-Corpus legendary', of the same type as that described above for Canterbury. A fair proportion of the Cotton-Corpus texts are present, but there are also many additions, both of Anglo-Saxon and of non-native saints' Lives. The former are Abbo's *passio* of St Edmund, the Life of St Birinus, the Life of Eadburh of Lyminge[85] and an account of the miracles of Eadburh, apparently found only in this manuscript,[86] Dominic's Life of Ecgwine, and (added, in a hand of the fifteenth century, to the original table of contents) a now lost Life of Æthelberht, king and martyr.[87] Since Hereford P. VII. 6 is probably only a small portion of a much larger legendary with Lives for the entire liturgical year, it is not easy to reach a firm decision about where the legendary was compiled, whether at Hereford, or at Worcester *for* Hereford, as M. R. James supposed.[88] The presence of a Life of St Ecgwine may indicate a connection with Worcester. Such a connection would imply a close relationship with the Worcester legendary, although any conclusion is hindered by the fact that only the November/December portion of the Hereford legendary survives. Close scrutiny of the texts common to both is required.

There is evidence for the existence of a multi-volume legendary at the Old Minster, Winchester, compiled or at least copied, in the first half of the twelfth century, on the basis of a Frankish collection of saints' Lives similar to the 'Cotton-Corpus legendary'. All that remains of this Winchester legendary is the section covering the period from the end of June to the beginning of August, preserved in London, BL, Arundel 169, fos. 2^r–103^v; but extrapolation from the contemporary contents list (fo. 2^r) of this surviving portion of the sanctoral (29 texts listed for July alone) implies a (hypothetical) legendary of some considerable size, covering the entire liturgical year.[89] The attribution to Winchester can for the

---

[84] The contents of the MS are listed by R. A. B. Mynors and R. M. Thomson, *Catalogue of the Manuscripts of Hereford Cathedral Library* (Woodbridge, 1993), pp. 110–12; cf. A. T. Bannister, *A Descriptive Catalogue of the Manuscripts in the Hereford Cathedral Library* (Hereford, 1927), pp. 172–7.   [85] *BHL* 2384a.

[86] See H. Fros, 'Inédits non recensés dans la *BHL*', *AB* cii (1984), 163–96, 355–80, at p. 182.

[87] The Life was, to judge from the contents-list, a later addition, perhaps on loose sheets of vellum, which could easily have become detached and lost.

[88] See pp. lxxvii–lxxviii below.

[89] See Lapidge and Winterbottom, *Wulfstan*, pp. clxviii–clxxi, for a list of contents.

present remain only a conjecture, based on the presence in this fragmentary legendary of the Lives of two Winchester saints, Swithun and Æthelwold. In any case, it is reasonably safe to imagine that the legendary represented by Arundel 169 was the end-product of activity similar to that conjectured above for the Canterbury legendaries and Hereford P. vii. 6.

A three-volume legendary, now Lincoln Cathedral Library 149 and 150 (dated to the second half and the middle of the twelfth century respectively)[90] + Gloucester Cathedral Library 1 (of the early thirteenth century), may have belonged to Leominster Priory, Herefordshire.[91] This collection displays a further expanded and modified form of the core-material of 'Cotton-Corpus legendary', with yet more English saints added, such as Milburh, Chad, Edward king and martyr, Cuthbert, Dunstan, Alban, Æthelthryth, Æthelberht, Augustine of Canterbury, Swithun, Æthelwold, Oswald king and martyr, Edmund, Kenelm, and Edward the Confessor.

London, Gray's Inn 3,[92] written in the early twelfth century, possibly at St Werburg's Abbey, Chester, preserves a collection of Lives very similar to that of the Leominster legendary.[93] Only the first volume remains, but two leaves inserted into the manuscript in the early sixteenth century supply an alphabetical list of the contents of the surviving volume and three others, now lost.[94] London, BL, Cotton Tiberius D. iii, written in the late twelfth or early thirteenth century at an unknown centre in England, seems also to be just one part of a large collection of saints' Lives, and displays very strong affinities, in terms of the selection and form of the texts included, with the last two named legendaries.[95]

It is likely that the multi-volume legendary came to be an essential part of the library of almost every religious house, although relatively few have survived in a complete form. We may yet find

---

[90] Contents listed in R. M. Thomson, *Catalogue of the Manuscripts of Lincoln Cathedral Library* (Woodbridge, 1989), pp. 115–19.

[91] Ker, *Medieval Manuscripts*, ii. 934–9.   [92] Ibid. i. 52–5.

[93] See esp. Thomson, *Catalogue*, p. 117, items 49 and 52.

[94] There are some striking similarities between the contents of the former third volume of the Chester legendary and those of Hereford P. vii. 6. See G. Philippart, 'Catalogues récents de manuscrits', *AB* lxxxviii (1970), 188–211, at p. 195. Unfortunately, since only the Lives for February to June survive in Gray's Inn 3, and those for November and December in Hereford P. vii. 6, the nature of the relationship of the two legendaries cannot be defined more clearly.

[95] Cf. Ker, *Medieval Manuscripts*, p. 54, items 58 and 59.

traces of them. For example, in a list of the books held at Glastonbury, of about 1170,[96] the following entry appears: 'Septem uolu-
mina de passionibus sanctorum per totum anni circulum', and in
another catalogue of 1247–8 from the same house, the seven 'Passionalia mensalia' are listed according to the first Life appearing in
each volume.[97]

Wilhelm Levison attempted to supply a 'family tree' of the
earlier manuscripts of the 'Cotton-Corpus legendary', based on his
examination of the Merovingian Lives which he edited for the
Monumenta Germaniae Historica.[98] The formulation of patterns of
relationships between whole groups of texts may have important
implications for any work on the textual history of an individual
Vita.[99] It would, however, be a massive endeavour to collate all the
constituent texts of several legendaries. Many of the observations
made above represent the beginning of that work, but a more
detailed study of the contents and relationships of the surviving
English legendaries remains to be carried out. Such an investigation needs also to include some examination of the degree of
uniformity in the treatment of the texts in a given collection—at the
simplest level, abridgement, but also other more subtle forms of
intervention.[100]

(v) *Evidence for the Liturgical Function of Legendaries*

It is important when considering the role which legendaries played
in the dissemination of saints' Lives to give some attention to the
functions such compilations were intended to fulfil. The guiding
principle of the very earliest collections of *passiones* may well have
been the imperatives of the liturgy.[101] In eleventh-century England,

---

[96] Printed by T. W. Williams, *Somerset Mediaeval Libraries* (Bristol, 1897), p. 50.

[97] Ibid. 69.

[98] 'Conspectus codicum hagiographicorum', *MGH*, SRM vii. 545–6.

[99] Cf. the remarks of Philippart, *Légendiers*, p. 104, on the possibility of establishing a *stemma codicum* of legendaries.

[100] See Dolbeau, in *Hagiographie*, p. 20. B. de Gaiffier, 'A propos des légendiers latins', *AB* xcvii (1979), 57–68, at pp. 59–60, stressed the need for caution when speaking of a compiler or editor of a given collection of saints' Lives. As regards the importance of considering a collection of Lives as a whole and studying the working-methods of the 'collectors', cf. comments of Richard Sharpe concerning the collections of Irish saints' Lives which he has examined, in *Medieval Irish Saints' Lives: An Introduction to Vitae Sanctorum Hiberniae* (Oxford, 1991), esp. pp. 88–90.

[101] See B. de Gaiffier, 'La lecture des Actes des Martyrs dans la Prière liturgique en Occident', *AB* lxxii (1954), 134–66.

as elsewhere, the formal liturgical context for the reading of saints' Lives was the night office. This, on weekdays and the feast-days of saints of lower rank (according to the particular observance of the religious house in question), consisted of a single nocturn, which included three lessons (only one in summer), either from the Bible, a homily (which could be exegetical), a sermon (either on a particular saint, or of a more generally exhortatory nature), or from a saint's Life. Sundays and feast-days were marked by an office made up of three nocturns, each containing four lessons (only three in communities of secular clergy).[102] Hence, the feast-day of a saint could be celebrated in a variety of different ways, according to the degree of veneration in which he or she was held—either by four (or three) readings taken from the relevant life, or eight, or twelve.

Obviously enough, the ordering of Lives according to the liturgical calendar could be taken as a sign of the basic function of a legendary, but it is also the most logical and practical means to control such a large body of material—if you know the feast-day of the saint whose *Vita* you wish to read, it should in theory be easy enough to find in a legendary disposed calendrically.[103] A clearer sign of the specifically liturgical application of legendaries could be the marking-up of texts into the appropriate number of lections of suitable length, to make the reader's task easier.[104] Contrary to expectation, the English legendaries which we have just discussed offer disappointingly little (or, at best, rather ambiguous) evidence of this kind, and it is therefore difficult to be certain about the purpose for which they were actually compiled.[105]

---

[102] See the description of the constitution of the night office by J. B. L. Tolhurst, *The Monastic Breviary of Hyde Abbey, Winchester*, 6 vols., HBS lxix–lxxi, lxxvi, lxxviii, and lxxx (1932–42), vi. 7–14; and also by Gneuss, in *Learning*, p. 120.

[103] See P. Salmon, *L'Office divin au Moyen Age: Histoire de la formation du bréviaire du IXe au XVIe siècle*, Lex Orandi xliii (Paris, 1967), p. 28. For the idea that the importance of the liturgy has been exaggerated, see the discussion in Dolbeau, 'Notes sur l'organisation', pp. 30–1, and Philippart, *Légendiers*, pp. 30–2.

[104] Cf. Gneuss, in *Learning*, p. 125. Another type of evidence for the way legendaries are used would be notes in the manuscripts or in surviving book lists of where the book was stored; cf. M. Lapidge, 'Surviving booklists from Anglo-Saxon England', in *Learning*, pp. 33–89, at 35.

[105] Cf. the comments concerning the case of Continental legendaries by Philippart, *Légendiers*, pp. 22–3, and Dolbeau, in *Hagiographie*, p. 18. See also the discussion of the uses of hagiography in 11th-cent. Flanders by B. de Gaiffier, 'L'Hagiographie et son public au XIe siècle', in *Études critiques d'hagiographie et d'iconologie*, pp. 475–507; and cf. V. Leroquais, *Les Bréviaires manuscrits des Bibliothèques Publiques de France*, 5 vols. (Paris, 1934), i, pp. l–li.

The example of the earliest manuscript of the 'Cotton-Corpus legendary' is interesting. None of the Lives was originally copied out with divisions which are very obviously intended to be lections for the night office, and only very few of the texts were so marked out subsequently.[106] In both Nero E. I and CCCC 9 there are a few instances of annotation in a hand nearly contemporary with that of the Latin text. This annotator supplied Old English interlinear directions to the reader, indicating where to begin reading ('foh on'), and where to stop ('læt'), and what portions to omit ('ofer-hefe').[107] In some places the Latin text was also slightly altered to ease the passage between the portions to be read out.[108] This marking is, however, of a distinctly desultory nature, no clear pattern has yet been discerned to explain the choice of texts to be annotated, and certainly not one that could be related to the sanctoral observed at Worcester in the eleventh century. But the matter may reward more detailed investigation.

There is just as little evidence for the marking-out of lections in the legendaries of the twelfth century. To consider specific examples of texts, namely the *Vitae* edited here, not one surviving manuscript of *Vita S. Birini*,[109] and only one of *Vita S. Rumwoldi* appears to have been divided into lections.[110] As an example of just one legendary, Oxford, Bodleian Library, Fell 2 (the last volume of the St Augustine's legendary) has lections marked by a hand perhaps slightly later than that of the text, in just eight out of the forty-six Lives it now contains.[111] It is evident that the entire contents of a large legendary, such as the one of which Arundel 169 is just a small section, could not all have been read out as part of the

---

[106] In CCCC 9 *Vita S. Rumwoldi* was at some point divided into three sections, by crosses marked in the margin. The texts relating to the Blessed Virgin were divided into lections by a 12th- or 13th-cent. hand; as were some four or five other texts, such as *Passio S. Lucie*, *Translatio SS Benedicti et Scholastice*, *Passio S. Calesti pape*.

[107] Most of the instances of annotation are noted by Ker, *Catalogue*, p. 41, no. 29; and by A. S. Napier, *Old English Glosses, chiefly unpublished*, Anecdota Oxoniensia (Oxford, 1900), p. xx.

[108] A good example of this can be seen in CCCC 9, pp. 219 and 220.

[109] This Life was, in three of its earliest witnesses, apportioned into thirteen roughly equal chapters with chapter headings, but thirteen is not a standard number for lessons intended to be read at the night office.

[110] The single exception is the copy of *Vita S. Rumwoldi* in CCCC 9 which at some time after copying seems to have been marked up in the margins with three crosses which indicate a rough division of the text into reading-portions.

[111] These are the Lives of SS Martin, Edmund, Cecilia, Clement, Andrew, Nicholas, Lucy, and John the Evangelist.

liturgy, otherwise every single day would have been a feast-day. For some days of the year, more than one Life would be available.[112] Perhaps some texts were never read out, but it seems more plausible that the context in which legendaries were used was, in fact, frequently non-liturgical; that is, reading aloud in the refectory, in chapter, or during spells of manual labour, or for private meditative study.[113] There are occasionally clues which help us to form some picture of what was going on. For example, the twelfth-century (Leominster?) legendary contained partly in Lincoln Cathedral 149 has a table of contents with some annotations made not long after the manuscript was written. One such reads: 'Kal. ianuarii. Post euangelium Legitur in Ref⟨ectorio⟩ Vita Sancte Eufrosine. Require in alio uolumine.'[114] It is also worthwhile noting the case of a set of lections for the feast of St Dunstan, composed during the first decade or so of the eleventh century by Adelard of Ghent.[115] Adelard interspersed responsories between the lections he composed, having in mind a specifically liturgical use for his Life of Dunstan. In several of the surviving copies of Adelard's work, the responsories have been entirely omitted, or copied as if they were part of the lections around them, and the lections have been run together to form a continuous text, contrary to the original intention.[116]

Conclusions about the evidence for the liturgical use of legendaries do need to be controlled by some consideration of what can be discovered about the use of *libelli*,[117] and saints' Lives in smaller groups. The evidence is similarly mixed, at least in the case of the Lives edited here. It is interesting to find, for example, that one of the early witnesses to *Vita S. Birini*, namely Oxford, Bodleian Library, Digby 39, of the late eleventh or early twelfth century, is bound up with a booklet (a *libellus*?) of Birinus material, which

---

[112] Cf. the comments on textual 'acquisitiveness' on p. xxiii above.

[113] On the variety of uses made of legendaries, see Philippart, *Légendiers*, pp. 112–21, and Dolbeau, in *Hagiographie*, p. 30.

[114] On reading in the refectory, see de Gaiffier, 'A propos des légendiers', pp. 62–3.

[115] Adelard, *Vita S. Dunstani*, ed. W. Stubbs, *Memorials of St Dunstan*, RS lxiii (1874), pp. 53–68.

[116] E.g. in Lincoln, Cathedral Library 149, Gray's Inn 3 and London, BL, Cotton Tiberius D. III. By contrast, in London, BL, Cotton Nero C. VII, part of the Christ Church legendary, the twelve lections of Adelard's Life are marked out separately; it would have been surprising not to find a text of the Life of Dunstan being used liturgically at Canterbury.

[117] Cf. Dumville, *Liturgy*, p. 108.

includes eight clearly-divided lections taken from Bede, *HE* iii. 7, on Birinus and the bishops who succeeded him.[118] This evidence may imply that at Abingdon, where this manuscript was apparently written, *Vita S. Birini* was not intended to be read out at the night office, but at some other occasion, possibly in the refectory, or in private, whereas the lections from Bede were read at the nocturns instead. Alternatively, the older lections may have been superseded by the new *Vita*.[119]

Among the three saints' Lives here edited, the only clear-cut example of lections specifically marked out is in the earliest witness to *Vita S. Kenelmi*, Oxford, Bodleian Library, Douce 368, of Winchcombe provenance. The eight lections were signalled in the margin, with roman numerals, by a hand contemporary with the text. The same scribe had, in like manner, marked two sections of the copy of Bede's *HE* which precedes *Vita S. Kenelmi* in the manuscript, namely the description of the life of King Oswald, and that of Cuthbert. In both cases, eight lections were marked for reading out.[120] A codex containing Bede's *HE*, a genealogy of Mercian kings (including Kenelm), and one single saint's Life does not, on the face of it, seem much like a typical liturgical book. Overall, it is clear that the evidence for the use of hagiographical manuscripts of all types, in the liturgy, requires some further examination, not least on account of the additional evidence that may be gleaned for the dissemination of a given saint's liturgical cult, and for the types of audience that hagiography was able to reach.

(vi) *The Revival of Anglo-Latin Hagiography in the Eleventh Century*

We must now proceed to an examination of the cultural and intellectual context in which the Lives edited here should be viewed.[121] The hagiography of the later eleventh century in England cannot be discussed without a brief consideration of what might be termed the 'mini-revival' of the later tenth century, if only for

---

[118] See below, p. lxvi.

[119] See p. lxx below.

[120] If this book may rightly be assigned, from its inception, to Winchcombe, it is to be wondered why only eight, and not twelve, lections were signalled in *Vita et miracula S. Kenelmi*, given the status Kenelm's feast must have had. See below, p. cxxvi.

[121] What follows makes no claim to be an exhaustive history of 11th-cent. hagiography and its development, but the intention is to sketch an outline, and to uncover some of the reasons why saints' Lives began to be written in such numbers, in order to provide a background to the composition of the three texts edited in this volume.

purposes of comparison. At that time, after a hiatus of nearly 200 years, there was a burst of hagiographical activity, closely related to the renewal of Benedictine monasticism gradually imposed over the second half of the century, and to the key executors of that reform. Part of the motivation behind the hagiography composed then may indeed have been to proclaim the virtues and benefits of the Benedictine way of life.[122] This flurry of texts seems also to have come about at least in part as a result of Continental influence upon the late Anglo-Saxon Church.

At Winchester, for example, Lantfred (previously a monk of Fleury) composed a *Translatio et miracula S. Swithuni* in about 975, to commemorate the translation of Swithun in 971.[123] This work was subsequently rendered into a 3,386-line hexametrical poem, *Narratio metrica de S. Swithuno*, by Wulfstan of Winchester, between the years 992 and 994 (final form after the translation of Æthelwold in 996).[124] Perhaps surprisingly, there is no evidence that a Life of Swithun was produced at this period, to complement the miracles. Possibly because the saint had only just been 'invented', that is, rediscovered for the first time (supposedly under miraculous circumstances), too little was known about his life for the task to be regarded as worth attempting. No such scruple burdened the mind of the anonymous hagiographer who produced *Vita S. Swithuni* a century later, any more than a parlous lack of information prevented him from writing at length about Birinus. Wulfstan and Lantfred's works on Swithun were largely superseded by recomposition of the same set of miracles, with the addition of more recent ones, and the accompanying Life of Swithun. This anonymous prose work survives in a good many more manuscripts than either that of Lantfred or that of Wulfstan, and could be argued to have outdone them in its popularity.

[122] E.g. Byrhtferth's *Vita S. Oswaldi*—cf. S. Millinger, 'Liturgical devotion in the *Vita S. Oswaldi*', in *Saints, Scholars and Heroes, Studies in Medieval Culture, in honour of C. W. Jones*, 2 vols., ed. M. H. King and W. M. Stevens (Ann Arbor, MI, 1979), i. 239–64.

[123] Part of the text was edited by E. P. Sauvage in *AB* iv (1885), 367–410, which supplemented the edn. in *ActaS*, July, i. 328–30. See the edn. in preparation by M. Lapidge, *The Cult of St Swithun*, Winchester Studies, iv (2) (Oxford, forthcoming); and cf. Lapidge and Winterbottom, *Wulfstan*, p. l.

[124] Ed. M. Huber, *Sanctus Swithunus: Miracula Metrica auctore Wulfstano monacho*, Beilage zum Jahresbericht des humanistischen Gymnasiums Metten (Metten, 1906); and A. Campbell, *Frithegodi monachi Breuiloquium uitae beati Wilfredi et Wulfstani Cantoris Narratio metrica de Sancto Swithuno* (Zürich, 1950), pp. 65–177. See Lapidge and Winterbottom, *Wulfstan*, pp. xx–xxii.

Ælfric of Eynsham, in writing his Old English Life of Swithun at the close of the tenth century, did make a token effort in the direction of describing the saint's life before passing on to the translation and miracles (drawn from Lantfred's account). He made it clear that he had found no material to go on:[125]

His dæda næron cuðe ærðan þe hi god sylf cydde . ne we ne fundon on bocum hu se bisceop leofode on þysre worulde . ærðan þe he gewende to criste . þæt wæs þæra gymeleast þe on life hine cuþon . þæt hi noldon awritan his weorc and drohtnunge þam towerdum mannum ðe his lif mihte ne cuðon .[126]

This seems to be a fairly accurate description of the state of affairs which confronted many of those who set out to write about the Anglo-Saxon saints in the eleventh century. The products of the late tenth-century revival of hagiography dealt mainly with more manageable subjects. Thus, for example, Wulfstan wrote his *Vita S. Æthelwoldi* with first-hand knowledge of the subject, who had been his abbot and his master,[127] and shortly afterwards, in 1006, Ælfric of Eynsham wrote an abbreviation of Wulfstan's 'biography', dedicated to Bishop Cenwulf (who only held office during the year 1006) and the monks at Winchester (where he himself had been a pupil of Æthelwold).[128]

Ramsey abbey seems also to have been the focus for a certain amount of hagiographical activity in the late tenth century. Another monk from Fleury, Abbo, who visited Ramsey abbey for two years (985–7) as a teacher, was moved by Dunstan's oral account of the martyrdom of Edmund, to write his *Passio S. Eadmundi regis et martyris*.[129] Abbo's prologue claimed that his information derived ultimately from an eyewitness account of Edmund's martyrdom. His *Passio* enjoyed a wide circulation and was not as

---

[125] Skeat, *Ælfric's Lives of Saints*, i. 442.

[126] 'His deeds were not known, before God himself manifested them, neither have we found in books what kind of life the bishop led before he went to Christ. It was carelessness on the part of those who knew him in life, that they did not choose to write down his doings and conduct (*conuersatio*) for future generations who did not know his power.'

[127] Ed. Lapidge and Winterbottom, *Wulfstan of Winchester*.

[128] Ælfric's Life of Æthelwold is edited by M. Winterbottom, *Three Lives of English Saints* (Toronto, 1972), pp. 17–29, and again in Lapidge and Winterbottom, *Wulfstan*, pp. 70–80. The arguments for the relationship of Ælfric's *Vita* to Wulfstan's are also set out there, pp. cxlvii–clv.

[129] Ed. Winterbottom, *Three Lives*, pp. 67–87. See M. Mostert, *The Political Theology of Abbo of Fleury* (Hilversum, 1987) pp. 40–5, for the theory that the *Passio* was actually composed after Abbo's return to Fleury.

quickly superseded as many of the products of the late tenth-century period of hagiographical enthusiasm. Supplementary writings on Edmund, such as Herman's large collection of miracles, appeared in plenty after the eleventh century.[130] Ælfric translated Abbo's text into Old English.[131]

It has been demonstrated conclusively that another two of the texts added to the beginning of Nero E. 1, part 1, namely *Vita S. Oswaldi*,[132] and *Vita S. Ecgwini*,[133] were in fact the work of Byrhtferth, who was certainly at Ramsey in the early eleventh century writing his *Enchiridion* or *Manual*,[134] a bilingual explanation of computus.[135] Byrhtferth had been a pupil of Abbo, who may have communicated to him some enthusiasm for hagiography. It is a possibility that Byrhtferth undertook the task of writing about Ecgwine, patron saint of Evesham, at the request of Ælfweard, the abbot of that house from 1014 and formerly a monk of Ramsey. The prospective hagiographer may have travelled to Evesham in an attempt to gather material for the work in hand. As we shall see, such a practice seems to have been common among hagiographers of the later eleventh century. It is fairly evident from the resulting *Vita* that strikingly little useful information about Ecgwine's actual life was forthcoming, since Byrhtferth went to extraordinary lengths to find things to say, including a long description of the apostolic descent. His idiosyncratic Latin style meant that his Life of Ecgwine did not enjoy a wide circulation (the copy in Nero E. 1 is the only one to survive) and by the close of the eleventh century it had been superseded by Dominic of Evesham's *Vita S. Ecgwini*, found, for example, in the Hereford legendary.[136] The *Vita S. Oswaldi* was also later to be reworked.

At Canterbury, a foreigner, Frithegod, was commissioned to produce a poem honouring St Wilfrid, whose relics had been

---

[130] See T. Arnold (ed.), *Memorials of St Edmund's Abbey*, 3 vols., RS xcvi (1890–6), i. 26–92.

[131] Ed. G. I. Needham, *Ælfric: Lives of Three English Saints* (London, 1966), pp. 43–59.

[132] Ed. Raine, *HCY* i. 399–475. The *Vita* is datable from the mention of Ælfric, archbishop of Canterbury (p. 452), who held office from 995–1005.

[133] Ed. J. A. Giles, *Vita quorundum Anglo-Saxonum* (London, 1854), pp. 349–96. The text is roughly datable by the author's reference to the millennium: 'nos uero qui in ultima millenarii sumus parte et ultra progressi' (p. 387).

[134] Ed. S. J. Crawford, *Byrhtferth's Manual (A.D. 1011)*, EETS, os clxxvii (1929).

[135] M. Lapidge, 'Byrhtferth and the *Vita S. Ecgwini*', *Mediaeval Studies*, xli (1979), 331–53.

[136] Ed. M. Lapidge, 'Dominic of Evesham, *Vita S. Ecgwini, episcopi et confessoris*', *AB* cxiv (1978), 65–104.

brought to Canterbury from the wrecked minster at Ripon, in about 948 or shortly after.[137] In his *Breuiloquium uitae Wilfridi*, Frithegod followed very closely the prose *Vita S. Wilfridi* written by Stephen of Ripon in the early eighth century.[138] In this respect, Frithegod was more fortunate than Byrhtferth in having an early account on which to base his own work. The one disadvantage with Frithegod's work, dubbed elsewhere 'the "masterpiece" of Anglo-Latin hermeneutic style',[139] was that he was so concerned to write in an ostentatious and obscure style, that the result is hard reading. By the end of the eleventh century, the *Breuiloquium* had been replaced by Eadmer's somewhat more approachable Life of Wilfrid.

Another product of late tenth-century Canterbury is the *Vita S. Dunstani*, dedicated to Ælfric, archbishop of Canterbury (995–1005), by an unnamed author, who gives his name in abbreviated form as 'B'.[140] Whoever he was, B. wrote a difficult, hermeneutic Latin, and it is hardly surprising that not many manuscripts of his work survive (and one of those, London, BL, Cotton Cleopatra B. XIII, fos. 59–90, of the early eleventh century is an extensively revised version made at St Augustine's). A short time later, between about 1005 and 1012, Adelard, a monk of St Peter's, Ghent, composed a set of lections and responsories for the feast of St Dunstan, which enjoyed a far wider circulation.[141]

From this very brief outline, it is clear that, to some extent, the groundwork for the revival of interest in hagiography in the second half of the eleventh century was done in the later part of the tenth century. The eleventh-century hagiographers were obviously familiar with the works written at the end of the previous century and

[137] See M. Lapidge, 'A Frankish Scholar in tenth-century England: Frithegod of Canterbury/Fredegaud of Brioude', *ASE* xvii (1988), 45–65.

[138] Frithegod's poem has been edited three times: by J. Mabillon, *Acta Sanctorum Ordinis S. Benedicti*, 9 vols. (Paris, 1668–1771), saeculum III, pars prima (1672), pp. 171–96 + saeculum IV, pars prima (1677), pp. 722–6, repr. in *PL* cxxxiii. 981–1012. Also by Raine, *HCY* i. 105–59; and by Campbell, *Frithegodi*, pp. 1–62. The closing dedication to Archbishop Oda of Canterbury, who died in 958, provides the later limit for the composition of the poem, and the likely date of the removal of Wilfrid's relics from Ripon in 948 the earlier.

[139] M. Lapidge, 'The hermeneutic style in tenth-century Anglo-Latin literature', *ASE* iv (1975), 67–111, at p. 78.

[140] *BHL* 2342, ed. Stubbs, *Memorials*, pp. 3–52. See Lapidge, 'Hermeneutic style', pp. 81–3; and also M. Lapidge, 'B. and the *Vita S. Dunstani*', in *St Dunstan: His Life, Times and Cult*, ed. N. Ramsay, M. Sparks, and T. Tatton-Brown (Woodbridge, 1992), pp. 247–59.

[141] Ed. Stubbs, *Memorials*, pp. 53–68.

strove to improve upon the efforts of their predecessors. Since, however, the majority of their writings are datable to the second half of the eleventh century (in other words after the Norman conquest), we cannot ignore the fact that between these two periods of activity there lies a yawning gap of some fifty years, during which virtually no Lives seem to have been composed. Such a lack cannot be explained simply in terms of the non-survival of manuscripts. There were, perhaps, a few exceptions to the overwhelming silence, such as the lost Life of St Ivo by Wythman (abbot of Ramsey 1016–20), which Goscelin claimed to be reworking in his *Vita S. Yuonis*.[142] Although Wythman's work could be taken as but one example out of many texts from that period which are now lost to us, further examination of the saints' Lives written by Goscelin ought to sound a note of warning against such an extrapolation. For he seems generally to have been quite careful to describe the nature of the sources upon which he had drawn to compose the many texts certainly attributed to him, and *Vita S. Yuonis* is the only place where he refers to another named hagiographer. Indeed there is but one other occasion when Goscelin referred to a pre-existing Life of a saint about whom he was writing, and that is in his *Vita S. Mildrethe*.[143]

Perhaps during the first half of the eleventh century there were other preoccupations. But it has also been suggested that, generally speaking, the Anglo-Saxons may have been disinclined to record the Lives of their saints, as Ælfric hinted in his Old English Life of Swithun. We must concede that the 'negligentia' of past ages was something of a standard topos in hagiography, which Ælfric was probably echoing, but still, the fact that the initiative for the fresh stirrings of hagiography in England in the tenth century seems to have lain with foreigners, or those influenced by them, may be significant.[144] It seems highly likely that the same is true also of the hagiography of the eleventh century.

In the past, scholars have concluded that post-conquest Anglo-

---

[142] Written at Ramsey in the late 1080s; *PL* clv. 81.

[143] See D. W. Rollason, *The Mildrith Legend: A Study in Early Medieval Hagiography in England* (Leicester, 1982), pp. 60 and 108.

[144] See C. E. Fell, 'Edward King and martyr and the Anglo-Saxon hagiographic tradition', in *Ethelred the Unready: Papers from the Millenary Conference*, ed. D. Hill, British Archaeological Reports, British Series lix (1978), 1–14; and cf. J. Campbell, 'Some twelfth-century views of the Anglo-Saxon past', in *Essays in Anglo-Saxon History* (London, 1986), pp. 209–28.

Latin hagiography sprang into life as a consequence of the scepticism of incoming Norman ecclesiastics.[145] On the one hand, it is possible that the roots of the revival lay a little deeper than that, with the earlier arrival of Lotharingian and Flemish ecclesiastics such as Herman (bishop of Ramsbury, 1045–55, and Sherborne, 1058–78), Leofric (bishop of Exeter, 1046–72), Giso (bishop of Wells, 1061–88), Walter (bishop of Hereford, 1061–79) and the scholars Goscelin and Folcard, both of Saint-Bertin. We have already seen that a Flemish collection of Lives of universal interest was introduced into England possibly in the 1050s, and perhaps stands as a token of the more abstract cultural import, namely a different set of attitudes towards the appropriate commemoration of the saints. On the other hand, there must also be a better explanation than scepticism for the undeniable link between the arrival of the Normans and the large-scale production of Anglo-Latin saints' Lives.[146] It may be safer to think in terms of cultural assimilation; a desire on the part of the newly arrived Norman clergy, to see the Lives of the Anglo-Saxon saints properly recorded in writing, in a fitting style, coupled with the wish to consolidate their own position by accepting, taking over, and manipulating the cults of England's patron saints.[147] This could be a two-sided affair, insofar as those persons (whether Anglo-Saxon or not) with a personal or professional interest in the matter may also have been anxious to encourage and commandeer the earthly, but often very powerful, patronage of the Norman ecclesiastical hierarchy, not only for indigenous saints, but also for the centres with which their relic-cults were associated.

(vii) Eleventh-century Anglo-Latin saints' Lives

It is intriguing to speculate upon the difference that would have been made to the history of Anglo-Latin hagiography and to our knowledge of the Anglo-Saxon saints if Goscelin and Folcard of Saint-Bertin had both stayed at home. The former was possibly

[145] Cf. the summary by S. J. Ridyard, 'Condigna veneratio. Norman attitudes to Anglo-Saxon saints', Anglo-Norman Studies, ix (1987), 179–206; and also Campbell, in Essays, p. 210.

[146] Consider, for example, the case of Vita et miracula S. Kenelmi composed possibly by Goscelin, and apparently during the regime of Winchcombe's first Norman abbot; see pp. xci–cx below.

[147] Cf. Ridyard, 'Condigna veneratio', pp. 204–6.

one of the most prolific hagiographers at work in eleventh-century England,[148] and a very high proportion of extant Lives from that milieu have either been attributed to him with certainty, or at some time in the past been assigned to him, rightly or wrongly.[149] Patently, the canon of Goscelin's works has still to be established once and for all, and a detailed analysis of his vocabulary and style is urgently required.[150] A study of this kind will be essential before the development of Latin hagiography in eleventh-century England can be charted fully.[151] Relatively little scholarly attention has been paid to the œuvre (admittedly much smaller) of Goscelin's confrater Folcard.[152] Particularly useful would be an overall investigation of the extent to which we can speak of a Saint-Bertin school of hagiographical writing, an earlier product of which may well have been the anonymous author of the so-called *Encomium Emmae Reginae*.[153]

From a brief examination of Goscelin's writings, it is possible to form some impression of the circumstances in which the eleventh-century 'revival' of hagiography was initiated. Goscelin came to England under the aegis of Herman, the Lotharingian bishop of Ramsbury and Sherborne, in about 1058, and joined that bishop's household. Apart from a *Vita S. Amelberge*, which he may have

---

[148] The career of Goscelin has been treated in several places, notably by F. Barlow in Appendix C of *The Life of King Edward who rests at Westminster*, 2nd edn., OMT (1992), pp. 133–49, and by C. H. Talbot, 'The *Liber Confortatorius* of Goscelin of St Bertin', *Studia Anselmiana*, xxxviii, Analecta Monastica, 3rd series (Rome, 1955), pp. 1–117, at pp. 5–22; also A. Wilmart, 'Ève et Goscelin,' *Revue Bénédictine*, xlvi (1934), 414–38, and l (1938), 42–83.

[149] Lists of Goscelin's works (of quite varied length) occur in *Histoire littéraire de la France*, par des religieux de la Congrégation de S. Maur (Paris, 1738–1876), viii. 660–77; Talbot, '*Liber Confortatorius*', p. 13; A. Wilmart, 'La Légende de Sainte Édithe en prose et vers par le moine Goscelin', *AB* lvi (1938), 5–101, 265–307, at p. 5 n. 1; M. L. Colker, 'Texts of Jocelyn of Canterbury which relate to the History of Barking Abbey', *Studia Monastica*, vii (2) (1965), 383–460, at p. 384; Barlow, *The Life of King Edward*, pp. 146–9; and T. J. Hamilton, 'Goscelin of Canterbury; a critical study of his life, works and accomplishments', Ph.D. thesis (University of Virginia, 1973), pp. 123–4.

[150] There is much analysis in Hamilton's unpublished dissertation on Goscelin, confined largely to the securely attributed works; little consideration, however, seems to have been given to the possibility of a development in style over the twenty or so years of Goscelin's working life.

[151] Cf. Barlow, *Life of King Edward*, p. 133.

[152] Cf. the surveys in *Histoire littéraire de la France*, viii. 132–8; and Barlow, *Life of King Edward*, pp. lii–lix.

[153] Ed. A. Campbell, *Encomium Emmae Reginae*, Camden 3rd Series, lxii (London, 1949). See Campbell's comments on the identity of the encomiast, pp. xix–xxiii.

written before leaving Saint-Bertin,[154] the earliest Life which can certainly be attributed to Goscelin is that of St Wulfsige. This was apparently begun at the request of Herman and the monks at Sherborne, but only completed after the bishop had died in 1078, and dedicated probably to Bishop Osmund (1078–99), Herman's successor and a figure of some political and ecclesiastical power, as William I's former chancellor.[155] Goscelin does not seem to have found any earlier Life of Wulfsige at Sherborne, but claimed to have assembled his account from the traditions collectively stored in the memories of the members of the community.[156]

The composition of his fulsome *Vita S. Edithe* in about 1080 seems also to have been stimulated initially by the personal interest of Goscelin's patron Herman, as well as that of successive abbesses of Wilton (several of whom he would have been acquainted with, as sometime chaplain to the nuns); he claimed that Edith's renown had even come to Herman's attention while he was still a monk at Saint-Bertin.[157] Yet again, the work was not actually completed until after Herman's death, and was dedicated to Lanfranc, archbishop of Canterbury (1070–89).[158] Interestingly enough, Goscelin chose to list precisely the reasons why he felt that Lanfranc should be interested in a Life of Edith, emphasizing her connections with Canterbury, and, after a few phrases flattering to that primate, commended the saint to his patronage as a 'margaritam non porcis conculcandam'.[159] While it would be

---

[154] *BHL* 323; *ActaS*, July, iii. 87–98. The attribution depends upon a cross-reference in the *Vita S. Werburge* to a miracle about geese: 'tale prorsus miraculum in Vita beatissime uirginis Amelberge, quam nostro stylo recudimus, legitur' (*PL* clv. 97). *Vita S. Amelberge* does indeed have a similar miracle concerning wild geese, but so too does *Vita S. Milburge* (Lincoln Cathedral Library, 149, fo. 85ʳ), which may have been the work of Goscelin; it is just possible that Goscelin was actually referring to the latter, but that the two names were confused by a later scribe; cf. Talbot, '*Liber confortatorius*', p. 8, contradicted by H. P. R. Finberg, *The Early Charters of the West Midlands*, 2nd edn. (Leicester, 1972), p. 200 n. 1.

[155] The Life is printed from the only known MS, Gotha I. 81, by C. H. Talbot, 'The Life of Saint Wulsin of Sherborne by Goscelin,' *Revue Bénédictine*, lxix (1959), 68–85. Significant modifications to Talbot's work, and to his dating of the text, were suggested in the review by P. Grosjean, *AB* lxxviii (1960), 197–206, at pp. 201–6. Grosjean felt that the Life must in fact be counted among Goscelin's latest writings, although the phrase in the dedicatory preface 'mors uelocioribus alis illum [scil. Herman] mihi preripuit et te cui scribam iuuentus aquile restituit' (Talbot, p. 73) seems most applicable to Osmund. Cf. Barlow, *Life of King Edward*, p. 140.

[156] Talbot, 'St Wulsin', p. 73.

[157] Wilmart, 'La légende', pp. 37–8.

[158] Ibid. 34 and 38. [159] Ibid. 38–9.

arguing too far to claim this as evidence of Lanfranc's famed scepticism towards Anglo-Saxon saints, Goscelin's words could be interpreted as an instance of the way hagiography might have been used, at least in part, to commend a saint, and thereby the centre of her cult, to the patronage of the powerful.

Just as at Sherborne, Goscelin claimed that he was working principally from a trustworthy oral source, namely the nuns and abbesses of the convent, 'quarum et parentele et religiose uite non minorem fidem quam libris noscuntur habere'.[160] This was not the whole story, however, since, although no explicit reference is made to an earlier Life of Edith, it seems that some of the miracles which had occurred more recently at Wilton had been recorded on the spot 'patriis literis', that is, in Anglo-Saxon.[161]

If there is any validity in the conjectures made about *Vita et miracula S. Kenelmi* further on in this book, that text would actually displace *Vita S. Wlsini* as Goscelin's earliest attributed work in England, and was apparently composed under the regime of the first Norman abbot of Winchcombe. Although it remains unclear who can have instigated its production, or to whom its preface was addressed, *Vita et miracula* nevertheless seems to fit into the picture being built up here—composed probably without reference to an earlier Life of the saint, based upon anecdotal evidence and a few surviving documents, some of them in Anglo-Saxon, and apparently commending Kenelm and his cult to a superior figure.[162] A possible obstacle to the attribution of *Vita et miracula S. Kenelmi* could be that, unlike in the case of his works on Wulfsige and Edith, there is no obvious reason why Goscelin, based in Herman's diocese, should have been involved with the cult of a saint tucked away at Winchcombe, in the diocese of Worcester. Another Life, which, it has been suggested, may have been composed by Goscelin at this period, is *Passio S. Eadwardi regis et martyris*, written presumably for Shaftesbury.[163] The text is in many ways very comparable to *Vita et miracula S. Kenelmi*, in describing the death of an innocent royal martyr, and being accompanied by a selection of miracles (albeit far fewer than those concerning Kenelm). There again we run up against Bishop Herman, who is purported to have

---

[160] Wilmart, 'La légende', p. 37.
[161] Ibid. 39 and 292.   [162] See below pp. xcvii, cviii.
[163] *BHL* 2418; ed. C. E. Fell, *Edward, King and Martyr*, Leeds Texts and Monographs, NS (Leeds, 1971); on authorship, see esp. p. xx.

been the witness to the healing of a blind man at Edward's shrine.[164]

A good deal of the hagiography which Goscelin went on to write after he left Sherborne diocese seems to have been commissioned in commemoration of a recent translation of relics. This is the case with his group of Lives written for Barking, which were probably completed shortly after 1087, when a triple translation apparently occurred: [165] *Vita S. Wlfhilde*, *Translatio S. Wlfhilde*,[166] *Vita et uirtutes S. Ethelburge uirginis*,[167] *Lectiones de S. Hildelitha* and *Translatio uel eleuatio SS. uirginum Ethelburge Hildelithe ac Wulfilde*.[168] The Lives of Wulfhild and Æthelburh were dedicated to Maurice, bishop of the diocese of London (1086–1107), in which Barking was situated.

Perhaps Goscelin's most substantial work was that which he carried out at St Augustine's, Canterbury, to which he had migrated in about the year 1089. Once he was established there, his hagiographical skills were soon brought to bear upon the enormous business of recording and commemorating the grand programme of translations made in 1091.[169] The texts he composed concern mainly St Augustine: *Historia maior de aduentu S. Augustini*,[170] and *Historia maior de miraculis*,[171] *Historia minor de uita S. Augustini*,[172] *Historia minor de miraculis*,[173] *Historia translationis S.*

---

[164] Fell, pp. 14–15.

[165] The evidence for this date lies in the fact that the translation of the three Barking saints was celebrated on 7 March, according to the calendar of that house; see *The Ordinale and Customary of the Benedictine Nuns of Barking Abbey*, ed. J. B. L. Tolhurst, 2 vols., HBS lxv (1927–8), i. 3, and ii. 200. Goscelin, in his account of the translation (Colker, 'Texts', p. 443), said that it took place on Laetare Sunday: 'dies dominica quae est quadragesimae media', which fell on 7 March in 1087 (though also in 1092)—cf. *Handbook of Dates for Students of English History*, ed. C. R. Cheney (London, 1978), pp. 96–7.

[166] Ed. M. Esposito, 'La vie de sainte Vulfhilde par Goscelin de Cantorbéry', *AB* xxxii (1913), 10–26, and again by Colker, 'Texts', pp. 418–34.

[167] Ed. Colker, 'Texts', pp. 398–417.

[168] Ibid. 435–52.

[169] The relationship between the writings of Goscelin and the translations which took place at Canterbury in 1091 is discussed by R. Sharpe, 'Goscelin's St Augustine and St Mildreth: Hagiography and Liturgy in Context', *Journal of Theological Studies*, xli (1990), 502–16.

[170] *BHL* 777; ed. d'Achery and Mabillon, *Acta Sanctorum O.S.B.* (Venice, 1733), i. 485–520, and in *ActaS*, Maii, vi (3rd edn.) 372–92, and *PL* lxxx. 43–94.

[171] *BHL* 779, printed d'Achery and Mabillon, *Acta Sanctorum*, i. 520–43, and *ActaS*, Maii, vi (3rd edn.) 393–407.

[172] *BHL* 778; printed H. Wharton, *Anglia Sacra* (London, 1691), ii. 51–71, and *PL* cl. 743–64. Goscelin stated that this abbreviated version was intended for the wider audience of those not belonging to the community at St Augustine's (cols. 743–4).

[173] *BHL* 780. Cf. Hardy, *Catalogue*, i. 195–6, no. 540.

Augustini et aliorum sanctorum,[174] but also Augustine's successors at Canterbury,[175] and St Mildreth (*Vita S. Mildrethe*, *Translatio et miracula S. Mildrethe*, and *Libellus contra inanes S. uirginis Mildrethe usurpatores*).[176] Goscelin seems to have completed his task finally in 1098 or 1099, when the *Historia translationis* was finished.[177]

We have touched here upon only a portion of the saints' Lives Goscelin may actually have written for various houses. The itinerant period of his career remains to be worked out clearly (if such a thing can ever be achieved), so that his time at Ramsey, where he wrote his *Vita S. Yuonis*,[178] and his sojourn at Ely can be fitted in with his other known activities at Barking and St Augustine's.[179] Further work is required on the group of Lives of women saints connected with Ely which may be Goscelin's work, namely those of Seaxburh,[180] Wihtburh,[181] and Eormenhild;[182] as well as on two other Lives which seem to be his work, but cannot yet be readily fitted into his itinerary, namely *Vita S. Werburge*[183] and *Vita S. Milburge*.[184]

Goscelin's compatriot Folcard seems to have come to England at roughly the same time, and was appointed abbot of Thorney (1069), where he stayed for some sixteen years.[185] While still at

---

[174] *BHL* 781; printed in *ActaS*, May, vi (3rd edn.) 408–39, and partly in *PL* clv. 13–46.

[175] Lives of Laurence, Mellitus, Justus, Honorius, Deusdedit, and Hadrian; almost all unpublished—see Barlow, *Life of King Edward*, p. 147.

[176] Respectively *BHL* 5960, ed. Rollason, *Mildrith Legend*, pp. 108–43; and id., 'Goscelin of Canterbury's account of the translation and miracles of St Mildrith (*BHL* 5961/4): an edition with notes', *Mediaeval Studies*, xlviii (1986), 139–210; and M. L. Colker, ed., 'A hagiographic polemic', *Mediaeval Studies*, xxxix (1977), 60–108.

[177] *PL* clv. 15–16: 'Codicellus est recentis translationis signorumque ipsius . . . quae diuersis locis per hoc fere ab ipsa translatione septennium . . . clare patrata noscuntur.'

[178] The dedication is 'frater Goscelinus rectori Hereberto' (Herbert Losinga, abbot from 1087 to 1091), *PL* clv. 84; *Miracula S. Yuonis*, also largely by Goscelin, are printed by Macray, *Chronicon Abbatiae Rameseiensis*, RS lxxxiii (1886), pp. lix–lxxv.

[179] It is recorded that when he was there he wrote a now lost 'prosa' for the feast of St Æthelthryth, in the time of Abbot Simon (1082–94); see E. O. Blake, *Liber Eliensis*, Camden 3rd Series, xcii (London, 1962), p. 215 (ii. 133).

[180] *BHL* 7693. See Blake, *Liber Eliensis*, pp. xxiv, xxix, and xxxiv; and London, BL, Cotton Caligula A. viii, fos. 104ʳ–116ᵛ.

[181] *BHL* 8979. See Blake, *Liber Eliensis*, pp. xxiv and xxxvii.

[182] *BHL* 2611. See Blake, *Liber Eliensis*, pp. xxiv and xxxiv.

[183] *BHL* 8855–6; printed *ActaS*, Feb. i. 386–90, and *PL* clv. 97–110.

[184] The Life (accompanied by an account of the miracles attending the invention of Mildburh at Wenlock, by Odo, cardinal bishop of Ostia), still unpublished, occurs in Lincoln Cathedral 149, fos. 83ᵛ–88ᵛ, London, BL, Addit. 34633, fos. 206ʳ–216ᵛ and partly in Lambeth Palace Library, 94, fo. 169ʳ⁻ᵛ. See H. P. R. Finberg, *The Early Charters of the West Midlands*, 2nd edn. (Leicester, 1972), pp. 199–200.

[185] See *The Ecclesiastical History of Orderic Vitalis*, ed. M. Chibnall, 6 vols. (OMT, 1969–80), xi. 17.

Saint-Bertin, Folcard had already composed a Life of the patron saint, in 1050 or shortly after,[186] and the two Lives of Anglo-Saxon saints which are certainly his work are those of St John of Beverley,[187] commissioned by Bishop Ealdred of York (1061–9),[188] and that of St Botwulf, dedicated to Walkelin, bishop of Winchester (1070–98).[189] In the prologue of the latter, Folcard gave an affecting account of his fondness for Thorney, to which he clung 'ut asinus uel bos ad presepe Domini', and how he was moved to write about Botwulf: 'Videns autem sanctos in eadem basilica pausantes, nulla scriptorum memoria commendatos, indignatus antiquitati, quae de eis addiscere potui, tuis auribus primum offerre uolui, ne rusticior sermo, nullo suffultus defensore, derisioni expositus, emulorum cachinnum potius optineret quam auditum.'[190] One strongly senses that this is a call for patronage, as much for Folcard himself as for Botwulf and the cult at Thorney.[191]

At the same time as Goscelin was busy at St Augustine's, others at Canterbury had begun seriously to take up the cause of Anglo-Saxon saints, namely Osbern and Eadmer, both Englishmen, and both writing at, and mainly for, Christ Church. A certain amount of their work was taken up with rewriting earlier Lives, for example Osbern's Life of Dunstan,[192] which Eadmer subsequently reworked again,[193] and also Eadmer's Life of Wilfrid.[194] But new ground was also covered. The well-known story of the circumstances which led to Osbern's composition of his Life of Ælfheah demonstrates the thoughtful care (but ultimately, open-mindedness) with which Norman churchmen such as Lanfranc approached the cults of the Anglo-Saxon saints.[195] Both Osbern and Eadmer were occupied with filling in, as it were, the gaps in Canterbury's knowledge of her own ecclesiastical history: thus Osbern produced a now-lost Life of Archbishop Oda, and Eadmer composed Lives of Peter, the first abbot of St Augustine's,[196] of

---

[186] ActaS, Sept. ii. 604–13. [187] Ed. Raine, HCY i. 239–91.
[188] See p. xcvii below for speculative comments about Ealdred's interest in Anglo-Saxon saints.
[189] ActaS, June, iii. 402–3. The prologue was published by Hardy, Catalogue, i (1) 373.
[190] Hardy, Descriptive Catalogue, i (1) 373.
[191] The preface to the Life of John, addressed to Ealdred, has an even more plaintive tone; cf. HCY i. 240. [192] Stubbs, Memorials, pp. 69–161.
[193] Ibid. 162–249. [194] Raine, HCY i. 161–226.
[195] See Ridyard, 'Condigna veneratio', pp. 200–1; Lanfranc's qualms about Ælfheah were reported by Eadmer in his Vita S. Anselmi, ed. Southern, pp. 50–4.
[196] Wilmart, 'Noua Opuscula', pp. 354–61.

Bregwine, the eighth-century archbishop of Canterbury,[197] and of Archbishop Oda.[198] Part of Eadmer's enthusiasm for such work must have sprung from a kind of sentimentality about Canterbury's, indeed England's past.[199] Their concern was also to record the manifestation of the powerful favour the saints bestowed upon Canterbury in the form of the many miracles worked at their shrines.[200] Thus, to complement their respective Lives of Dunstan, both Osbern and Eadmer included a full dossier of miracles for Dunstan, and Eadmer also wrote up those associated with the relics of St Ouen, of which Christ Church claimed to be in possession.[201]

Plainly there was also some interest at Worcester in the proper recording of the Lives of the Anglo-Saxon saints. We have already noted that various texts were appended to the Worcester copy of the 'Cotton-Corpus legendary'. It is possible that St Mary's, Worcester was in some way involved with the production of *Vita et miracula S. Kenelmi*, in the 1070s.[202] Somewhat later, apparently at the request of the monks at St Mary's, Eadmer produced a new *Vita et miracula S. Oswaldi*, drawing upon Byrhtferth's earlier work.[203] Although the text is now lost, we discover from William of Malmesbury's later version that an Old English Life of Wulfstan II was composed shortly after his death by his chaplain Coleman.[204]

Alongside these Lives concerning whose authorship and origins we can be fairly confident, there is a host of eleventh-century Anglo-Latin hagiography, which remains unattributed and unaccounted for. Some of these texts can clearly be associated with particular centres and with a specific concern to record and dignify

---

[197] B. W. Scholz, 'Eadmer's Life of Bregwine, Archbishop of Canterbury', *Traditio*, xxii (1966), 127–48.

[198] Wharton, *Anglia Sacra*, ii. 78–87; *PL* cxxxiii. 933–44.

[199] Cf. R. W. Southern, *St Anselm: A Portrait in a Landscape* (Cambridge, 1990), pp. 406–9.

[200] It seems that both Osbern and Eadmer were filled with curiosity about the nature and origin of the many relics that must have filled the church at Canterbury; see the account of their investigation of the shrines at Christ Church, carried out at Osbern's instigation, which Eadmer included in his *De reliquiis S. Audoeni* (Wilmart, 'Nova opuscula', p. 367). Cf. Southern, *Portrait*, p. 318.

[201] See Wilmart, 'Les reliques', and 'Nova opuscula', pp. 185–6; and Ker, 'Un nouveau fragment'.

[202] See below, pp. cii–ciii, cx.

[203] Ed. Raine, *HCY* ii. 1–40 and *Miracula*, pp. 41–59; this was begun after the death of Wulfstan in 1095.

[204] R. R. Darlington, ed., *The Vita Wulfstani of William of Malmesbury*, Camden 3rd Series, xl (London, 1928), p. 2.

the cults of the saints resting there. *Vita S. Birini* and *Vita et miracula S. Swithuni*, whether composed at Winchester or Sherborne,[205] are nevertheless the formal commemoration of Winchester's principal patron saints, mirroring Goscelin's more substantial dossier of materials composed for St Augustine's in the 1090s. Possibly datable to the same period is *Vita S. Erkenwaldi*, which proclaimed London's patron saint.[206] From perhaps a little earlier in the century there is the *Vita Prima S. Neoti*, which was apparently concerned mainly with establishing the claim of St Neots, Huntingdonshire to possess the relics of that saint.[207] Many more texts which contribute to a general impression of an eleventh-century revival in hagiography are even less readily datable, and it is at present difficult to know what should be made of them severally. *Vita S. Rumwoldi*, for example, seems on the face of it to be commending the reader's attention to the site of Rumwold's resting, at Buckingham.[208] Yet closer examination suggests that this unique text was in some ways as concerned to justify the veneration of an infant saint, as to promote local interests. Other Lives that await closer study are the *Passiones* of King Æthelberht of Hereford,[209] of the brothers Æthelberht and Æthelred who rested at Ramsey,[210] of Osgyth,[211] and of Wigstan.[212]

At this juncture it seems appropriate briefly to raise a point of interest which arises from a survey of the Lives of the Anglo-Saxon saints, namely the concept of the 'saintly cousinhood'.[213] It is noticeable that sanctity runs in the family; thus Goscelin's *Vita et uirtutes S. Ethelburge* reminds us that the saint's brother was St Eorkenwald, his *Vita S. Edithe* that she was the sister of the martyred Edward,[214] and *Vita S. Mildrethe* and *Vita S. Werburge*

[205] See below, pp. lviii–lx.

[206] *BHL* 2600, ed. and trans. E. G. Whatley, *The Saint of London. The Life and Miracles of St. Erkenwald* (Binghamton, 1989). Whatley decided against the earlier attribution of this text to Goscelin, on stylistic grounds (pp. 16–19).

[207] D. Dumville and M. Lapidge (eds.), *The Anglo-Saxon Chronicle: A Collaborative Edition*, xvii: *The Annals of St Neots with Vita Prima Sancti Neoti* (Woodbridge, 1985), pp. 111–42. Perhaps datable to the mid-11th cent. (p. xcvi).

[208] See below, pp. clx–clxi.

[209] See M. R. James, 'Two Lives of St Ethelbert, king and martyr', *English Historical Review*, xxxii (1917), 214–44.

[210] Cf. Rollason, *Mildrith*, pp. 90–104.

[211] See D. Bethell, 'The Lives of Osyth of Essex and St Osyth of Aylesbury', *AB* xcix (1970), 75–127.

[212] Ed. W. D. Macray, *Chronicon Abbatiae de Evesham*, RS xxix (1863), pp. 325–37.

[213] Cf. Campbell, *Essays*, p. 218.   [214] Wilmart, 'La Légende', p. 40.

incorporate what is known as the 'Kentish royal legend', in which the reader is introduced to the extended family that produced the sisters Mildrith, Mildburh, Mildgyth and the little saint Merefin; the sisters Æthelthryth, Wihtburh, and Seaxburh (and her daughters Eorcongota and Eormenhild).[215] Similarly *Vita S. Rumwoldi* connects that infant saint to the Mercian royal line, by making him a grandson of King Penda;[216] the so-called 'First Essex Life' of St Osgyth makes her also a grandchild of Penda,[217] among whose children may be numbered SS Cyneburh and Cyneswith. The 'Kentish royal legend' is enshrined in an Anglo-Saxon tract, *þa halgan*, which is found in two manuscripts alongside another document, known as the *Secgan*, a quite comprehensive list of the resting-places of the Anglo-Saxon saints.[218] The earlier of the two copies of these tracts seems to have been written in about 1031,[219] but the texts themselves may have been composed somewhat earlier; what is certain is that Goscelin knew and used at least the first of these tracts, possibly in a Latin translation,[220] and may also have seen the *Secgan*. To Goscelin and his contemporaries, arriving in England in the second half of the eleventh century, works such as *þa halgan* and *Secgan* would have provided an exciting starting-point for researches into the possibilities of the Anglo-Saxon past, and for the formal codification of the multitude of saints whose earthly lives and heavenly patronage left their mark throughout the churches and countryside of England, and in the memories of its inhabitants.

[215] Rollason, *Mildrith*, pp. 114–16; cf. the family tree on p. 45, and Ridyard, *Royal Saints*, p. 50.

[216] See below, pp. clxii–clxiii.

[217] Cf. the comments of C. Hohler on the proliferation of Penda's daughters and the foundation of minsters, in 'St Osyth and Aylesbury', *Records of Buckinghamshire*, xviii (1966–70), 61–72, at p. 63 n. 15. See also Ridyard, *Royal Saints*, pp. 134–5.

[218] The full titles are *Her cyð ymbe þa halgan þe on Angelcynne restað* and *Secgan be þam Godes sanctum þe on Engla lande ærost reston*; both ed. F. Liebermann, *Die Heiligen Englands* (Hanover, 1889); cf. also D. Rollason, 'Lists of saints' resting-places in Anglo-Saxon England', *ASE* vii (1978), 61–93.

[219] London, BL, Stowe 944; see Rollason, 'Lists', p. 61.

[220] Known as *De sanctis* (ed. Liebermann, *Heiligen*, pp. 2–20) and translated at St Augustine's; see Colker, 'Hagiographic polemic', pp. 63–4.

2. ST BIRINUS OF DORCHESTER-ON-THAMES AND *VITA SANCTI BIRINI*

(i) *St Birinus*

THE earliest recoverable account of the mission of St Birinus, apostle of Wessex, is to be found in Bede, *HE* iii. 7, upon which *Vita S. Birini* is based. Bede did not provide any date for the arrival of Birinus, but in the *Anglo-Saxon Chronicle*[1] we find the following entries defining the limits of his sojourn in England:

[634] AN. dcxxxiiii Her Birinus biscep bodude Westseaxum fulwuht.
[650] AN. dcl Her Ęgelbryht of Galwalum æfter Birine þam romaniscan biscepe onfeng Wesseaxna biscepdome.

Some kind of early West-Saxon annals might lie behind the information included in the *Anglo-Saxon Chronicle*. However, no more details about Birinus are available to us now than those which have been relayed by Bede,[2] namely that he was sent by Pope Honorius I to continue the conversion of England, and on the way was consecrated bishop in Genoa, by Asterius, archbishop of Milan. On arrival in England, he found the Gewisse, or West Saxons, still so pagan that he abandoned his original intention of penetrating deeper into the region, and began his evangelization there in Wessex. Having converted and baptized the king of the West Saxons, Cynegils, and many of the people of the area, Birinus was granted Dorchester-on-Thames (Oxon.) as his see. Since Birinus's exact origins and extraction remain obscure, it is not certain what exact form his name should take, whether Berin or Birin, and consequently the Latinized form is used here throughout, to avoid confusion.[3]

---

[1] *The Anglo-Saxon Chronicle. A Collaborative Edition*, general editors, D. N. Dumville and S. Keynes, iii: *MSA*, ed. J. M. Bately (Cambridge, 1986), pp. 28–9.

[2] Bede probably acquired his scant knowledge of Birinus from Daniel, bishop of Winchester (*c.*705–44). See J. M. Wallace-Hadrill, *Bede's Ecclesiastical History of the English People: A Historical Commentary* (OMT, 1988), pp. 97–8, and K. Harrison, *The Framework of Anglo-Saxon History to A.D. 900* (Cambridge, 1976), p. 135.

[3] Cf. J. C. Field, *Saint Berin The Apostle of Wessex* (London, 1902), pp. 42–56, where the form 'Berin' is argued for, as a name of Teutonic origin related to 'Beorn', on the

It does not seem possible to provide a very precise date for the composition of *Vita S. Birini* from internal evidence alone. The way in which Æthelwold is referred to—'Euoluto autem multo tempore beatus Athelwoldus magne religionis et auctoritatis uir, qui et ipse uigesimus sextus in honore episcopatus successor a Deo factus est' (c. 21)—suggests that the episcopacy of Æthelwold (*ob.* 984) lay well in the past. Oxford, Bodleian Library, Digby 39, the earliest manuscript which preserves *Vita S. Birini*, is datable to the very end of the eleventh century or the beginning of the twelfth, and thus provides a later time-limit for the composition of the text. As will be seen below, external evidence based upon the probable authorship of the Life may offer a more precise dating than this rather broad sweep of about a century.

(ii) *The Style, Latinity and Sources of* Vita S. Birini

The vocabulary of *Vita S. Birini* is largely free from the kind of archaisms, neologisms, and Grecisms which characterized the Latinity of some Anglo-Latin authors of the later tenth century. The author's stylistic pretensions lay elsewhere. There is a marked predilection for polysyllabic nouns and adverbs, but virtually all of those used are well attested in either Classical or Late Latin. As regards syntax, although the periods are often rather long, they consist not infrequently of accumulated short parallel clauses, bound together by rhyme (of one or more syllables)[4] or assonance, so that the structure and sense are clear enough. These short parallel clauses are often used climactically. Quite frequently, the pattern seems to be three short phrases in asyndeton, followed by a fourth, longer clause, in which the wave of tension breaks, so to speak; for example, 'Flat aura, uentus insurgit, deseuit mare, nauis unda tumultuante succutitur' (c. 9), and 'Cadunt idola, fana sternuntur, franguntur simulachra, omnis eorum cultus aut minuitur aut dampnatur' (c. 14).

---

assumption that the saint was of Lombardic descent. See E. Förstermann, *Altdeutsches-namenbuch*, 3 vols. (Bonn, 1900), i, s.v. 'Bera'.

[4] On rhymed prose in general see K. Polheim, *Die lateinische Reimprosa* (Berlin, 1925), and in particular pp. 373–6, and pp. 422–5 on the widespread use of rhyme in hagio-graphy. The extensive use of rhymed prose in the 11th-cent. hagiography of Flanders is noted by de Gaiffier, 'L'hagiographie dans le Marquisat', pp. 437–44. A relatively early example of rhymed-prose hagiography in England is Lantfred's *Translatio et miracula S. Swithuni*.

Many examples of the use of rhyme could be furnished from every page, and also of alliteration. Another particularly prominent feature of the rhetorical style of *Vita S. Birini* is the use of rhythmical *cursus*,[5] which, combined with the extensive use of rhyme, gives the text a strongly poetic tone.[6] The word order was, needless to say, often determined by the dictates of rhyme and rhythm but never contorted to the extent that the text becomes unintelligible. Certainly, hyperbaton is one rhetorical device not favoured by the author.

What is perhaps most remarkable about *Vita S. Birini* is the thoroughly pompous and verbose rhetorical style. The hagiographer contrived, with some skill and imagination, to work up a rather terse report in Bede's *HE*, into a fairly lengthy piece, without adding any significant information about Birinus except his two supposed miracles. Much of the rest is hagiographical commonplace, such as the description of the early life and virtues of the saint, or mere padding and rhetorical amplification, often of the most desperate kind.[7] At times, the impression one gains is that the principal aim was to produce as many pages of text as possible to glorify the saint, or so many minutes' worth of reading aloud, and in as dignified and striking a style as possible.

The whole is decked out with a variety of rhetorical adornments. As well as the employment throughout of rhyme and assonance, as already mentioned, the following figures may be noted:

(*a*) antithesis (often quite extended); for example, the rejoicing exile, who leaves the multitudes of the city, but has the One God dwelling in the city of his heart (c. 6); the bellicose conqueror whose conquest did not last contrasted with the peaceful conqueror whose conquest is eternal (c. 8); the king made servant to the King, and the king's servants made kings (cc. 18–19).

[5] When the sentence-endings of *Vita S. Birini* were analysed according to the system devised by T. Janson, *Prose Rhythm in Medieval Latin from the 9th to the 13th Century* (Stockholm, 1975), his four principal configurations were found to occur (apparently by design rather than by accident) with the following frequency: p 3p, 29%; p 4pp, 20%; pp 4p, 14%; and p 4p, 4%; making a total of 67%. The further inclusion of various by-forms (such as p 1 2, and p 1 3pp) increases this figure to about 80% (*planus*: 36%; *tardus*: 24%; *velox*: 16%; *trispondiacus*: 4%).

[6] Cf. the comments of Barlow on Goscelin's style, 'He does not spare his words and the prose often sounds like verse' (*Life of King Edward*, p. li).

[7] Just two of the many examples of the latter are the account of Birinus's departure from Rome (c. 6) and the discussion of how Birinus happened to stay for three days where he had put to shore (c. 14).

(*b*) epanaphora; for example, the five successive sentences beginning 'Exiuit . . .' (c. 6); the repetition of 'Iste' (c. 7); repetition of
'Stabat' (c. 12).

(*c*) asyndeton; the description of the sea voyage, where a sense of
urgency and swift movement is required, supplies several examples, and two instances of a tricolon in asyndeton: 'Insistunt
naute remigio, portus in uoto est, illum uultu manu sermone
requirunt, periculum dampnum mortem se declinare contendunt'
(c. 9); 'Tenduntur carbasa, antenne curuantur, concutiuntur remi,
omnia nauis armamenta laborant' (c. 12).[8]

(*d*) word-play; such as, the play on the name of Pope Honorius (c.
4); on 'exulo' and 'exulto' (c. 6); and 'furo' and 'fero' (c. 20).

(*e*) apostrophe; for example, the address to Peter and Paul (c. 1);
and to Britain (cc. 7 and 20), inspired by an apostrophe to Rome in
Leo the Great's homily; to Birinus (cc. 11 and 19).

(*f*) There are numerous examples of chiasmic construction; to
note just a few: 'magnificus pater, pastor egregius' (c. 1); 'seueritatis exemplar, speculum honestatis, religionis liber, pagina sanctitatis' (c. 2); 'flat aura, uentus insurgit' (c. 9); 'Gemit hostis,
inimicus dolet' (c. 14).

As has already been noted, Bede, *HE* iii. 7, was the principal
source of information about Birinus upon which the hagiographer
seems to have been dependent. The relevant portions are quoted
almost verbatim, either with acknowledgement of the source, 'sicut
uenerabilis Beda refert' (c. 17), or not. It is just possible that some
earlier written account, which has not survived, was available too,
perhaps deriving from Dorchester, but there is no conclusive evidence to indicate that such was the case.[9] Thus we cannot now
determine the origin of the two miracles, of Birinus walking on
water, and healing the blind and deaf woman. Such stories may
have circulated as oral traditions, which the hagiographer
endowed with some sort of structure and narrative coherence. It is
noteworthy, however, that both of them, as recounted in *Vita S.*

---

[8] Cf. the comments above on climactic phrases.

[9] See the section below on the cult of Birinus. Field, *St Berin* (pp. xiv–xv), was
mistaken in supposing that the three lections for the Translation of Birinus in the York
Breviary were the antecedent of *Vita S. Birini*, and composed shortly after 984. The
lections look much more like a drastic abbreviation of the *Vita*; see *Breviarium ad usum
insignis ecclesie Eboracensis*, ed. S. W. Lawley, 2 vols., Surtees Society lxxi, lxxv (1880–3),
ii. 532–3.

Birini, are strongly biblical in flavour. The possibility cannot be excluded that the author simply invented the miracles to make up for a lack of material,[10] but evidence will be adduced below which may indicate the contrary.[11]

In constructing his text, the hagiographer cast his net quite widely, drawing not only on biblical texts, but on a considerable variety of other material. Quite a few sources have already been detected, but doubtless many more still remain to be identified. The author evidently had sufficient familiarity with the Classical Latin poets, Vergil, Horace, and Lucan, to be able to draw upon their work for his description of the sea (c. 9), and he may also have known some form of commentary on Vergil's *Aeneid*.[12] He was also clearly rather fond of biblical exegesis, and used it as a means of amplification on several occasions: the three-score strong men of Israel (c. 3), good preachers who are like the golden poles which supported the Ark of the Covenant (c. 4), and two other portions of the Song of Solomon—the chinks in the rock (c. 14) and the crowning of the preacher (c. 19). In just a few cases it is possible that certain turns of phrase were also drawn directly from exegetical texts, such as Cassiodorus on the Psalms, or Jerome on Isaiah, and from Isidore's *Sententiae*. Two reminiscences of Sulpicius Severus, *Vita S. Martini* (c. 3) indicate that the author clearly regarded himself as following the Sulpician tradition of hagiography, with which he would undoubtedly have been conversant.

One text which was plundered quite heavily is a homily by Leo the Great (*Sermo* lxxxii) for the feast of SS. Peter and Paul, which may have been well known to an inmate of an institution whose dedication was to those particular saints (such as the Old Minster, Winchester), through use in the liturgy at Petertide.[13] This particular sermon of Leo the Great was included for the feast of Peter and Paul, in the homiliary compiled towards the end of the eighth century, by Paul the Deacon, at the behest of Charlemagne.[14] It is fairly certain that the collection had been introduced into Anglo-Saxon England by the tenth century, and although none of the

---

[10] Compare *The Earliest Life of Gregory the Great*, ed. B. Colgrave (Lawrence, KA, 1968), pp. 76 and 128–30 for the persistently apologetic tone of a hagiographer working several hundred years before our author with a similar paucity of material.

[11] See §iv below.   [12] Cf. note on c. 7, p. 15.

[13] See commentary on c. 1, p. 2 below.

[14] See R. Grégoire, *Homéliaires Liturgiques Médiévaux. Analyse de Manuscrits* (Spoleto, 1980), p. 461, no. 46.

surviving homiliaries of eleventh-century date may be ascribed to Winchester, there is some likelihood that *Sermo* lxxxii would have been familiar to the writer of *Vita S. Birini* by means of an Office homiliary of some sort.[15] He also uses another homily, by Peter Chrysologus, on John the Baptist, which may have been in the same compilation.[16] Overall, the available evidence indicates that the author of *Vita S. Birini* was a widely-read man.

(iii) Vita S. Birini *and* Vita S. Swithuni

Two of the surviving manuscripts in which *Vita S. Birini* has been transmitted also preserve the anonymous *Vita S. Swithuni* directly alongside:[17] in London, BL, Cotton Tiberius D. IV, part 2, fos. 111ʳ–112ᵛ, followed by *Miracula S. Swithuni* (fos. 112ᵛ–121ᵛ);[18] and in Oxford, Bodleian Library, Digby 112, fos. 1ʳ–4ᵛ, with a condensed version of the first part of *Miracula* (fos. 4ᵛ–5ʳ).[19] *Miracula S. Swithuni* seems to have been written as a companion piece to *Vita S. Swithuni*, probably by the same author, since most of the surviving manuscripts containing the former text also preserve the latter. A comparison of the *Vitae* of the two Winchester saints, and *Miracula S. Swithuni*, strongly suggests that the same hagiographer was responsible for all three texts. There are some very close verbal parallels. For example:

Vita S. Swithuni	*Vita S. Birini*
c. 1, Swithunus pater et pastor in ecclesia Die futurus	c. 1, Birinus, magnificus pater pastor egregius oritur Rome, futurus ciuis ciuitatis eterne

[15] For a list of the surviving homiliaries, see Gneuss, 'Liturgical books', at p. 124.

[16] See commentary on c. 2, p. 4 below.

[17] *BHL* 7943, printed by E. P. Sauvage, '*Vita Sancti Swithuni* Wintoniensis episcopi auctore Goscelino, monacho Sithiensi', *AB* vii (1888), 373–80, from Evreux, Bibliothèque municipale 101 L. A critical edition of *Vita S. Swithuni* is in preparation by M. Lapidge, *The Cult of St Swithun*, Winchester Studies, iv (2) (Oxford, forthcoming). I am very grateful to him for allowing me to use a typescript of his editions.

[18] The full version of the *Miracula S. Swithuni* is not listed in *BHL*, but cf. T. D. Hardy, *A Descriptive Catalogue of Materials relating to the History of Great Britain and Ireland*, 3 vols. RS (London, 1862), i (2). 514 (no. 1079). *Miracula S. Swithuni* has never been printed in full. Part of the selection of miracles preserved in the 14th-cent. MS Gotha, Forschungsbibliothek I. 81, was published by P. Grosjean, 'De codice hagiographico Gothano', *AB* lviii (1940), 90–103 and 177–204, at pp. 187–96. A critical edition of all fifty-six miracles will be included in Lapidge, *The Cult of St Swithun*.

[19] On this condensed version, see below, p. lvii.

Vita S. Swithuni

susceptum humiliter uiriliterque portauit

c. 2, ad honorem sacerdotii prouectus est

ordinem morum magisterium uite

c. 2, Ministerii autem huius perceptione sollicitus, curabat seipsum ministrum probabilem Deo semper offerre, operarium inconfusibilem se non remisse exhibere, uerbum ueritatis catholice et recte tractare

c. 3, factum est ut opinionis suauissime odor de prato sanctitatis ipsius emanans

quem rex euocatum multimoda indagatione perlustrans

quia sullimioribus potestatibus obediendum esse secundum apostolum et legebat et sciebat

c. 4, Euoluto igitur aliquanto tempore, supradictus episcopus

omnis etas, omnis sexus, uniuersa conditio

c. 5, Suscepta denique benedictione

archiepiscopo magne auctoritatis et religionis uiro nomine Celnodo

honore pontificali honorifice sullimatus

Vita S. Birini

c. 4, uidebat illum humiliter suscipere fideliterque complecti

c. 3, ad culmen sacerdotalis honoris euectus est

c. 2, magisterium uite, ordo iustitie

c. 20, Curabat sollicite seipsum probabilem exhibere Deo operarium inconfusibilem, recte tractantem uerbum ueritatis.

c. 4, Suauissime igitur opinionis illius odor longe lateque . . . cepit emanare

quem multa et sapienti indagatione perlustrans

c. 6, quia sciebat ex precepto apostoli omnem animam potestatibus sullimioribus esse subdendam

c. 21, Euoluto autem multo tempore, beatus Athelwoldus

c. 19, Omnis etas, uterque sexus, uniuersa conditio

c. 6, Benedictione denique suscepta

c. 21, Athelwoldus, magne religionis et auctoritatis uir

c. 5, episcopali gradu honorifice sullimato

Miracula S. Swithuni

c. 1, de ubi iacebat debere leuari intra ecclesiam loco

digniori honorificentius tumulandum

c. 4, loco eminentissimo intra ecclesiam honorificentius apponitur collocatum

c. 21, in ecclesia beatorum apostolorum Petri et Pauli

honorifice tumulauit

in eadem ecclesia iuxta maius altare honorificentius collocauit

Miracula S. Swithuni	*Vita S. Birini*
c. 6, quas et calamitas miserande paupertatis urgebat et infortunium cecitatisluce priuabat	c. 15, quam iam per multum tempus calamitas geminata uastabat
c. 7, sine omni dilatione reparatur uisus optatus	c. 16, uitio surditatis eliso subitus reparatur auditus
c. 15, die illucescente clarus in eo reparatur intuitus	
c. 1, intimare contendit	c. 14, nidificare contendit
c. 32, redire contendit	c. 15, ire contendit
c. 34, reuerti contendit	c. 17, ire contendit

Beyond these striking parallels, the general prose style of all three texts is inescapably similar,[20] including the use of rhyme and rhythm, and the accumulation of parallel phrases, although on the whole *Vita S. Birini* is decidedly the most ornate and verbose of all. *Vita S. Swithuni* does not include, for example, material comparable to the lengthy apostrophes to Peter and Paul, Britain, and Birinus. An explanation for this difference in narrative style may lie in the fact that the relatively short *Vita S. Swithuni* (just over 1,600 words, in eight lections) is accompanied by the *Miracula*. There is no surviving account of any posthumous miracles of Birinus—it is possible that there never was one. The rather inflated verbosity, and consequent length, of *Vita S. Birini*, when compared with *Vita S. Swithuni*, might be regarded as arising from the need to make up, as it were, for the lack of a complementary 'Miracula S. Birini'.

The attribution of *Vita S. Birini* to the author of *Vita et miracula S. Swithuni* may help to close up the wide limits stated above for the date of the composition of the former. However, the dating of the Swithun material is itself a somewhat complicated matter. The fifty-six *Miracula* of Swithun were evidently composed as a complementary piece to the *Vita*, and probably by the same author, to judge from the uniformity of Latin prose style throughout. The first forty miracles are based closely upon Wulfstan of Winchester's *Narratio metrica de Sancto Swithuno*,[21] composed probably between about 992 and 994.[22] The other sixteen miracles seem to

---

[20] Sufficiently so, I believe, to exclude the possibility that the author of *Vita S. Birini* had a copy of someone else's *Vita S. Swithuni* before him to plunder for material, or *vice versa*.   [21] *BHL* 7947; ed. Campbell, *Frithegodi*, pp. 65–177. See p. xxxiv above.   [22] See Lapidge and Winterbottom, *Wulfstan*, p. xxii.

have been composed afresh to describe events which occurred at Winchester and Sherborne and on the Isle of Wight during the course of the second half of the eleventh century. The mention of certain prominent individuals supplies evidence for the date of composition. For example, Ealdred, archbishop of York, who *ob.* in 1069, is referred to as 'uenerande memorie',[23] and similarly bishop Walkelin of Winchester is 'uenerabilis memorie' (*ob.* 1098).[24] Durand, sheriff of Hampshire around the year 1096, is also referred to in the final miracle.[25] The year 1098 thus appears to be the *terminus post quem* for the *Miracula*.

The earliest surviving manuscript of the complete set of *Miracula*, London, BL, Cotton Tiberius D. IV, part 2 (fos. 112ʳ–121ᵛ) is datable on palaeographical grounds to about 1100, or to the very early years of the twelfth century.[26] Hence the last sixteen *Miracula* of Swithun would have to have been composed close to the year 1100. It follows then that if the same author was also responsible for *Vita S. Birini* and *Vita S. Swithuni*, then they must have been written at roughly the same date, as a single project. On the other hand, it is possible that there was more than one stage of composition. Oxford, Bodleian, Digby 112,[27] preserves, between *Vita S. Swithuni* and *Vita S. Birini*, a 'condensed' version of chapters 1, 2 and 4 of the *Miracula*, which simply describes the translation of Swithun by Æthelwold.[28] Although the only copies of this condensed translation account are both probably a little later in date than the earliest copy of the full set of miracles in Tiberius D. IV, they may actually represent an earlier version, composed together with the two *Vitae*. Subsequently the same author could have adumbrated his own description of the translation of Swithun in order to work it in with the forty miracles he was adapting from Wulfstan's verses, with the addition at the same time of the sixteen freshly composed miracles, thus bringing the account right up to

[23] Miracle no. 43.

[24] Miracle no. 52.

[25] See J. A. Green, *English Sheriffs to 1154*, PRO Handbooks, xxiv (London, 1990), p. 44 and *Regesta Regum Anglo-Normannorum*, ed. H. W. C. Davis, R. H. C. Davis, H. A. Cronne, and C. Johnson, 4 vols. (Oxford, 1913–69), ii, nos. 403, 407.

[26] See the description of the MSS of *Vita S. Birini* below, pp. lxxvii–lxxix.

[27] Winchester, s. xii ⁱⁿ.

[28] At fos. 4ᵛ–5ʳ. The same 'condensed' text was copied, in the early 12th cent., on to some originally blank pages at the end of London, BL, Royal 15. C. VII, a late 10th- or early 11th-cent. MS written at the Old Minster, Winchester, and containing Lantfred's *Translatio et miracula Sancti Swithuni* and Wulfstan's *Narratio metrica de Sancto Swithuno*.

date.[29] If this were the case, then the date of the composition of *Vita S. Birini* and *Vita S. Swithuni* (and the short translation account) need not be as late as *c.* 1100. An occasion which could have stimulated the production of a Life of Swithun (and one of Birinus), was the retranslation of his feretory from the Anglo-Saxon minster, about to be demolished, into the partially completed Norman church, in July 1093.[30] During the demolition work the following year, relics of Swithun 'aliorumque plurimorum sanctorum' (perhaps including Birinus) were discovered under the high altar, and presumably translated into the new minster building.[31] This can only remain, for the time being, a conjecture: the lack of any reference to the supposed translation of 1093 in *Miracula S. Swithuni* is rather surprising.[32] It is probably safe to say at least that *Vita S. Birini* was composed towards the close of the eleventh century.

Vita S. Swithuni has in the past been attributed to Goscelin of Saint-Bertin,[33] and this conjecture should now be examined in the light of what has already been said here. There are just a few turns of phrase in various works of Goscelin, such as *Vita S. Edithe*,[34] *Vita*

---

[29] It is of course possible that the addition of the last sixteen miracles was a third and separate stage of the process, although no surviving MS preserves the text in that state (i.e. with only forty miracles).

[30] See R. N. Quirk, 'Winchester Cathedral in the Tenth Century', *Archaeological Journal*, cxiv (1957), 28–68, at pp. 60–1, and *Winchester in the Early Middle Ages. An Edition and Discussion of the Winton Domesday*, ed. M. Biddle, Winchester Studies, i (Oxford, 1976), p. 308. One might compare with this the great series of translations which occurred at St Augustine's, Canterbury in 1091.

[31] These events are recorded in *Annales de Wintonia* printed by H. R. Luard, *Annales Monastici*, 5 vols., RS xxxvi (London, 1864–9), ii. 37–8. It is uncertain how trustworthy that account is, given that Luard printed the annals (from 1066 onwards) from London, BL, Cotton Domitian A. xiii, which was apparently copied from annals in Oxford, Bodleian Library, Bodley 91, made for Hyde Abbey, Winchester, rather than the Old Minster; see A. Gransden, *Historical Writing in England c.550–c.1307* (London, 1974), p. 411; and N. Denholm-Young, 'The Winchester-Hyde Chronicle', *The English Historical Review*, xlix (1934), 85–93.

[32] This fact might support the conjecture, noted below (p. lix), that *Miracula S. Swithuni* was composed at Sherborne rather than Winchester.

[33] Sauvage, in the introduction to his edition of *Vita S. Swithuni* (p. 373), wrote, 'Goscelini hanc esse narrationem concludere est'. On Goscelin's work in England, see pp. xl–xliv above. In the first edition of Barlow, *The Life of King Edward* (NMT, 1962), *Vita S. Swithuni* was listed under works whose attribution to Goscelin is discredited (p. 111), but it has been omitted altogether in the second edition.

[34] Compare, for example, with c. 7 of *Vita S. Birini*, the similar use there of such metaphors as 'consurgens aurora' (Wilmart, 'La Légende', p. 41); 'matutina stella' and 'sol iusticie' (p. 42); and with c. 1, 'duo candelabra lucentia ante faciem suam' (p. 57).

et uirtutes S. Ethelburge,[35] *Vita S. Yuonis*,[36] *Historia maior de aduentu S. Augustini*,[37] which are similar to those found in *Vita S. Birini* and *Vita S. Swithuni*, but for the most part they are commonplaces of hagiography and widely-used biblical tags, and no striking verbal echoes have hitherto come to light. Of the three Winchester texts, *Vita S. Birini* is closest in style to the prose of Goscelin at its most inflated and ponderous, abounding in rhyming parallel phrases, but does not on the whole display the kind of vocabulary which seems to go hand in hand with such pomposity.[38] In sum, it is difficult to assemble a particularly convincing argument for Goscelin's authorship on grounds of style and vocabulary.[39]

The conjectured dating of the Winchester texts must also be matched up with Goscelin's movements. When he first came to England in about 1058, Goscelin was attached to the household of Herman, bishop of Ramsbury and Sherborne (1058–78), acted for a time as chaplain to the nuns at Wilton, and would then have been in the appropriate part of the country to be able to turn his attention to the saints of Winchester. In this connection, two facts about *Miracula S. Swithuni* are worth noting. One of the surviving manuscripts of Wulfstan's *Narratio metrica de S. Swithuno* (on which, it will be recalled, the first forty *miracula* were based), Oxford, Bodleian Library, Auct. F. 2. 14 was apparently at Sherborne.[40] Moreover, among the additional sixteen miracles of Swithun added to the rewriting of Wulfstan's poem are included several which relate to a statue of Swithun at Sherborne.[41] Hence, one could construct a scenario in which Goscelin, while still under the patronage of Herman, might have been commissioned to put together a suitable hagiography of Swithun and Birinus, but not have completed that work until a good deal later, for whatever

---

[35] Compare 'sole iustitie' and 'oriens ex alto uisitauit' (Colker, 'Texts', p. 402).

[36] *PL* clv. 81–90. Compare the word-play 'Yuo Domini iuit ad Dominum qui exiuit a Patre et uenit in mundum . . .' (col. 84), with that in c. 6 of *Vita S. Birini* on 'exulo/exulto'. A couple of other parallels are noted in the commentary.

[37] Compare the reference to *Felix Roma*, and her two sons Augustine and Gregory, 'haec duo magna mundi luminaria' (*PL* lxxx. 50); the apostrophe to Augustine (col. 51), and the mention of the 'barbara lingua Britannie' (col. 66).

[38] Cf. the brief comments on Goscelin's style by Rollason, 'Translation', pp. 141–3.

[39] Compare the case of *Vita et miracula S. Kenelmi* considered below.

[40] Cf. Gneuss, 'List', no. 535 (dated s. xi²).

[41] cc. 44–6, 53. Cf. the suggestion that *Miracula S. Swithuni* may in fact have been composed at Sherborne, in M. Lapidge, 'The origin of CCCC 163', *Transactions of the Cambridge Bibliographical Society*, viii (1981), 18–28, at p. 22.

reason.[42] If it is correct to extrapolate to all three texts the late dating of the last few *miracula* of Swithun, then Goscelin would have been putting the finishing touches to this task at broadly the same time as he was drawing to a close his massive engagement with the fit commemoration of the relic-translations of 1091 at St Augustine's, Canterbury.[43]

To return briefly to matters of style, if the scenario just described were to be the right one, it is a little surprising to find that, at least as preserved, neither *Vita S. Birini* nor *Vita S. Swithuni* has a preface or dedication. Almost all Goscelin's well-attested works have introductory remarks of some kind. This, combined with the absence of external evidence to verify the above conjecture, and the lack of convincing textual evidence, must mean an adjournment—perhaps a permanent one—of any attempt to insert the Winchester texts into the canon of Goscelin's writings. The point remains valid, however, that if *Vita et miracula S. Swithuni* and *Vita S. Birini* were to have been written in the later 1090s as a result of retranslations at Winchester, they constitute a parallel, even if on a somewhat smaller scale, to developments at St Augustine's, Canterbury.

(iv) *The Cult of St Birinus*

Bede concluded his account of Birinus with a brief notice of the translation of the prelate's body from Dorchester to Winchester by Hædde (bishop of Winchester, 676–705). We cannot now determine the precise date of this translation, but the reason for such an action was presumably that the authorities felt it inappropriate that the apostle and first bishop of the West-Saxon see should rest anywhere other than at the new centre of ecclesiastical power, Winchester (established in about 648). Perhaps also, because Dorchester had fallen into Mercian hands, it seemed essential to rescue the remains of the West-Saxon patron saint.[44] Despite the fine phrases of *Vita S. Birini* (c. 21), the translation was probably as

---

[42] Cf. Goscelin's apology in the prologues of both *Vita S. Edithe* and *Vita S. Wlsini*, for only completing the text after Herman, who had instigated the composition of both, had died (Wilmart, 'La Légende', p. 38; and Talbot, 'Saint Wulsin', p. 73).

[43] He seems to have completed the last of the Canterbury texts only in 1099; see Sharpe, 'Goscelin's St Augustine', p. 516.

[44] Cf. D. P. Kirby, 'Problems of Early West-Saxon History', *English Historical Review*, lxxx (1965), 10–29, at p. 13.

much for the benefit of Winchester, as it was for the increased honour and glory of Birinus. After all, the birth of Winchester's great patron-saint-to-be, Swithun, lay over a century in the future. The main focus of Birinus's cult thus became Winchester.

The principal feast of Birinus, that of his deposition, on 3 December, is already to be found in one liturgical calendar from the north country, datable to the ninth century, namely that preserved in Oxford, Bodleian Library, Digby 63.[45] This could provide an indication that his cult was already widely known, but that early calendar might well have commemorated Birinus simply because Bede included an approving account of his deeds (as is the case for most of the other Anglo-Saxon saints named in the Digby 63 calendar). Apart from this calendar, there is no evidence upon which to construct a history of the cult of Birinus between the occasion of the supposed translation to Winchester and the later tenth century.

On 15 July 971, Bishop Æthelwold of Winchester translated the remains of St Swithun, and the rebuilding of the Old Minster at Winchester was commenced possibly in the same year, or in those following. The dedication and consecration of the new building works (which had just got underway) took place on 20 October 980.[46] From 980 onwards the east end of the Old Minster was reconstructed and extended, and at about that time the remains of Birinus were translated again and placed by Æthelwold 'iuxta maius altare' (c. 21 of the *Vita*).[47] It was probably then that the feast of the translation of Birinus (celebrated in conjunction with that of Cuthbert) was instituted on 4 September. Certainly the translation is not commemorated in the earlier calendars Digby 63 and Salisbury, Cathedral Library 150,[48] but, along with the feast of the deposition, it is found in almost every English monastic calendar surviving from the eleventh century.[49] The deposition

[45] See Wormald, *English Kalendars*, no. 1.

[46] See M. Biddle, '*Felix Urbs Winthonia*: Winchester in the Age of Monastic Reform', in *Tenth-Century Studies*, ed. D. Parsons (London and Chichester, 1975), pp. 123–40. Æthelwold's building-work was described by Wulfstan, *Vita S. Athelwoldi* (c. 40); see Lapidge and Winterbottom, *Wulfstan*, p. 61.

[47] Wulfstan, *Narratio metrica*, *Epistola specialis*, 261–2, mentioned the presence of Birinus's remains in Æthelwold's new building.

[48] Wormald, *English Calendars*, no. 2; south-west England, perhaps Shaftesbury, datable to the third quarter of the 10th cent.

[49] Birinus is also included in a large number of litanies; see M. Lapidge, *Anglo-Saxon Litanies of the Saints*, HBS cvi (1991), p. 305. Such evidence requires to be handled with

and translation of Birinus are recorded in five surviving pre-Conquest calendars from Winchester.[50] Both feasts are also recorded in two calendars originating from unidentified centres in the West Country,[51] in one copied at Salisbury,[52] one from Christ Church, Canterbury,[53] from Sherborne,[54] three from Worcester,[55] and one from Bury St Edmunds,[56] as well as in the calendar in the early eleventh-century sacramentary known as the Missal of Robert of Jumièges.[57] London, BL, Cotton Vitellius A. xviii (Wells, 1061–88), and Oxford, Bodleian Library, Douce 296 (Crowland, s. xi^{med}) alone of the surviving eleventh-century calendars mark only the deposition of Birinus.[58] The evidence of pre-conquest calendars implies that Birinus had come, by the end of the eleventh century, to enjoy widespread commemoration, but may be more of a testimony to the influence of the Winchester calendar over those compiled at other centres. It remains to be seen from an examination of other liturgical books whether the cult of Birinus extended much beyond nominal commemoration, further afield than Winchester.

It is not the intention here to provide a detailed analysis of every single surviving liturgical document pertaining to the cult of St Birinus, but rather to attempt to draw a more general picture of the context in which *Vita S. Birini* was composed and circulated. There is a fairly substantial body of material intended for use in the

care, insofar as litanies are, by nature, cumulative and grounded upon a mentality of intercessory acquisitiveness, and thus can offer only very general information about the veneration of many of the saints included in them.

[50] Wormald, *English Kalendars*, nos. 9–12: London, BL, Cotton Titus D. xxvii (New Minster, s. xi$^{2/4}$)—this MS also preserves a litany which includes Birinus; Cambridge, Trinity College, R. 15. 32 (New Minster, s. xi^{in}); London, BL, Arundel 60 (New Minster, s. xi^2)—Birinus occurs in a litany here too; and London, BL, Cotton Vitellius E. xviii (New Minster, s. xi^{med}). Nos. 11 and 12, the latest of the Winchester calendars, both also mark the Octave of the deposition of Birinus on 10 December, probably a sign of increased promotion of the cult at Winchester during the second half of the century.

[51] Ibid. nos. 3, London, BL, Nero A. ii (s. xi), and 6, Cambridge, UL, Kk. 5. 32 (s. xi^2).

[52] Ibid. no. 7; London, BL, Vitellius A. xii (s. xi^2).

[53] Ibid. no. 13; London, BL, Arundel 155 (s. xi^{in}). Note, however, that Birinus does not occur in no. 5, the calendar added between 988 and 1008 at Christ Church, to the so-called Bosworth Psalter.

[54] Ibid. no. 14; CCCC 422 (possibly written at Winchester for Sherborne, AD 1060/1), which also includes Birinus in two litanies (Lapidge, *Litanies*, nos. viii. i and viii. ii).

[55] Wormald, *English Kalendars*, nos. 16–18; Oxford, Bodleian Library, Hatton, 113 (s. xi^2); CCCC 391 (s. xi^{ex}), which also includes Birinus in a litany; and CCCC 9 (AD 1061).

[56] Ibid. no. 19; Vatican City, Biblioteca Apostolica Vaticana, Reg. lat. 12 (possibly written at Canterbury for Bury, s. xi$^{2/4}$), also including Birinus in a litany.

[57] Ed. H. A. Wilson, HBS xi (1896), p. 16.

[58] Wormald, *English Kalendars*, nos. 8 and 19.

liturgy on the feasts of Birinus, preserved in manuscripts datable to the eleventh century.[59] It is probable that these texts were composed initially for use at Winchester, with a few exceptions, which will be discussed further on. Mass-sets for the feasts of the deposition and translation are preserved in two sacramentaries, the so-called New Minster Missal,[60] and the one apparently written (at Canterbury) for the use of Bishop Giso of Wells (1061–88), in London, BL, Cotton Vitellius A. xviii.[61] The Missal of Robert of Jumièges includes a set for the deposition only,[62] and parts of the same set occur also in the fragmentary Anglo-Saxon missal, now Oslo, Riksarchivet, Lat. fragm. 209, nos. 1–6 + 239, nos. 6–7.[63] Collects for both feasts are found also in the collectar known as the 'Portiforium of Wulstan', written at Worcester in about 1065, but based upon a Winchester exemplar.[64] Tropes for use during mass on the feast of the deposition of Birinus are included in the Winchester Tropers,[65] along with a sequence commemorating Birinus and another linking Birinus with Swithun.[66]

[59] The liturgical material commemorating Birinus is discussed in detail by A. Corrêa, in a forthcoming study, 'A mass for St Birinus in an Anglo-Saxon missal from the Scandinavian mission-field', a copy of which she has kindly given me in advance of its publication.

[60] Ed. D. H. Turner, HBS xciii (1962), pp. 189 and 155–6 (s. xi²). Somewhat puzzlingly, the former set is preceded in the manuscript by another mass-set (comprising collect, secret and postcommunion) for Birinus, headed 'II Kl. NO. SEPT. TRANSLATIO S. BYRINI EPISCOPI' (id. pp. 188–9), despite the fact that it is among proper mass-sets for December feasts. The set does not seem to occur elsewhere.

[61] Printed as part of the appendix to *The Leofric Missal*, ed. F. E. Warren (Oxford, 1883), pp. 303–7, the mass-set for Birinus at p. 306. This sacramentary has signs of having been copied from a Winchester exemplar.

[62] Ed. Wilson, pp. 229–30. See J. B. L. Tolhurst, 'Le Missel de Robert de Jumièges, sacramentaire d'Ely', *Jumièges: Congrès scientifique du XIIIᵉ centenaire*, 2 vols. (Rouen, 1955), i. 287–93; and C. Hohler, 'Les Saints insulaires dans le missel de l'archevêque Robert', ibid., pp. 293–303, on the disputed origin of this sacramentary, whether Ely, Peterborough, or Winchester.

[63] Roughly s. xi³/⁴. See Corrêa, 'A mass for St Birinus', appendix II. Only the collect and secret are preserved.

[64] Ed. A. Hughes, 2 vols., HBS lxxxix–xc (1958–60), pp. 150 and 141.

[65] The two tropers, CCCC 473 and Oxford, Bodleian Library, Bodley 775, both written at the Old Minster, Winchester, in the early and mid-11th cent. respectively, were edited by W. H. Frere, *The Winchester Troper*, HBS viii (London, 1894). See also A. E. Planchart, *The Repertory of Tropes at Winchester*, 2 vols. (Princeton, NJ, 1977), and A. Holschneider, *Die Organa von Winchester* (Hildesheim, 1968). Cf. the discussion in Lapidge and Winterbottom, *Wulfstan*, pp. xxxi–xxxiii.

[66] D. Schaller and E. Könsgen, *Initia Carminum Latinorum saeculo undecimo antiquiorum* (Göttingen, 1977), no. 1808; U. Chevalier, *Repertorium Hymnologicum*, 6 vols. (Louvain, 1892–1921), no. 3606; ed. *AH* xl. 154–5 (no. 171). See the discussion of the sequences in the Winchester Tropers, in Lapidge and Winterbottom, *Wulfstan*, pp. xxxiv–xxxvi.

The evidence of the Missal of Robert of Jumièges, of Vitellius A. xviii, and of the 'Portiforium', points to the transmission of the liturgical cult of Birinus beyond the confines of Winchester to a few other centres in England. This is supported by the somewhat surprising preservation only in three benedictionals deriving apparently from Christ Church, Canterbury, of two different blessings for use on the feast of the deposition of St Birinus.[67] It is possible that the presence of these blessings in Canterbury books may be attributable originally to the personal devotion of Ælfheah, archbishop of Canterbury from 1005 to 1012, who before his elevation had been bishop of Winchester.[68]

Two other groups of material preserved in eleventh-century manuscripts call for closer attention here. First to be considered is an incomplete set of versicles, responds, and antiphons for the Office on the feast of St Birinus (presumably the deposition), which has been discovered at fos. 74^r–76^r of New York, Pierpont Morgan Library, 926. The manuscript is a miscellaneous collection of liturgical texts copied, in all probability, at St Albans, at various stages during the second half of the eleventh century.[69] The materials relating to Birinus do not survive elsewhere, and consist of nine responsories for Matins (beginning acephalously), five antiphons for the psalms at Lauds, the antiphon for the Benedictus at Lauds, part of that for the Magnificat at Vespers, and eight antiphons also for use at Vespers.

Hartzell has conjectured that the responsories, as set out in this manuscript, were designed for use at a secular rather than monastic office, since rubrics, added in the margins in a hand of slightly later date than that of the main text, seem to divide the nine surviving responsories into groups of three, for use at the three nocturns of Matins. The monastic night office on a feast day would have required three sets of four responds and versicles, to match the twelve lessons.[70] Thus Hartzell takes this as an indication that

---

[67] One in London, BL, Harley 2892 (s. xi^1), ed. R. M. Woolley, *The Canterbury Benedictional*, HBS li (1917), p. 118; listed in *Corpus Pontificalium Benedictionum*, ed. E. Moeller, 4 vols., *CCSL* clxii, clxii A–C (Turnhout, 1971–9), no. 1058; and one in both CCCC 146 (s. xi^{in}) and Paris, BN, lat. 987, part 2 (s. xi^2); Moeller, no. 1500.

[68] See Lapidge and Winterbottom, *Wulfstan*, p. cxxxix.

[69] K. D. Hartzell, 'A St. Albans Miscellany in New York', *Mittellateinisches Jahrbuch* x (1975), 20–61; the portion pertaining to Birinus is discussed at pp. 38–42 and printed at pp. 58–9. Cf. R. M. Thomson, *Manuscripts from St Alban's Abbey, 1066–1235* (Woodbridge, 1982), p. 9.

[70] See the description of the office in Tolhurst, *Monastic Breviary*, vi. 7–14.

the responsories derived originally from Dorchester, which was until about 1140 a community of secular canons: 'if this conjecture is correct, then the Office would be divided in a way which suggests a secular liturgy and not a monastic one, something that if the Office were originally written at Birinus's cathedral of Dorchester would be most acceptable to monks at St Albans'.[71] A desire to commemorate Birinus at St Albans could have stemmed from the fact that until 1072, that house was in the Dorchester diocese. If Hartzell is correct in his conjecture, then the items in the St Albans miscellany are significant as being the only surviving evidence for a liturgical cult of Birinus at Dorchester before the twelfth century.

A single piece of textual evidence which may support the conjecture that the responsories were composed for use at Dorchester is the phrase 'Preclarus antistes birinus in *hac* sede annis pluribus floruit piis doctrinis et actibus', referring to Dorchester as being 'here', although 'hac' might just as easily refer back to the explicit mention of 'urbis dorcensis cathedra' in the previous respond. On the other hand, no reference is made to the translation of Birinus's relics to Winchester by Hædde, a fact which it might not have suited the community at Dorchester to have acknowledged.[72] It would be difficult to show that the responsories, as preserved, derived from eleventh-century Winchester if Hartzell's assumption, that the acephalous respond at the beginning of the fragment was in fact always the first one, is indeed correct. We should, in the case of a Winchester origin, expect twelve sets of responds and versicles, divided into three groups of four, not three. Nevertheless, the possibility of a Winchester origin cannot be ruled out altogether, since it is not beyond the bounds of imagination that material composed initially for the monastic office could have been rewritten for secular use.

Another approach to the responsories is to evaluate the information they offer about Birinus. Most of the very brief narrative could have been gathered from Bede alone, except for the miracle referred to in the fifth respond: 'In conspectu gentilium nouum dogma mirantium inuocans nomen domini cece et mute mulieri uisum uocemque reddidit.' This is presumably the same miracle as that which is described in cc. 15–16 of *Vita S. Birini*, where the woman is 'ceca et surda', and is able to speak, although only

---

[71] 'St Albans miscellany', p. 39.
[72] Cf. the 13th-cent. developments described below, p. lxxii.

incoherently. There is, however, no reference to the miracle of Birinus walking on water. The St Albans miscellany, as noted above, has been dated to the second half of the eleventh century and could therefore pre-date the composition of *Vita S. Birini* (if there is any validity in what has been said above about the late date of the *Vita*). Consequently that fifth responsory may be a shred of evidence for an account of the Life of Birinus additional to Bede's, either written or preserved only in oral tradition. Such a narrative might have been the basis upon which the anonymous author built up his *Vita*. The account, in whatever form, could have already reached Winchester by the late eleventh century, or possibly, the author of the *Vita* could have had recourse to Dorchester while searching for material with which to begin composition.

The other group of liturgical materials pertaining to Birinus which merit closer examination are those included in Oxford, Bodleian Library, Digby 39, a manuscript which also contains probably the earliest copy of *Vita S. Birini*.[73] The manuscript is thought to have been written at the Benedictine Abbey of St Mary's, Abingdon. It would not be surprising to find evidence of a liturgical commemoration of Birinus at this house, as it had close ties with Winchester, particularly since the time of Bishop Æthelwold, who had served as abbot of Abingdon from about 954 until his elevation to the episcopate. And in any case, Abingdon lies not far from Dorchester, Birinus's own episcopal seat.

Part four of Digby 39 (fos. 50^r–56^v) constitutes a distinct codicological unit, written in a single hand probably datable to the last quarter of the eleventh century, and composed of the following:

(1) Bede, *HE* iii. 7, in its entirety, divided (by crosses marked in the margin) into eight lections presumably for reading aloud at Matins. The presence of these lections may be significant as an indication that at the time when they were copied out, no other version of the Life of Birinus was available at Abingdon for reading at the office on his feast day.[74] The entire text of iii. 7 was copied out but only a small portion of it actually relates to Birinus—much is taken up with describing his successors at Dorchester, Wine, Agilbert, and Leuthere.

[73] See pp. lxxiv–lxxv below for a detailed description of the physical constitution of Digby 39.

[74] Alternatively, it could be argued that these lections provide proof that *Vita S. Birini* was never composed with the need for lessons at Matins in mind at all, or at least, that it was not used in that way.

(2) A homily for the feast of Birinus with the rubric 'SEQVITVR OMELIA IN EIVS SANCTA FESTIVITATE SOLLEMPNITER RECITANTA' (*sic*), not known to survive elsewhere.[75] This homily was almost certainly composed originally for use at Winchester, in view of specific references such as, 'sed in istam post Dei prouidente gratia translatus urbem; nobis non nostris meritis sed gratuita sola diuina precedente clementia, ad patrocinium et solatium donatus atque concessus est', and the warning 'ne tanti patris *presentia* iudicemur indigni'.[76] The homilist at one point says, 'audiuimus itaque cum Deo dilecti sacerdotis gesta licet breuiter legerentur, quantam in omni bonitate habuit deuotionem; audiuimus quoque magnam et mirabilem et uere laudabilem cordis eius in Domino constantiam quando . . .'. Since the homily in this manuscript was copied by the same scribe straight after the eight lections, the natural assumption is that 'audiuimus' must refer to those same lections, to which 'licet breuiter' applies aptly enough. The hand in which these liturgical materials was copied appears to be somewhat earlier than that in which *Vita S. Birini* was written, but can probably be dated to the last quarter of the eleventh century. If the composition of the *Vita* may correctly be assigned to the closing years of the century, then the homily might be assumed to be an earlier testimony to an account of the Life of Birinus. If, on the other hand, the composition of *Vita S. Birini* is earlier than conjectured above, then the homily could conceivably have been composed by the same author as the *Vita*, or by someone who was familiar with it.

It is perhaps possible to test some of these hypotheses by an analysis of the style of the homily and the information about Birinus which it contains. While there is a marked preference for emphatic alliteration, the accumulation of relatively short rhyming parallel clauses is much less prominent than in the *Vita*; indeed, comparatively speaking, the homilist's use of rhyme is by no means thoroughgoing. There are no verbal parallels to speak of, certainly none as striking as those which unite *Vita S. Birini* and *Vita S. Swithuni* under one authorship. To compare, for example, the ways in which Birinus is referred to in the two texts:

---

[75] Since the homily has never been published, a transcription is provided as Appendix B below.

[76] If this text was indeed copied for use at Abingdon, no attempt was made to adapt it to the point of view of that community.

whereas in the *Vita*, the saint is consistently called 'beatus Birinus', very frequently 'beatus antistes', 'uir apostolicus', and 'pastor', none of these epithets occurs in the homily, and Birinus is never 'beatus', but rather 'sanctus' (not once applied directly to Birinus in the *Vita*) or 'sanctissimus'. It could be argued that there are themes in both texts which seem to be the result of a similar thought-process. For example, the contrast drawn in the homily between Augustine's 'team' mission to a convert who dragged his heels, and Birinus's single-handed and seemingly straightforward act of conversion, is not unlike the antithesis set up in the *Vita* between the arrival and successes of Birinus in England and the forays of Julius Caesar. But the similarity is not strong enough to be compelling. On the whole, although it must be acknowledged that the same author could have chosen to employ a distinct 'voice' for a more overtly didactic work, there is insufficient evidence to demonstrate that the homily was composed by the author of *Vita S. Birini*.

The question of whether the anonymous homilist could have been writing with *Vita S. Birini* to hand must probably also be answered in the negative. For although there is a reference to miracles, 'Vel quid non potest pietatis precibus impetrare in celis, qui tantis in mundo claruit miraculis? Sed omnibus miraculis maior est euangelice predicationis instantia, et sancte claritatis in corde flagrantia', it is only a vague one, and no mention is ever made of the specific wonders of walking on water and healing the blind and deaf woman which are recounted in the *Vita*. Furthermore, it is debatable whether 'cum . . . gesta licet breuiter legerentur' could be an accurate description of *Vita S. Birini*.

This homily, then, may itself represent an earlier attempt to amplify the terse record of Birinus's deeds supplied by Bede, or was based on a pre-existing account or brief Life, now lost, but similar in content to that extrapolated from the responsories copied at St Albans. A firm conclusion does not seem possible, nor can a precise date be ascertained for the composition of the homily.

The other items in Digby 39 are: (3) a mass-set for the translation of Birinus and (4) for his deposition.[77] These mass-sets are different from those in the liturgical books referred to above, and

---

[77] Printed in the appendix to Warren, *Leofric Missal*, p. 307.

are not attested in any other surviving manuscript. Since Digby 39 was probably copied at Abingdon, they might have been composed specifically for use there, or alternatively, they represent an earlier phase in the liturgical cult of Birinus which was imported to Abingdon, but was soon superseded at Winchester. The fact that the preceding homily was copied out apparently unadapted for use at Abingdon may suggest that the mass-sets were also imports.

(5) Formerly, a metrical hymn followed the mass-sets, but only the rubric remains, at the very bottom of fo. 56ᵛ: 'CARMEN IVBILATIONIS PER ALPHABETI LITTERAS DE SANCTO BIRINO METRICE COMPOSITVM, ET IN EIVS LAVDEM VBICVMQVE VOLVERIS PRO GAVDIO DEPOSITIONIS SVE QVE EST DIE .III. NONARVM DECEMBRIVM.'[78] The text has been lost, and *Vita S. Birini*, copied on a fresh quire by a different scribe, now follows. However, a hymn which fits the rubric well is 'Agmina sacra poli iubilent modulamine dulci', composed probably by Wulfstan of Winchester,[79] and found with four other hymns to Æthelwold and Swithun, in Rouen, Bibl. mun. 1385 (U. 107), a manuscript written at Winchester in the late tenth century, and also with some variation in Alençon MS 14 (dated to the twelfth century). All the hymns are abecedarian, epanaleptic (paraceteric) poems. It is interesting that certain of the themes chosen by Wulfstan are similar to those found in *Vita S. Birini*, for example, lines 9–12,

> Exsul ad hunc populum qui uenit ab urbe Quiritum
> Pro Christo pergens exsul ad hunc populum,
> Fortis et armipotens Kynegils quo tempore regnat
> Barbarie frendens, fortis et armipotens.

with which may be compared the description of Birinus as an exile from Rome in c. 6, and the reminiscence of Gregory the

---

[78] The rubric itself may be incomplete at the end since the phrase 'et in eius laudem ubicumque uolueris . . .' does rather call for some kind of verb, perhaps a gerundive to match 'recitanta' in the rubric of the homily.

[79] Printed in *AH* xlviii. 12–14, no. 2; it is listed by Schaller and Könsgen, *Initia*, no. 474; and Chevalier, *Repertorium*, no. 729. See also C. Blume, 'Wolstan von Winchester und Vital von Saint-Évroult, Dichter der Lobgesänge auf die heiligen Athelwold, Birin und Swithun', *Sitzungsberichte der K. Akademie der Wissenschaften in Wien*, clxvi (3) (Vienna, 1903), 9–12; and H. Gneuss, *Hymnar und Hymnen im Englischen Mittelalter* (Tübingen, 1968), pp. 247–8.

Great (probably via Bede), 'barbarum frendere' in c. 20. Compare also lines 21–2,

> Liber adest populus sub longo tempore seruus,
> Nunc famulans Domino liber adest populus.

with the description of the baptism of the West Saxons in c. 19. The author of *Vita S. Birini* may thus have had Wulfstan's hymn in mind. The fact that this hymn, composed in the late tenth century, was formerly among the materials assembled in Digby 39 could be taken as evidence for the date of the other items—in other words, they too could have originated in the same milieu, been passed on to Abingdon, and recopied there in the second half of the following century. But this is pure conjecture.

Some tentative conclusions must now be drawn from the above examination of liturgical documents. The cult of Birinus was of high status at late-Anglo-Saxon Winchester, where the majority of liturgical texts commemorating the saint must have been generated, and whence the liturgical cult must have permeated to some other centres. In addition, a written account of the Life of Birinus, expanding Bede's brief notice, may have existed at Dorchester by the second half of the eleventh century and could also have been known at Winchester, and therefore drawn upon by the author of *Vita S. Birini*. How early such an account might have been in circulation is an even more debatable point, in view of the ambiguous evidence presented by Digby 39. It is perhaps worth noting at this point that in Paris, BN, lat. 5362, a collection of texts copied around the year 1100, either in England or in Normandy, there are excerpts from the first part of Bede, *HE* iii. 7, pertaining to Birinus (at fo. 70^{r-v}).[80] It has been suggested that this manuscript is a later copy of a hagiographical commonplace-book put together by Ælfric of Eynsham, for subsequent use in his own writings.[81] A translation of exactly the same Bedan excerpts relating to Birinus occurs in Ælfric's Old English Life of Oswald.[82] Paris, BN, lat. 5362 also includes an abbreviation of Lantfred's *Translatio et miracula S. Swithuni*, which Ælfric used for

---

[80] See *Catalogus codicum hagiographicorum latinorum antiquiorum saeculo xvi qui asseruantur in Bibliotheca Nationali Parisiensi*, 4 vols., *Subsidia Hagiographica*, ii (Brussels, 1889–93), ii. 354–66.

[81] See Lapidge and Winterbottom, *Wulfstan*, pp. cxlviii–cxlix.

[82] Skeat, *Lives of Saints*, ii. 132–4.

his Life of Swithun.[83] This may imply that whereas Ælfric had
Lantfred's account to draw upon for his own work on Swithun, no
such source, beyond what could be gleaned from Bede, existed at
late tenth-century Winchester in the case of Birinus.

The evidence for a continuing cult of Birinus beyond the eleventh
century, as provided by post-Conquest liturgical calendars, is
rather mixed. The only calendars still marking both the translation
and the deposition of Birinus are from Abbotsbury,[84] and Ely,[85]
and perhaps that from Chertsey, which marks the translation as a
feast of twelve lessons, but of which the November and December
portions of the calendar are now missing, so that it is no longer
possible to determine whether the deposition was also originally
included.[86] The deposition of Birinus seems still to have been
commemorated at Abingdon,[87] St Albans,[88] Crowland,[89] Dunster[90]
and Muchelney in Somerset.[91] There is no surviving calendrical
evidence of later commemoration of Birinus at St Augustine's
(despite the presence of *Vita S. Birini* in Fell 2) or Christ Church,
Canterbury, or Chester (despite the former presence of *Vita S.
Birini* in the St Werburg's legendary).

Among the surviving missals dating from after the eleventh century,[92] only that from Hereford includes a proper mass-set for

---

[83] Ibid. i. 440–70.

[84] F. Wormald, *English Benedictine Kalendars after AD 1100*, 2 vols., HBS lxxvii, lxxxi
(1939–46), no. 1; Cotton Cleopatra B. IX, *c*.1300, translation: 'iii lc.' and deposition:
'xii lc.'.

[85] Ibid. no. 12; London, BL, Harley 547 (s. xiii), translation: 'iii lc.' and deposition:
'xii lc.'; although the Ely breviary, Cambridge, UL, Ii. 4. 20, provides only collects for
both feasts and no lections.

[86] Ibid. no. 6; Oxford, Bodleian, lat. lit. e. 6. (s. xiv¹).

[87] Ibid. no. 2; Cambridge, UL, Kk. i. 22 (s. xiii^ex), a twelve-lection feast. By the early
twelfth century Abingdon had apparently acquired a relic of Birinus, through the good
offices of Abbot Faricius (1100–17); see *Chronicon Monasterii de Abingdon*, ed. J. Stevenson, 2 vols., RS ii (1858), ii. 158.

[88] Wormald, *Benedictine Kalendars*, no. 3; Oxford, New College 358 (s. xiii²).

[89] Ibid. no. 8; London, Lambeth Palace, 873 (s. xv).

[90] Ibid. no. 10; London, BL, Addit. 10628, 'xii lc.' (s. xv^ex); Dunster was a cell of Bath
Abbey, which claimed to possess a relic of Birinus—see *Two Cartularies of the Priory of St
Peter at Bath*, ed. W. Hunt, Somerset Record Society, vii (1893), pp. lxxv–lxxvi.

[91] Wormald, *Benedictine Kalendars*, no. 17; London, BL, Addit. 43405 (*c*.1300).

[92] Cf. the summary of contents in *Missale Westmonasteriense*, ed. J. W. Legg, 3 vols.,
HBS i, v, xii (1891–7), iii. 1406–628.

Birinus.[93] As regards lections for the three nocturns of the night office on the saint's feast day, there are only two surviving sets. The York breviary includes three lections, derived from *Vita S. Birini*, for use on the feast of the translation of Birinus.[94] A possible reason for the inclusion of Birinus there, is that York claimed at some time to possess a relic of Birinus.[95] A longer set is preserved in the breviary of Hyde Abbey and will be discussed below in the description of abbreviated witnesses to *Vita S. Birini*.

The impression is that the liturgical cult of Birinus scarcely survived beyond the eleventh century, except in a few places, some of which can be demonstrated to have had a particular reason to commemorate him. In addition to those already noted, just a few places claimed to possess some kind of relic of Birinus:[96] Reading,[97] Salisbury,[98] and Shrewsbury.[99] There is little evidence to indicate that Birinus had a particularly flourishing popular cult; even at the place which claimed to house his body he was largely overshadowed by Swithun. Such a conclusion is perhaps supported by the fact that there are no known church-dedications to Birinus of any antiquity.[100]

In 1224, the community of Augustinian canons at Dorchester suddenly decided at long last to stake a claim to possess the true relics of St Birinus, 'scripture Bede obuiantes'. The story is interesting for what it reveals about later attitudes towards the authority of a written document of such venerable standing as Bede's *Historia Ecclesiastica*. Appended to the abbreviated version of *Vita S. Birini* made by John of Tynemouth, is an account of how the pope's permission was sought to translate the body of Birinus, and of how Pope Honorius III wrote back, instructing Archbishop

---

[93] *Missale ad Usum percelebris ecclesiae Herfordensis*, ed. W. G. Henderson (Leeds, 1874), p. 222, consisting only of a collect, secret and postcommunion, which are all different from those found in the 11th-cent. liturgical books already mentioned.

[94] Ed. Lawley, ii. 532–3 (from a breviary printed in Venice in 1493).

[95] J. Raine, *Fabric Rolls of York Minster*, Surtees Society, xxxv (1859), pp. 150–3, and id. *HCY* iii. 106–10.

[96] See I. G. Thomas, 'The cult of saints' relics in medieval England', unpublished Ph.D. thesis (London, 1974).

[97] Unprinted list, c. 1200, in the cartulary London, BL, Egerton 3031, fos. 6ᵛ–8ʳ.

[98] C. Wordsworth, *Ceremonies and Processions of the Cathedral Church of Salisbury* (Cambridge, 1901), pp. 33–40.

[99] H. Owen and J. B. Blakeway, *A History of Shrewsbury*, 2 vols. (London, 1825), ii. 42–3.

[100] See F. Arnold-Foster, *Studies in Church Dedications or England's Patron Saints*, 3 vols. (London, 1899); Dorchester's Roman Catholic Church, built in 1849, was given the dedication of St Birinus.

Stephen Langton to look into the case.[101] Visions and miracles were adduced as proof, and finally a tomb was opened up, revealing the vested body of a bishop—the abbot declared that he was sure it was Birinus, and, so the account claims, wriggled around the difficulty of Bede's story of the translation by saying 'in cronicis scribuntur non solum que uidentur, sed et que audiuntur'. A hermit living near Oxford supposedly heard a voice explaining everything to him with the resounding words, 'Birinus in pauimento, Bertinus retro ostium'. The account describes Bertinus as 'episcopus decimus post Birinum'. That position was in fact occupied by Dudda (781–5), and it is possible that Beornstan (twenty-second in succession) was intended, although then the chronology of the whole affair becomes suspect, because Beornstan died in 934, long after Hædde or Bede's time.[102] Possibly at the root of this lies the fact that, on the day after the feast of the translation of Birinus on 4 September, the feast of St Bertin, the seventh-century abbot of Sithiu, was commemorated.[103]

Nevertheless, John of Tynemouth's account states that the pope decreed that Hædde had translated Bertin, and that 'quod Beda de Bertino scripsit, fuerit de Birino receptum, nomine scriptorum negligentia uiciato'.[104] Cautiously enough, however, it is noted that Honorius issued the condition that, should Langton find at Winchester any record of miracles brought about through intercession to Birinus, the case should be abandoned. No other source indicates whether the matter was indeed finally settled, after Langton had made his investigations. Less than a century previously, so *Annales de Wintonia* claimed, the relics of Birinus, along with those of Swithun and three others, had been retranslated.[105] Regardless of what Langton might have found at Winchester (which is not

---

[101] *NLA* i. 119–22; see below p. lxxxiii. Cf. J. E. Sayers, *Papal Government and England during the Pontificate of Honorius III (1216–27)* (Cambridge, 1984), p. 40; *A Calendar of Entries in the Papal Registers illustrating the History of Great Britain and Ireland*, ed. W. H. Bliss *et al.* (HMSO London, 1893–), i. 95, 103; and P. Pressutti, ed., *Regesta Honorii Papae III*, 2 vols. (Rome, 1888–95); ii. 4847 and 5601.

[102] See *HBC*, p. 223.

[103] The feast occurs in virtually every pre-conquest calendar (see Wormald, *English Kalendars*).

[104] There does not seem to be any record of a papal missive giving quite such explicit approval to the canons at Dorchester; the second letter on the subject from Honorius III to Stephen Langton, dated 1225, contains the sentence 'mandat ut hii super huiusmodi facto ueritatem inquirant, et si inuenerunt locum Bedae esse uitiatum, ipsis abbate et conuentui petitam licentiam concedant' (Pressutti, ii. 5601).

[105] Luard, *Annales Monastici*, ii. 54, s.a. 1150. See p. lviii above.

recorded), in 1320 a splendid marble shrine for Birinus's remains was erected at Dorchester,[106] of which only fragments survive to the present day.[107] In the light of this incident, it is somewhat surprising that no written account of miracles worked by Birinus at either Dorchester or Winchester has yet been discovered.

Shortly after the controversy over the relics (perhaps as a consequence thereof), possibly in 1227, the court poet Henry of Avranches composed a metrical version of the Life of St Birinus, 'Et pudet et fateor quia turgeo magna professus', loosely based upon *Vita S. Birini*, and dedicated to Peter des Roches, bishop of Winchester 1205–38.[108] The poem adds little to our knowledge of Birinus, of his cult at thirteenth-century Winchester, or of the transmission of *Vita S. Birini*. A heavily abbreviated version of *Vita S. Birini*, translated into Middle English, and possibly composed at some centre in the south-west, found its way into a handful of manuscripts of the South English legendary, all datable to the later fourteenth or early fifteenth centuries, and from south-western England.[109]

(v) *The Manuscripts of* Vita S. Birini

The following manuscripts preserve the whole of the *Vita S. Birini*:

A = Oxford, Bodleian Library, Digby 39 (*SC* 1640), fos. 57^r–74^v. This codex, now containing 111 folios,[110] is a compilation of originally separate booklets; part one, of three quires (fos. 1–23^v), was written by two scribes in the early twelfth century, and contains *Passio S. Thecle uirginis*[111] and *Passio S. Blasii episcopi et martyris*;[112]

---

[106] The shrine was described by Ranulph Higden in his *Polychronicon*, ed. J. R. Lumby, 9 vols., RS (1865–86), vi. 4.

[107] See H. Addington, *Some Account of the Abbey Church of St Peter and St Paul at Dorchester*, reissued with additional notes by W. C. MacFarlane (Oxford and London, 1860), pp. 63 and 137. Cf. N. Pevsner and J. Sherwood, *Oxfordshire*, BofE (1974), p. 581. In 1535, the year before Dorchester Abbey was dissolved, revenues from Birinus' shrine were valued at £5; see the *Valor Ecclesiasticus*, ed. J. Caley, 6 vols., RC (1810–34), ii. 170.

[108] Cambridge, UL, Dd. 11. 78, fos. 113^v–125^v and Oxford, Bodleian Library, Bodley 40, fos. 43^v–52^v, unprinted; see J. C. Russell and J. P. Hieronymus, *The Shorter Latin Poems of Master Henry of Avranches relating to England*, Medieval Academy of America, Studies and Documents, i (Cambridge, Mass., 1935).

[109] Unprinted; see M. Görlach, *The Textual Tradition of the South English Legendary* (Leeds, 1974), pp. 208–9.

[110] Page measurement: 187 mm. × 110 mm.; written area: 152 mm. × 85 mm.; single columns of 24 lines.

[111] *BHL* 8020.   [112] Cf. *BHL* 1370.

part two (fos. 24–39ᵛ), of the late eleventh or possibly early twelfth century, contains Hermann's *Miracula S. Eadmundi*;[113] part three, a single quire (fos. 40–49ᵛ), contains a sermon by Fulbert of Chartres on the nativity of the Virgin,[114] written in a Continental hand, of perhaps the late eleventh century, with *Translatio Beati Iacobi apostoli* added afterwards,[115] in an early twelfth-century English hand.

Part four is composed of Bede, *HE* iii. 7, divided into eight lections (fos. 50ʳ–52ʳ), then a homily for the feast of Birinus (fos. 52ʳ–56ʳ), followed immediately by mass-sets for the translation and deposition of St Birinus (fos. 56ʳ⁻ᵛ).[116] Immediately below, on the bottom six lines of fo. 56ᵛ, there follows the rubric for a now-lost hymn to Birinus, possibly, 'Agmina sacra poli iubilent modulamine dulci'.[117] This hymn consists, in the two surviving copies, of fifty-four lines; if it were to have been copied into the present manuscript at the same rate (in fos. 50ʳ–56ᵛ) of twenty-eight lines per page, then it need only have occupied just less than one complete folio. The codicology of Digby 39 supports this conjecture, since the first quire of this part of the manuscript has only seven folios, whereas the next four have eight each. There would then have been room for the 'Incipit' rubric for *Vita S. Birini*—none now survives in this manuscript. All these documents pertaining to Birinus were copied in a hand datable to the last quarter of the eleventh century.

Part five begins at fo. 57ʳ, the start of a fresh quire (the pages are ruled with four fewer lines than those of the previous quire), containing *Vita S. Birini*, in a different and slightly later hand, of the very end of the eleventh century, or, more likely, the early twelfth. From fo. 62ᵛ onwards (beginning mid-sentence), the hand of a second scribe can be distinguished, and from there on, the two seem to have worked in collaboration, alternating every page or so. The second scribe finished off *Vita S. Birini* on fo. 74ᵛ, line 18, and continued immediately below with Osbern's *Vita S. Ælfegi* (fos. 4ᵛ–89ᵛ).[118] The remaining two parts of the manuscript date from the later twelfth century, and, apart from some miracles of the Virgin Mary (fos. 93–9ʳ), contain non-hagiographical material.[119]

---

[113] *BHL* 2395.   [114] *Sermo* iv, *PL* cxli. 320–4.

[115] See Fros, 'Inédits', p. 191, 'Post Saluatoris nostri . . .'.

[116] See § iv above for a discussion of these liturgical materials.

[117] See the discussion of this hymn in § iv above.

[118] *BHL* 2518, incomplete at the end.

[119] See W. D. Macray, *Catalogi codicum manuscriptorum bibliothecae Bodleianae pars nona* (Oxford, 1883), cols. 35–6.

On fo. 1ᵛ there is a fourteenth-century inscription of ownership, at the top and bottom of the page: *Liber beate Marie Abbendon, quicunque eum alienauit sit anathema* and it seems reasonable to suppose, at least, that the various parts of the codex were put together, or indeed copied, at the Benedictine Abbey of the Blessed Virgin Mary, Abingdon.[120]

D = Oxford, Bodleian Library, Digby 112 (*SC* 1713), fos. 5ᵛ–17ʳ. The manuscript is a small collection of saints' Lives, in two sections.[121] The first part contains the *Vita S. Swithuni* (fos. 1–5ʳ),[122] *Vita S. Birini*, a traveller's description of Constantinople,[123] a copy of *Passio S. Marci Euangelistae*,[124] Bede's *Historia abbatum*,[125] and *Vita S. Ceolfridi*,[126] *Vita S. Ecgwini*,[127] *Vita S. Maximi*,[128] *Vita S. Eucharii*,[129] *Vita S. Eustasii* by Jona of Bobbio,[130] *Vita S. Burgundofare*,[131] *Vita S. Saluii episcopi*,[132] and *Vita S. Indracti*.[133] The first quire of part one was written by one scribe, and then a second scribe took over somewhat abruptly at the beginning of the next quire, part of the way through a sentence of *Vita S. Birini* (fo. 11ʳ). The second scribe wrote the whole of the rest of part one. The hands appear to be roughly contemporary, and may be dated to the first quarter of the twelfth century.

Part two, written at some time in the second half of the twelfth century, consists of Rhygyfarch's *Vita S. Dewi archiepiscopi*,[134] and *Passio S. Christophori martiris*,[135] followed by various verses and epitaphs by Godfrey of Cambrai, prior of Winchester (1082–1107).[136] The presence of both the *Vita S. Swithuni* and the *Vita S. Birini* in part one, together with the poetry of a prior of Winches-

---

[120] See Gneuss, 'List', p. 38, where Digby 39 is dated to s. xiᵉˣ.

[121] Page measurement: 232 mm. × 155 mm.; written area: 176 mm. × 111 mm., single columns of 30 lines. See the description in Macray, *Catalogi codicum*, cols. 125–7.

[122] *BHL* 7943, followed by a condensed version of the *Miracula S. Swithuni*.

[123] See K. N. Ciggaar, 'Une description de Constantinople traduite par un pélerin anglais', *Revue des études byzantines*, xxxiv (1976), 211–67.

[124] *BHL* 5281.   [125] *BHL* 8968.   [126] *BHL* 1726.

[127] *BHL* 2434b, ed. M. Lapidge, 'The Digby-Gotha recension of the Life of St. Egwine', Vale of Evesham Historical Society, *Research Papers*, vii (1979), 39–55.

[128] *BHL* 5850.   [129] *BHL* 2660.   [130] *BHL* 2773.

[131] St Fara; *BHL* 1487.   [132] *BHL* 7472.

[133] *BHL* 4271; see M. Lapidge, 'The Cult of St. Indract at Glastonbury', in *Ireland in Early Mediaeval Europe: Studies in Memory of Kathleen Hughes*, ed. D. Whitelock, D. Dumville, and R. McKitterick (Cambridge, 1982), pp. 179–212.

[134] *BHL* 2107.   [135] Not in *BHL*.

[136] See A. G. Rigg, *A History of Anglo-Latin Literature 1066–1422* (Cambridge, 1992), pp. 17–20.

ter, Godfrey, in part two, suggests that Digby 112 may have been written and compiled at Winchester.[137]

G = Gotha, Forschungsbibliothek I. 81, fos. 113^r–118^v. This manuscript is a large collection of English and British saints' Lives,[138] made at an as yet undetermined English centre, and written by a single hand, of the second half of the fourteenth century.[139] Considering its significance, this compilation, which preserves versions of certain Lives of Anglo-Saxon saints not now known from any other source, deserves, and may indeed reward, a closer examination.[140]

H = Hereford, Cathedral Library, P. VII. 6, fos. 134^v–139^r.[141] The feast days of the fifty saints' Lives in this manuscript fall in November and December, suggesting that the present codex is only the final volume of a large and comprehensive legendary, arranged according to the liturgical calendar.[142] The selection, and form, of the Lives included in the manuscript indicate that this legendary belongs to the 'family' of the so-called Cotton-Corpus legendary, a collection of Lives for the whole liturgical year, which may have been based on an originally Frankish compilation, and is found in several English manuscripts from the eleventh century onwards.[143]

In addition to the inscription inside the front cover, *De armariolo maioris ecclesie Herefordensis*, the codex contains, on the back fly-leaf, a price-mark, *precii XLs*, apparently put in by the same scribe who, in *c.* 1300, wrote valuations into some forty of the manuscripts in Hereford Cathedral library. It is quite likely that P. VII. 6 has always been at Hereford. The entire manuscript, including the list of contents on fo. 1^r, was written by one scribe, whose hand, roughly datable to the mid-twelfth century, is to be found in at least

---

[137] See M. Lapidge, 'The medieval hagiography of St Ecgwine', Vale of Evesham Historical Society, *Research Papers*, vi (1977), 77–93, at p. 88.

[138] 230 fos.; page measurement: 313 mm. × 230 mm.; double columns. The contents of Gotha I. 81 are described by Grosjean, 'De codice Gothano'.

[139] D. Dumville and M. Lapidge (eds.), *The Anglo-Saxon Chronicle: A Collaborative Edition*, xvii: *The Annals of St Neots with Vita Prima Sancti Neoti* (Woodbridge, 1985), pp. lxxix–lxxx, and Lapidge and Winterbottom, *Wulfstan*, p. clxxv.

[140] I hope to make this MS the subject of a subsequent study.

[141] 249 fos.; page measurement: 412 mm. × 280 mm.; written area: 309 mm. × 185 mm.; double columns of 44 lines.

[142] Cf. Mynors and Thomson, *Catalogue*, pp. 110–12; and Bannister, *Catalogue*, pp. 172–7.

[143] On the Cotton-Corpus legendary and Hereford P. VII. 6, see pp. xxvi–xxvii above.

one other manuscript (P. VIII. 7, a homiliary) in the library at Hereford Cathedral. M. R. James, writing in the introduction to Bannister's catalogue of the library, suggested that P. VII. 6 and P. VIII. 7 may have been copied at Worcester (or possibly Evesham) for Hereford, on account of the presence of a Life of St Ecgwine in the legendary.[144] It is not certain that there can have been a working scriptorium at Hereford at this time.[145] As already stated, the earliest surviving copy of the 'Cotton-Corpus legendary', preserved in London, BL, Cotton Nero E. 1 and CCCC 9, was probably written in Worcester, in the third quarter of the eleventh century. Thus it is not inconceivable that the legendary of which Hereford P. VII. 6 is the last remnant, could indeed have been copied from, or rather compiled with reference to, the legendary at Worcester. Only a detailed examination and collation of the contents of both legendaries could come anywhere near to supporting such a hypothesis.[146]

T = London, BL, Cotton Tiberius D. IV, pt. 2, fos. 105^v–110^v. This is a collection of forty-five saints' Lives, arranged only sporadically according to the liturgical calendar, now bound as two volumes.[147] It was badly damaged in the Cottonian fire in 1731, so that text is lost or illegible in some places. The majority of the contents are the Lives of confessors (only five martyrs included together near the end of the collection), many of whom are Frankish saints such as Vedast, Amand, Walaric, Medard, Richier, Audoen, and Philibert.[148] The manuscript was evidently made by several scribes, writing at about the end of the eleventh or the beginning of the twelfth century. At the end of the collection (that is, at the end of the present part two), four Lives of English saints were added, all

---

[144] Bannister, p. vii.

[145] See Mynors and Thomson, *Catalogue*, p. xix.

[146] Other evidence suggests that the matter is complex. M. Chibnall, discussing the surviving MSS of the earliest version of the Life of St Evroul (*BHL* 2376b), suggests that the copy in Hereford P. VII. 6 may have been copied from that in Oxford, Bodleian Library, Fell 2, part of the early 12th-cent. legendary from St Augustine's, Canterbury; see *The Ecclesiastical History of Orderic Vitalis*, iv. 363–4.

[147] Page measurement: 345 mm. × 235 mm., written area: 310 mm. × 190 mm., double columns. See the description of this MS in Lapidge and Winterbottom, *Wulfstan*, pp. clxxvii–clxxix.

[148] The contents are listed in T. Smith, *Catalogus librorum manuscriptorum bibliothecae Cottonianae* (Oxford, 1696), repr. and ed. C. G. C. Tite (Woodbridge, 1984), pp. 27–8. See also J. Planta, *A Catalogue of the Manuscripts in the Cottonian Library, Deposited in the British Museum* (London, 1802), p. 39.

in one hand which appears to be of the first quarter or so of the twelfth century: *Vita S. Birini*, *Vita* and *Miracula S. Swithuni* (fos. 111ʳ–121ᵛ), Wulfstan's *Vita S. Æthelwoldi* (fos. 121ᵛ–130ᵛ),[149] and Osbern's *Vita S. Dunstani* (fos. 130ᵛ–153ʳ).[150] An account of the miracles of St Laurence came at the end of the book as it was constituted in the early twelfth century (fos. 153ʳ–157ʳ).

The addition of the Lives of three saints with an especial Winchester connection, namely Birinus, Swithun, and Æthelwold, suggests the possibility that the manuscript might have been written at the Old Minster there, particularly when considered in conjunction with the evidence provided by the presence of nine leaves (part 2, fos. 158–66) including a copy of Æthelwulf's *De abbatibus*.[151] These nine leaves were originally part of an early eleventh-century manuscript containing a copy of Bede, *HE*, now Winchester, Cathedral Library, 1.[152] That manuscript was probably written at Winchester, and so if the nine leaves were transferred there too, then a Winchester provenance for Tiberius D. IV, the new home of the Æthelwulf's poem, is implied.[153]

A mutilated copy of *Vita S. Birini* is to be found in: **C** = London, BL, Cotton Caligula A. VIII, fos. 121ʳ–124ᵛ. The constitution of this codex,[154] which is made up of twelve distinct parts of various origins and dates, is rather complicated.[155] The hagiographical portions include Eadmer's *Vita S. Wilfridi*,[156] a copy of *Vita S. Werburge*,[157] a set of lections for the feasts of SS Seaxburh and Eormenhild,[158] the *Miracula S. Wihtburge*,[159] *Vita S. Sexburge*,[160] and Lives of Benedict and Scholastica, Mary Magdalene and Katherine. The remains of *Vita S. Birini* constitute part six of the manuscript, and are followed immediately by Wulfstan's *Vita S. Æthelwoldi*, also fragmentary.

The text of *Vita S. Birini* breaks off at the end of fo. 122ᵛ, and

---

[149] *BHL* 2647. [150] *BHL* 2344.

[151] A. Campbell, *Æthelwulf: De Abbatibus* (Oxford, 1967), pp. ix–x.

[152] Ker, *Catalogue*, p. 465, no. 396.

[153] See Holschneider, *Die Organa*, pp. 19–20.

[154] Page measurement: 227 mm. × 165 mm., single columns.

[155] The parts of the MS are discussed and described in detail in Lapidge and Winterbottom, *Wulfstan*, pp. clxxi–clxxiv.

[156] *BHL* 8893. [157] *BHL* 8855.

[158] Cf. *BHL* 7693 and *BHL* 2611. [159] *BHL* 8980.

[160] *BHL* 7693. This and the preceding material relating to Wærburh, Seaxburh, Eormenhild, and Wihtburh may have been composed by Goscelin of Saint Bertin.

what follows at fo. 123ʳ is discontinuous, and from a later section of the *Vita*. The amount of text omitted (c. 5 'Perscrutatus' to c. 11, 'Vestigando consilium') would be sufficient to fill two folios, and so it appears that fos. 121–4 were once the outer leaves of a quire of four, and that the two inner leaves have fallen out. The text breaks off again, mid-sentence at fo. 124ᵛ (ending with c. 15, 'inmurmurat uoce'), and the remainder is now lost. A further four or five leaves would have been required to reach the end of the text of the *Vita* as preserved in the other surviving manuscripts. The ragged aspect of both these portions, and the fragments of the Life of Æthelwold, suggest that at one time the leaves were on the outer ends of a codex, but it is no longer possible to determine whether they were originally part of the same manuscript, or where they were written. The presence elsewhere in the compilation of material relating to saints connected with Ely, namely, Seaxburh, Wærburh, Eormenhild, and Wihtburh, may offer some clue as to the place where the parts of Caligula A. VIII were, at least, put together.

The remains of *Vita S. Birini* are the work of two scribes, the first writing fos. 121ʳ–123ᵛ (line 19), the second fos. 123ᵛ (line 20) to 124ᵛ. The script is very similar to that of the *Vita S. Æthelwoldi* which follows the *Vita S. Birini*, and has the generally upright and narrow aspect characteristic of the late eleventh and early twelfth century.

There is evidence for the existence of another, now lost, manuscript of *Vita S. Birini*. London, Gray's Inn, 3 is part of an early twelfth-century legendary which may have been written at St Werburg's Abbey, Chester.[161] An alphabetical list of the Lives contained in that volume, and in three others, now missing, is to be found on inserted paper fly-leaves (fos. ii and iii), in an early sixteenth-century hand. The list includes a reference to the volume in which each Life occurred, and a folio number. It shows that in the former volume three, at folio 22, there was a copy of a Life of Birinus, occupying at least five folios. The format of the surviving volume of the legendary is double columns, with 40 lines of text per page, and so, if the missing third volume had had a similar format, five folios would have been just enough to accommodate a full text of *Vita S. Birini*.[162]

---

[161] See Ker, *Medieval Libraries*, p. 49, and the description in Ker, *Medieval Manuscripts*, i. 52–5.

[162] Compare Hereford P. VII. 6, where, at the rate of 44 lines per page, in double columns, *Vita S. Birini* occupies just under five fos. (134ᵛ–139ʳ).

(vi) *Abbreviated versions of* Vita S. Birini

The abbreviated versions of *Vita S. Birini* are as follows:

B = Oxford, Bodleian Library, Bodley 509 (*SC* 2672), fos. 135^v–138^v. Most of this manuscript (fos. 1–130) is taken up with material concerning Thomas Becket, in various hands of the thirteenth century.[163] The remainder was possibly once a separate manuscript, the contents of which are a sermon for the feast of St John *ante Portam Latinam*, *Vita S. Birini*, sermons for the feast of St Peter *ad uincula*, and of the *Cathedra Petri*, the *Inuentio S. Crucis*, and the Lord's Nativity, all written in the same thirteenth-century hand. The presence of the account of the life, translation and miracles of Thomas Becket may indicate a Canterbury origin for this codex, but there is no supporting evidence. The text of *Vita S. Birini* is, in this manuscript, very drastically abbreviated, to supply only the bare bones of the 'story', omitting the whole of cc. 7 and 8, and virtually all of cc. 1, 2, 4, 6, 11, 12, and 14–20.

F = Oxford, Bodleian Library, Fell 2 (*SC* 8690), pp. 263–8. This manuscript, containing saints' Lives for November and December, was probably once the final part of a multi-volume legendary, of which London, BL, Arundel 91, is the penultimate volume.[164] Only these two portions now survive. The legendary was written at St Augustine's Abbey, Canterbury, and, to judge from the upright and prickly appearance of the script, during the first third of the twelfth century.[165] It is possible that the St Augustine's legendary was copied from a now fragmentary legendary written at Christ Church, Canterbury in the early eleventh century.[166] The December portion of the latter is lost, but may well have included either a complete, or abbreviated, copy of *Vita S. Birini*.[167]

Fell 2 has been mutilated by the removal of many of the historiated initials which decorated the beginning of almost every Life in

---

[163] Page measurement: 188 mm. × 152 mm., written area 135 mm. × 122 mm.; single columns of 20 lines. Cf. A. G. Watson, *A Catalogue of Dated and Datable Manuscripts in Oxford Libraries, c.435–1600*, 2 vols. (Oxford, 1984), i. 18 (no. 96), and references there.

[164] 232 fos.; page measurement: 334 mm. × 230 mm.; written area: 260 mm. × 170 mm.; double columns of 37 lines.

[165] See Ker, *Medieval Libraries*, p. 42, and Ker, *English Manuscripts*, p. 30. And see pp. clxxiii–clxxiv below on Arundel 91. [166] See pp. xxiv–xxv.

[167] The relationship of these two Canterbury legendaries is discussed below, pp. clxxxiii–clxxxiv.

the legendary; in some places the whole folio has been torn away, in others a square has been cut out, which hampers the identification of the texts included in the collection. The text of *Vita S. Birini* was very drastically abbreviated. Although both of these abbreviations remain unpublished, it seems unnecessary to print them here. However, the portions omitted in each have been listed in Appendix (A), in order to clarify what will be said below about the relationship of **B** and **F** to the other witnesses.

Another very heavily abbreviated version of *Vita S. Birini* is to be found in the breviary of Hyde Abbey (previously the New Minster), Winchester, preserved in Oxford, Bodleian, Rawlinson, Liturg. e. 1*, and Gough Liturg. 8, datable to the late thirteenth or early fourteenth century. There are four lections for the feast of the translation (shared with St Cuthbert) and eight for the deposition, all taken from the *Vita*.[168] Too much has been omitted from the source, by abridgement, for these lections to contribute much to our knowledge of the text, but an isolated variant reading suggests that the lections derive from a version related in some way to those found in **B** and **F**.[169]

(vii) *Indirect Witnesses*

London, BL, Lansdowne 436, a fourteenth-century compilation of English saints' Lives, written at Romsey Abbey (Hants.),[170] includes a redaction of *Vita S. Birini* (fos. 30ʳ–31ᵛ).[171] Although clearly indebted to *Vita S. Birini* (to judge from the overall shape of the narrative, and a few phrases copied verbatim), the Life has not only been abridged, but also extensively rewritten. This is the case with many of the Lives included in Lansdowne 436, which merits a more detailed study than it has hitherto received, since it preserves some Lives of Anglo-Saxon saints not now surviving in any earlier form, and may represent the work of a single redactor.

Another version of *Vita S. Birini* occurs in the fourteenth-century compilation of English, Irish, British and Scottish saints'

---

[168] Tolhurst, *Monastic Breviary*, iv, fos. 337ʳ and 396ʳ–397ʳ respectively.
[169] See p. lxxxv below.
[170] An *ex libris* inscription on fo. 1ᵛ, 'Iste Liber est de Lib. Eccles. S. Marie et S. Ethelflede Virg. de Romesey' establishes the ownership.
[171] The contents of this MS are described by P. Grosjean in 'Vita S. Roberti Noui Monasterii in Anglia abbatis', *AB* lvi (1938), 334–60, at pp. 335–9. See also *A Catalogue of the Lansdowne Manuscripts in the British Museum* (London, 1819), p. 121.

Lives made by John of Tynemouth, and entitled *Sanctilogium Angliae, Walliae, Scotiae et Hiberniae*, now only surviving in one manuscript, London, BL, Cotton Tiberius E. 1, which was badly damaged during the Cotton fire of 1731. John's collection was ordered according to the liturgical calendar, and antiphons and collects were included for each saint. An anonymous compiler re-arranged all the Lives in alphabetical order, omitting the liturgical material, and this arrangement, now preserved in three fifteenth-century manuscripts, was printed by Wynkyn de Worde in 1516.[172] The long text of *Vita S. Birini* has been so severely abbreviated that any attempt to determine how it relates to the other full witnesses to the text is fruitless. An account (apparently not preserved else-where) of the thirteenth-century controversy at Dorchester con-cerning the whereabouts of Birinus's body, was added to the end of the Life by Tynemouth.[173]

(viii) *The Relationship of the Manuscripts*

None of the manuscripts can have been copied directly from any other, since each has some significant errors or omissions not found in the others, for example:

A: c. 7, *commutatio* for *commutationem*; c. 8, *dum* for *de*; c. 11, *in celis* for *incedis*; c. 19, omission of *ubi*; c. 20, omission of *de*, and *habitores* for *habitatores*; c. 21, *a populo* for *apostolo*. Other variant readings unique to **A**, which cannot however be said to constitute errors, c. 8, *uenit* for *creuit*; c. 11, *potuerunt* for *poterunt* (the Vulgate text being cited, from the *Song of Songs*, actually reads *potuerunt*, in the perfect tense, whereas the other witnesses have the verb in the future tense), and c. 20, *decantare* for *cantare*.

Elsewhere,[174] it has been suggested that the unique variant read-ing in **A**, of *operatum* for *operatus* (c. 16), is clearly the more plaus-ible and therefore preferable. This does not have to be the case, because either reading can fit the context. The reading *operatum* requires to be interpreted as a passive participle, meaning 'having been brought about, effected', not unknown in medieval latinity, whereas the most common use of 'operor' is as a deponent verb—'I work'.[175] The author of the *Vita* clearly knew that 'operor' is, or can

[172] Repr. *NLA*. [173] *NLA* i. 118–22.
[174] Townsend, 'An Eleventh-Century Life of Birinus', pp. 135–6.
[175] See *TLL*, under 'operor'.

be, deponent, since he used it only a few phrases before: *qui imitatus Dominum suum immo operatus per Dominum suum.* . . . Although to read *operatum* would in one sense follow the train of thought *dixit et factum est* . . ., the sentence could be open to another interpretation. The rhetorical style of the whole text, which has been discussed above, displays a tendency towards balancing parallel phrases, but also sometimes towards antithesis, an emphasis upon duality of function, and word-play. The sentence we are considering could be interpreted thus: *qui imitatus Dominum suum*—who (1) imitated his Lord, since he said and it was done, an echo of the creation in Genesis, ch. 1—*dixit et factum est*, and then *immo operatus per Dominum suum*—nay rather, (2) worked *through* his Lord, since he willed and brought about, i.e. did the working himself—*uoluit et operatus est*.

C: c. 1, *enim* for *eum*, and *religiosius* for *religiosus*; c. 3, *effectus* for *euectus*; c. 11, *eam* for *eum*.

D: c. 2, *eelum* for *celum*, *carnis* for *carnalis*; c. 3, omission of *qui*; c. 4, *suauitate* for *suauiter*, omission of *honore*, omission of *ut astutia*, *simplitatas* for *simplicitas* and *simplicita* for *simplicem*; c. 5, *secus* for *secutus*; c. 6, *exulat* for *exultat*; c. 7, *demonium* for *demonum*; c. 8, omission of *eam in perpetuum* . . . *in eternum*; c. 10, *disposionis* for *dispositionis*, *proditor* for *proditur*, *deadem* for *de eadem*; c. 15, *lenocinantur* for *lenocinatur*; c. 17, *pugnandi* for *pugnaui*; c. 18, omission of *belli*, *reri* for *regi*, *cultrum* for *cultum* and *est* for *e*; c. 19, *gententem* for *gentem*; c. 20, omission of *subditos*, and *finem* for *fidem*.

H: c. 3, *et promptus* for *expromptus*; c. 4, addition of *et* after *emanare*, and *testamenti* for *testimonii*; c. 5, omission of *ex* after *maxima*; c. 6, *ergo* for *uero*, *inhabitem* for *habitem*, *meliorem* for *optimam*; c. 7, commutatione for *commutationem*; c. 8, *uincit* for *uicit*, *subegit* for *subiecit*; c. 10, *putantes* for *putabant*; c. 11, *effectus* for *effectum*, *euacuatur* for *uacuatur*; c. 14, omission of *humiliter*; c. 16, *correpta* for *correcta*; c. 17, addition of *et* after *intrepidus*.

T: c. 1, *caritate* for *claritate*; c. 2, omission of *ubi* after *thesaurum*; c. 3, *prepararet* for *perciperet*; c. 4, *que* instead of *ut astutia*, and *instruunt* for *instruant*; c. 5, *perscrutatis* for *perscrutatus*, *qualitate* for *qualitatem*, and *euangelii predicatorem* for *euangelium predicaturum*; c. 7, *denuntiat* for *denuntiet*; c. 8, *deficit* for *deficis*; c. 11, *incremento* for *cremento*; c. 13, *oculantur* for *osculantur*, *euuangelicam* for *ecclesiasticam*, *per fidem* for *perficere*; c. 14, *surgit ecclesia* for *surgunt ecclesie*; c. 17, *deseruiens* for *deseuiens*, *hostiam* for *bestiam*, *fide* for *fine*; c. 20, *didicant* for *didicerat*, *fuerit* for *furit*, *deducens* for *deduceret*, *cominatum* for *comitatum*.

G: c. 1, omission of *ecclesie*; c. 2, *singulo* for *cingulo*; c. 3, omission of *suum propter timores nocturnos . . . femur* by homoeoteleuton; c. 6, *potest* for *potestati* and omission of *qui Deum inhabitantem . . . habebat* and *intraret . . . orbem* by homoeoteleuton.

B and **F**, the abbreviated versions of the Life, are clearly independent of one another, since each preserves sections omitted by the other. Furthermore, it cannot be shown that either **B** or **F** was directly dependent upon any of the other witnesses. **F** does, however, share several variants with **G** alone, namely, c. 4, *interim* for *uiritim*, and omission of *sint* after *luce*; c. 5, *itaque* for *igitur*, *magna* for *maxima*; c. 14 addition of *praedicans ibi diem a quo omnis dies*; c. 15, *ergo* for *etenim illi*; c. 21, omission of *nostri* before *Hedde*. On every occasion when **G** shares a variant reading with one other witness, **F** is absent. On the other hand, there are only two instances where **F** shares a variant with one other witness, both in c. 21: *Wentanam* shared with **H**, and *a populo* shared with **A**. It may be that these two instances are coincidental correspondences, in particular the second one (since it is not difficult to confound *apostolo*, abbreviated to 'apło', and *a populo*, shortened to 'a popło'). If they are, then it would be possible to regard **F** and **G** as deriving from one hyparchetype (γ), and thus to abandon their individual readings and only report the shared readings. Such a step may be inadvisable, in view of the fact that **F** represents a considerably abridged version of the Life.

Since **B** is an even more abbreviated version of *Vita S. Birini* than **F**, its affiliations are harder to determine. **B** is close to **F** and **G** in one salient variant, that is, in c. 9, where **F** and **G** have *insula sisteretur*, **B** has *insula insisteretur* (the abbreviated version in the Hyde breviary also has *insula sisteretur*). **B** and **G** share one other variant, in c. 11, offering *auctorem* for *ductorem*, but **F** is absent. In no other instances, where present, does **B** follow **F** and **G**, and consequently it cannot derive from the hypothetical γ. An hyparchetype (β) could, however, be conjectured for γ and **B**. As with **F**, in all cases where **G** shares a variant reading with one of **A**, **C**, **D**, **H**, or **T**, then **B** is absent, so that those shared readings do not count against the conjectured hyparchetype β. Again, the fact that **B** is such an abbreviated version of *Vita S. Birini* means that this can only remain a very hypothetical relationship. The one instance where there is disagreement between **F**, **G**, and **B**, is over the name of Birinus's see. **F** and **G** read, in error, *Dorkinga* and *Dorkynga* respectively (with **A**), whereas **B** reads *Dorcacestra*. It is possible that β also read *Dorkinga*, which was corrected by the scribe of **B** (or of its exemplar). The highly conjectural relationship thus far described is summarized by the *stemma* in Figure 1. It is just possible that the recension represented by **B**, **F**, and **G** represents a form of *Vita S. Birini* which reached Canterbury in the early part of the twelfth century.

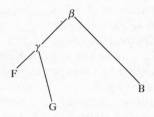

Figure 1

A much more complicated task is to connect the hypothetical recension (β) just described, to the other witnesses. **G** shares at least one variant reading with every one of **A**, **C**, **D**, **H**, and **T**. The largest number are those common to **C** and **G** alone, namely, c. 3, *ordinem* against *ordine*, c. 14, *in piis Christi* for *in Christi piis*; c. 15, *obstrusit* for *obstruxit*.

It may be best to turn aside for a moment and attempt to draw up the possible relationships between **A**, **C**, **D**, **H**, and **T**. These witnesses fall roughly into two groups. **A**, **C**, and **D** have certain features in common, such as c. 4, *effecto* for *effectu*, *benedictum* for *bene dictum* (both insignificant variants, admittedly), plus inclusion, in only these three, of the chapter headings. **A** and **D**, however, share two variant readings: c. 8 *comperas* for *comparas* (**C** absent) and c. 14 *hiemi* for *hiems*. Neither **A** and **C** alone, nor **C** and **D**, share readings. Thus the three cannot derive directly from one single exemplar.

Certain variants, which either **A** or **D** shares with at least one other witness, may stand in the way of assigning to **A** and **D** a common exemplar or hyparchetype; for example, c. 3, *lectum* **D** (before correction) and **G**; c. 5, *inmensum* for *in inmensum* **DFGH**; c. 11, *placuerat* for *placauerat* **DG**; c. 14, *Dei* for *diei* **DT**; c. 17, *priusquam* for *postquam* **AG**; and c. 20, *Dorkinga* **AFG**. On the other hand, **H** and **T** share two minor variant readings: c. 12, *repperit* for *reperit*, and c. 20, *lectioni* for *lectionis*, but certain other variants, such as c. 7, *resplenduit* for *resplendeat* **GT**; *bellatur* for *bellaturus* **GH** and c. 18, *amplectens* for *amplexans* in **FGH**, may preclude the possibility that these two witnesses shared a common exemplar or hyparchetype.

The complicating factor here may be that some contamination of witnesses has taken place, particularly in the case of the latest manuscript, **G**, which could have been prepared from a collation of more than one exemplar (or copied from an exemplar which had been thus collated). It is perhaps noteworthy that in two cases **G** preserves a reading which appears as a later correction to **T**: c. 3, *ordinem* for *ordine* **CG** and **T** after correction; c. 16, *interim* **G** and **T** after correction.

Matters are also not helped by the fact that so many of the variant readings are relatively insignificant, or could quite easily have been arrived at independently by more than one witness. Examples of this are: c. 5, *in inmensum* against *inmensum* (where the Vulgate passage being cited has *in immensum* twice); c. 7, *bellatur* in **GH**, where only the suspension mark for '-us' has been omitted; c. 11, *placuerat* for *placauerat* **DG**; c. 14, *Dei* for *diei* **DT**; c. 17, *priusquam* for *postquam* **AG**; c. 18, *amplectens* against *amplexans*. Consequently, it seems almost impossible to construct with absolute confidence a *stemma codicum* which includes all the witnesses. Figure 2 is a very conjectural *stemma*, taking into account that which has just been stated about the possibility of disregarding a certain class of variants, which could have arisen coincidentally in more than one witness.[176] Needless to say, at every branch of the textual history which this *stemma* is an attempt to summarize, further exemplars, now lost, could have intervened, making the relationships between the surviving witnesses even less direct than they might seem.

Since they represent very heavily abbreviated versions of *Vita S. Birini*, the variant readings of **B** and **F** have only been supplied in the critical apparatus where they support what would otherwise

---

[176] Conjectural hyparchetypes are represented by δ, μ, and θ.

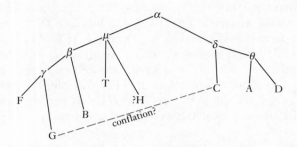

Figure 2

appear as unique variants in other witnesses (in particular **G**). The apparatus would become impossibly chaotic if every single variant of **B** and **F** were to be included. Many of them arose from the redactors' efforts to make seamless connections where portions of the full text had been omitted. Another way of signalling these shared variants would have been by reference to the hyparchetypes β and γ referred to above, but, as already stated, since the *stemma codicum* can only remain very conjectural, such a measure may seem over-hasty.

(ix) *Previous Editions of* Vita Sancti Birini

Vita S. Birini has only been edited once before, by D. Townsend.[177] His edition is defective in various respects. The critical apparatus has been keyed to the Latin text by reference to line numbers, yet the lines of the text have, rather unfortunately, not been numbered, which does not make for easy inspection of variants, and in one case (p. 156, line 554—where the word *de* appears twice) leads to complete ambiguity. In several places, readings are wrongly reported, or the manuscripts have been misread, for example, (p. 138, line 6) **A** is said to read 'pro ea', but the manuscript very clearly reads 'βea', the abbreviation for 'postea' (fo. 57ʳ; c. 1); on p. 151, line 390, **A** is said to read 'est igitur', whereas the manuscript has 'est k' (fo. 68ᵛ; c. 15); p. 156, line 564, 'penis' where all witnesses clearly read 'peius' (c. 20). At p. 157, line 604, 'a populo' is in fact only supported by **A** and **F** (c. 21, note e), and does not readily make sense in the context, because of 'suo' at the beginning of the phrase, whereas 'apostolo', the majority reading, is perfectly intelligible.

---

[177] 'An Eleventh-Century Life of Birinus of Wessex', *AB* cvii (1989), 129–59.

3. ST KENELM OF WINCHCOMBE AND VITA ET MIRACVLA SANCTI KENELMI

(i) St Kenelm

'By God! I hadde levere than my sherte | That ye hadde rad his legende, as have I,' cries Chaucer's cockerel, Chauntecleer, as he recounts the tale of Kenelm's premonitory vision to his hen, Pertelote, thereby testifying to the lasting popularity of that saint's story.[1] The legend of St Kenelm runs as follows: on the death of his father, King Coenwulf, the 7-year-old Kenelm was designated heir to the throne, fulfilling the wish of both Coenwulf and the populace. However, Kenelm's elder sister, Cwoenthryth, desired the position herself, and plotted the child's murder with Æscberht, his tutor. Kenelm had a premonitory dream, interpreted by his nurse. The tutor took the child hunting in Clent forest, and after a feverish search for a suitably secluded spot, cut Kenelm's head off, and buried his corpse under a thorn tree. Subsequently, the whereabouts of the body were miraculously revealed to the wider world, and Kenelm's remains were removed to Winchcombe to be enshrined. Miracles proceeded both from his tomb and from the holy well which sprang up at the site of the murder.

There is no mention of either Kenelm or Cwoenthryth in the *Anglo-Saxon Chronicle*, where the death of Coenwulf in 821 is followed immediately by the accession of Ceolwulf.[2] It is difficult securely to establish the identity of the saint from any surviving documentary evidence independent of the legend recounted above. For example, several charters connected with Winchcombe and datable to between 803 and 811 were attested by a Cynhelm 'princeps' or 'dux'.[3] The fact that the name does not occur again after 811 suggests that this Cynhelm may have died in about that year. The Life of Kenelm claims that the saint was 7 years old when his father died in 821, which is hardly consistent with

---

[1] Geoffrey Chaucer, 'The Nun's Priest's Tale', lines 3120–1, ed. F. N. Robinson, *The Riverside Chaucer*, gen. ed. L. D. Benson, 3rd edn. (Oxford, 1987), p. 257.

[2] *ASC* s.a. 819.

[3] S 106; 'princeps' in S 1260 and 168; 'dux' in S 1187, 161, 40, 159, 163, 164, 165, 167, ranging in date from c.801 to 811.

someone who was apparently already of an age to witness a charter in 803.[4] Either there were two Cynhelms (or a Coenhelm and a Cynhelm), both perhaps members of Coenwulf's family, which seems a little unlikely,[5] or the events described by the Life of St Kenelm must be regarded as very largely fictitious. The evidence of charters independently establishes the existence of Cwoen-thryth, daughter of Coenwulf, as an abbess of Minster-in-Thanet.[6]

The Latin Life of St Kenelm exists in two recensions, the first a set of lections preserved in a single fragmentary manuscript from Worcester, which will for convenience be referred to as *Vita brevior*,[7] and secondly, the *Vita et miracula*,[8] found in eight manuscripts, and transmitted also in several abbreviated versions.[9] *Vita brevior* describes only the martyrdom of Kenelm, whereas *Vita et miracula* goes on to recount the circumstances of the recovery of his body, its journey back to Winchcombe, the demise of Cwoen-thryth, and then a selection of posthumous miracles up to the author's own time. It is the latter with which we shall be prin-cipally, though not exclusively, concerned here.

(ii) *The Dating and Latinity of* Vita et miracula

The evidence for the date of the composition of *Vita et miracula* may be gathered from within the text. In his preface, the author acknowledges the help of Eadgyth, the wife of the Confessor, in collecting information about Kenelm.[10] Furthermore, the impres-

---

[4] Cf. W. Levison, *England and the Continent in the Eighth Century* (Oxford, 1946), pp. 249–59, at 249; and E. S. Hartland, 'The Legend of St Kenelm', *Transactions of the Bristol and Gloucestershire Archaeological Society*, xxxix (1916), 13–65, at p. 16.

[5] This was the assumption of J. Armitage-Robinson, *Somerset Historical Essays* (London, 1921), p. 38, swiftly dismissed by Levison, *England and the Continent*, p. 250.

[6] See commentary on c. 1 below.

[7] *BHL* 4641m, subdivided in the MS into eight lections of which only seven survive. In *BHL* (supplement), the text was given the title *Vita antiquior*, on the basis of the work of R. von Antropoff, 'Die Entwicklung der Kenelm-Legende' (Inaugural-Dissertation zur Erlangung der Doktorwürde der Philosophischen Fakultät der Rheinischen Friedrich-Wilhelms-Universität zu Bonn, 1965), mainly because the lections are preserved in a MS some fifty years older than the earliest surviving witness to *Vita et miracula S. Kenelmi*.

[8] *BHL* 4641n, p and r.

[9] See §§ ix–x below for a detailed description of the MSS of these two texts.

[10] It is noteworthy that the anonymous author of the *Vita S. Ædwardi* claimed similarly to have acquired information for his work through conversation with Eadgyth (Barlow, pp. 59–60), although this is hardly surprising when he was researching for a Life of her husband.

sion is that Eadgyth was still alive at the time of writing. Hence, the composition of the text (or at the very least, the preface) must fall between 1045, the date of Eadgyth's marriage to Edward, and her death in December 1075.[11] It seems fairly certain that the *Vita* and most of the *Miracula* were conceived as a single unit.[12] The preface promises some account of Kenelm's miracles: 'Nec desunt adhuc uisiones et reuelationes super eo sanctissime. Porro in huius fine textus tam recentia et late nota referemus signa', and those which follow fit the description well enough. Furthermore, the narrative style and Latinity of the *Vita* and the *Miracula* are uniform. In any case, no surviving manuscript preserves the *Vita* alone. The phrase 'pauca ex multis moderni et nostri temporis' at the end of c. 17, implies a distinction between miracles of relatively recent times, and those of the author's own day. Hence, the chapters which follow, while keeping to a broadly thematic order (punitive miracles, then healings), seem simply to be arranged in chronological order, with no perceptible change in style. If we are correct in this assumption of unity, then the date-limits for composition can be narrowed. After several chapters apparently all describing the abbacy of Godwin (1042–53), c. 27 refers to Godric as 'abbate proximo' (1054–66), and then c. 28 mentions what must be a different man, 'presenti patri monasterii', presumably Galandus (1066–75).[13] The date of the composition of *Vita et miracula* may thus be narrowed to between 1066 and 1075,[14] during the regime of its first Norman abbot.

Turning to the matter of the style and Latinity of *Vita et miracula*, it may be noted first of all that one of the prominent features of the text is the extensive use of rhyme, mostly monosyllabic, but also disyllabic, linking two or more segments of a sentence, which are sometimes quite carefully balanced. Consider, for example: 'Legitur . . . epistol*a*, que uiolenter absconditum in Angli*a* celitus prodiderit in Rom*a*' (preface); 'qui celo teste erat martyriz*atus* celo teste est declar*atus*' (with homoeoptoton); 'Quem . . . abscidere nitebatur inhumanitas beluin*a*, illum prodebat . . . pecualis diligenti*a*'

---

[11] See commentary below.

[12] Comparison of the fullest witnesses to the *Miracula* suggests that c. 31, not included in every MS, may have been a subsequent addition, quite possibly by the same author. See p. cxxxii below.

[13] See *Heads*, p. 79.

[14] Cf. Brett, 'The use of universal chronicle', p. 280, where the dates 1069–75 are suggested.

(c. 8); 'Nec ei cessit in uacu*um*, tanti itineris perrexisse spaci*um*' (c. 31). Rhyme is combined with liberal application of alliteration,[15] and assonance,[16] to create, at times, a strongly poetic tone, eminently suited to reading aloud. Other rhetorical figures employed are asyndeton (in a tricolon)[17] and antithesis.[18] Rhythm also seems to have been used; about 64 per cent of the sentence-endings were furnished with one of the four principal types of rhythmical *clausulae*.[19]

These features notwithstanding, the narrative proceeds with few digressions, no pious exclamations and apostrophes such as occur in *Vita brevior* (cc. 3 and 4) or, for example, in *Vita S. Birini*. The prose style is restrained and simple, almost terse at times. Even the preface, often the platform for a slightly more grandiose style,[20] is relatively unpompous in tone, except perhaps for 'ipsa rebellatrix obstinatia'. There is none of the heaping up of parallel phrases such as we have observed to be a feature of *Vita S. Birini*. Given the exigencies of rhyme and rhythm, the syntax is mostly uncomplicated, presenting few difficulties. It is terseness which occasionally leads to some obscurity, for example, 'Kenelmum abducit in siluam gratia uenandi, quasi oblectandum amore studii paterni' (c. 5), where the gerundive 'oblectandum' must depend upon 'Kenelmum', and a pronoun would have facilitated understanding. The following from the preface is similar: 'Legitur per totam patriam epistola, que uiolenter absconditum in Anglia celitus prodiderit in Roma', where 'absconditum' is made to stand alone as the object of the verb.

Although one or two unusual words are to be found in *Vita et miracula*, the vocabulary is not over-obscure, and selection seems sometimes to have been dictated by the desire for rhyme.[21] There are no neologisms and but one Graecism, the very common

[15] e.g. 'puer expergiscens . . . preuenit . . . prophetica . . . paruulis prestante . . .' (c. 6); 'ad primum peruertendo eum, fraterne felicitati efficeret pernitiosum' and 'hunc uersum ore uoueret uenefico' (c. 16), and the alliterating pairs, 'interpretationis et intelligentie', 'luminaribus et lampadibus' (c. 3); 'attracta et allecta' (c. 9).

[16] e.g. 'Angl*o*rum pign*o*ra' (c. 1); 'se*uo* li*uo*re' (c. 2).

[17] 'ira indignatione felle' (c. 16); 'cecorum surdorum claudorum' (c. 13).

[18] For example 'inhumanitas beluina . . . pecualis diligentia' (c. 8); 'que obfuscabatur in Anglica patria, clarius emicuit in arce mundi Roma' (c. 10); 'reatum suum tacendo prodidit, quem loquendo defenderat' (c. 19).

[19] *Planus*: 22%, *tardus*: 15%, *trispondiacus*: 14%, and *velox*: 13%, including admissible by-forms. On prose rhythm, see p. li above.

[20] Cf. e.g. the preface to *Vita S. Rumwoldi*.

[21] Cf. 'obstinati*a*'—see commentary on p. 53.

'charismata'. More unusual words, parallels for which can nevertheless readily be supplied,[22] are: 'cantilena' (preface); 'etatula' (c. 1); 'pusio' (c. 5); 'lanista' (c. 6); 'rebellatrix' (preface); 'pecualis' (c. 8); 'almifluus' (c. 13)—they are by no means numerous, and there is nothing in any way comparable to the sophistications of the late tenth-century hermeneutic texts.[23] The author had a certain enthusiasm for agentive nouns in '-or', for example, 'censor', 'approbator' (preface); 'procurator' (c. 2); 'proditor', 'imitator' (c. 5); 'percussor' (c. 8); 'fraudator' (c. 19); and 'altor' (c. 23), though none of these is especially unusual. One noticeable characteristic of style is the use of the subordinative conjunction 'quatinus' ('quatenus'), which occurs eight times, most frequently with similar force to 'ut' in a final or causal clause.

As far as can be determined, relatively few non-biblical sources seem to have been used in the composition of *Vita et miracula*, apart from a smattering of poetic phrases, noted in the commentary, and the proverb derived ultimately from Boethius' *Consolation of Philosophy*. The author was reasonably well-versed in earlier hagiography, and made use of his knowledge. For example, he drew upon Gregory of Tours' account of the fight over St Martin's body to describe the competition between the men of Gloucester and the men of Worcester (cc. 14–15). He may also have had some specific model for his description of Kenelm as a cephalophoric saint, perhaps a Life of St Denis of Paris, or St Just.[24] Other narrative motifs are familiar, both from earlier hagiography, and also in roughly contemporary Lives, for example, the soul ascending as a dove, the column of light, the holy wells, as well as some of the posthumous miracles, such as the chained penitent.[25] It is, however, seldom possible to establish a direct borrowing from another text. In the case of the miracles of Kenelm, it is to be wondered how far they reflect the hagiographer's ideas about what ought to be included in a saint's 'repertoire', rather than actual events at Winchcombe, Clent, and elsewhere.

(iii) *The Authorship of* Vita et miracula S. Kenelmi

To judge from the way in which the layout of the monastic buildings at Winchcombe is described (apparently with some accuracy

---

[22] See commentary.   [23] See Lapidge, 'The hermeneutic style'.
[24] On cephalophoric saints, see the commentary to c. 7.
[25] See commentary for parallels.

when compared with present-day archaeological investigation), the author of *Vita et miracula* either was a member of the community, or had visited the site.[26] Very little more can be discovered about his identity—the reference to Queen Eadgyth implies a passing acquaintance with her, or an opportunity to have met her, perhaps during the period of her retirement to Wilton after the death of Edward in 1066. Perhaps it should also be assumed that he was able to read Old English, if 'cantilena et Anglica scripta', in the preface, alluded to a source which the author had used himself.

Another source of information acknowledged in the preface is Wulfwine, monk of Worcester and pupil of Oswald (d. 992). It so happens that a Wulfwine, 'clericus' and later 'presbiter', is to be found among the signatories of several charters pertaining to Worcester preserved in Hemming's cartulary. The name first appears in about 981 and for the last time in 1017.[27] Possibly it is the same Wulfwine who occurs at 6 February in the obit list of a mid-eleventh-century calendar prefixed to the homiliary Oxford, Bodleian Library, Hatton 113 and 114.[28] Since Wulfwine did not appear as a signatory after 1017, he may have died in that year.

At this point, it seems appropriate to evaluate the evidence offered by the version of the preface to *Vita et miracula* found uniquely in the thirteenth-century manuscript, Oxford, Bodleian Library, Bodley 285 [= **B**].[29] We are told that Wulfwine (there given the cognomen Winnoc, not attested elsewhere) left his 'memoranda' to brother Ælfwine, who was still alive at the time of writing.[30] In every other manuscript, it is stated that Wulfwine left his 'memoranda' to 'nobis', that is, presumably, the author. The

---

[26] See commentary on c. 16. He may also, conceivably, have had an informant with detailed knowledge. It should be noted that the author never explicitly refers to himself as an inmate of Winchcombe.

[27] S 1343, 1344, 1349, 1346, 1350, 1351, 1352, 1353, 1354, 1356–8, 1359–63, 1365–6, 1367, 1369, and 1381.

[28] The witness-lists and obit lists have been reproduced by I. Atkins, 'The Church of Worcester from the Eighth to the Twelfth Century, Part II', *The Antiquaries Journal*, xx (1940), 1–38, 203–29, esp. pp. 9–15, and 30; on the obit list see also *The Leofric Collectar*, ed. E. S. Dewick and W. H. Frere, 2 vols., HBS xlv, lvi (1914–21), ii. 601–2.

[29] Described below, §x.

[30] '... quidam Vuigornensis monachus beati Osuualdi Eboracensis archiepiscopi discipulus nomine Vulfuuinus et Winnoc cognomine. Hec suo ordine a maioribus audita, fratri Alfuuino adhuc superstiti fide certissima reliquit memoranda.' As originally punctuated in the MS, with a capital 'h' on 'Hec', this leaves the preceding sentence beginning 'Inter plures' without a verb, which might suggest that what follows is in fact an interpolation, added in rather carelessly.

logical equation would therefore be that the aforesaid Ælfwine =
'nobis' = the author of *Vita et miracula*. It has been suggested that
the reference to Ælfwine was an interpolation made by a later
scribe who wanted to preserve the author's name.[31] Such an
assumption does not take account of the words 'adhuc superstiti',
which require the interpolation to have been made during
Ælfwine's lifetime. The name Ælfwine is not elsewhere attested as
that of the author of any surviving texts, either vernacular or Latin,
but, considering the number of eleventh-century saints' Lives
transmitted anonymously, that, in itself, is not an obstacle. If, however, the intention had indeed been to record the name of the
author, this interpolation would seem a rather diffident manner in
which to do it.[32]

Alternatively, Ælfwine was simply another stage in the process
of handing on Wulfwine's 'memoranda'. In that case, 'adhuc
superstiti' begins to have some force, because the fact that Ælfwine
was still living at about the time *Vita et miracula* was composed
brought the line of transmission right up to date. The point of the
reference to Wulfwine had presumably been to provide well-
established authority and authentication for the content of *Vita et
miracula*. Whoever the author was, he would have been anxious to
ensure that the story should not be seen as merely the fruit of his
own imagination, but as an account gleaned from someone still
alive, though now very old, who had, in his turn, received it from
Wulfwine, who had heard it from his elders, and so on.[33] One
might therefore ask why Ælfwine's name should apparently have
been supplied only by one late witness. **B** preserves several unique
variants which seem to be scribal interventions, the work of a
minor redactor, rather than actual errors in copying.[34] Some, perhaps all, of these may have occurred at quite an early stage in the
transmission of the text. Certainly, this must be true of the information about Ælfwine, an addition intended to modify, on better

---

[31] Suggested by P. A. Hayward, in his unpublished dissertation, 'The Kenelm
Legend in Context: A Study in the Hagiography of Eleventh-Century England' (University of Auckland, MA diss., 1990), pp. 37–8, a typescript of which he has very kindly
lent to me.

[32] Cf. Antropoff, p. 94 n. 1, 'der Autor der Hauptfassung hätte der Nennung seines
eigenen Namens wohl kaum die Worte "adhuc superstiti" hinzugefügt, und daher wird
Alfwinus nur ein Gewährsmann gewesen sein.'

[33] Compare Abbo of Fleury's prefatory account of the way in which he learnt about
Edmund's martyrdom, in his *Passio S. Edmundi*, ed. Winterbottom, *Three Lives*, p. 67.

[34] See p. cxxxii below.

evidence, what had already been said about sources. Some alterations could even, just conceivably, represent an authorial revision
of *Vita et miracula*. It is hard to see why such information should
have been omitted from an archetype by every other surviving
witness.

We cannot be certain of the identity of Ælfwine, nor yet how
accurately the name was transmitted in **B**. One way to interpret the
reference to him would be to take 'frater' in the religious sense, and
suppose that he was just old enough to have had some contact with
Wulfwine (perhaps before 1017), but was still alive as late as the
1070s. The verb 'reliquit', however, need not imply direct personal
contact. Inspection of the same range of documents in which the
aforementioned Wulfwine occurs, produces no Ælfwine at Worcester before the last quarter of the eleventh century.[35]

Of course, Ælfwine need not have been a member of the
Worcester community. Comparable documentation is not available with which to construct a list of the inmates of Winchcombe
during the eleventh century. An identification which has been put
forward, is Ælfwine, abbot of Ramsey between 1043 and 1079 or
1080, and formerly prior.[36] Certainly, if 1066–75 is the correct date-
range for the composition of *Vita et miracula*, and the additional
clause in **B** was only put in shortly afterwards, then Abbot Ælfwine
could indeed still have been 'superstes', although only barely of an
age to have had personal contact with Wulfwine. If he had been
born at around the year 1000, he could conceivably have known
Wulfwine as a novice. Furthermore, Abbot Ælfwine of Ramsey
would have been well placed to be in touch with Queen Eadgyth,
having been sent by King Edward as a royal ambassador to the
Council of Rheims in 1049,[37] to Rome in 1062–5,[38] and possibly
also to Saxony (1054?).[39] After such exertions, Ælfwine's health
failed and he was obliged to relinquish his responsibilities,
remaining abbot only in name.[40] Elsewhere, it has been suggested
that this Ælfwine was actually the author of *Vita et miracula*, bearing in mind the close link between Kenelm and Ramsey, which will
be discussed below.[41] Yet it would perhaps be rather surprising not
to find him referred to as 'abbas', even if he had already, in practi-

---

[35] Atkins, 'The Church of Worcester', pp. 9–29.   [36] See *Heads*, pp. 61–2.
[37] Macray, *Chron. Rames.*, p. 170.   [38] Ibid. pp. 176–7.
[39] Cf. Barlow, *English Church*, pp. 87 and 118.   [40] Macray, *Chron. Rames.*, p. 177.
[41] Hayward, 'Kenelm legend in context', pp. 37–8.

cal terms, relinquished the position. In sum, it seems, at present, impossible identify Ælfwine adequately, but it is fairly safe to say that he was not the author we are seeking.

The composition of *Vita et miracula* has previously been ascribed to the ubiquitous Flemish hagiographer Goscelin,[42] and the evidence for this must now be considered. Like the author of *Vita et miracula*, Goscelin may have had some acquaintance with Queen Eadgyth, both as a member of Herman's household, and also as the nuns' chaplain at Wilton, to which community the queen retired after Edward's death. He was still based in the West Country during the period from 1066 to 1075, during which *Vita et miracula* seems to have been composed.[43] It is easy enough to imagine that Goscelin could have travelled up to Winchcombe, and thus have gained some familiarity with the layout of the monastery, as well as having an opportunity to consult such documents as may have been available there. The circumstances which would have led to Goscelin undertaking such a commission can only remain a matter for conjecture.[44] It is just conceivable, for example, that the link (admittedly tenuous) between Goscelin and Kenelm lies in the person of Ealdred, sometime bishop of Worcester.[45] For a brief period, between about 1053 and 1058, this man (formerly a monk at Winchester) successively combined his position at Worcester with the oversight of Winchcombe abbey (between the death of Abbot Godwine and the election of Godric), and then of the see of Ramsbury (during the period of Herman's absence at the monastery of Saint-Bertin, *c.* 1055–8). He must already have been acquainted with Herman, Goscelin's patron, since they both represented the king at the Easter synod at Rome in 1050. Although by the time of the composition of *Vita et miracula* Ealdred had relinquished the bishopric of Worcester, he may have passed on an interest in the cult of Kenelm to Herman, who instigated Goscelin's work on the Lives of Wulfsige and Edith.[46]

[42] E.g. in the list of Goscelin's works proposed by Talbot, '*Liber Confortatorius*', p. 13. Cf. Hardy, *Catalogue*, i. 508, referring to the *Vita brevior*.

[43] Cf. Barlow, *The Life of King Edward*, pp. xlvi, 137–9.

[44] It is at least worth noting that, in his *Liber Confortatorius*, lib. iv, Goscelin, in describing the flocks which Christ will gather up at the end of time, enumerates the kings and rulers who will be there, starting with David, and including 'sancti quoque reges Britannie Osuualdus, Edmundus, Kenelmus, Ethelbertus, Edgarus, Eduuardus' (Talbot, p. 113).

[45] See Barlow, *English Church*, pp. 86–90 for an account of Ealdred's career.

[46] Cf. the record of Ealdred's veneration of Swithun, noted in Lapidge, 'CCCC 163',

Von Antropoff rejected out of hand the possibility of ascription to Goscelin, principally on the grounds that he would have named himself in the prologue.[47] Although it is true that Goscelin often included his own name in his dedicatory prefaces,[48] he was by no means consistent in doing so.[49] The most compelling evidence is, however, that of narrative style and vocabulary. A close reading of Goscelin's well-authenticated works reveals a good many word-combinations which are strikingly reminiscent of, though seldom identical with, phrases in *Vita et miracula*. For example, *Vita et miracula* c. 22, 'Nec mora, reuersus ad se reseratis oculis profluente sanguine hausit diem, mirabatur ignotas rerum species, mundi amplitudinem, lucis nitorem', is undeniably similar to Goscelin, *Historia maior de miraculis S. Augustini* c. 49, 'noua luce infusa haurit lumen ubique diffusum. Miratur lucis candorem, mundi decorem, tam diuersas rerum formas et species', 'reseratis oculis ceco lux infunditur';[50] likewise, compare *Vita et miracula* c. 25, 'Debilem quoque repentem per humum quis digne referet erectum? O erumnam et necessitatem humanam!' with Goscelin, *Historia translationis S. Augustini* i. 3, 'O miserandam cladis humanae condi-tionem! Non poterat hec ... suas erumnas proloqui';[51] *Vita et miracula* (preface), 'Porro in huius fine textus tam recentia et late nota referemus signa, ut ea calumniari non possit ipsa rebellatrix obstinatia', with Goscelin, *Vita S. Wlsini* c. 12, 'Quem ... ne ab hiis qui obstinatiores sunt ad credendum temeritatis forte calumpniar-etur adhuc frequentioribus uirtutum choruscationibus diuina manus ... declarat';[52] and *Vita et miracula* c. 26, 'cui exesum et liuentem uterum molli cera abbatis refouit benignitas, donec

---

p. 22. Note also the presence of Kenelm in the calendar in CCCC 422 (Wormald, *English Kalendars*, no. 14), often thought to be from Sherborne (*c.*1061); the entry reads 'Sancti Kenelmi MARTIRIS', which could be a sign that the feast was regarded as of some importance.

[47] Cf. Antropoff, 'Kenelm Legende', p. 94 n. 1, 'Es gibt aber nicht den geringsten Anhaltspunkt für die Annahme, daß Goscelin entweder die Hauptfassung geschrieben hat (Goscelin hätte sich sicher im Prolog genannt) oder daß die gemeinsame Quelle der Fassung C und der Hauptfassung von ihm verfaßt wurde'.

[48] E.g. *Vita S. Ethelburge* (Colker, 'Texts', p. 398); *Vita S. Yuonis* (*PL* clv. 81); *Historia translationis S. Augustini* (*ActaS* Maii, vi. 408A).

[49] Cf. *Vita S. Wlsini* (Talbot, 'St Wulsin', p. 73); *Vita S. Mildrethe* (Rollason, *Mildrith Legend*, p. 108).

[50] *ActaS*, Maii, vi. 405D.   [51] *ActaS*, Maii, vi. 414B.

[52] Talbot, 'St Wulsin', p. 80. These and several other examples are noted in the commentary to the text below.

rediret sanitas. Excusso etiam ferro ab alterius brachio medietas circuli supra chorum fratrum euolauit, reliqua uero medietas inueniri non potuit', with Goscelin, *Miracula S. Yuonis*, 'gratias abbati et fratribus refuderit, maxime quod egrotantem tanta benignitate refouerint',[53] and *Miracula S. Edithe* c. 18, 'alterius ferrum de exeso brachio penitentis excussum super ipsius sancte liberatricis euolauit scrinium'.[54]

Some of these correspondences could, of course, be dismissed as coincidental, and arising from the treatment of the stock narrative features of hagiography. A control on this kind of comparison might be to look at the way standard miracles are described not only in *Vita et miracula* and by Goscelin, but also by other hagiographers. Thus, for instance, we might consider the healing of a cripple in *Vita et miracula* c. 25:

Debilem quoque repentem per humum quis digne referet erectum? O erumnam et necessitatem humanam! Ligneas soleas cauatis truncis alligauerat genibus pro coturnis pedalibus, et calciatis ligno poplitibus, nitebatur pro gressibus. Scabellula pro bacillis suppeditabant manibus et egre sustentabant labile corpus. Videres hominem ad celestia contemplanda sublimatum, peccati conditione in reptile conuersum.

With this, compare sections of Goscelin, *Historia maior de miraculis S. Augustini* cc. 3–6:[55]

Quid uirum dixi, qui manibus nitens pro pedibus similior erat reptili quam homini? . . . iter legebat manuum scabellulis aut manibus scabellatis, mutato scilicet usu, in morem natantis uel reptantis, manus et lacerti gressus captabant, poplites fallentibus uestigiis suppeditabant . . . curuatum uidebatur reptile cum prodiret. Ecce Adam Dei imago, cum per ambitionem non per gratiam appetit similis esse Deo, comparatus est non modo iumentis et quadrupedibus, uerumetiam lutosis reptilibus.

Also very similar is *Miracula S. Yuonis*, 'Quidam de proximo uico curuus et distortus erat ut quadrupes duobus scabellulis praenitendo incederet';[56] and parts of *Historia maior de miraculis S. Augustini* cc. 52–5, 'alterum a pedibus contortum et contractum ire manibus pro gressibus debilitas compulerat'; 'qua te trahebas per humum tamquam languidum reptile?'; 'manualibus scabellulis

[53] Macray, *Chron. Rames.*, pp. lxvii–lxviii.
[54] Wilmart, 'La Légende', p. 293.
[55] *ActaS*, Maii, vi. 394–5.
[56] Macray, *Chron. Rames.*, p. lxv.

innitens, attracto corpore humi serpens';[57] and *Vita S. Wlfhilde* c.
11, 'quae ulnis et genibus ut humanum reptile aduenisset'.[58] One
might then compare the following: Osbern, *Miracula S. Dunstani* c.
9, 'Aut quo modo factum in te miraculum, Elwarde, narrabo?
hominem giganteae magnitudinis si repentem te in terra tota mole
corporis per triginta annos pondus non premeret grauissimae
infirmitatis', and c. 13, 'Epheborum aliquis prope ciuitatem mane-
bat, ita a puero debilitatus, ut a lumbis ac deorsum per totum
emortuus duobus inniteretur bacillis, totius corporis post se
trahentem medietatem';[59] Herman, *Liber de Miraculis S. Edmundi* c.
18, 'Talibus interest quaedam infirma, sic cingulo tenus inferius
debilitata, sic pedibus ac cruribus frustrata ut scabellulis in manibus clunibusque uteretur pro pedibus';[60] Eadmer, *Vita S. Bregwini*
c. 8: 'quidam ambulandi officio carens, ambabus manibus singulis
scabellis innitens, genibus pro pedibus utens, crura ac pedes
intortos post tergum trahens',[61] and *Miracula S. Dunstani* c. 13,
'quidam sibi ipsi a renibus et deorsum pene inutilis duobus baculis
pro pedibus utebatur';[62] and Lantfred, *Translatio et Miracula* c. 30,
'Venit denique ... quidam debilis, claudus utroque pede et sic
curuatus egritudine, ut penitus non posset sese de loco remouere,
nisi binis sustentaretur scabellis'. Although there are necessarily
some items of vocabulary common to all these descriptions, on the
whole, the account in *Vita et miracula* and those by Goscelin seem
to be the most alike, for example in stating so explicitly the reptile
nature of the cripple. A similar exercise could be undertaken for
the story of the chained penitent which occurs in several places, or
with miracles concerning candles.[63]

It has to be conceded that generally, the prose style of *Vita et
miracula* is somewhat terser, less ornate than most of Goscelin's
known work. Yet, like many another author, Goscelin must have
been capable of modulating his voice, as it were, and of using
different stylistic registers according either to that which was
required of him, or to that which he felt to be appropriate. Within
his securely attributed canon, it is possible to observe Goscelin

[57] *ActaS*, Maii, vi. 406 A–E.
[58] Colker, 'Texts', p. 431.
[59] Stubbs, *Memorials*, pp. 135 and 139–40.
[60] Arnold, *Memorials*, p. 49.
[61] Scholz, 'Eadmer's Life of Bregwine', p. 143.
[62] Stubbs, *Memorials*, p. 231. Cf. also c. 8 (p. 227).
[63] See commentary on *Vita et miracula* cc. 26 and 29.

doing this; *Vita S. Wlsini* is by no means as pompous as the texts relating to St Augustine, *Vita S. Yuonis* crisper than *Vita S. Edithe*; the range of materials composed for Barking show some variation in style and degree of amplification. One might also think in terms of a gradual evolution in Goscelin's prose style over the years of his sojourn in England. To conclude, if *Vita et miracula S. Kenelmi* were to have been written by Goscelin, and if the proposed dating of the text is correct, then it would be one of the earliest known works of that prolific hagiographer. Obviously, the evidence available at present falls just short of absolute proof and is open to debate, but the case for admitting this text into the canon of his works does seem quite strong.

(iv) *The Relationship of* Vita brevior *to* Vita et miracula

The present discussion of *Vita et miracula* cannot proceed without some consideration of *Vita brevior*, since the two are almost certainly related. Precise dating of the latter is difficult. The single surviving copy was written in a script datable to around the third quarter of the eleventh century,[64] but there is nothing within the text from which to establish a *terminus post quem*.[65] An analysis of Latinity may be the only means (and not the safest). For example, the style of *Vita brevior* is not discernibly 'hermeneutic', as there are no notable Graecisms, neologisms or archaisms. The same fondness for agentive nouns in '-or' as was noted in the case of *Vita et miracula* may be observed: 'nutritor', 'interemptor', 'exsequutor', 'seductor' and 'procurator' (all attested elsewhere). Rhyme was also used to some extent. The fact that the Latinity of *Vita brevior* is not vastly different from that of *Vita et miracula* may suggest that it is not much older.

Vita brevior, as preserved, was evidently intended for use in the liturgy, having been divided into eight lections, for a feast of twelve lections, of which the last four would be taken either from the Bible, or from some homiletic or exegetical text. The fact that there are only eight and not twelve 'proper' lections implies that the feast was not of the very highest rank.[66] The lections

---

[64] See p. cxxi below for a description.

[65] Antropoff, 'Kenelm-Legende', inclined towards a date during the first half of the 11th cent., but for no especially convincing reasons (pp. 50 and 59–60).

[66] On lections, see Gneuss, 'Liturgical books', p. 120, and Tolhurst, *Monastic Breviary*, vi. 7–14. St Kenelm's day was marked as a feast of twelve lections in the

commemorate Kenelm specifically in the context of his martyrdom at Clent, because, although the place is not referred to by name, attention is drawn to the chapel and the holy well there: 'Vbi ergo martyr occubuit . . . ibi nunc est oratorium et uirtutum Dei locus, ibi fons sacer emanauit . . .' (c. 8). Furthermore, the translation is not mentioned, indeed Winchcombe is only referred to indirectly, 'Ibi etiam, sicut et ubi nunc in Christo requiescit exuberante gratia Dei liberantur uarii infirmi . . .' (c. 8). Clent's claim to be the source of just as many miracles as Winchcombe is noted.

If these lections were intended for use at Worcester, then they may reflect the particular interest of St Mary's in the chapel and well at Clent, which might have come about partly through the brief period of ownership which St Mary's apparently exercised over Clent.[67] The community at Worcester would in any case have been quite likely to commemorate a saint the supposed site of whose martyrdom lay near by. Furthermore, it should be noted that, albeit briefly, in the hiatus between the death of Abbot Godwine in 1053, and the appointment of Godric the following year, Winchcombe was apparently in the hands of Ealdred, bishop of Worcester (c. 1044–62).[68] There does seem, in the eleventh century at least, to have been some interest at Worcester in the hagiography of local saints, since the single surviving copy of Byrhtferth's *Vita S. Ecgwini*, composed for Evesham, is preserved as an addition to the Cotton-Corpus legendary in London, BL, Cotton Nero E. I.[69]

Whether or not *Vita brevior* had been written at Worcester for use there, it appears also to have been known at Winchcombe, because portions occur as the antiphons and responsories for the Office on the feast of Kenelm in the Winchcombe breviary, Valenciennes 116.[70] Antropoff concluded from this that *Vita brevior* had actually been composed for use at Winchcombe, but was superseded by *Vita et miracula*.[71] Another view might be that some form of *Vita brevior* was acquired from Worcester for use at Winch-

---

Worcester calendar in CCCC 391, dated to between 1064 and 1069, ed. Wormald, *English Kalendars*, no. 17. On the dating, see P. R. Robinson, *Dated and Datable Manuscripts, c.737–1600, in Cambridge Libraries*, 2 vols. (Woodbridge, 1988), i, no. 157.

[67] See commentary on c. 7 below. [68] Cf. *Heads*, p. 79.

[69] See pp. xxi–xxii above.

[70] Fos. 208ʳ–211ʳ; see Appendix E below.

[71] 'Kenelm-Legende', p. 122, where this is suggested as a reason for the lack of surviving witnesses to *Vita brevior*.

combe, prior to the composition of a more appropriate and up-to-date text. Whatever the case may be, the surviving copy of *Vita brevior* may also have fallen out of use in the liturgy at Worcester by the early twelfth century when a portion of *Vita et miracula* was squeezed into the spaces below and to the side of the folio containing the concluding lection.[72]

As it survives, *Vita brevior* corresponds roughly to cc. 1–5, 7–8 of *Vita et miracula*. Each tells broadly the same story, although certain differences, both of detail and of emphasis, require examination. There are, nevertheless, too many close verbal similarities between these texts for them to be utterly independent accounts, as the following parallel passages demonstrate.[73]

Vita brevior	*Vita et miracula*
(c. 2) forma, perfusus diuina dilectione et gratia, Deo et hominibus amabilis erat aetatula.	(c. 1) speciosus forma et illustrante superna gratia amabilis Deo et hominibus florebat etatula.
(c. 5) Omni ergo intentione insidiabatur eius sanguini sicut Herodias Iohanni, uel sicut Iezabel Helie, et sicut Cain extincto Abel regnum querebat fraterno sanguine	(c. 2) insidiabatur illi ut Herodias Iohanni ut Helie Iezabel ut Cain Abel
(c. 6) quia non est perniciosior pestis ad nocendum quam familiaris inimicus	(c. 2) quia non est pernitiosior pestis quam familiaris inimicus
(c. 8) in siluam quasi ad uenandi oblectationem	(c. 5) in siluam gratia uenandi, quasi oblectandum amore studii paterni
(c. 8) Cum ita duceretur ad uictimam agniculus Christi	(c. 5) ut agnus ductus ad uictimam
(c. 8) Sed qui solo teste celo est iugulatus, celo teste per columpnam lucis ex diuina bonitate postmodum est reuelatus.	(c. 8) Denique qui celo teste erat martyrizatus, celo teste est declaratus, quatinus fulgida lucis columna ab ethereis arcibus sepe uideretur super eum effusa.

---

[72] See description on p. cxxi below.

[73] Several short phrases are to be found in both texts and have not been listed here, but are signalled in the commentary below, and in the text of *Vita brevior*. The two versions of Kenelm's dream are also virtually identical (*Vita brevior*, c. 7 and *Vita et miracula*, cc. 3–4).

Vita brevior	Vita et miracula
(c. 8) Abscisum est igitur caput Kenelmi natalis et innocentiae candore lacteum, unde lactea columba aureis pennis euolauit in celum dum ipse propriis palmulis extensis reciperet caput abscisum, ut appareret preciosa in conspectu Domini mors sancti sui.	(c. 7) caput Kenelmi lacteum septennis, ut dictum est, paruuli absciditur, quod ipse protinus extensis palmulis excepisse memoratur, . . . ut in conspectu Domini pretiosa mors sancti sui commendetur. Hinc et lactea columba aureis pennis transuolasse ethera merito creditur . . .
(c. 8) ibi fons sacer emanauit, qui adhuc fideli populo et potum et salutem inpendit.	(c. 13) In assumptione autem almiflue glebe . . . fons sacer emersit qui hactenus in riuum effluit et multis . . . salutem impendit.

A task of greater complexity is to determine the precise nature of the textual relationship. The fragmentary survival of *Vita brevior* precludes a confident conclusion, and various discrepancies need to be taken into account. For example, in *Vita brevior*, Æscberht is said to have ordered a swineherd to murder Kenelm.[74] Such ignominy increases the pathos of the saint's death.[75] In *Vita et miracula* the murder is described at greater length and Æscberht emerges more strongly as an evil character (compare cc. 5–7 with c. 8 of *Vita brevior*), an impression reinforced by his portrayal as the dealer of the death-blow. The drawing-out of the event heightens the drama and tension of the account in *Vita et miracula*,[76] but may also have been in order to accommodate a reference to Kenelm's miraculous ash-tree.[77]

A less significant difference is that in *Vita brevior*, more time seems to elapse between the death of Coenwulf and the murder of Kenelm; events move on more swiftly in *Vita et miracula*. Furthermore, Cwoenthryth is depicted, in the former, as already being in control, before the murder of Kenelm: 'quia septennis fere adhuc puericia nondum preualebat, Quendrytha soror maior natu serpentina astutia regia iura preripiebat.' The difference of emphasis between the two texts is a symptom

---

[74] Compare c. 8 with *Vita et miracula* c. 7.
[75] Compare in *ASC* s.a. 755, the murder, in revenge, of Sigebryht: 'hiene an swan ofstang æt Pryfetes flodan'.
[76] The author employed suspense as a narrative effect elsewhere; cf. cc. 25–6.
[77] In c. 6.

partly of the discrete purposes for which they may have been composed, relating to the same cult but at two different sites, and
partly, perhaps, of the kind of context in which they were intended
to be read. As already noted, *Vita brevior* betrays a concern to highlight the cult at Clent, despite the fact that Kenelm's body lay elsewhere. The author of *Vita et miracula*, on the other hand, seemed
anxious to justify the translation and to emphasize the saint's
protecting and curative power at Winchcombe. There is no hint of
competition, since *Vita et miracula*, although including an account
of how the men of Worcester were supposedly worsted by the men
of Gloucester, does mention healings at the well at Clent, and later
miracles on a trip back there with the relics; and *Vita brevior* refers,
albeit indirectly, to the miracles wrought at Winchcombe.

Vita brevior, as preserved, was conceived with the liturgy more
specifically in mind than *Vita et miracula*.[78] Hence, where the
former is generally homiletic in tone and replete with pious
sentiment (non-narrative 'padding'),[79] the latter includes circum-
stantial details, which occasion the only deviations from the narrative (an almost anecdotal style).[80] Thus *Vita brevior* devotes
considerable attention to the 'theological' reasons for Kenelm's
martyrdom, contrasting God's intentions for the boy with those of
his earthly father, Coenwulf, with frequent recourse to biblical
citation (c. 2). A case is thereby presented for the boy's sanctity: he
is very definitely not a saint simply because he was murdered;
rather, he was murdered, because his saintly innocence had to be
preserved. There is no hint of this in *Vita et miracula*, where the
principal preoccupation seems to have been the translation to
Winchcombe, and the fact of Kenelm's sanctity was, so to speak,
taken as read. *Vita brevior* also lingers longer over Cwoenthryth's
twisted machinations, painting a more vivid portrait of her wicked-
ness than the sketchy view offered in *Vita et miracula*.[81]

The textual relationship between these two redactions could be

[78] It should, however, be recalled that the earliest surviving MS of *Vita et miracula*,
Oxford, Bodleian Library, Douce 368, had, at some point after the text was copied, been
marked out into eight lections, presumably for liturgical use—see description § x—and
that portions of the text were also used as lections in the breviary, Valenciennes 116.

[79] See esp. cc. 2, 3, and 4.

[80] cc. 3, 6, 7. Cf. Antropoff, 'Kenelm-Legende', pp. 120–2. See e.g. De Gaiffier,
'L'Hagiographie et son public', pp. 475–6, 481–8, on the various uses made of *Vitae*.
And also J. M. H. Smith, 'Oral and written: saints, miracles and relics in Brittany, c. 850–
1250', *Speculum*, lxv (1990), 309–43, at p. 319.

[81] Compare cc. 5 and 6 with c. 2 of *Vita et miracula*.

construed in several ways. In view of the difficulty of adjudicating between the alternatives, each requires to be considered carefully. Rurik von Antropoff, in his unpublished study of both texts, opted for a common source as the best explanation.[82] He felt that the lections must be older,[83] but noted that, where there are close parallels between the two texts, *Vita brevior* frequently has a slightly longer form of words—as can be seen from some of the examples given above, notably the second and third, and the dream section. He concluded that the author of *Vita brevior* often added to the common source, whereas the author of *Vita et miracula* was largely conservative in approach. His argument hinged particularly upon the form of the proverb, 'quia non est perniciosior . . .', deriving ultimately from Boethius (c. 2), where *Vita brevior* (c. 6) has two extra words. Antropoff attempted to demonstrate, by reference to a late English version of the proverb, that the author of *Vita et miracula* preserved the usual form, as he found it in the conjectured common source, and that, had he been copying from *Vita brevior*, he would have included *ad nocendum*.[84] Antropoff failed to identify the ultimate origin of the proverb, and hence was unaware that *Vita brevior* actually follows Boethius by including *ad nocendum*.[85] This weakens his particular argument. To posit a common source is, in some ways, the safest approach to the present problem, although it does leave one with unanswerable questions about the nature and date of that now-lost text.

A second, more economical, hypothesis is that the author of *Vita et miracula* drew directly upon *Vita brevior*, expanding some parts and suppressing much.[86] Hence, *Vita brevior* could be one of the 'plures testes etiam ueteranos fideles ab antiquioribus deductos', perhaps even the 'memoranda' of Wulfwine. Such a neat conclusion would provide an early date (possibly before 1017) for the *Vita brevior*, which could then be counted among the saints' Lives written at the time of the Benedictine reform. Just such neatness should, however, also be viewed with extreme caution.

[82] 'Kenelm-Legende', pp. 50–9 and 120–2. He named the two versions 'Fassung C' (*Vita brevior*) and 'Die Hauptfassung'.

[83] Ibid. 50, 59–60. His conclusion was grounded partly on the impression that the *Vita brevior* lections are incomplete at the end as well as at the beginning, which seems unlikely, considering the physical constitution of the MS (see below). His further assumption was that a longer text (meaning *Vita brevior*) is bound to be older.

[84] Ibid. 54–6. [85] See commentary on c. 2.

[86] This is the view put forward by Hayward, 'Kenelm Legend in Context', pp. 19–20. Accordingly, he names the two recensions *Vita prima* and *Vita secunda*.

Inspection of the narrative construction of *Vita et miracula* can support the theory that the author used a form of *Vita brevior*. For example, the section 'Tali modo ... consiliati' (c. 2) seems to follow somewhat abruptly upon the brief account of Cwoenthryth's overtures to Æscberht, whereas it fits in well after the direct speech in *Vita brevior* (c. 6). One might conclude that the author of the former, choosing to omit the speech, wrote a précis of its content, and, by 'cut and paste', copied the summarizing biblical pastiche 'Tali modo . . .' almost verbatim. The same could be said of 'Quem cum ueneno . . .' which seems rather a *non-sequitur*, but may have been an attempted summary of 'Omnia temptauit . . . absumeret' (*Vita brevior*, c. 5). Kenelm's dream, and some of the parallel passages listed above, in which *Vita brevior* has a slightly longer form of words, point to the same conclusion, for abbreviation is generally a more straightforward task than expansion.[87]

It is perhaps surprising that the author of *Vita et miracula*, confronted with *Vita brevior* as a source, should have chosen to omit so much of the early part of that text, concerning divine intentions for Kenelm, and the events leading up to the murder. An argument based on the simple desire to abbreviate is problematic considering the length of the murder-scene when compared with that in *Vita brevior*.[88] One might also ask why the swineherd should have been dispensed with in *Vita et miracula*, except to serve artistic ends, as noted above.

The further question of whether *Vita brevior* could actually be Wulfwine's 'memoranda' must also be addressed, as of some importance for the dating of that text. It is not clear exactly what is meant by 'memoranda',[89] whether a Life of Kenelm, or simply brief notes of what was known about the saint. As already suggested above, Wulfwine was mentioned for a specific reason.[90] Just conceivably, 'memoranda' did not refer to a written text at all. The preface goes on to mention documents: 'Sed et cantilena et Anglica scripta plura memorant inde probabilia . . .', and the intention could have been to draw a distinction between 'memoranda',

---

[87] Cf. the discussion of the relationship between Ælfric's *Vita S. Æthelwoldi* and that of Wulfstan, in Lapidge and Winterbottom, *Wulfstan*, pp. cxlvi–clv.

[88] Cf. Antropoff, 'Kenelm-Legende', p. 57: 'Die Möglichkeit, daß die Hauptfassung den ersten Teil der Fassung C zusammengefaßt hätte, scheidet deshalb aus, weil diese Kürzung dem Anliegen ihres Autors zuwider laufen würde.'

[89] Literally, 'things worthy to be called to mind', or 'worthy to be mentioned'.

[90] § iii.

meaning anecdotes passed on orally by an old monk, and written documents.[91] The verb 'reliquit' does, however, imply something concrete. Yet if Wulfwine had indeed written a Life of Kenelm, it seems slightly odd that such a work should be referred to so obliquely. Despite the admittedly allusive tone of the preface, one might still have expected the author of *Vita et miracula* to state explicitly that he was rewriting an older Life of Kenelm, whether by Wulfwine or not.[92]

Yet another construction of events is that the compiler of *Vita brevior* used *Vita et miracula* as a source, omitting that which did not serve his purpose, and expanding, with passages of pious sentiment, to compensate. There is, after all, no evidence to date *Vita brevior* any earlier than the period suggested for *Vita et miracula* (1066–75). If, for the sake of argument, one supposed that a version of the Life of Kenelm was required for liturgical use at Worcester, *Vita et miracula* might have seemed inappropriate in its content and length, and was accordingly adapted, removing that which was perceived to be irrelevant, and filling out the remainder with rhetorical flourishes of piety. Some features of *Vita brevior* point towards this hypothesis; for example, the brief list of posthumous miracles at the end (c. 8). This includes a reference to those bound with iron, as described in *Vita et miracula* (c. 26): 'Ibi etiam sicut et ubi nunc requiescit . . . liberantur uarii infirmi, soluuntur ferro aut debilitate uinculati', which might lead one to conclude that the compiler of the lections was summarizing the content of Kenelm's *Miracula*.[93] There are, nevertheless, two places where the textual evidence could be argued to militate against the dependence of *Vita brevior*. The biblical quotation 'preciosa in conspectu Domini' was reproduced more accurately in *Vita brevior* (c. 8) than in *Vita et*

[91] Cf. e.g. Goscelin's care in distinguishing between types of source material; in *Vita S. Edithe*, he outlined the nature of his oral sources, and their reliability: 'cetereque presentes matres, tam fideles quam generose, inter reliqua que ipse oculis conspexere, affirmant confidenter cum aliis idoneis testibus ea que ab his uenerabilibus matribus audiere . . .', but also mentioned certain written documents (Wilmart, 'La Légende', pp. 37 and 39). Compare the prefatory remarks in his *Vita S. Yuonis*, 'Ab inuentione uero eius reuelationes et prodigia, quae hic praecessor [Wythman] scribit, tam oculis uisa quam fidelium testimonio comprobata, adhuc pene omnium fratrum Ramesiensium . . . cordibus, memorabilius quam in libro sunt scripta et scriptis luculentius memorant aliqua praetermissa' (*PL* clv. 81).

[92] One might compare the way in which Goscelin referred explicitly to Wythman's lost work on Ivo, in the preface to *Vita S. Yuonis* (*PL*, clv. 81).

[93] Compare the way in which they were summarized at the end of Tynemouth's redaction of *Vita et miracula*, noted below, § xii.

miracula (c. 7), where it was rearranged to achieve a rhyme at the end of the clause. Moreover, as we have already noted, *Vita brevior* gives a more correct rendering of the proverb from Boethius. The fact that both of these are quotations could indicate a way out of this difficulty, since it is not beyond the bounds of imagination to suppose that the redactor could have recognized the sources and amended from memory. The difference of detail concerning the man who dealt Kenelm his death-blow is perhaps less readily explained away.

Finally, I should like to put forward one last hypothesis concerning the relationship of these two texts, one which has not previously been considered, namely that they were actually the work of a single author (and hence that *Vita brevior* may also have been written by Goscelin). We have already noted how little the two texts differ in Latinity, and how they offer closely similar turns of phrase. In some ways *Vita brevior* displays features which can be paralleled in Goscelin's well-attested Lives, such as the apostrophe to Coenwulf in the third lection, and the 'purple' passage of address to the martyr in the terms of the Song of Songs, in the fourth.[94] Included among the materials Goscelin composed for Barking in the late 1080s, are two versions of a *Translatio SS. Ethelburge, Hildelithe ac Wlfhilde*, both of them sets of twelve lections, but one a good deal shorter than the other.[95] He seems to have written both versions—they contain many of the same phrases and follow the same narrative pattern. While these Barking texts cannot be detected offering discrepant information which could be compared with the detail about the swineherd, they do present a parallel to what may have been going on with *Vita et miracula* and *Vita brevior*. The former could have been composed for use at Winchcombe, and at the same time adapted for use at Worcester;[96] the presence in the Valenciennes breviary responsories of some of the same material as occurs in *Vita brevior*,[97] might even suggest that they were composed also at that juncture. This can only remain an unsupported conjecture (not least because *Vita brevior* is

---

[94] Cf. the prologue to *Vita S. Edithe* (Wilmart, 'La Légende', p. 35).

[95] Colker, 'Texts', pp. 435–52.

[96] It is not inconceivable that *Vita brevior* was actually composed for use at Winchcombe, and was passed on to Worcester, though it would perhaps be surprising in that case to find only eight lections, rather than the twelve which full veneration of the patron saint would surely require.

[97] See pp. cii and cxxx.

only partially preserved), and may seem too neat a solution to our problem.

(v) *The Origins of the Cult of St Kenelm*

The versions of the Life of Kenelm must be considered in the context of the development of the cult, before any attempt is made to draw a conclusion about their relationship. The implications of the second proposition are important. If *Vita brevior* was composed for use at Worcester and subsequently employed by the author of *Vita et miracula*, it is to be wondered what version of the Life of Kenelm had existed at Winchcombe before, either for use in the liturgy, or for reading at other times. *Vita brevior*, as preserved, seems scarcely appropriate for the purpose, and yet was evidently known at Winchcombe in some form, at least by the time the Valenciennes breviary was compiled, during the early twelfth century. The author of *Vita et miracula* alluded very vaguely to pre-existing, possibly vernacular sources, but it is doubtful whether an Old English Life of Kenelm could confidently be extrapolated from his comments. The fact that *Vita et miracula* was apparently composed during the regime of Winchcombe's first Norman abbot must probably be regarded as significant. Perhaps the inappropriateness of *Vita brevior*, or something similar to it, occasioned the commissioning of a new Life and a set of up-to-date miracles, as part of the sweeping of the new broom. Alternatively, until the mid-eleventh century, the cult of Kenelm at Winchcombe had been maintained without the necessity being felt for any detailed Latin Life of the saint at all.[98] When the matter of composing such a thing was looked into, Worcester may have seemed an appropriate direction to turn for information (because of the Clent connection), and upon enquiry, *Vita brevior* was forthcoming, as a model for the new text. A Worcester source of some kind, in the person of Wulfwine, is certainly acknowledged in the preface of *Vita et miracula*.

Stories of murky events at the time of Coenwulf's death were, conceivably, still being told at Winchcombe in the eleventh century, and fabulous tales, preserved only by oral tradition, may have grown up in connection not only with the tomb of a fairly young member of his family, but also with various topographical

---

[98] Cf. Smith, 'Oral and Written', p. 343.

features (springs and an ash-tree). The retrospective formulation in writing of the details of the legend of Kenelm would account for the considerable confusion in *Vita et miracula* regarding facts such as the age of Kenelm, the status of Cwoenthryth, and the name of the pope who would have been at Rome at the time of Coenwulf's death. It is also important to bear in mind that, for the period of hiatus between the dispersion of the monastic community in 975 (see below), and the abbacy of Godwine (1043 onwards), little is known of what went on at Winchcombe, or of how a cult of Kenelm might have been maintained.

The community at Winchcombe was revived by Oswald of Worcester in about 969,[99] and it is demonstrable that the cult of Kenelm only took on a coherent form at that time. As will be seen from the survey in the next section, there is little available evidence for any formal, liturgical, veneration of Kenelm before the middle of the tenth century. One phrase in the preface of *Vita et miracula* goes some way to support the conjecture: 'sancti patres Dunstanus et Adeluuoldus ipseque sacer Osuualdus ceterique sancti patres nunquam celebrassent nec coli consensissent, nisi dignum cognouissent.' In other words, the cult of Kenelm had the sanction of the principal churchmen involved in the Benedictine reform. There is a strong likelihood that a key figure in the formulation and development of Kenelm's sanctity was Germanus, the first abbot of the reformed community at Winchcombe, introduced from Ramsey by Oswald.[100] Coming originally from Winchester, and having also spent some time at Fleury, Germanus may have had particular ideas about saints and their cult, and perhaps felt that Winchcombe required a heavenly patron with a formalized relic cult. There may have been some attempt, at that time, to put together a hagiographical dossier for Kenelm, as was beginning to be done for other saints, for example, at Winchester.[101]

It was not long, however, before the Winchcombe community was uprooted by the anti-monastic reaction which followed the

[99] *Heads*, p. 78, gives 970; cf. *VCH, Gloucestershire*, ii. 66; and G. Haigh, *The History of Winchcombe Abbey* (London, 1950), p. 25.

[100] Germanus went briefly to Westbury-on-Trym first of all. See *Heads*, p. 78; C. Hart, *The Early Charters of Northern England and the North Midlands* (Leicester, 1975), pp. 337–8; and M. Lapidge, 'Abbot Germanus, Winchcombe, Ramsey and the Cambridge Psalter', in *Words, Texts and Manuscripts. Studies in Anglo-Saxon Culture Presented to Helmut Gneuss on the Occasion of his Sixty-fifth Birthday*, ed. M. Korhammer (Woodbridge, 1992), pp. 99–129, at 117–26.

[101] See pp. xxxiv–xxxv above.

death of King Edgar in 975. Germanus returned for about three years to Fleury, before being summoned to Ramsey, where he remained until 992, when he was made abbot of Cholsey.[102] While at Ramsey, Germanus probably maintained his position as abbot 'in exile', particularly since the community there was, at the time, only under the charge of prior Eadnoth.[103] The enthusiasms of Winchcombe, specifically the veneration of Kenelm, probably shifted to Ramsey with Germanus. The presence of Kenelm in several liturgical manuscripts of uncertain provenance may be due to Germanus' direct influence and could thus provide grounds for assigning their origin to Ramsey (rather than Winchcombe).[104]

Again during this period of exile at Ramsey, there may have been some effort to write down a Life of Kenelm. There is certain proof of hagiographical activity at Ramsey at about the turn of the tenth century, in the form of Byrhtferth's works on Oswald and Ecgwine.[105] Traces of a continuing tradition in the earlier eleventh century can be discerned in Goscelin's preface to his *Vita S. Yuonis*, where, as already noted, he referred to a previous Life of Ivo by Wythman, abbot of Ramsey between 1016 and 1020. Any Life of Kenelm which might have been written at Ramsey during Germanus's time there does not seem to have survived; at least, it would be difficult to demonstrate securely that *Vita brevior* could have been composed as early as 975–92. In any case, as has already been noted, the *Vita brevior* lections give the impression that, wherever they were to be used, Clent was the primary focus. Such an emphasis is not consistent with the conjectured importation of the Winchcombe-based cult to Ramsey, by Germanus. It is not impossible, however, that materials of some kind, relating to Kenelm, and dating originally from the time of Germanus, may have survived at Ramsey, and thus one configuration of events could be that, when it was decided at Winchcombe to put together a new Life of Kenelm, information was sought from Ramsey as well as Worcester. An earlier Life of Kenelm could even have been available. Such a text could conceivably contend for the title of Antropoff's common source for *Vita brevior* and *Vita et miracula*. On the other hand, it may seem ill-advised to multiply the numbers of supposedly lost saints' Lives from Anglo-Saxon England.

---

[102] *Heads*, p. 39. The rest of the Winchcombe community also fled to Ramsey.
[103] *Heads*, p. 61.
[104] See Lapidge, 'Abbot Germanus', pp. 100–16.   [105] See p. xxxvi above.

Any attempt to reach further back into the history of the cult of Kenelm becomes highly speculative. It has been suggested that veneration of Kenelm arose at an early date for reasons of local politics, that the cult may, in other words, have been connected with the dynastic struggles of the Mercian line, or with a desire to condemn either Cwoenthryth's act specifically, or regicide in general.[106] At the same time the cult appears quite as likely to have taken its form most coherently over a century after the saint's supposed murder and to have arisen to a large extent from the basic desire to have a saint as protecting (and royal) patron, perhaps formalized as a result of Continental influence at late tenth-century Winchcombe, and parallel to developments at other centres, such as Winchester.[107]

To return, finally, to the vexed question of the relationship of the two Lives of Kenelm: considering the matter on the whole, the contention here is that the third and fourth hypotheses are in fact the most plausible, and that *Vita brevior* and *Vita et miracula* were quite probably the work of one man, or at the very least, that the former was an abbreviated reworking of the latter, to serve slightly different purposes.

(vi) *The Liturgical Cult of St Kenelm*

Whatever might be said of the true identity of Kenelm, or the origin of his cult, there is little doubt that the saint had already become quite widely commemorated by the early eleventh century, to judge from the liturgical evidence. The earliest extant calendar to mark the feast of St Kenelm on 17 July is that in Salisbury Cathedral 150, written somewhere in south-western England during the second half of the tenth century.[108] Kenelm was included in the so-called Metrical Calendar of Ramsey, composed at some time during the final decade of the tenth century, and his

---

[106] Cf. Rollason, 'The Cults of murdered royal saints', pp. 9–10, 15 and 21; A. Thacker, 'Kings, saints, and monasteries in pre-Viking Mercia', *Midland History*, x (1985), 1–25, at pp. 8–12; and Ridyard, *Royal Saints*, pp. 247 and 249.

[107] It is intriguing to note that, according to Lantfred, *Translatio et miracula S. Swithuni*, c. 1, the revelation of the 'invention' of St Swithun's body was connected with one Eadsige, a secular cleric and kinsman of Æthelwold, who, having been expelled from the Old Minster in 964, 'nunc Winchelcumbe degit'.

[108] Wormald, *English Kalendars*, no. 2: 'Cynelmi martyris'.

inclusion was very probably due to the influence of Germanus.[109] The fact that Kenelm is not commemorated in the somewhat earlier calendar in Oxford, Bodleian Library, Digby 63, thought to derive from the North Country and datable to the ninth century,[110] may suggest that the cult had not yet been established long enough to reach wide recognition at that date. The feast is marked in virtually all the calendars surviving from the eleventh century,[111] except two of apparent West Country origin.[112]

Liturgical calendars can, however, only supply a limited insight into the extent to which a saint was venerated, and we must turn to the surviving service-books for confirmation. In those for the monastic Office, there is evidence to suggest that Kenelm eventually received widespread commemoration. The breviary of Hyde abbey contains three lections for St Kenelm's day,[113] as does that of Hereford[114] and Sarum,[115] and also the set of 'legenda' compiled by Bishop John Grandisson in the fourteenth century, for use at Exeter.[116] These sets of lections were drawn, without exception, from *Vita et miracula*, and are all preceded by the same collect.[117]

In the case of books for use at mass, it is also the examples from after the eleventh century which provide the clearest evidence of the popularity of Kenelm's liturgical cult. The earliest surviving mass-set for the feast of Kenelm, including collect, secret, preface,[118] and postcommunion, occurs in the sacramentary, Orléans, Bibliothèque Municipale, 127 (105), written at Winchcombe, or

[109] Ed. M. Lapidge, 'A tenth-century metrical calendar from Ramsey', *Revue Bénédictine*, xciv (1984), 326–69; 'Purpureis sanctis iunctus Koenelmus in arce' (line 71). Another calendar in a MS possibly connected with Ramsey, but which had reached Fleury by the early 11th cent., namely Paris, BN lat. 7299, ff. 3–12 (s. x/xi), also commemorates Kenelm.

[110] Wormald, *English Kalendars*, no. 1.   [111] Ibid. nos. 3, 6, 9–20.

[112] Ibid. nos. 7 (Salisbury) and 8 (Wells). The feast of Kenelm appears as a 13th-cent. addition to the latter.

[113] Tolhurst, *Monastic Breviary*, iv, fos. 295^{r-v}.

[114] Ed. W. H. Frere and L. E. G. Brown, 3 vols., HBS xxvi, xl, xlvi (1904–11), ii. 248.

[115] Ed. F. Procter and C. Wordsworth, 3 vols. (Cambridge, 1879–86), iii, cols. 497–502. Salisbury Cathedral claimed to possess a relic of Kenelm, according to a 15th-cent. list in the processional, Salisbury Cathedral Library 148, printed in Wordsworth, *Ceremonies and Processions*, p. 36.

[116] Ed. H. E. Reynolds, *Legenda Sanctorum: The Proper Lessons for Saints' Days according to the Use of Exeter* (London, 1880), ii (2), fasc. ii, fos. 84^{v}–85^{r}. See also *Ordinale Exon.*, ed. J. N. Dalton et al., 4 vols., HBS xxxvii–xxxviii, lxiii, lxxix (1909–40), iii. 283–4.

[117] See pp. cxxxv–cxxxvi below on the lections.

[118] Listed in E. Moeller, *Corpus Praefationum*, 5 vols., CCSL clxi, clxi A–D (1980–1), ii. 1213, and cf. 1214.

possibly Ramsey, in the second half of the tenth century.[119] Otherwise, of extant eleventh-century manuscripts, only the so-called Missal of Robert of Jumièges, Rouen, Bibliothèque Municipale, 274 (Y. 6), includes the same proper mass-set, as an addition at the beginning of the codex.[120] The 'Portiforium of St Wulstan' provided three collects for St Kenelm's day.[121] Moving on from the eleventh century, the same mass-set is also to be found (though without the proper preface) in the missals of Hereford,[122] Sarum,[123] Sherborne,[124] and Westminster.[125]

Kenelm is to be found in several surviving litanies,[126] although, as has already been noted, it is not safe to make too many inferences about such evidence. Exceptions to this are the litanies found in Orléans, Bibliothèque Municipale, 127 (105), the sacramentary mentioned above,[127] and Cambridge, UL, Ff. 1. 23, the early eleventh-century 'Cambridge Psalter'.[128] In the latter, the names of St Peter and St Kenelm are the only ones in the entire list to be rubricated, while St Benedict occurs in capitals. Among the confessors, Kenelm is the first English saint in the list (in 25th place, after the proto-martyr, Stephen). These shreds of evidence imply that the litany was composed for use at Winchcombe, and thus that the manuscript as a whole was written there. But they are not absolute proof.[129] The manuscript could conceivably have originated at Ramsey, where Kenelm was also venerated.[130]

---

[119] This sacramentary will be further discussed below. Cf. L. Delisle, 'Mémoire sur d'anciens sacramentaires', *Mémoires de l'Institut national de France, Académie des Inscriptions et Belles-Lettres*, xxxiii (1) (1886), 211–18, and V. Leroquais, *Les sacramentaires et les missels manuscrits des bibliothèques publiques de France*, 3 vols. (Paris, 1924), i. 89 (no. 35).

[120] Ed. Wilson, pp. 5–6 (cf. Warren, *Leofric Missal*, pp. 283–4). Mass-sets for four other English saints, Edward king and martyr, Guthlac, Botolph, and Alban were also added to the beginning of this book.

[121] Ed. Hughes, ii. 132. Cf. the calendar in that MS, where the day was marked as a feast of twelve lections; Wormald, *English Kalendars*, no. 17.

[122] Ed. Henderson, pp. 285–6.   [123] Ed. J. W. Legg (Oxford, 1916), p. 291.

[124] Property of the Duke of Northumberland, on loan to the British Library, Loan 82, s. xiv/xv.

[125] Ed. Legg, *Missale Westmonasteriense*, iii. 1566.

[126] Lapidge, *Litanies*, nos. I, VI, VIII. i, IX. i, XII, XVI. ii, XXI, XXII. i, XXIII, XXIV, XXVIII, XXXII, XXXVI, XLV.

[127] Ibid. XXVIII.   [128] Ibid. I.

[129] Cf. Gneuss, 'List', no. 4. See also E. Temple, *Anglo-Saxon Manuscripts* (1976), no. 80.

[130] See Lapidge, 'Abbot Germanus', esp. pp. 100–3, 126–9. But cf. D. N. Dumville, *English Caroline Script and Monastic History: Studies in Benedictinism, A.D. 950–1030*, Studies in Anglo-Saxon History, vi (Woodbridge, 1993), pp. 79–85, for the suggestion that this MS, and Cambridge, UL, Kk. 5. 32, may have been written at Canterbury or Cholsey.

In the litany in the Orléans sacramentary, Kenelm appears with even greater prominence, second only to St Stephen in the list of martyrs, and with his name in capital letters. The manuscript is known to have reached Fleury by the early eleventh century, and the only other saints accorded such prominence are SS Benedict and Scholastica, and the martyrs of Agaune (Maurice and companions). It has been suggested that the sacramentary was originally written at Winchcombe, on account of the prominence accorded to Kenelm, and travelled thence to Fleury.[131] On the other hand, Ramsey could quite plausibly be the place of origin, with Germanus providing the link between Kenelm, Ramsey and Fleury.[132]

A further manifestation of the veneration of Kenelm at Ramsey may be the hymn 'O Kenelme, martyr alme', which occurs immediately after *Vita et miracula* in Bodley 285, fo. 83ᵛ.[133] The chance preservation of the hymn only in a manuscript assigned to Ramsey by no means constitutes infallible proof that it was composed there, and the attribution can only remain conjectural. The hymn takes the form of a rhythmical imitation of septenary trochaics (= 4p + 4p + 7pp), with lines rhyming in pairs, and also with internal rhyme between the two halves of the first hemistich;[134]

> O Kenelme, martyr alme, Merciorum gloria,
> Rex sublimis, tua nimis dulcis est memoria
> Nam precellis, fauo mellis, gratia dulcedinis
> Atque rosis speciosis, flore pulchritudinis . . .

The rhyme-scheme may indicate that the hymn is datable to the twelfth century.[135]

---

[131] Gneuss, 'List', no. 867; and Temple, *Anglo-Saxon Manuscripts*, no. 31. The origin of this MS is discussed at length by D. Gremont and L. Donnat, 'Fleury, le Mont St-Michel et l'Angleterre à la fin du Xᵉ et au début du XIᵉ siècle, à propos du manuscrit Orléans 127', in *Millénaire monastique du Mont-St-Michel*, i, *Histoire et vie monastique*, ed. J. Laporte (Paris, 1966), pp. 751–93. Cf. Lapidge, 'Abbot Germanus', pp. 103–6.

[132] Ker, *Medieval Libraries*, p. 111, rejected Orléans 127 from the list of Winchcombe MSS; but cf. Dumville, *English Caroline Script*, p. 58 n. 259 and id., *Liturgy*, pp. 80–1.

[133] Ed. Blume, *AH* lv (1922), p. 239, no. 212. The hymn is not listed by Chevalier, *Repertorium*, or by Schaller and Könsgen, *Initia*. Blume noted that the rubric in the MS is 'legatur', commenting, 'demnach ist zweifelhaft, ob ein Reimgebet oder eine Sequenz vorliegt'.

[134] This verse-form is described by D. Norberg, *Introduction à l'étude de la versification latin médiévale*, Studia Latina Stockholmensia, v (Uppsala, 1958), pp. 114–16; and id., *Les vers latins iambiques et trochaïques au Moyen Age et leurs répliques rythmiques* (Stockholm, 1988), pp. 96–124.

[135] Other examples of similarly rhyming 'septenarii' are late; see Norberg, *Introduction*, p. 45.

The evidence of all these liturgical books implies that during the eleventh century full commemoration of Kenelm may have been confined mainly to centres with a specific interest in him, namely Winchcombe, Ramsey and Worcester, but that subsequently the saint's feast began to be observed quite widely. The number of post-Conquest calendars which include Kenelm is a testimony to the enduring nature of that popularity. Some have a commemoration only, such as those from Abbotsbury, Chester, Crowland, and Muchelney,[136] while others mark 17 July as a feast of three lections, such as Abingdon, St Albans, Chertsey, Gloucester, and Westminster;[137] and a few as a feast of twelve lections, namely Dunster, Evesham and Malmesbury,[138] and Worcester.[139] A further witness to the saint's popularity is the inclusion of a Middle English Life of Kenelm in the South English Legendary, translated from the *Vita et miracula* at an unidentified centre in the south-west, in the later thirteenth century.[140]

(vii) *The Old English Kenelm Couplet*

Additional evidence for wider knowledge of the legend of Kenelm is provided by an Old English couplet, purporting to be the content of the letter delivered by a dove to the pope, revealing Kenelm's resting-place. This couplet is preserved by several of the witnesses to *Vita et miracula*, either at the appropriate point in the Latin text (c. 11), as in **G** and **H**, or as a marginal annotation (**J** and probably also **P**).[141] It is repeated by several thirteenth-century chroniclers as part of their own redactions of *Vita et miracula*.[142] Furthermore, it is preserved independently on the recto of the first folio of Cambridge, Pembroke College 82.[143] The note, written in a later twelfth-century hand (thus making this the earliest surviving witness to the couplet), runs:

> In clench qu becche under ane þorne
> liet Kenelm kinebern heved bereved.

[136] Wormald, *Benedictine Kalendars*, nos. 1, 7, 8, and 17.

[137] Ibid. nos. 2, 3, 6, 14, and 15. [138] Ibid. nos. 10, 13 and 16.

[139] Oxford, Magdalen College 100, an early 13th-cent. psalter (marked as twelve-lection feast). And likewise in the calendar appended to the gradual and antiphoner, Worcester Cathedral Library F. 160, of the beginning of the 13th cent.

[140] See p. cxxxviii below.

[141] See the description of **P** below, § x. [142] See below, § xiii.

[143] M. R. James, *A Descriptive catalogue of the manuscripts contained in Pembroke College Library* (Cambridge, 1905), pp. 70–2. Contents include *Vita S. Alexis* and Bede, *HE*.

A thirteenth-century hand added: 'Versus dompni Iohannis primi abbatis de sancto albano' (John de Cella, abbot of St Albans, 1195–1214):

> In clenc sub spina iacet in conualle bouina
> uertice priuatus kenelmus rege creatus.

This Latin version occurs also in the bottom margin of fo. 48ᵛ of **G** (the page where the story of the beheading is told), with the slight variation 'kenelmus rex quia creatus'. Pembroke 82 is thought to have belonged to Tynemouth Abbey, a cell of St Albans.[144] A possible reason for an interest in Kenelm at Tynemouth is that in about 1073 or 1074, a mission set out to Jarrow and Tynemouth, the members of which were Ealdwine, prior of Winchcombe, Ælwig and Reginfrid, both from the community at Evesham.[145] This could also have been the reason for the interest in Kenelm at St Albans, of which John de Cella's Latin couplet is one manifestation. By the thirteenth century, St Albans was claiming to possess a relic of Kenelm.[146]

Interestingly, a trace of this couplet may be found in *Secgan be þam Godes sanctum*,[147] the list of resting-places, which includes Kenelm, in the early eleventh-century portion, as 'cynebearn' (not all the saints in the list were furnished with comparable epithets). The compiler could have known a version of the couplet, and have echoed it in his list, either consciously or unconsciously. Thus, if the dating of the portion of *Secgan* which includes Kenelm is correct, there may be reason to suppose that the couplet was already in circulation by the early eleventh century. The words 'Legitur per totam patriam epistola . . .' in the preface to *Vita et miracula* may be an allusion to this apparently commemorative couplet (or 'cantilena'), but we cannot now determine what its purpose and origin could have been. It has been tentatively suggested that the couplet in fact represents the last remnants of a vernacular Life of Kenelm, which had been used by the author of

[144] Ker, *Catalogue*, p. 124.

[145] See Symeon, *Historia ecclesiae Dunhelmensis*, ed. T. Arnold, 2 vols., RS lxxv (1882–5), i. 110.

[146] In a 13th-cent. list appended to the chronicle in London, BL, Cotton Claudius E. IV, printed in *Gesta Abbatum S. Albani*, ed. H. T. Riley, 3 vols., RS xxviii (1867–9), iii. 539–45.

[147] Ed. F. Liebermann, *Die Heiligen Englands* (Hanover, 1889), pp. 17–18. Cf. D. W. Rollason, 'Lists of saints' resting-places in Anglo-Saxon England', *ASE* vii (1978), 61–93.

Vita et miracula.[148] Another explanation is that the couplet was recited by pilgrims to the shrine at Winchcombe, and might even have been composed for that purpose, in order to encourage, or formalize, lay participation in the rites of Kenelm's feast.[149]

(viii) *Churches Dedicated to St Kenelm*[150]

It is not clear how some of the following churches should have come to be dedicated to Kenelm, or, in any case, how old each dedication is. They are perhaps simply a further sign of the popularity of the saint. All lie within a 60 km. radius of Winchcombe (or in the case of the Worcestershire dedications, near Clent), apart from the last.

(*a*) Alderley, Gloucestershire
Held at Domesday by Miles Crispin, and by Wigot of Wallingford, sheriff of Oxfordshire, under Edward the Confessor.[151]

(*b*) Sapperton, Gloucestershire
The present church here has a few traces of Norman work.[152] There was a tradition that Kenelm's body rested here on the way to Winchcombe,[153] highly unlikely considering how far south of any possible route Sapperton lies.[154]

(*c*) Clifton-on-Teme, Worcestershire
The oldest part of the present fabric is the thirteenth-century west tower.[155] Clifton was held at Domesday by Osbern, son of Richard

---

[148] Cf. R. M. Wilson, *Lost Literature of Medieval England* (London, 1952), pp. 99–100; and C. E. Wright, *The Cultivation of Saga in Anglo-Saxon England* (London, 1939), p. 104.

[149] A conjecture by W. de G. Birch, noted in D. Royce, *Landboc siue Registrum monasterii beatae Mariae Virginis et sancti Cenhelmi de Winchelcumba*, 2 vols. (Exeter, 1892–1903), i. viii. Cf. W. Haubrichs, *Heiligenfest und Heiligenlied im früher Mittelalter. Zur Genese mündlicher und literarischer Formen in einer Kontaktzone laïkaler und Klerikaler Kultur*, in *Feste und Feiern im Mittelalter. Paderborner Symposion des Mediävistenverbandes*, ed. D. Altenburg, J. Jarnut and H. H. Steinhoff (Sigmaringen, 1991), pp. 133–43, where Continental examples of vernacular pilgrim-chants are discussed. Haubrichs suggests that although such hymns may have originated within popular (and orally transmitted) veneration, the written forms in which they have been preserved were clerical compositions intended to channel, even restrain, lay participation in the solemnities at shrines (pp. 142–3).

[150] Cf. Arnold-Forster, *Church Dedications*, i. 174–5.

[151] *DB, Glos.*, 64. 3 (i. 169c).

[152] D. Verey, *Gloucestershire. I: The Cotswolds*, BofE (1970), p. 386.

[153] *VCH, Gloucestershire*, ix. 98, n. 50.

[154] On the possibility that the church was formerly dedicated to St Dunstan, see p. 77 below.

[155] N. Pevsner, *Worcestershire*, BofE (1968), p. 122.

Scrope, and formerly by King Edward.[156] A spurious charter, dated 930, records King Æthelstan's grant of Clifton to Worcester.[157]

(d) Upton Snodsbury, Worcestershire
A building extensively restored 1873–4, but with windows of the thirteenth and fourteenth centuries.[158] It was a chapelry of the church of the Holy Cross, Pershore, until 1427,[159] probably granted by Edgar to Pershore in 972.[160] In 1086, Upton Snodsbury was held by St Peter's, Westminster.[161]

(e) Enstone, Oxfordshire
This was owned by Winchcombe Abbey at the time of the Confessor,[162] and probably earlier.[163] A Saxon church formerly stood on this site.[164] The earliest portion of the present building is the south aisle, probably added in about 1180 to the Saxon church.

(f) Minster Lovell, Oxfordshire
The existing building is of fifteenth-century date, but the cruciform layout betrays the form of the earlier church.[165] Furthermore, the name of the place indicates that it was originally a minster, although the date and circumstances of the foundation are not known. By the late twelfth century the church belonged to the Benedictine abbey of Ivry.

(g) Hinton Parva, Dorset
Here again, although the church was largely rebuilt in the neo-Norman style in 1860, a few Norman fragments survive, including, over the door, a sculpture thought by some to be of St Kenelm.[166]

(h) There is an isolated reference, in a will of 1529, to an altar or image of Kenelm in the church of St John the Evangelist, Wyke Dyve, in Northamptonshire.[167]

[156] DB, Worcs., 19. 3 (i. 176d).
[157] S 406 = BCS 700, cf. H. P. R. Finberg, The Early Charters of the West Midlands (Leicester, 1972), p. 108 (no. 275).   [158] Pevsner, Worcs., p. 283.
[159] See VCH, Worcestershire, iv (1971), p. 211.   [160] S 786 = BCS 1282.
[161] DB, Worcs. 8. 11 (i. 174d).   [162] DB, Oxon. 11. 1 (i. 157a).
[163] See the confirmation of Winchcombe's estates in a bull of Pope Alexander III (1175), ed. Royce, Landboc, i. 25–9.
[164] J. Sherwood and N. Pevsner, Oxfordshire, BofE (1974), p. 593.   [165] Ibid. 706.
[166] J. Newman and N. Pevsner, Dorset, BofE (1972), p. 229. This is rather a long way from Winchcombe, but compare c. 23, 'ad Stertel' which may refer to Sturthill in Dorset.
[167] R. M. Serjeantson and H. Isham Longden, 'The Parish churches and religious houses of Northamptonshire. Their dedications, altars, images and lights', Archaeological Journal, lxx (1913), 217–452, at p. 439.

(ix) *The Manuscript of* Vita brevior

Cambridge, Corpus Christi College, 367, part 2, fos. 45^r–48^r. This is a composite codex made up of miscellaneous fragments, including Ælfric's version of Bede's *De temporibus* and a collection of Old English homilies, bound up together in about 1575.[168] The copy of the *Vita brevior* occupies just one quire, of which the first folio has been lost, since the text begins part way through the second of eight lections.[169] It was written in a single hand of the third quarter of the eleventh century, probably at Worcester.[170] There was originally a blank space after the eighth lection, at first covered with a maze design. Almost immediately, the verso of fo. 48 was filled with an Old English list of eleven books, in a hand of about the third quarter of the eleventh century, possibly that of Coleman (d. 1113).[171] This was followed by an Old English account of the vision of Leofric of Mercia (d. 1057) in a late eleventh-century hand.[172] Consequently, it may reasonably be conjectured that there were only ever intended to be eight lections to *Vita brevior*. At the conclusion of the eighth lection, an early twelfth-century hand has added, over the top of the maze, a portion of *Vita et miracula* as if to continue where the *Vita brevior* left off.[173] Since the verso of the page had already been filled, this later material was squeezed in partly below the original text, and partly into the outer margin of the page, in smaller script. The concluding words of the eighth lection were probably altered in order to dove-tail into the addition. As a consequence of subsequent trimming, some of the text in the outer margin (three or four letters in every line) has been lost.

A brief account of the Life of Kenelm, apparently drawn from the *Vita brevior*, is preserved in the Worcester annals known as the

---

[168] A detailed list of the contents of this MS is to be found in M. R. James, *Descriptive Catalogue of the Manuscripts in the Library of Corpus Christi College, Cambridge* (Cambridge, 1912), ii. 202; and also in Ker, *Catalogue*, nos. 62–4.

[169] Page measurement: 214 mm. × 139 mm.; written area: 179 mm. × 111 mm.; single columns.

[170] See E. A. Macintyre, 'Early twelfth-century Worcester Cathedral Priory with special reference to the manuscripts written there', D.Phil. thesis (Oxford, 1978), p. 202.

[171] Ibid. 42.

[172] See A. S. Napier, 'An Old-English Vision of Leofric, Earl of Mercia', *Transactions of the Philological Society* (1907–10), 180–8.

[173] Possibly the hand is that of John of Worcester; see Macintyre, 'Early twelfth-century Worcester', p. 219.

Chronicon ex Chronicis,[174] and (almost verbatim) in the early twelfth-century compilation from Winchcombe, London, BL, Cotton Tiberius E. IV, at fo. 15ʳ, as part of the Winchcombe annals (fos. 1–27ᵛ), which probably derive substantially from Worcester.[175]

Rex Merciorum S. Kenulfus,[176] post multa bona que in sua uita gessit opera, ad beatitudinem que in celis est transiuit in[177] perennem, filiumque suum sanctum Kenelmum septennem regni reliquit heredem. Sed paucis mensibus euolutis germane sue Quendrythe insidiis, cuius seuam conscientiam dira cupido regnandi armarat, ausu crudelitatis ab Asceberto, nutritore suo cruentissimo, in uasta syluaque nemorosa sub arbore spinosa occulte traditur iugulo; uerum qui solo teste celo est iugulatus, celo teste per columpnam lucis postmodum est reuelatus. Absciditur caput Kenelmi natalis et innocentie candore lacteum, unde lactea columba aureis pennis euolat in celum. Post cuius felix martyrium, Ceolwulfus [178]patruus eius[178] regnum suscepit Merciorum.

A further, very fragmentary witness to the *Vita brevior* is provided by some of the antiphons and responsories for the Office of St Kenelm in the early twelfth-century Winchcombe breviary, Valenciennes, 116 (fos. 208ʳ–211ʳ).[179]

(x) *The Manuscripts of* Vita et miracula S. Kenelmi

B = Oxford, Bodleian Library, Bodley 285 (*SC* 2430), fos. 80–83ᵛ. This manuscript is an early thirteenth-century collection of saints' Lives, not arranged in any calendrical order.[180] Only from the nature of the contents can a conjecture be made as to where the manuscript might have been written. Goscelin's *Vita S. Yuonis*, written for, and dedicated to, Abbot Herbert Losinga (1087–90/1) is included, and with it, the only surviving copy of his *Miracula S. Yuonis*.[181] These texts were written purposely to celebrate the 'inuentio' of Ivo at Ramsey which took place in the early eleventh century. At the end of the *Miracula S. Yuonis*, on fo. 108ʳ, are the

---

[174] R. R. Darlington, P. McGurk (eds.), and J. Bray (trans.), *The Chronicle of John of Worcester*, vol. ii, *The Annals from 450 to 1066* (OMT, 1995), pp. 238–40.

[175] Ed. R. R. Darlington, 'Winchcombe Annals, 1049–1181', in *A Medieval Miscellany for Doris Mary Stenton*, ed. P. M. Barnes and C. F. Slade, Pipe Rolls Society, xxxviii (1962), pp. 111–37.

[176] Kenulphus in *Chronicon*.   [177] Omitted in *Chronicon*.

[178] ... [178] Omitted in *Chronicon*.   [179] See p. cxxx below.

[180] Page measurement: 366 mm. × 270 mm.; written area: 270 mm. × 197 mm.; 183 fos., double columns of 36 lines.

[181] *BHL* 4622 and 4623.

additional words 'Hec qui descripsit deuotus quique rescripsit, |
Yuo sacer, de te placeat Dominoque tibique', the specific piety of
which may also suggest a Ramsey origin. The manuscript also contains a version of the *Passio beatorum martyrum Ethelredi atque Ethelbricti*, possibly also by Goscelin, and not found elsewhere.[182] The
text includes an account of their translation to Ramsey by Oswald,
and may thus serve as a further indication that the manuscript was
written at Ramsey Abbey.[183] Eadmer's Life and miracles of St
Oswald, the first abbot of Ramsey, is also included in the collection.[184] At the conclusion of *Vita et miracula S. Kenelmi*, in the
bottom margin of fo. 83^v is a short septenary hymn to Kenelm,
beginning, 'O Kenelme, martyr alme, | Merciorum gloria,' written
out on specially ruled lines. It does not survive elsewhere.[185] A
Winchcombe provenance for this manuscript was suggested by
Canon Raine to explain the presence of *Vita et miracula S. Kenelmi*
and of the hymn.[186] But as has already been shown above, the
presence of a Life of, and hymn to, Kenelm in a Ramsey manuscript does not require explanation. A copy of *Vita et miracula* could
have reached Ramsey in the eleventh century, and have subsequently been used as the exemplar for the thirteenth-century copy
presently under discussion.

The manuscript appears to have been written by three or four
roughly contemporary hands. The *Vita et miracula* is the work of
one scribe, who writes an early form of gothic, still quite rounded,
without very pronounced lozenge-shaped tops to the minims, but
with a tendency towards lateral compression. The first two named
characteristics are especially noticeable on fo. 83^v where the first
column contains the conclusion of *Vita et miracula*, and the second
column is the beginning of Osbern's *Vita S. Dunstani*,[187] written by
a different scribe, whose hand is very much more angular and
gothic in aspect. Other features which point towards a dating early
in the thirteenth century are the use of the uncrossed tironian 'et'
symbol, and the placing of the first line of script above the top
ruled line. The hymn to St Kenelm is written in a smaller, more
cursive, script, possibly by a different scribe—perhaps the same

---

[182] *BHL* 2641.

[183] Ker, *Medieval Libraries*, lists this MS under Ramsey Abbey with a query. Rollason,
Mildrith, p. 89, accepts the Ramsey origin, as does Bethell, 'Lives of St Osyth', p. 77 (the
MS also contains *Vita S. Osgithe, BHL* 6352).

[184] *BHL* 6375 and 6376.   [185] See above, p. cxvi.

[186] *HCY* ii. x.   [187] *BHL* 2344.

one who provided the 'explicit' rubric at the very bottom of the page.

C = Cambridge, Corpus Christi College 367, part 2, fo. 48^r. As noted above, a small portion of *Vita et miracula S. Kenelmi* was added in an early twelfth-century hand to the end of the eight lections which constitute the *Vita brevior*.

D = Oxford, Bodleian Library, Douce 368 (*SC* 21943), fos. 79^r–83^v. This large and finely executed manuscript containing Bede's *HE*, a genealogy of the Mercian kings, which includes Kenelm, and the *Vita et miracula S. Kenelmi*, was probably written at or for Winchcombe Abbey in the third quarter of the twelfth century.[188] Pasted on to the modern flyleaf is a fifteenth-century *ex-libris* inscription: 'In hoc uolumine continetur liber uenerabilis bede presbiteri in libro ecclesiastice historie gentis anglorum quod quidem uolumen pertinet ad monasterium Winchelcombense.'[189] The entire manuscript appears to have been written by one scribe, except for the final miracle of Kenelm (Appendix C, below), which was added slightly later, on fo. 83^v. This extra material is unique to **D**, being the description of the fire which devastated Winchcombe Abbey in 1149 or 1151. The text breaks off mid-sentence at the bottom of fo. 83^v, just at the start of a fresh miracle attending Kenelm's relics on their journey. This folio is the last of a quire of eight, so we may suppose that either an entire quire, or, more likely, a few extra folios, employed to complete the miracles, have been lost. A note by Francis Douce on the modern fo. 84 suggests that 'much cannot be wanting' from the text—working on the assumption, not verifiable, that this supposed Winchcombe version is not likely to be much longer than the other known witnesses.

The principal scribe writes an upright, compact minuscule of later twelfth-century type. Certain corrections have been made to *Vita et miracula*, in a hand only a little later than that of the text itself (possibly even contemporary). The initial 'd' of the *Vita* is handsomely historiated, depicting a crowned figure, presumably Kenelm, seated on a throne, holding a sceptre in his left hand and a sprouting branch, or perhaps a lily, in the other, and attended by

---

[188] Page measurement: 409 mm. × 273 mm.; written area: 300 mm. × 180 mm.; 83 fos., double columns of 45 lines. See Ker, *English Manuscripts*, pp. 7, 41, and 50.

[189] This is the form of words which Ker, *Medieval Libraries*, p. 198, records as being found usually on a label on the back cover of Winchcombe MSS.

a bird bearing something in its beak—perhaps the letter delivered to the pope in Rome. The decorative foliage surrounding the figure of Kenelm extends outside the bow of the capital 'D', and under one curled leaf is a bodiless head—which may have been intended to represent the martyr's head 'sub spino', although such heads are a not uncommon decorative feature in manuscripts of this period.[190] The text written by the second scribe (c. 32) was evidently intended to have the same coloured initials as the rest of the *Vita*, since a space has been left for one, in two places, but, for whatever reason, the necessary letters were never added. The second scribe cannot have been writing very much later than the first—the date of the fire at Winchcombe, 1149 or 1151, gives a *terminus post quem* for the additional miracle. The fact that this material has been added straight on to the preceding text without any intervening *explicit* may imply that very little time elapsed between the writing of the main body of text and the additional miracles, reported perhaps only a short while after they had occurred. The *Landboc* of Winchcombe, fo. 84, preserves a document by which a son was renewing his father's grant to the people of Postlip,[191] and, as an explanation for the loss of the previous grant, an account, with close verbal similarities to this miracle, is given of the Winchcombe fire.[192] The monastery is stated to have lost all its books and charters. We are therefore obliged to assume that Douce 368 was written after this time, that is, in the second half of the twelfth century. When discussing the status of the text of the *Historia Ecclesiastica* in Douce 368, which falls into a group of 'conflate' manuscripts, Mynors stated that although on inspection he was unable to find any particular textual indications, it remained for him 'only a probability' that this text was copied from the eleventh-century copy, London, British Library, Royal 13. C. v from St Peter's Abbey, Gloucester.[193]

If it is the case that the Douce Bede was copied from a Gloucester manuscript, it is just as possible that, after the depredations of the fire, a version of the Life of St Kenelm, now lost, had also to

---

[190] For a comparison of this initial with illuminations from the same geographical area, and of similar date, see A. Heimann, 'A twelfth-century manuscript from Winchcombe and its illustrations. Dublin, Trinity College, MS. 53', *Journal of the Warburg and Courtauld Institutes*, xxviii (1965), 86–109, esp. pp. 108–9.

[191] Ed. Royce, i. 83.   [192] For the text, see Appendix C.

[193] Colgrave and Mynors, *Bede's Ecclesiastical History*, p. lii; and Plummer, *Baedae Opera Historica*, i, pp. cxiv–cxvii.

be acquired for copying, from some other scriptorium (perhaps also from Gloucester) and that this version was duly updated with the most recent miracle to have occurred at Winchcombe. If the destruction of the buildings of Winchcombe Abbey and their contents was as complete as described in the miracle and in the above-named grant, then it is to be wondered how quickly any kind of scriptorium can have been established or re-established. Only ten years before the fire, the monastery had been sacked by Miles of Gloucester in the wars of Stephen's reign.[194] Under such circumstances, it may be that there was no active scriptorium at all at Winchcombe for some time, and that manuscripts intended for use at the abbey had had to be copied elsewhere.

The text of the *Vita* in this manuscript is partly marked out into lections, presumably for use at the night office on the feast of St Kenelm. The first eight lections are signalled by the word 'Lectio', abbreviated, and with the appropriate roman numeral either in the outer margin or in the area between the two columns of text. The ends of the fourth and the eighth lections are marked by the words 'Tu' and 'Tu autem', as the cue for the customary formula 'Tu autem Domine miserere nobis' said after every lesson.[195] Lection 1 = cc. 1–2 (but originally just c. 1); 2 = cc. 3–4 (originally cc. 2–4); 3 = c. 5; 4 = c. 6 (from 'Verum ubi puer'); 5 = c. 8; 6 = c. 9; 7 = c. 10; 8 = cc. 11–12. These divisions correspond, to some extent, to the lections in the breviary Valenciennes 116.

An intriguing annotation, by a hand later than the main text, perhaps of the early thirteenth century, in the margin of fo. 80^r, is 'sed credimus' intended for insertion after 'ascensure anime tue gloria' (c. 4). This seems to refer to the corresponding point in *Vita brevior*, where the seventh lection includes the words 'Heu quam timeo arborem illam succisam, pie indolis tue presignare iacturam. *Sed credimus* quia recipiet te clementia dei . . .'. It is not entirely clear why those words were put in the margin—possibly a copy of *Vita brevior* came into the hands of a thirteenth-century scribe who attempted to compare it with the text he already had, and to make annotations, although there is no sign of any such activity elsewhere in **D**. However, the presence of this one annotation may

---

[194] See, *The Chronicle of John of Worcester, 1118–40*, ed. J. R. H. Weaver, Anecdota Oxoniensia (Oxford, 1908), pp. 56–7.

[195] Earlier in the MS, the same hand also marked out, in exactly the same fashion, eight lections concerning the life of Oswald (*HE* iii. 9 and 12–13), and eight describing the life of Cuthbert (*HE* iv. 27–8).

indicate that the *Vita brevior* was available in some form at Winch-combe.[196]

G = Gotha, Forschungsbibliothek 1. 81, fos. 47ᵛ–50ᵛ. A large collection of British and English saints' Lives dated to the third quarter of the fourteenth century, but as yet unlocalized.[197]

H = London, British Library, Harley 3037, fos. 157ᵛ–163ʳ. This manuscript, of unknown origin,[198] contains 150 folios of Latin homilies, followed by *Vita et miracula S. Kenelmi*, Archanaldus, *Vita beati Maurilii andegauorum episcopi*,[199] a sermon on the translation of St Andrew, and *prima pars prologi in Vita domini Gerardi Prioris primi de karitate* which breaks off part way through.[200] The texts were copied by two different but roughly contemporary romanesque hands datable to the second half of the thirteenth century.

J = Oxford, St John's College 149, fos. 72ᵛ–81ᵛ. This codex contains a miscellaneous collection of saint's Lives and other texts;[201] hagiographical items include Ailred's *Historia de uita et miraculis S. Edwardi*,[202] Abbo of Fleury's *Passio S. Eadmundi*,[203] *Passio S. Christiane uirginis*,[204] *Passio SS. Spei, Fidei et Charitatis*,[205] *Pauca de uirtutibus beati Gregorii Neocaesariensis episcopi*,[206] the *Visiones* of Elizabeth, abbess of Schonau (*ob.* 1165),[207] *Passio S. Margarete uirginis*,[208] *Passio SS. Virginum undecim milium apud Coloniam*,[209] and nine lections for the feast of St Cyriac and his companions.[210] The manuscript was copied by various scribes of the earlier thirteenth century, at an as yet unidentified scriptorium. The *Vita et miracula Sancti Kenelmi* was written by one scribe throughout.

[196] For further evidence of this see below, on Valenciennes 116.
[197] Described above, p. lxxvii.
[198] Page measurement: 445 mm. × 215 mm.; written area: 206 mm. × 146 mm.; 211 fos., double columns of 28 lines.
[199] *BHL* 5731.
[200] See *A Catalogue of the Harleian Manuscripts in the British Museum*, 2 vols. (London, 1808), ii. 727.
[201] Page measurement: 207 mm. × 146 mm.; written area: 152 mm. × 100 mm.; 205 fos., single columns of 25 lines. The contents are listed by H. O. Coxe, *Catalogus codicum manuscriptorum qui in collegiis aulisque Oxoniensibus hodie adseruantur*, 2 vols. (Oxford, 1852), ii. 45.
[202] *BHL* 2423.   [203] *BHL* 2392.   [204] *BHL* 1756.
[205] *BHL* 2970.   [206] *BHL* 3677.   [207] *BHL* 2485.
[208] *BHL* 5306.   [209] *BHL* 8430a.
[210] Roughly corresponding to *BHL* 2059a.

L = London, British Library, Lansdowne 436, fos. 88^r–91^r.[211] Many of the texts in this collection of English saints' Lives are in a very much abbreviated form—indeed often almost completely rewritten. The *Vita et miracula S. Kenelmi* was, however, shortened simply by omitting all but the first five miracles. The text is divided into twelve *capitula*.

P = Gloucester, Cathedral Library 1, fos. 113^r–115^v. This early thirteenth-century collection of forty-eight saints' Lives is probably the third volume of a set, of which Lincoln, Cathedral Library 149 and 150 are the first and second volumes respectively.[212] The compilation of texts in this third volume starts in calendrical order, beginning with St Lambert (17 September), and reaching as far as St Eloi (1 December). The only English saint included thus far is Edmund, king and martyr. After the Life of St Eloi, the selection becomes random, with Kenelm (17 July), followed by the translation and miracles of James the Great (25 July), and then leaping to Edward the Confessor (5 January), and so on. Presumably these randomly assembled texts were acquired or discovered only after the orderly collection had been either compiled or copied from another passional—there is no break in the continuity of script or layout. Ker suggested that the three-volume set belonged to Leominster Priory in Herefordshire,[213] a cell of Reading Abbey, to judge from the attention given to St James—his translation and miracles are included, and among the latter, paragraphs about suppliants to the apostle at Reading, some of which are only known from this manuscript.[214]

The collection is written mostly by one scribe, apart from the first few folios. The script is probably of the first quarter or so of the thirteenth century, being an early form of gothic book-hand or 'textualis rotunda', with some lateral compression, but without the distinctive lozenge-shaped minim-tops. The minims are finished with a simple horizontal stroke, a fairly archaic feature by that

---

[211] See above, p. lxxxii, for a description.

[212] Page measurement: 393 mm. × 280 mm.; written area 305 mm. × 195 mm.; ii + 194 + i fos., double columns of 48 lines. The contents are listed by Ker, *Medieval Manuscripts*, ii. 934; cf. p. xxviii above.

[213] *Medieval Manuscripts*, ii. 939, and *Medieval Libraries*, Supplement to 2nd edn., ed. A. G. Watson (London, 1987), p. 44.

[214] The conjecture is supported by the fact that the codex was given to Gloucester Cathedral by Foulk Wallwyn (d. 1660) of Hellens, just 20 miles from Leominster; see Ker, *Medieval Manuscripts*, p. 938.

time. The crossed tironian symbol for 'et' is used frequently though not exclusively—this feature became virtually standard in the second half of the thirteenth century. The text of *Vita et miracula* has been subject to a certain amount of alteration, some apparently 'official' correction (contemporary), but also some later annotation by an early fourteenth-century hand. Examples of this later 'correction' are the addition in the margin of fo. 114^r of the name of what is evidently considered to be the right pope, namely 'Leo secundus', and also the addition above the line of the name of the archbishop of Canterbury, Wulfred, at the top of fo. 114^v. Conceivably, this later corrector had before him another copy of the *Vita et miracula* which he was comparing with his own text, rather than emending *ad lib*.

In the margin by the description of the dove delivering the letter to the pope (fo. 114^r), there was originally a sketch of a bird holding a strip of parchment in its beak. The parchment evidently once had writing on it, but the whole sketch seems to have been intentionally erased so that only a faint outline remains. Thus it is not possible to tell whether the writing on the parchment was the Old English couplet found in **GHJ**, or the Latin couplet, or a different text again.

V = Valenciennes, Bibliothèque Municipale, 116 (109), fos. 208^v–210^v. This breviary was written in the third quarter of the twelfth century almost certainly at, or for, Winchcombe abbey,[215] since St Kenelm and also St Peter are given very great prominence. In the calendar (fos. 1–7), at 17 July we find the entry, 'Occidit absque dolis KENELMVM fraude sororis',[216] in blue capitals, with the name of the saint in red, blue and green capitals. The votive mass 'De reliquiis' has the prayer: 'Propiciare, quesumus, Domine, nobis famulis tuis per beati Kenelmi martyris tui et aliorum sanctorum tuorum, quorum reliquie in presenti requiescunt ecclesia, merita gloriosa.'[217] In the sanctoral, the Office for the feast of

---

[215] Page measurement: 188 mm. × 134 mm.; 269 fos., double columns. Described by V. Leroquais, *Les Bréviaires manuscrits des bibliothèques publiques de France*, 5 vols. (Paris 1934), iv, no. 883.

[216] The same line is found also in the Metrical Calendar of Winchcombe, in London, BL, Cotton Tiberius E. iv, on which see M. Lapidge, 'A tenth-century metrical calendar from Ramsey', *Revue Bénédictine*, xciv (1984), 326–69. No other parts of the metrical calendar are reproduced in the Valenciennes calendar.

[217] Fo. 32^r.

Kenelm has twelve lections, which are taken from *Vita et miracula S. Kenelmi*. The text was divided up as follows: lection 1: c. 1; lection 2: c. 3; lection 3: c. 5; lection 4: c. 6; lection 5: c. 7 up to 'commendetur'; lection 6: c. 8; lection 7: c. 9; lection 8: c. 10; lection 9: c. 11; lection 10: c. 12; lection 11: c. 13 and c. 14 up to 'auferrent'; lection 12: c. 14 'Altercantibus' onwards, and c. 15. The antiphons and responsories of the Office for Kenelm in **V** are of interest because in many cases they contain phrases strongly reminiscent of the *Vita brevior* preserved in **C**.[218]

Thomas Smith's catalogue of the Cottonian collection lists a *Passio Sancti Kenelmi regis anglorum et martyris* amongst the contents of London, BL, Cotton Otho C. XVI, one of the manuscripts which suffered severe damage in the fire of 1731.[219] The handwritten annotations (copied from notes made by Sir Frederic Madden) to the list of damaged and destroyed manuscripts appended to the report made by a parliamentary committee in 1732, give account of the remaining leaves of Otho C. XVI.[220] Of item 7, the Life of Kenelm, large portions are said to have survived. It seems that whatever did remain when Madden examined the manuscript, was subsequently lost in a fire at the museum bindery in 1865, since nothing of it is available for inspection now.

A further witness to a small portion of the *Vita et miracula S. Kenelmi* has recently been brought to light by Richard Sharpe, who, upon discovering *miracula* of St Tecla (apparently patron of Llandegley, Radnorshire), appended to a copy of the Life of St Thecla, Anthiochene martyr, in Lambeth Palace Library 94, noticed that two of the miracles have been transferred virtually *verbatim* from those of Kenelm.[221] The sections in question are cc. 20 and 22; minimal alterations have been made to the text, substituting Tecla's name, replacing 'Peyletona' and 'Anglia' with 'Radenoura' and 'Wallia', and turning 'abbas Goduuinus cum fratribus' into 'sacerdos cum clericis'. Of the witnesses to *Vita et miracula*, the text of the Tecla miracles most closely resembles that

---

[218] See Appendix **E**.
[219] Smith, *Catalogus librorum*, ed. Tite, p. 74. Planta, *Catalogue*, simply reports, of Otho C. XI–XVI, 'desiderantur' (p. 369).
[220] Reproduced in *Catalogus librorum*, ed. Tite (unpaginated).
[221] 'Some medieval *miracula* from Llandegley (Lambeth Palace Library, MS. 94, fols. 153ᵛ–155ʳ)', *Bulletin of the Board of Celtic Studies*, xxxvii (1990), 166–76.

of **D**,[222] but also **P**.[223] Sharpe comments that there may be sources for other parts of the Tecla miracles yet to be identified, and indeed so, since the brief preface is taken almost entirely from the closing section of Goscelin's unprinted *Vita et miracula S. Mildburge*.[224] Lambeth Palace Library 94, containing saints' Lives for January and February, is evidently the first, and only surviving, volume of a legendary. The last item in the manuscript is the above-mentioned *Vita et miracula S. Mildburge*, now incomplete at the end. In considering the possibilities for the composition of the miracles of Tecla, Sharpe has suggested that, as the compiler worked through the *Passio S. Thecle*, he may have been reminded of a local St Tecla, known to him, and may accordingly have assembled a brief account of her miracles, cheerfully plucking material from the texts he was using to put together his legendary, possibly copying from some other large compilation. Thus it is quite conceivable that he had before him a legendary containing the Lives of Thecla, Mildburh and Kenelm, and equally that one of the now-lost volumes of his 'new' legendary contained a copy of the *Vita et miracula S. Kenelmi*.

(xi) *The Relationship of the Manuscripts*

Three significant variants divide the witnesses into two broad groups. In c. 10, **B**, **G**, and **L** agree in calling the pope, to whom the dove made its delivery, *iunior Siluester papa* rather than *Leo papa iunior*, named in all the other witnesses (except **P**, where no pope is named). The parchment delivered by the dove is described in these same three witnesses as *cedulam* rather than *scedulam*, which is found in all other witnesses (although *cedulam* is simply a later form of the same word). In c. 12, the name of the archbishop of Canterbury, Wulfred, is omitted by **BGL** (but also by **P**). The fact that **B** and **G** terminate at the same point, namely at the end of c. 30, and have very similar closing sentences, may also be regarded as significant. **L** terminates well before, but relative brevity is characteristic of that manuscript. Also, in c. 16, **BGL** read *iussisse* where all other witnesses have *iussisseque*. From this much it

[222] Cf. ibid. 168 n. 1.
[223] The Tecla version of c. 22 supplies the personal name 'Leffius', which occurs in **D** as 'Lifsius' but in **P** as 'Leoffius'.
[224] Cf. *BHL* 5959b and c; preserved in Lincoln Cathedral Library, 149, fos. 83ᵛ–87ʳ and London, BL, Addit. 34633, fos. 206ʳ–216ʳ.

appears that **B**, **G**, and **L** represent a distinct recension of the text, and none of them seems likely to have been copied directly from **D**, the earliest full witness to *Vita et miracula*. **G** and **L** cannot be shown to derive directly from **B**, because of its unique variants; for example, c. 3, *somnium* for *somnum*; c. 5, *esse* for *fuisse*; c. 6, omission of *cunis et*, *proferente* for *pronuntiante*; c. 8, *frustra estimatus* for *nequicquam ratus* and so on. An alternative explanation for the apparently close relationship would therefore be that **B**, **G**, and **L** have a common exemplar (at the simplest level), which had *Silvester iunior papa* and not *Wulfredum*, and ended at c. 30. Almost certainly, this is an oversimplification of the relationship, and at least one stage, represented by a now-lost witness, will have intervened between **BGL** and their common ancestor. In particular, **B** seems to derive from an exemplar which contained certain additions and alterations, such as the clause concerning Wulfwine and Ælfwine, made only a short time after the composition of *Vita et miracula* (see above). However, for now, the conjectural hyparchetype of **BGL** will hereafter be designated β.

This leaves **CDJHPV**, whose relationship seems no less complex. The common features of these witnesses are the extra miracle, c. 31 (not **C** and **V** which terminate much earlier), the reading *Leo papa iunior* and the inclusion of *Wulfredum*. The style of c. 31 seems to be uniform with the rest of *Vita et miracula*, and it may therefore have been added by the author, shortly after the completion of the text as represented by the ancestor of **B** and **G**. Perhaps at the same stage it was felt necessary to alter the name of the pope to one putatively less anachronistic[225] and to insert the name of the archbishop of Canterbury.

Since **D** is the earliest full text of *Vita et miracula*, the first approach to this group should be to consider whether any of the other witnesses in this group could have been copied from it, directly or at some remove. We shall consider **V** first. The text of the breviary lections is virtually identical to that of **D**. It is noteworthy that in several places **V** preserves variants which have obviously been emended away in **D**. For example, in **D** we find *Pyriford* (c. 14), where the 'f' has been written over an erased 'u', and in **V** we find *Pyriuord*. Similarly *Glauescestrensibus* (c. 14) and

---

[225] If this occurred at Winchcombe, the emendation could have been influenced by the fact that the pope whose privilege confirming the possessions of Coenwulf seems to have been preserved there, was styled 'Leo papa iunior'; see commentary below, p. 64.

Glauescestrenses (c. 15) in **D** have been emended from *Glauestensibus* and *Glauenses* respectively, the readings preserved by **V**. **V** also reads *Clentho* with **D** (cc. 7 and 11). Apart from these variants, it should be noted that **V** omits 'iunior' from *Leo papa iunior* (c. 10), and also omits the name of the archbishop of Canterbury, Wulfred. All the remaining variant readings of **V** (about 14) are unique to that manuscript, and several came about as part of the process of dividing the text up into appropriate portions, and tying up loose ends where sections of text were omitted. Hence it seems quite likely that **V** actually derives from **D** (or perhaps from a common exemplar), and for this reason its variants have not been included in the critical apparatus.

C, actually the earliest witness to *Vita et miracula*, preserves only a small portion of the text, but where present parallels **D** very closely, and could well have derived from a common exemplar.

H and the slightly older **P** share certain readings which suggest that neither of them can have been copied directly from **D**; for example, *Aschebert(us)* in the preface and cc. 2 and 5; *Eadgitha* (preface); *natalium* for *natalicium* (c. 2); the addition of a rubric to signal the beginning of the miracles (c. 17); *dilecti Dei* (c. 20); *tamen poterat* (c. 23). **P** displays several unique variants which are not shared by **H**, and consequently cannot have served as the exemplar of **H**. But it is possible that the two witnesses derived from a common exemplar (π). This exemplar may have had the Old English Kenelm-couplet copied into the margin, and whereas the scribe of **H** interpolated this into his text, the scribe of **P** preferred to incorporate it in a sketched illustration of the messenger dove in the margin.

Very few of the variant readings of **J** are shared by another witness (just three shared with **L**), but it is interesting to note that, as well as sharing alone with **D** the designation of the prologue as 'prefatio', **J** also reproduces the place-name forms found in **D** (rather as **V** does). For example, in c. 14, **J** alone reads *Glauecestre* with **D**; *Glauescensibus* (c. 14), *Glauenses* (c. 15) and *Pyriuord* (c. 14) are also found in **J**. **J** could, then, have been copied from **D**, but one other variant may point to the likelihood of a common exemplar: in the preface, **J** has *æðelwoldus*, a form which more accurately reproduces the Old English name (as do **H** and **P**) than does *Adeluuoldus* in **D**.

To connect these various groups of witnesses is a complicated matter, not least because on several occasions those from the β recension share readings with those from the other group. Possibly, such shared variants came about through the collation of two or more copies of the text. However, in many cases, the variant readings are relatively minor and could by coincidence have been introduced into the text independently. Examples of this type of variant are **HL**: *Wigorniensis*, **BH**: *cantilene* for *cantilena* (preface); **BHL**: *etheris* for *ethereis* (c. 8); **HL**: omission of *etiam* (c. 10); **BHP**: reversal of *Dei dilecti* (c. 20).

A link between **BGL** and **D** is indicated by the phrase *ipsius quoque passio sacra Parisius perhibetur haberi descripta* found in the preface in **BL**. At the same place in **D**, there is an erasure of about a line and a half of text. Virtually nothing can now be deciphered of what was erased, but some form of words similar to, indeed identical to those found in **B** would fit the space perfectly, and would correspond to the minute remnants of the erased ascenders and descenders. It is possible that the 'Parisius' clause was present in the author's first version of *Vita et miracula*, which ended at c. 30, and from which **B**, **G**, and **L** all derive indirectly.

Shortly after the completion of this version, an extra miracle (c. 31) was perhaps added, and some emendations were made to the text (such as the pope's name), although the 'Parisius' clause was left in; we shall call this version δ. Possibly, the conjectured common exemplar of **H** and **P** (π) was copied from δ, omitting the obscure 'Parisius' clause. **C**, **D**, and **J** may also have been copied from δ.[226] The 'Parisius' clause could have been erased in this common exemplar after the copying of **D** (**C** does not include the preface), but before the copying of **J**. Perhaps the Kenelm couplet was copied into the margin of δ after **C** and **D** were copied from it.

These highly conjectural relationships are summarized in the following *stemma codicum*. It should be borne in mind that at every stage it is impossible to be certain how many intervening exemplars have been lost.

---

[226] Note that **P** occasionally has readings similar to **D** pre-correction, such as *somnum* (c. 3), *Cunuto* and *Niuuentuna* (c. 18), and *Peiletuna* (c. 20). It also follows **D** in the form of the name, *Wincelcumbe* (cc. 3, 15, 17, 31), but not in *Clento*. Of the **CDJHP** group, these two witnesses are the closest in date.

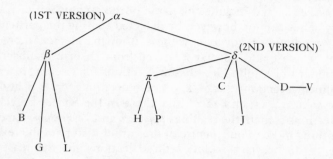

(xii) *Abbreviated Versions of* Vita et miracula

A version of the *Vita et miracula* is to be found in John of Tyne-mouth's *Sanctilogium Anglie*.[227] The text has been heavily abbreviated and, in the process, extensively rewritten, but part, or all, of cc. 1–16, 18, 20, 22–4, 26–8, and 31 are preserved. In particular, the *Miracula* have been greatly abridged, the last five being reduced to one summarizing sentence, or even a single clause, for example, 'quendam ferro accinctum liberauit, contractum gressibus resti-tuit, cecum illuminauit', which dispenses at a stroke with cc. 26–8.[228] The version is therefore of little use in reconstructing the history of the transmission of *Vita et miracula*. Tynemouth clearly had access to a version of the text extending as far as c. 31, which immediately eliminates **B**, **G**, and **L** from the list of possible exemplars. In any case, Tynemouth gave the name of the pope as *Leo papa iunior* in c. 10, contrary to the reading of **BGL**, and supplied the name of the archbishop, Wulfred, in c. 12, which they all fail to do. However, it does not seem possible to demonstrate that any of the surviving manuscripts served as Tynemouth's exemplar.

Further evidence for the dissemination of *Vita et miracula S. Kenelmi* is offered by the sets of lections found in the liturgical books already mentioned. The Sarum breviary provides three quite lengthy lections for the feast of St Kenelm,[229] including all of

[227] *NLA* ii. 110–13. See p. lxxxiii above.
[228] *NLA* ii. 113.
[229] Ed. Procter and Wordsworth, iii. 497–502.

cc. 1, 2, 5, 6, 8–12. The lections were evidently drawn from a version of *Vita et miracula* closely similar to the branch of witnesses which includes **D (V)**, **H, J**, and **P**, since they preserve the reading, *Leo papa iunior*, and include the name of the archbishop of Canterbury. They cannot, however, be detected sharing the particular variant readings of any one witness (though, in fact, there is nothing which could not have derived from **D**, or a manuscript very similar to it). John Grandisson's lections for Exeter preserve the following: lection 1: cc. 1, 2, 5, and 6; lection 2: cc. 6, 8, and 9; lection 3: cc. 10, 11, and 12.[230] Like those in the Sarum breviary, these lections contain the readings *papa Leo* and *Wylfridum*, but can add nothing more to our picture of the earlier history of the text.

The Hyde breviary includes three lections for the feast of Kenelm,[231] which, although heavily abbreviated, derive ultimately from a copy of *Vita et miracula* (lection 1: cc. 1, 2, 5; lection 2: cc. 5, 6, 7; lection 3: cc. 7, 8, 12, and 13). Such brevity means that it is impossible to determine how these lections relate to other witnesses.

(xiii) *Indirect Witnesses to* Vita et miracula

The popularity of the legend of Kenelm ensured that an account of his Life found its way into many of the chronicles of the later medieval historians.

There is a version of *Vita et miracula* in an anonymous historical and hagiographical compilation probably made at St Albans or one of its cells (perhaps Wallingford) in about the second quarter of the thirteenth century, and surviving only in what appears to be the author's autograph manuscript.[232] The Chronicle treats extensively of several saints besides Kenelm, and Vaughan supposed the author to have drawn upon a set of 'Legenda sanctorum'.[233] Certainly, at the end of his account of Kenelm, the author wrote 'si quis uult plenius erudiri, querat ubi legenda eius plenius explicatur'.[234] None of the Lives concerned, including that of Kenelm,

[230] Reynolds, *Legenda Sanctorum*, ii (3), fasc. ii, fos. 84ᵛ–85ʳ, three lections, up to 'solempniter transportatur'. See also *Ordinale Exon.*, ed. Dalton, iii. 283–4.

[231] Ed. Tolhurst, *Monastic Breviary*, iv, fos. 295ʳ⁻ᵛ.

[232] London, BL, Cotton Julius D. vii, fos. 10–33. Ed. R. Vaughan, 'The Chronicle Attributed to John of Wallingford', *Camden Miscellany*, xxi, Camden 3rd Series, xc (London, 1958). The portion relating to Kenelm is at pp. 13–16 and 66–7.

[233] Ibid., p. x.

[234] Ibid. 16. Cf. similar comments on pp. 17 and 23, regarding Botwulf and Edmund respectively.

seems to have been copied directly from any known version, but there are just enough passages transferred *verbatim* to give some clue to the nature of the source.[235] The order of *Vita et miracula* (cc. 1–16) was followed fairly closely, and later on in the Chronicle, a single miracle was included, as pertaining to the reign of Cnut (c. 18). For example, Kenelm's account of his vision is reproduced almost word for word.[236] The chronicler probably had before him some version of the *Vita et miracula* allied to the group **BGL**, since he gave the name of the pope as *Siluester papa iunior,*[237] and also omitted the name of the archbishop of Canterbury.[238] In addition, he was able to supply the Kenelm-couplet: 'In Cleng Cubeche under ane þorne lith Kenelm kenebern eweð beireuueð' (p. 15). Unfortunately, it does not seem possible to demonstrate that any of the surviving manuscripts of *Vita et miracula* were used by the chronicler. It is not inconceivable, however, that a copy of the text was available at St Albans, particularly since the house claimed to possess a relic of Kenelm.[239]

Both in his *De Gestis Regum Anglorum*[240] and his *Gesta Pontificum Anglorum,*[241] William of Malmesbury gave an almost identical account of the Life of St Kenelm, which, although freely rewritten, clearly derived ultimately from the *Vita et miracula.* Roger of Wendover, another historiographer working at St Albans, also incorporated some account of Kenelm into his work, completed between 1231 and 1234.[242] He drew largely upon William of Malmesbury's version of the *Vita et miracula*, although there are a few verbal reminiscences of the original text, in the description of Cwoenthryth's psalter.[243] Thus it is quite likely that Roger actually used the same source as the anonymous 'Wallingford' chronicler in order to expand what he had found in William of Malmesbury. He was able to supply three versions of the Kenelm couplet, the vernacular one, a translation of it similar to that found in *Vita et miracula*, and John de Cella's versification.[244] Matthew Paris

---

[235] Compare the discussion of the anonymous chronicler's use of the *Vita Prima S. Neoti* in Dumville and Lapidge, *Annals of St Neots*, pp. cxxi–cxxiii.

[236] 'Visum est mihi . . .' (c. 3); Vaughan, 'Chronicle', p. 13.

[237] c. 10; Vaughan, 'Chronicle', p. 15.   [238] c. 12; Vaughan, 'Chronicle', p. 15.

[239] Cf. § vii above, on interest in Kenelm at St Albans.

[240] Ed. W. Stubbs, 2 vols., RS xc (London, 1887–9), i. 262–3.

[241] Ed. N. E. S. A. Hamilton, RS lii (London, 1870), pp. 294–5.

[242] *Chronica, siue Flores Historiarum,* ed. H. O. Coxe, 4 vols., English Historical Society, viii (London, 1841–4), i. 273–5.

[243] Ibid. 274.   [244] See pp. cxvii–cxviii above.

copied Roger of Wendover's description of Kenelm's passion almost verbatim.[245]

Ranulph Higden, a Benedictine monk of St Werburg's, Chester, writing during the first half of the fourteenth century, drew explicitly upon William of Malmesbury for his account of Kenelm.[246] However, he also had available a copy of the Kenelm couplet in both the vernacular version and the Latin of the *Vita et miracula*.

A Middle English version of the Life of Kenelm, closely based upon *Vita et miracula*, is to be found in the 'L' (Glos./Oxon.) redaction of the South English legendary, and reflects the continuing popularity of the story in the late thirteenth and fourteenth centuries.[247] On only a few occasions does this Middle English text supply information not to be found in *Vita et miracula*, for example, in lines 251–6, where it is stated that the monks of Winchcombe built a chapel of St Kenelm on Salter's Hill.[248]

Richard of Cirencester's *Speculum Historiale de Gestis Regum Anglie*, written at some point in the fourteenth century, contains a very full version of *Vita et miracula S. Kenelmi* (book 11, chapter 67).[249] Apart from the preface, the entire text up to 'infixos habuerat' (c. 31) is present. The text is, for the most part, close to that of **D**, except for the three distinguishing variants of the group **BGL**. It is possible that Richard had access to, or had seen on his travels, more than one copy of the *Vita*, and was able to compare and conflate different versions, to achieve what seemed the 'best' text.[250] A careful study of Richard's treatment of the other *Vitae* included in his *Speculum*, and of the contents of the library at Westminster where he was working, would be a necessary first step in determining the status of this witness. Richard also included three

---

[245] *Mattaei Parisiensis Monachi S. Albani Chronica Maiora*, ed. H. R. Luard, 7 vols., RS lvii (London, 1872–83), i. 373.

[246] *Polychronicon Ranulphi Higden Monachi Cestrensis*, ed. J. R. Lumby, 9 vols., RS xli (London, 1865–86), iv. 304–8.

[247] Ed. C. Horstmann, *The Early South-English Legendary*, EETS, os lxxxvii (1887), pp. 345–55; C. D'Evelyn and A. J. Mill, *The South English Legendary*, EETS, os ccxxxv, ccxxxvi, ccxliv (1956–9), i. 282–91; and also J. A. W. Bennett and G. V. Smithers, *Early Middle English Verse and Prose*, 2nd edn. (Oxford, 1968), pp. 97–107. A shorter version, independently derived from *Vita et Miracula*, occurs in the 'G' (Worcs./Warks.) redaction. See Görlach, *Textual Tradition*, pp. 35, 51–4, and 179–80.

[248] Bennett and Smithers, p. 106.

[249] Cambridge, UL, Ff. 1. 28, fos. 102ᵛ–107ᵛ; ed. J. E. B. Mayor, 2 vols., RS xxx (1863–9), i. 309–21.

[250] For an account of the life and activities of, and sources used by, Richard of Cirencester, see the introduction to Mayor's edn. of the *Speculum*.

other saints' Lives, those of Offa (c. 61), Ethelbert (c. 64), and Edmund (c. 70), in a similarly lengthy form.

(xiv) *Previous Editions of* Vita et miracula

The *Vita brevior* and *Vita et miracula S. Kenelmi* have been edited only once before, as the appendix to an unpublished German doctoral dissertation, by Rurik von Antropoff.[251] The principal disadvantage of von Antropoff's edition is its inaccessibility. There are occasional inaccuracies in his reading of the manuscripts, and he seems to have been unaware of the existence of **P**. In the fourth volume of the July portion of *Acta Sanctorum*, the Bollandists reproduced only Tynemouth's abbreviation of *Vita et miracula*.[252]

---

[251] 'Die Entwicklung der Kenelm-Legende', pp. xxxiii–xxxvi and iv–xxiv respectively.

[252] *ActaS*, Iulii, iv. 300–1.

4. ST RUMWOLD OF BUCKINGHAM AND *VITA SANCTI RVMWOLDI*

(i) *St Rumwold*

EMBARKING upon an account of St Rumwold, Thomas Fuller (1608–61), having battled with the identity of the saint, exclaimed in exasperation, 'Reader, I request thee to take this ... on my credit for thy own ease, and not to buy the truth of so difficult a trifle with the trouble I paid for it.'[1] Even now, the cult of Rumwold of Buckingham remains shrouded in obscurity. The eleventh-century *Vita S. Rumwoldi* (*BHL* 7385) describes the three-day life of a Mercian infant saint, born the grandson of King Penda (632–55), and son of an unnamed king of Northumbria. He was enabled miraculously to speak at birth, confessing the faith, demanding baptism and communion, and preaching on wisdom and the Trinity, before predicting his own death and giving instructions as to where his body was to rest, naming first his birth-place, King's Sutton, then Brackley, and finally Buckingham. The story is preserved by no other surviving source and we are obliged to turn immediately to liturgical documents for the first recoverable references to the saint.

(ii) *The Liturgical Evidence*

The earliest evidence for a cult of St Rumwold is provided by liturgical calendars which preserve a commemoration of the saint's feast on 3 November, namely those found in Salisbury Cathedral 150,[2] London, BL, Cotton Nero A. II;[3] and London, BL, Addit. 37517.[4] From these we may reasonably infer that the cult was known in some form before the end of the tenth century. Rumwold is to be found not only in the calendar in the Winchester psalter, London, BL, Arundel 60 (fos. 2–7^v),[5] but also as the seventeenth of

---

[1] Fuller, *The History of the Worthies of England*, ed. P. A. Nuttall, 3 vols. (London, 1840), i. 194.

[2] Wormald, *English Kalendars*, no. 2 (s. x^2), 'Rumuualdi', mistakenly labelled as a martyr.   [3] Ibid. no. 3, 'Rumpaldi'.

[4] Ibid. no. 5, Canterbury (s. x^{ex}), 'Rumpaldi', entered under 2 Nov., instead of 3.

[5] Ibid. no. 11, Winchester, New Minster (s. xi^2), 'Rumpaldi'.

the confessors in the litany in that manuscript (fos. 130^r–132^v).[6] His feast on 3 November is marked as a later eleventh-century addition to the Worcester calendars in Oxford, Bodleian Library, Hatton 113, and CCCC 9, possibly by the same hand.[7] It is likely that these additions were made at roughly the same time as *Vita S. Rumwoldi* was copied at Worcester as an addition to the legendary in CCCC 9.[8] Such a gesture could be construed in several ways: the bringing of a copy of the *Vita* to that house could have stimulated the saint's insertion into the annual round of commemorations, or conversely, the nominal introduction of Rumwold's cult could have aroused sufficient curiosity to warrant the acquisition (perhaps even composition) of a text describing his claim to sanctity. As with so many other aspects of the cult of Rumwold, both of these conjectures lack supporting evidence.

St Rumwold is not to be found in any existing martyrologies, and is very seldom commemorated in surviving post-Conquest calendars, apart from the one from Worcester mentioned above, and one in a late twelfth- or early thirteenth-century psalter, Cambridge, St John's College 233 (K. 30), of unknown origin, where the entry 'Rumaldi Archiep' occurs against 3 November.[9] In addition to these, Rumwold's name also occurs in the calendars of two fifteenth-century books of hours, Oxford, Bodleian Library, Rawlinson liturg. g. 1 (*SC* 15833) and Bodleian Library, Liturg. 299 (*SC* 30618).[10] Overall, Rumwold's cult does not appear to have gained wide ecclesiastical acceptance, and was soon largely abandoned and forgotten. 28 August was apparently marked at Brackley as the date of the translation of Rumwold's remains thither,[11] but

---

[6] Lapidge, *Anglo-Saxon Litanies*, p. 68.

[7] Wormald, *English Kalendars*, nos. 16 and 18, both 'Rumuuoldi'. Rumwold is also included in the calendar in the early 12th-cent. Worcester MS, Cambridge, St John's College, 42 (B. 20); see M. R. James, *A Descriptive Catalogue of the Manuscripts in the Library of St John's College, Cambridge* (Cambridge, 1913), pp. 57–64.

[8] St Nicholas was also added to the December portion of the CCCC 9 calendar in the same hand and *Vita S. Nicolai* was another of the texts added to the legendary; see above p. xxii.

[9] See James, *Descriptive Catalogue of the Manuscripts in the Library of St John's College*, pp. 271–3.

[10] Neither of these books can be assigned to any particular centre, though a connection with the diocese of Lincoln seems likely in both cases.

[11] R. Stanton, *A Menology of England and Wales or, Brief Memorials of the Ancient British and English Saints* (London, 1887), p. 419, although Stanton omitted to mention his specific source. Nicholas Roscarrock (*c.* 1549–1634), in his MS compilation of saints' Lives (Cambridge, UL, Addit. 3041, fo. 390^r), stated that the August feast was known 'by the warrant of the Register of Brackley', which I have been unable to trace.

no surviving calendar or martyrology preserves this secondary feast day.

Except for the aforementioned items, not a shred of liturgical evidence for the commemoration of Rumwold survives in England. Although Winchester, Canterbury and Worcester chose to acknowledge the memory of Rumwold, it appears that no necessity was felt for more elaborate commemoration. The only indication that Rumwold was commemorated other than nominally in any of these places is the fact that the Worcester copy of *Vita S. Rumwoldi* (CCCC 9) was at some stage marked out for three lections, possibly for use at nocturns.

The single surviving trace of Rumwold's liturgical cult is preserved in Sweden, in the fragments of a twelfth-century missal and of a breviary in the Swedish State Archives in Stockholm.[12] These fragments had, since the sixteenth century, served as wrappings for archival material relating to landholdings. Of the missal, only two leaves survive, containing mass-sets for November. Between those for St Eustace (2 November) and St Leonard (6 November), there is a fragmentary set for St Rumwold:[13]

SANCTI RVMWOLDI
Deus qui hodiernam diem gloriosi confessoris tui Rumwoldi sollempnitate declarasti, tribue quesumus, ut quicumque beneficia tua in eius ueneratione deposcimus, de quacumque necessitate pecierimus, ipso suffragante solatium capiamus.

SECRETA
Munera hec presentia altari tuo superposita omnipotens Deus, beato Rumwoldo interueniente[. . .]odorem suauitatis[. . .]perhennia. Per.

POSTCOMMVNIO
Sumpta domine quesumus libamina in honorem tui nominis immolata beati Rumwoldi meritis cuius sollempnia colimus nobis obtine[. . .]

The remaining parts of the mass were probably intended to be taken from the Common of a Confessor. The fragment of the breviary contains only the same collect for Rumwold as that found

---

[12] T. Schmid, 'Smärre Liturgiska Bidrag, XII', *Nordisk Tidskrift för Bok- och Biblioteksväsen*, xxv (1938), 98–110, at pp. 108–10. Cf. a review of this material by P. Grosjean in *AB* lix (1941), 344. See also J. Toy, 'The Commemorations of British Saints in the Medieval Liturgical Manuscripts of Scandinavia', *Kyrkohistorisk årsskrift* (1982), 91–103, at p. 100.

[13] Swedish State Archives CF Mi 697. The dots [. . .] indicate portions of the text now destroyed or illegible.

in the missal.[14] It is not known for certain where the missal and breviary were written, probably either Uppsala or Strängnäs, but the fact that both contain the same collects (not only in the case of Rumwold), suggests, at least, that they are of similar origin.[15] St Rumwold is not commemorated in any surviving Swedish liturgical calendar. Probably the feast was of relatively low grade, since only three portions of the propers for the mass are provided in the missal, and, apparently, only a collect and no lections for nocturns, in the breviary.

Although there had been previous attempts to evangelize Sweden, conversion was only carried out systematically during the eleventh century by English missionaries.[16] It must follow then that the liturgy of the Swedish Church was heavily influenced by England,[17] and that such a relationship probably involved the provision of the necessary books. These fragments do not square with the absence of Rumwold in liturgical manuscripts surviving in England. But since the prayers are unlikely to have been composed specifically for use in Sweden, they must derive from a centre in England which formerly venerated Rumwold liturgically. Possibly, the importation of the mass-set and collect to Sweden predated a decline in Rumwold's liturgical cult in England. There does not, however, seem to be any means of determining from which centre in England the prayers were transported.

(iii) *Relics of St Rumwold*

Apart from the bones of Rumwold which rested at Buckingham until the sixteenth century, there is only one very ambiguous record of a claim to possess his relics.[18] The fifteenth-century relic-list preserved in the processional, Salisbury, Cathedral Library, 148, at fos. 15ᵛ–19ᵛ, includes, 'A relike of Seint Rumwald' (fo. 16ᵛ), under the list of martyrs whose relics were claimed for

---

[14] Swedish State Archives CF Br 361.

[15] Schmid, *art. cit.*, without giving reasons, expressed the opinion that the texts could not be of Benedictine origin (p. 110).

[16] Cf. P. Sawyer, 'The process of Scandinavian Christianization in the tenth and eleventh centuries', in *The Christianization of Scandinavia*, ed. B. Sawyer, P. Sawyer, and I. Wood (Alingsås, 1987), pp. 68–77.

[17] See C. J. A. Oppermann, *The English Missionaries in Sweden and Finland* (London, 1937), pp. 121–2, on the inclusion of Anglo-Saxon saints in Swedish liturgical calendars; and cf. Toy, 'Commemorations', p. 91.

[18] See Thomas, 'Saints' Relics', p. 455.

Salisbury.[19] The word 'confessor' was later added in the margin, presumably to correct the error of including Rumwold among the martyrs. It is likely therefore that the original entry was actually intended for St Rombaut/Rumold of Mechlin, who was a martyr.[20]

The early eleventh-century list of saints' resting-places, *Secgan be þam Godes sanctum þe on Engla lande ærost reston*, includes an entry for Rumwold: 'Ðonne resteð sancte Rumwold on þare stowe, þe is gehaten Buccyngaham, neah þare ea Usan'.[21] Two post-Conquest lists of resting places, namely that contained in the twelfth-century *Chronicle of Hugh Candidus*,[22] and a fourteenth-century Anglo-Norman list, bound up at the end of the Breviate of Domesday,[23] include, in addition to Rumwold at Buckingham, reference to a Rumwald at 'Hah'.[24] This 'Hah' is possibly identifiable as Haugh in Lincolnshire,[25] but there is no other surviving reference to a second Rumwald.[26]

(iv) *The Cult of St Rumwold at King's Sutton*

In 1525, one Thomas Westall gave 8*d.* in his will, for the maintenance of the altar of St Rumwold in the parish church of King's Sutton (St Peter, or St Peter and St Paul).[27] The altar has long since disappeared, and, apart from Westall's donation, no documents alluding to the earlier veneration of St Rumwold at King's Sutton seem to be recoverable. The oldest portion of the fabric of

[19] Ed. Wordsworth, *Ceremonies and Processions*, p. 35.

[20] Compare this with the error in the calendar in Salisbury Cathedral 150, noted above, p. cxl. Relics of St Rombaut were claimed at Hyde Abbey and at Westminster Abbey; see Thomas, 'Saints' Relics', p. 454. On this saint, see pp. cli–clii, below.

[21] Liebermann, *Die Heiligen*, p. 13 (no. 19a).

[22] Ed. W. T. Mellows (London, 1949), pp. 59–64.

[23] Printed by T. D. Hardy and C. T. Martin (eds.), *Lestorie des Engles solum La Translacion Maistre Geffrei Gaimar*, 2 vols., RS xci (1888–9), i, pp. xxxix–xlii.

[24] Mellows, *Hugh Candidus*, p. 62, 'Et in Hah sanctus Rumuualdus'. Cf. 'Et in Bucingeham sanctus Rumoldus trium noctium puer', p. 61; Hardy and Martin, pp. xl and xli.

[25] Cf. a grant of 1042–55 to St Peter, *Hah* (Haugh, Lincs.); *The Early Charters of Eastern England*, ed. C. R. Hart (Leicester, 1966), p. 246.

[26] Cf. L. Butler, 'Church dedications and the cults of Anglo-Saxon saints in England', in *The Anglo-Saxon Church. Papers on History, Architecture and Archaeology in Honour of Dr H. M. Taylor*, CBA Research Report lx, ed. L. A. S. Butler and R. K. Morris (London, 1986), 44–50, at p. 47, where it is suggested that *Hah* = Buckingham, which flies somewhat in the face of the fact that 'Rumwold' appears *twice* in the list, once at Buckingham and once at this not certainly identified resting-place.

[27] Serjeantson and Longden, 'Parish Churches', pp. 354–5.

the present church is datable to the later twelfth century,[28] but it has been shown that there was probably an Anglo-Saxon church on the site.[29] There is evidence that King's Sutton was also formerly an ecclesiastical centre of some importance. Michael Franklin has argued that it was the site of an early minster church, with control over a large surrounding area, and the power to exact church-scot.[30] Furthermore, the present font in the church is apparently of early date. The medieval font was removed by the Victorians, but fortunately not before it had been recorded in two drawings (dating from between 1820 and 1840), and described as a rough-hewn tub-shaped bowl.[31] In 1923, the Victorian Gothic font was, in its turn, abandoned; a stone found in the churchyard was set up in its place and is still in use. Although somewhat shorter, the present roughly octagonal font-stone may well be a portion of the one sketched in the 1820s, since some of its dimensions match those in the description of the discarded font. There are numerous examples of Norman tub-shaped octagonal fonts, and the stone at King's Sutton could, in theory, date from the same century as *Vita S. Rumwoldi*.[32] Franklin suggested that the existence of an ancient font at King's Sutton could be proof that the church had possessed baptismal rights.[33]

In 1086, King's Sutton was a royal holding, and had previously been held by the Confessor.[34] It seems to have enjoyed the status of a royal vill, as the name suggests, and as the eleventh-century author of *Vita S. Rumwoldi* hinted was the case: 'Vocatur autem locus ille nunc ab incolis . . . Suthtunus, in quo etiam pagus situs est regie dignitati subministrans debita decreto tempore obsequia'

---

[28] N. Pevsner, *Northamptonshire*, revised B. Cherry, BofE, 2nd edn. (Harmondsworth, 1973), pp. 278–9.

[29] M. J. Franklin, 'The identification of minsters in the Midlands', *Anglo-Norman Studies*, vii (1984), 69–88, p. 85.

[30] Franklin, 'Identification', pp. 81–3; see also id., 'Minsters and parishes: Northamptonshire studies' (unpublished Ph.D. dissertation, Cambridge 1982), chap. 5, esp. pp. 261–9. Cf. J. Blair, 'Minster churches in the landscape', in *Anglo-Saxon Settlements*, ed. D. Hooke (Oxford, 1988), pp. 35–58, at 50; and id., 'Introduction: from minster to parish church', in *Minsters and Parishes: The Local Church in Transition, 950–1200*, ed. J. Blair, Oxford University Committee for Archaeology Monographs xvii (1988), pp. 1–19.

[31] See G. N. Clark, 'The legend of St Rumbold', *Northamptonshire Past and Present*, iii (1962), 131–5, at pp. 134–5, where one of the drawings is reproduced.

[32] Pevsner, *Northants*, p. 279; and see F. Bond, *Fonts and Font Covers* (Oxford, 1908; repr., London, 1985), pp. 144–205.

[33] 'Minsters and parishes', p. 267.   [34] *DB, Northants*, i. 8 (i. 219c).

(c. 6). How far back in time such royal connections stretch is difficult to determine.[35] It has been conjectured that as early as the Iron Age, King's Sutton lay at the centre of a substantial 'estate', comprehending Astrop and Walton.[36]

In Astrop, a hamlet on the north-eastern outskirts of King's Sutton, there is a spring known locally as St Rumbold's well. A mid-eighteenth-century edifice with a round niche presently houses the spring, in a valley to the south of a large mansion, Astrop Park.[37] In 1664, Dr Richard Lower and Dr Thomas Willis, on a journey to visit some patients, came across this spring. Returning subsequently, they carried out some experiments to test the powers of the water, and 'being persuaded of its efficacy, recommended it in their practice'.[38] John Aubrey told a different version, in which the discovery is attributed to Dr Willis alone, and to the year 1657. Willis is said to have noted the orange tinge to the stones in the stream and, upon testing the water, declared 'Ile not send my patients now so far as Tunbridge'.[39]

Whatever the truth of the matter, the spa had, by the middle of the eighteenth century, become a much-frequented resort, and Astrop could boast of a 'public ball every Monday and breakfast, cards, dancing and ordinary . . . every Friday during the season'.[40] In 1749, a replica well was set up, half a mile away from the first. It can still be viewed today, by the side of the minor road heading

---

[35] Franklin, 'Identification', p. 81, suggests, somewhat inaccurately, that *Vita S. Rumwoldi* 'postulates a *villa regia* here in the time of Penda', but the text describes the place of Rumwold's birth as 'quodam ameno prato' (c. 3), and only subsequently mentions the royal status of King's Sutton 'nunc', that is, at the time of writing. In c. 12 the hagiographer implies that all Rumwold's resting-places were, at the time of the saint's burial, relatively insignificant.

[36] F. Brown and C. C. Taylor, 'Settlement and land use in Northants: a comparison between the Iron Age and the Middle Ages', in *Lowland Iron Age Communities in Europe*, British Archaeological Reports, International Series, xlviii (1978), 77–89.

[37] See M. Valentine, *Holy Wells of Northamptonshire* (1984), p. 7; and J. E. B. Gover, A. Mawer, and F. M. Stenton, *The Place-Names of Northamptonshire*, EPNS x (Cambridge, 1933), p. 59; and Pevsner, *Northants.*, pp. 95–6.

[38] G. Baker, *The History and Antiquities of the County of Northampton*, 2 vols. (London, 1822–30), i. 703; see also W. Whellan, *History, Gazetteer and Directory of Northamptonshire* (Peterborough, 1849), and P. Whalley (ed.), *The History and Antiquities of Northamptonshire, compiled from the Manuscript Collections of the Late Learned Antiquary John Bridges*, 2 vols. (Oxford, 1791), i. 180.

[39] Baker, *History*, p. 703; J. Aubrey, *Letters written by Eminent Persons in the Seventeenth and Eighteenth Century to which are added . . . Lives of Eminent Men*, 2 vols. in 3 (London, 1813), ii (2). 585. A fascinating and detailed analysis of the properties of the waters of Astrop may be found in J. Morton, *The Natural History of Northamptonshire* (London, 1712), pp. 281–2.

[40] Baker, *History*, p. 704.

northwards out of King's Sutton, and the waters may yet be taken by those who dare.

Although Lower and Willis claimed to have discovered the spring, local memory apparently retained a tradition connecting it with Rumwold, and the physicians merely confirmed the healthfulness of the waters with the aid of science.[41] It has not proved possible to determine how far back such a tradition reaches, that is, whether the association with Rumwold is of any antiquity. Not inconceivably, the connection was, in fact, made only in the seventeenth century. That period saw the rise of gentlemanly interest in local antiquities, which, alongside natural history, found expression in county histories such as that based upon the work of Bridges.[42] Hence, the association between the local saint and the healing waters may simply have been a fanciful invention on the part of either the discoverers or those who first recorded the discovery.

Just a mile or so south-east of King's Sutton, in the now-deserted village of Walton Grounds, there was formerly a small chapel dedicated to Rumwold. Leland reported that 'St Rumoalde was born in this paroche [scil. King's Sutton]. There was of late a chappell dedicate to hym, standinge about a mile from Southtowne in the medes, defacid and taken downe.'[43] Already by the end of the eighteenth century, only two houses remained in Walton.[44] Foundations of the chapel could still be seen in the earlier part of the nineteenth century, in what was known as Chapel Field,[45] and all traces of the deserted village were only finally obliterated in the 1960s by heavy ploughing.[46] This long-gone chapel may have marked the supposed site of Rumwold's birth, in the fields, but, like the fabric itself, all record of the date at which the building was instituted has now vanished.

[41] Cf. the comments of R. C. Finucane on the rise of health spas as a substitute for shrines and relics as a focus not only for bodily renewal but for social diversion, in *Miracles and Pilgrims. Popular Beliefs in Medieval England* (London, 1977), pp. 215–16.

[42] Cf. S. Piggott, *Ancient Britons and the Antiquarian Imagination: Ideas from the Renaissance to the Regency* (London, 1989), pp. 21–7.

[43] Toulmin-Smith, *Itinerary*, ii. 38.

[44] Bridges, *History*, ed. Whalley, i. 180–1. See K. J. Allison, M. W. Beresford, and J. G. Hurst, *The Deserted Villages of Northamptonshire*, Department of English Local History Occasional Papers, xviii (Leicester University, 1966), pp. 47–8.

[45] Baker, *History*, p. 708.

[46] *Royal Commission for Historical Monuments: The County of Northamptonshire*, iv (London, 1982), p. 93.

(v) The Cult at Brackley and Buckingham

At Brackley (Northants), a well, known formerly as 'St Rumwold's Well', near the parish church (St Peter), is all that now marks the town's claim to have been Rumwold's second supposed resting-place.[47] Likewise, in Buckingham, about 600 yards from the parish church of St Peter, in Prebend End, there is a well of St Rumwold. The well-house is a small single-storey building, with a stone bearing the date 1623.[48] The well has given its name to Well Street, and near by is St Rumbold's Lane. No evidence is available from which to determine how long Rumwold's name has been attached to either of these wells. R. H. Hagerty, in his recent account of the cult of St Rumwold, implies that veneration at the shrine in Buckingham church was suppressed by Oliver Sutton (bishop of Lincoln, 1280–99) in 'around 1280'.[49] The reference he supplies to support this statement is a brief account of the cult of Rumwold written in the late nineteenth century.[50] There it is claimed that Sutton attempted to prohibit veneration at the above-mentioned well of St Rumwold, rather than at the shrine itself, although no authority or source was cited. There is no record in either the *Registrum Antiquissimum* of Lincoln Cathedral,[51] or among the surviving memoranda of Oliver Sutton, of an injunction referring specifically to either the well or the shrine at Buckingham.[52] Records of similar injunctions do exist; for example, that issued 'Contra uenerantes fontem de Lincelade', announcing that pilgrimage to the holy well at Linslade was forbidden on pain of

[47] Toulmin-Smith, *Itinerary*, ii. 37. Leland noted the existence of 'St Rumoaldes Welle' in Brackley, but confused the issue by adding 'wher they say that with in a fewe days of his birth he prechid', which, according to *Vita S. Rumwoldi* could only refer to Sutton, and not Brackley. Cf. Bridges, *History*, ed. Whalley, i. 143; and Gover *et al.*, *Place-Names of Northants*, p. 50.

[48] *Royal Commission on the Historical Monuments of England: The County of Buckinghamshire*, ii (1913), p. 74. Note that the well-house was erected just forty years before the 'rediscovery' of the well at Astrop.

[49] 'The Buckinghamshire saints reconsidered, 3: St Rumwold (Rumbold) of Buckingham', *Records of Buckinghamshire*, xxx (1988), 103–10, at p. 103.

[50] By A. Clear, in *The Buckinghamshire Miscellany, A Series of Concise and Interesting Articles illustrative of the History, Topography and Archaeology of the County of Buckingham*, ed. R. Gibbs (Aylesbury, 1891), p. 208.

[51] Ed. C. W. Foster and K. Major, 10 vols., Lincoln Record Society, xxvii–xxix, xxxii, xxxiv, xli, xlvi, li, lii, lxvii (Hereford and Lincoln, 1931–73).

[52] *The Rolls and Register of Bishop Oliver Sutton (1280–1299)*, ed. R. M. T. Hill, 8 vols., Lincoln Record Society, xxxix, xliii, xlviii, lii, lx, lxiv, lxix, lxxvi (Hereford and Lincoln, 1948–86).

excommunication,[53] and also 'Contra uenerantes fontem qui dicitur sancti Edmundi'.[54] Thus it is possible that a prohibition, which has not survived, was also laid upon Buckingham, or that pronouncements in general concerning superstition were taken to embrace all such wells and places of popular resort.

From the later Middle Ages there are numerous testimonies to the existence of a cult of Rumwold at the shrine, which was apparently situated at the east end of the south aisle of the old parish church of Buckingham.[55] One John Barton, in his will (dated 5 June, 1431), expressed a desire to be buried in St Peter's church, in 'St Rumbald's Isle [scil. aisle]', and required his brother to provide for a lamp to burn perpetually before the saint.[56] The same aisle of St Rumwold is referred to in the will (dated 1477) of Richard Fowler, Chancellor of the Duchy of Lancaster. Not only did that gentleman desire to rest there, but he also directed that the aforesaid aisle, already partly refitted, should be 'fully made and performed up perfitely in all Things att my Costs and Charge; and in the same Isle that there be made of new, a Toumbe of Shrine for the said Sainte, where the old is now standinge, and that it be made curiously with Marble, in Length and Breadth as shall be thought by myne Executors most convenient, Consideration had to the Rome [scil. room]; and upon the same Tombe or Shryne, I will that there be sett a Coffyn or a Chest, curiously wrought and gilte, as it apperteynith for to lay in the Bones of the same Saint.'[57]

When the vicarage was instituted at Buckingham in 1445, the document of institution stipulated: 'quod quilibet Vicarius perpetuus in dicta capella de Buckingham ... in eadem percipiat et habeat ... omnes et omnimodas oblaciones in quatuor festis principalibus ... et ad tumbam siue ad feretrum S. Rumwoldi in dicta capella qualitercunque obuenientes et prouenientes.'[58] In 1449, the guild of St Rumwold asked the King to grant them official recognition: 'Parochiani Ecclesiae SS. Petri et Pauli de Bokingham, a non modico tempore propriis sumptibus sustentarunt quandam pauperem fraternitatem, ob specialem deuotionem

---

[53] Ibid. vi. 186, issued 26 June 1299.
[54] Ibid. iii. 37, issued 26 August 1290.
[55] B. Willis, *The History and Antiquities of the Town, Hundred and Deanery of Buckingham* (London, 1755), p. 61.
[56] Ibid. 55.   [57] Ibid. 57–8.   [58] Ibid. 76–7.

quam habent ad gloriosum Christi Confessorem S. Romwaldum, cuius in Ecclesia praedicta translatum fuit.'[59]

It has not proved possible to recover earlier references to these arrangements at Buckingham, nor do any physical traces of the aisle and shrine of Rumwold survive today. The old parish church of St Peter was demolished in 1776, after the tower collapsed (the spire had already fallen in 1699), and the present building was erected between 1777 and 1781, on Castle Hill, slightly north-east of the original site.[60] It has recently been observed that, according to an engraving signed by Michael Burghers (d. 1727), the upper stage of the crossing tower of the old church at Buckingham showed decoration strongly reminiscent of that found on a group of Anglo-Saxon towers, including Brigstock, Barnack, and Earls Barton.[61] Certain features suggest that the Buckingham tower may have been a relatively late one, datable perhaps to the first half of the eleventh century, rather than the tenth.

Such a tower has been shown to have been a sign of high status in an Anglo-Saxon church, and as particularly characteristic of minsters in the Northamptonshire area. It cannot be stated with absolute certainty that Buckingham was an 'old minster' in the tenth and eleventh centuries, but the record of Domesday Book, showing that it was a substantially endowed church, strongly suggests that this was the case.[62] As such, then, Buckingham church would probably have been administered by a community of canons or priests.

According to the Domesday survey the church was held from Edward the Confessor by Wulfwig, bishop of Dorchester (1053–67), and retained by Bishop Remigius (1067–92) in 1086. In 1072, Remigius had begun the gradual process of transferring the see from Dorchester to Lincoln. In establishing the chapter of Lincoln along secular lines, at some time prior to 1092 (the dedication of the cathedral), he may have founded some prebends from the pre-

[59] *Calendar of Patent Rolls in the Public Record Office: Henry VI*, v, *1446–52* (London, 1909), p. 303.

[60] J. W. Bell, *The Parish Church of SS Peter and Paul, Buckingham*, 5th revised edn. (Buckingham, 1990), p. 5; and cf. N. Pevsner, *Buckinghamshire*, BofE (1960), pp. 73–4.

[61] I am grateful to John Blair, who kindly drew this to my attention, and gave me a draft copy of his unpublished article 'The lost late Anglo-Saxon church tower at Buckingham'. The engraving appears as the frontispiece in the Buckinghamshire County Museum copy of Willis, *History and Antiquities*—it has not been found in any other copies of that work.

[62] *DB, Bucks* B2 (i. 143a). Cf. Barlow, *English Church*, pp. 188–91.

existing endowments of the see of Dorchester, Buckingham church being amongst them.[63] Somewhat later, but before 1122, that prebend was augmented through the addition of the church of King's Sutton with land in Horley (Oxfordshire) by royal grant, and thereafter styled Sutton-cum-Buckingham.[64] This act of amalgamation has led to some confusion over the ecclesiastical status of Buckingham, since, whatever its value and mode of administration either before or afterwards, when the vicarage of King's Sutton was ordained in 1277, it was stated that the vicar shall be in receipt of 'duas marcas annuatim de capellis de Buk. et Horle pertinentibus ad ecclesiam memoratam [i.e. Sutton]'.[65] This seeming subordination of Buckingham to King's Sutton has caused some commentators to hesitate, in view of Buckingham's civil status.[66] It is, however, by no means clear that Buckingham had ever been exactly subordinate to King's Sutton, at least not before the later eleventh- or early twelfth-century rearrangements, nor in practical terms thereafter. Franklin has suggested that *Vita S. Rumwoldi* may be used as evidence of a much earlier connection between the two places,[67] although it must be borne in mind that the text is quite as likely to reflect almost exclusively eleventh-century concerns, a point to which we shall return below.[68]

(vi) *Churches Dedicated to Rumwold/Rumbold*

There are still several churches preserving a dedication to St Rumwold or Rumbold,[69] and evidence is available for others which have not survived. It must be borne in mind that any of these dedications could, in theory, be to St Rombaut/Rumold, the

[63] See *John le Neve: Fasti Ecclesiae Anglicanae 1066–1300* iii, *Lincoln*, compiled D. E. Greenway (London, 1977), pp. ix–x. Cf. *Registrum Antiquissimum*, i. 2–4 (authority to transfer the see).

[64] Grant of Henry I (1110–22); *Registrum Antiquissimum*, i. 33; cf. Greenway, *John le Neve*, iii. 99–100. The grant refers to 'ecclesias de Sutona', and it is not obvious which churches are intended by this, perhaps the chapel at Horley, or even the one at Walton Grounds.

[65] *Rotuli Ricardi Gravesend, episcopi Lincolniensis MCCLVIII–MCCLXXIX*, ed. F. N. Davis, C. W. Foster, and A. Hamilton Thompson, Lincoln Record Society Publications xx (1925), pp. 254–5.

[66] Cf. Willis, *History*, p. 79. Baker described the apparent dependency of Buckingham as 'an extraordinary and unique anomaly in the civil and religious institutions of the kingdom', *History*, p. 692; and cf. p. 696.

[67] 'Minsters and Parishes', pp. 265–6.

[68] § viii, p. clxi.

[69] Arnold-Forster, *Church Dedications*, i. 172.

patron saint of Mechlin (Malines) in Flanders. Although eleventh-century tradition claimed that this saint was Irish or Scots,[70] his name actually suggests an Anglo-Saxon origin, and he seems to have been a missionary who joined Willibrord in his work in the Brabant and in Holland, until he was (supposedly) murdered at Mechlin in about 775. There is little sign that St Rombaut was venerated in Anglo-Saxon England. Certainly his feast is not marked in any surviving pre-conquest calendar, nor is there other evidence for early liturgical commemoration.[71]

If all the following dedications were to be taken as authentically referring to Rumwold of Buckingham, they would be the mark of a remarkably widespread and popular cult, for which it is at present difficult adequately to account. The problem is, not least, one of determining the antiquity of each dedication. Note, however, that none of the places traditionally connected with Rumwold, that is, King's Sutton, Brackley, and Buckingham, preserves a dedication to that saint, nor is there evidence that any of them were so dedicated in the past. It has recently been suggested that the several dedications to Rumwold in the counties south of the Humber may be accounted for by the southwards missionary activities of St Wilfrid in the second half of the seventh century.[72] The contention that Wilfrid could have been acquainted with the cult of St Rumwold leans rather heavily upon the eleventh-century hagiographer's claim that the infant's father was a Northumbrian king, and as such remains decidedly in the realms of speculation.[73]

(*a*) Stoke Doyle, Northamptonshire, is dedicated to St Rumbald, probably because of its relative proximity to the main centres of

[70] The earliest witnesses to his cult are three early 9th-cent. Continental litanies, on which see B. de Gaiffier, 'Attestations anciennes sur le culte de S. Rombaut', *Sacris Erudiri*, xxvi (1983), 51–5. *Passio S. Rumoldi* (*BHL* 7381), composed in the 1090s by Theodoric of Saint-Trond, makes him of Scots origin, eventually to be murdered by two thieves who wanted his money; see *ActaS*, Iulii, i (1719), pp. 241–7. A later version (*BHL* 7383) claimed that he was the son of a Scots king, David, and became bishop of Dublin. He abandoned this post to become a missionary at Mechlin, where he was murdered by two men whose evil ways he had denounced in his preaching (*BHL* 7383; *ActaS*, Iulii, i. 177–8). His feast was generally kept on 1 July.

[71] On account of his supposed Scots origin, an abbreviated Life of Rombaut is to be found in the Aberdeen breviary—W. J. Blew, ed., *Breviarium Aberdonense*, 2 vols. (Edinburgh, 1854), ii. 16–17.

[72] Hagerty, 'Buckinghamshire saints', p. 108.

[73] See p. clxiii below.

the saint's early cult (it was held by the men of the cathedral church of Peterborough in 1086).[74]

(*b*) In Colchester High Street, there is still a church of St Runwald.[75]

(*c*) Dorset has three supposed dedications to a St Rumwold, one at Pentridge,[76] and one at Cann, a suburb of Shaftesbury.[77] There was also formerly a chapel in South Street, Dorchester, already gone by the beginning of the fifteenth century, called variously the chapel of 'S. Rowaldi' or 'S. Rumbaldi'.[78]

(*d*) One of the many churches in Winchester was dedicated to St Rumbold, but was also known as 'St Ruel' or 'Ruald'. The discovery of fragments of pre-Conquest sculpture at the site of St Ruel suggests that the church was an early foundation.[79]

(*e*) In Butwerk, an eastern suburb of Lincoln, there was once a church (now demolished) dedicated to St Rumbold.[80]

(*f*) An uncertain case is that of Rumboldswyke, near Chichester in Sussex.[81] The eleventh-century two-cell church is now dedicated to St Mary,[82] but may previously have been known as St Rumbold's.[83] It seems likely that there was at least a chapel or altar of St

---

[74] In 1531, one John Benett of Raunds, in his will, left money to send men on pilgrimage to Walsingham and several other destinations, including 'Seint Rumbold of Stok'; see Serjeantson and Isham Longden, 'Parish Churches of Northants', pp. 262 and 410.

[75] See P. Morant, *The History and Antiquities of the most ancient Town and Borough of Colchester* (London, 1748), ii. 9, and *VCH, Essex* ed. W. Page and J. H. Round, 10 vols. (1903–87), ii. 4.

[76] N. Pevsner and J. Newman, *Dorset*, BofE (1972), p. 312. Cf. *VCH, Dorset*, ed. W. Page, vols. ii and iii only (1908 and 1968), ii. 46.

[77] Pevsner and Newman, *Dorset*, p. 364. See also *Royal Commission on Historical Monuments: Historical Monuments of the County of Dorset*, 4 vols. (1962), iv. 65; and *VCH, Dorset*, ii. 46. See also A. D. Mills, *Place-Names of Dorset*, vols. i– , EPNS (1977–in progress), iii. 144, where the earliest recorded occurrence of the dedication is given as 1280 ('ecclesiam S. Rumbaldi').

[78] See Mills, *Place-Names of Dorset*, i. 349.

[79] See *Winchester in the Early Middle Ages*, ed. Biddle, p. 330.

[80] F. Hill, *Mediaeval Lincoln* (Cambridge, 1948; repub. Stamford, 1990), thought that the dedication must be to Rombaut/Rumold of Mechlin (p. 36).

[81] See A. Mawer and F. M. Stenton, *The Place-Names of Sussex*, 2 vols., EPNS (1929–30), i. 13–14. The place-name, recorded in *DB, Sussex* as 'Wiche' (11. 40; i. 24b), seems, in the 13th cent. (to which time the first attested longer forms of the name may be dated), to have acquired the prefix, 'Rumbald' or 'Rumbold'. All known forms of the name preserve the 'b', and not a 'w' or 'u'.

[82] I. Nairn and N. Pevsner, *Sussex*, BofE (1965), p. 170.

[83] Although see *VCH, Sussex*, ed. W. Page, vols. i–iv, vii, and ix (1905–37) and vol. vi, parts 1–3 (1980–7), at iv. 171: Rumboldswyke: 'originally, and frequently in later times, designated simply Wyke, and it is not known who was the Rumbold by whose name it

Rumbold in the church, since a will of one Richard Barnam (dated 1525) disposed money for the light of St Rumbold, and for the Fraternity of St Rumbold.[84]

(g) Another doubtful case is that of Romaldkirk in the North Riding of Yorkshire where the church is dedicated to St Romald.[85] It would be surprising to have found a Buckinghamshire or Northamptonshire saint in Yorkshire, even though his father was supposedly a Northumbrian king. It is just conceivable that the dedication refers either to Rombaut/Rumold of Mechlin, or to a former benefactor/founder of the church, long forgotten.

(h) There is a single surviving dedication to St Rumwold in Kent, at Bonnington, a church with a Norman chancel.[86] This, however, is not the only manifestation of an interest in Rumwold in that county, as will presently be shown.

(vii) *The Cult of St Rumwold in Kent*

It is recorded that there was a custom among the fishermen of Folkestone (at least until the early eighteenth century) to select the best and largest whitings from each boat, and sell them separately from the rest of the catch. They were known as 'rumbal whitings'. The proceeds of the sale of the whitings went towards a feast, called 'rumbal' or 'rumball', provided on Christmas Eve for his

was usually distinguished from about 1225 onwards'; and p. 172 n. 59, where the church is called St Mary's: 'the commonly-used title of St Rumbold is erroneous'.

[84] See R. Garraway Rice, *Transcripts of Sussex Wills*, ed. W. H. Godfrey, Sussex Record Society, xlv (Lewes, 1940–1), pp. 42–3.

[85] *VCH, Yorkshire North Riding*, ed. W. Page, 2 vols. and index (London, 1914–25), i. 117, 'Villa S. Reginaldi', 'Villa Sancto Romaldo'. Cf. *DB, Yorks.*: 'Rumoldescherce' (6N40; i. 310a) and A. H. Smith, *The Place-Names of the North Riding of Yorkshire*, EPNS v (1928), p. 309, 'Rumbald(e)kirke' (1184–1343) and 'Ecclesia S. Rum(b)aldi' (1244). But also *Feet of Fines for the County of York, 1218–31*, ed. J. Parker, Yorkshire Archaeological Society Record Series, lxii (1921), p. 23, 'S. Romundo'. Cf. Rombald's Moor below Ilkley, West Yorkshire, and Rombald's Lane in Ben Rhydding near Ilkley.

[86] N. Pevsner and J. Newman, *West Kent and the Weald*, BofE, 2nd edn. (1976), p. 173. See also J. Harris, *The History of Kent in Five Parts* (London, 1719), i. 45, and R. Kilburne, *A Topographie or Survey of the County of Kent* (London, 1659), p. 32, 'St Romwald'. Surviving 15th- and 16th-cent. wills set aside money for the maintenance of a light for St Rumwold, as recorded by A. Hussey, *Testamenta Cantiana* (London, 1907), p. 25. This dedication to an infant saint was humorously commemorated in 'The Blasphemer's warning: A lay of St Romwold', by R. H. Barham (1788–1845), in his *Ingoldsby Legends* (reissued, London, 1885).

crew by the master of each boat.[87] The earliest recoverable record
of this custom is in 1719, by John Harris,[88] who gave as his source
for the story 'the present Minister, Mr Sackett' (the parish priest of
Folkestone).[89] The same clergyman conjectured that 'rumbal' was
a corruption from 'Rumwold',[90] and that the whitings were originally intended as a yearly offering to that saint, 'to whom, he saith, a
chapel was once dedicated, and stood between Folkestone and
Hythe, but is long since demolished'.[91]

It has not proved possible to discover any earlier or independent
reference either to the custom of the fishermen of Folkestone, or to
the supposed chapel of Rumwold. All subsequent notices derive
from Harris's account. An exhaustive search has been made
through every available map and topographical account of the
area, and no trace of a chapel of Rumwold has hitherto come to
light. If it did exist, the significance to the fishermen of such a
building might have been that, standing on the coast between
Folkestone and Hythe, it served as a marker, or beacon, for naviga-
tion, for which they would have just cause to give thanks. There is
certainly nothing in *Vita S. Rumwoldi* which might indicate why the
saint should otherwise have been venerated by fishermen. However, the possibility cannot entirely be discounted that Mr Sackett
was indulging in fanciful antiquarian supposition (being aware of
the existence of St Rumwold's church not far away at Bonnington).
Harris himself hazarded a seemingly unsubstantiated guess that
there might also have been an altar of Rumwold in Folkestone
church, 'there being convenient places for setting such a Thing up,
at the East end of both the side Isles of the Chancel'.[92] It is by no

---

[87] The word 'rumbal' or 'rumbal whitings' passed into the Kentish dialect, and was
thus recorded by Dr Samuel Pegge in his 'Alphabet of Kenticisms', written in 1735–6;
ed. W. W. Skeat, 'Dr Pegge's manuscript alphabet of Kenticisms and collection of
proverbial sayings used in Kent', *Archaeologia Cantiana*, ix (1874), 50–177, at p. 96.

[88] *History of Kent*, i. 125. Repeated by E. Hasted, *The History and Topographical Survey of
the County of Kent*, 12 vols. (Canterbury, 1797–1801), viii. 175; and in *VCH, Kent*, ed.
W. Page, 3 vols. (London, 1908–32, repr. 1974), iii. 428.

[89] This is presumably John Sackette, vicar of Folkestone 1699–1753, rector of
Hawking 1713–53, vicar of West Hythe, 1732–53; see J. and J. A. Venn, *Alumni Canta-
brigienses. Part I: From the Earliest Times to 1751*, 4 vols. (Cambridge, 1922–7), iv. 2. Cf.
Hasted, *History*, xii. 134–5, where it is reported that Sackette was 'well known by his
publications as an antiquary and a poet'. It has not proved possible to discover whether
any of these 'publications' touched upon the cult of St Rumwold.

[90] With this development, one might compare that of the dedication of St Rumbold's
church, Cann, which seems in the 17th cent. to have been referred to occasionally as 'St
Romball's'; see Mills, *Place-Names of Dorset*, iii. 144.

[91] Harris, *History of Kent*, i. 125.   [92] Ibid., p. 125.

means clear from any of this that the St Rumwold referred to is definitely Rumwold of Buckingham, and not Rumold of Mechlin.

Particularly intriguing, but only a little more verifiable, is the story of the image of St Rumwold at the Cistercian abbey of Boxley in Kent. The fullest early (though by no means unbiased) account occurs in William Lambarde's *Perambulation of Kent*, first published in 1576.[93] Lambarde described with Protestant enthusiasm the famous abuses of the 'false Romish Foxes' at Boxley Abbey, which were uncovered upon the arrival of the Royal commissioners, after the surrender on 29 January 1538.[94] The most renowned was the so-called 'Rood of Grace', apparently an image of Christ contrived out of wood, glue, and paper, and so arranged that, by the means of cleverly concealed wires, it could be made to move its eyes and mouth. Thus were many pilgrims, the 'sillie lambes of Gods flocke', taken in.[95]

The fate of this Rood may be traced in letters of the time. One (dated 7 February 1538) from the commissioner, Jeffray Chamber, informed Cromwell of the discovery of the Rood during routine 'defacing' of Boxley and of its being conveyed to Maidstone to be displayed in the market place.[96] The Rood travelled thence to London, where, after providing entertainment at court, it was produced during a sermon preached by John Hilsey, bishop of Rochester, at St Paul's Cross on 24 February 1538, and then tossed to the mob, which tore the contraption to pieces.[97] The Rood of Grace became a useful justification for the dismantling of the monasteries, and stories about it show ever-increasing exaggeration. Lambarde, who would probably have been too young to see the thing for himself, was already able to give a much overblown account.

Lambarde proceeded to describe a further and somewhat less

---

[93] *A Perambulation of Kent: conteining the Description, Hystorie and Customes of That Shire written in the yeere 1570 by William Lambarde, of Lincolnes Inne, Gent* (1st edn., London, 1576; facsimile of 1826 edn., London, 1970).

[94] *Perambulation*, p. 205.   [95] Ibid.

[96] *Letters and Papers, foreign and domestic, of the reign of Henry VIII*, 21 vols. in 33 parts, ed. J. S. Brewer, J. Gairdner, and R. H. Brodie (London, 1862–1910), xiii (1). 79 (no. 231).

[97] *Letters and Papers*, xiii (1). 120 (no. 348), John Hoker of Maidstone to Johann Bullinger. Cf. C. Wriothesley, *A Chronicle of England during the Reigns of the Tudors, AD 1485–1559*, ed. W. D. Hamilton, 2 vols., Camden Society, NS (1875–7), i. 74–5 for a similar account. See J. Cave-Browne, *The History of Boxley Parish* (Maidstone, 1892), pp. 60–2; and P. H. Ditchfield and G. Clinch, *Memorials of Old Kent* (London, 1907), p. 59.

well-known 'illusion' at Boxley, namely an image 'untruly of the common sort called S. Grumbald for Sainct Rumwald ... the picture of a pretie Boy Sainct of stone, standing in the same churche.'[98] It was said that only those of clean living were able miraculously to lift the small but weighty image. The whole thing was a trick, whereby an 'engine fixed to the backe thereof' rendered the stone easily liftable by such pilgrims as had been seen to have given alms generously. At the approach of a more niggardly visitor, a brother concealed from sight was able 'by the meane of a pinne, running into a post' to secure the statue to the ground, 'so fast and unmoveable, that no force of hande might once stirre it'.[99]

This statue is not named or even referred to in the above-mentioned report of Jeffray Chamber, or in the accounts of either Hoker or Wriothesley. However, one John Finch, writing in 1538 to Conrad Humpard, having briefly described the fate of the Rood of Grace on 24 February, goes on to say, 'Bishop Latimer in the western part [of St Paul's] carried a small image in his hand, which the country people had said eight oxen could not move, and flung it out of the Church'.[100] This may be the same image to which Lambarde referred. Another letter, this time to Johann Bullinger, from Nicholas Partridge (dated 12 April 1538) refers to the presence of 'many other famous saints of wood and stone', inveighed against by Hilsey along with the Rood.[101]

Unlike the Rood, the history of whose arrival at Boxley Lambarde was able to relate in detail,[102] the origin of the image of Rumwold remains a mystery, as does the exact age of either of these conceits.[103] Lambarde contented himself with supplying a version of the Life of Rumwold from Tynemouth. He wrote, 'I my self cannot coniecture, what reason should move them, to make this S. Rumwald the Touchstone of cleane life and innocencie, unlesse it be upon occasion of a myracle that he did, in making two holy Priestes to lift a great stone easily, which before divers Lay persons could not stirre with all their strength and abilitie.'[104] Nothing is known of the final fate of the stone image, but it may have been hacked to pieces by zealous reformers.

---

[98] *Perambulation*, p. 209.   [99] Ibid., p. 210.
[100] *Letters and Papers*, xiii (1). 239 (no. 643).   [101] Ibid., pp. 283–5 (no. 754).
[102] Lambarde claimed to derive his information from an account by the inmates of Boxley, 'sometime by themselves published in print for their estimation and credite', *Perambulation*, p. 205.
[103] Cf. Cave-Browne, *History of Boxley*, p. 47.   [104] *Perambulation*, p. 211.

Needless to say, Lambarde's colourful account has the strong bias of a man writing only forty years after the Reformation. While his description of the Rood of Grace can be tested against other more sober versions and found to be somewhat exaggerated, it must be clear that the story of the Rumwold statue, although probably not a pure invention on Lambarde's part, was subject to a similar degree of embellishment. Yet one might wonder, with Lambarde, how and when the Cistercians at Boxley fixed upon the infant saint of Northamptonshire for their money-spinning venture. In this case there can be no confusion with Rumold of Mechlin, since Lambarde describes the image as being that of a child, a 'pretie Boy sainct'.

The Abbey of Mary the Virgin at Boxley was founded by William of Ypres in 1143, or possibly 1146.[105] By then the cathedral priory of St Andrew, Rochester, had been the patron of the parish church of Boxley (All Saints) for some years.[106] At the time of the Domesday survey, Boxley belonged to the bishop of Bayeux, but had previously been held by 'Alnod cilt'.[107] Æthelnoth *cild* was to be found in possession of land in several counties under Edward the Confessor, and is variously described as 'Alnod cild/cilt', 'Alnod chentiscus, teignus regis E,' or 'Alnodus cilt, teignus R. E.'.[108] It is striking that the single piece of land held by Æthelnoth in Northamptonshire should happen to be in Walton Grounds, where the chapel of St Rumwold formerly stood.[109] This man seems to represent the only retrievable, and admittedly tenuous, link between the Rumwold of King's Sutton and Lambarde's Rumwald of Boxley. Perhaps it was sheer coincidence that brought Boxley and Walton under a single ownership in the first half of the eleventh century. Quite why one of Edward's prominent thegns, holding land in several counties, should be involved with the cult of an obscure little saint remains unclear, and belongs to the realms of pure speculation. Nevertheless, it may be on account of these Kent connections that *Vita S. Rumwoldi* was eventually to

[105] See *Heads*. Also D. Knowles and N. Hadcock, *Medieval Religious Houses of England*, p. 116. 1143 in *Annales Wauerleienses*, in Luard, *Annales Monastici*, ii. 129–411, at p. 230.

[106] See *VCH, Kent*, ii. 154. Boxley had been conferred upon Rochester by Henry I; cf. Davis *et al.*, *Regesta Regum*, iii, no. 721.

[107] *DB, Kent*, 5. 102 (i. 8d).

[108] *DB, Bucks*, 4. 29; 36; 38 (i. 144d and 145a). See Von Feilitzen, *Pre-Conquest Personal Names*, p. 185.

[109] *DB, Northants*, 2. 6 (i. 220b); see p. cxlvii above, on the chapel at Walton.

be included in two Canterbury legendaries and in the fragment of a legendary from Rochester.[110]

(viii) *The Composition of* Vita Sancti Rumwoldi

The foregoing description of the manifestations of the cult of Rumwold leads to some tentative conclusions. Calendars show that the infant could already be numbered among the Anglo-Saxon saints by the late tenth century. However, the almost total lack of other surviving liturgical material, and the disappearance of Rumwold from calendars by the end of the eleventh century, suggest that the formal relic-centred cult failed to achieve the degree of higher ecclesiastical recognition or support required for wide dissemination and survival. Conversely, there are signs, albeit indistinct, that a more informal cult, based on oral traditions and not exclusively dependent upon the physical presence of relics, flourished and persisted in the Northamptonshire and Buckinghamshire region, and may even, in some form, have been transmitted into Kent. The origins and development of such veneration (and the extent of its connection with liturgical cult) seem impossible to trace, given the relatively late and uncertain nature of the evidence.[111] In particular, the tie between Rumwold's three supposed resting-places seems to elude definition.[112] The remaining task is to relate *Vita S. Rumwoldi* to such a mesh of speculation.

A *terminus ante quem* for the composition of *Vita S. Rumwoldi* is provided by the date of the earliest surviving copy, in CCCC 9, in a hand datable to about the third, or possibly last, quarter of the eleventh century.[113] There is nothing in the text itself which can be used to establish an earlier date-limit; as will be noted further on, the Latinity of the *Vita* probably cannot provide a dating of any greater precision. It is also uncertain for whom or by whom the text was composed, and where. The preface makes no reference to dedicatee or informants.

The stipulations made by Rumwold concerning his burial constitute the only internal evidence for the context in which *Vita S.*

---

[110] See § x below.

[111] The numerous church dedications add a further strand of complication, equally difficult to interpret.

[112] Cf. e.g. the connection of Freomund with Offchurch and Cropredy, as described in the early 12th-cent. *Vita S. Fremundi*.

[113] See the description below, pp. clxxiv–clxxv.

Rumwoldi should be viewed. His remains were to be placed first at King's Sutton, then moved after a year to Brackley, and after another year to Buckingham 'omni tempore' (c. 12). The author apparently intended to demonstrate that it was Rumwold's determined wish that his remains be translated. This concern was catered for throughout hagiography, with tales of saints appearing in visions to give instructions about their remains,[114] of relics becoming miraculously heavy at the spot where they were to rest,[115] or of martyrs carrying their decapitated heads miles from the scene of their murder.[116] Thus one might conclude that the aim of *Vita S. Rumwoldi* was to defend and publicize Buckingham's claim to possess the relics of Rumwold, in the face of counterclaims. Accordingly, an obvious place for the composition of the text would seem to be Buckingham itself. Presumably, prior to amalgamation with King's Sutton (and perhaps even thereafter), Buckingham church was still served by a small community of priests or canons, but it is difficult to evaluate the ability of such a community to engage in literary activity, except perhaps of the most modest kind. Furthermore, one might perhaps have expected Buckingham to reinforce its claim by a more detailed recital of posthumous miracles worked through Rumwold's relics than the brief list we have (c. 13). Alternatively, the *Vita* was composed on behalf of Buckingham, at another, unidentified, centre.

The question also remains whether (and why) the translation actually took place. Rumwold is not made to give a reason for desiring to be moved a few miles further south-east every year. Not infrequently in hagiography, the argument was that a saint's relics should not be allowed to moulder in obscurity, as a light under a bushel. One might compare the transfer of Birinus's body from Dorchester to Winchester by Hædde, 'indigne ferens tantam tamque pretiosam margaritam loci uilitate fuscari',[117] or indeed, the translation of Swithun by Æthelwold.[118] In such cases, the motivation is obvious enough, but we are not so well placed to discern the relative 'uilitas' of King's Sutton and Buckingham in

---

[114] e.g. Lantfred's *Translatio et miracula S. Swithuni* c. 1, and *Vita Prima S. Neoti* c. 17, ed. Lapidge, *Annals of St Neot's*, pp. 134–5.

[115] Ibid., p. 135; cf. *Translatio et miracula S. Odulphi*, ed. Macray, *Chronicon de Evesham*, pp. 318–19.

[116] e.g. Osgyth, and Denis; see below, pp. 60–1.   [117] *Vita S. Birini* c. 21.

[118] As described by Lantfred, *Translatio et miracula S. Swithuni*, and the later *Miracula S. Swithuni* (see above, p. xxxiv).

the seventh century. The likelihood is, however, that *Vita S. Rumwoldi* reflects concerns that are thoroughly eleventh-century. The description of such a chain of translations may simply have been a convenient convention by which to make a specific connection between the three places, for whatever reason.

Another hypothesis is that *Vita S. Rumwoldi* was composed primarily as an *apologia* for the very existence of the cult of an improbable three-day-old saint, at some remove, as it were, from the specific and localized concerns of Buckingham. The particularly defensive tone of the prologue, which rails against the false hissing of detractors who label recent hagiography as 'apochripha', goes some way to support the conjecture. However, the identity of the self-styled 'didascalos in plebe', the detractors, is not revealed, and it must be borne in mind that to some extent, phrases of this kind are one of the conventional features of hagiography.[119] The author made no reference to any kind of written source. Under the circumstances, it is reasonable to conclude that none was available to him, since he would surely have mentioned it in order to lend the weight of authority to his account. The conclusion would be that, until the composition of *Vita S. Rumwoldi*, traditions about the saint had only been preserved and transmitted orally, and that their authenticity was beginning to be questioned. As regards the detractors, since a preaching baby requires substantial suspension of disbelief by any standard, it seems unwise to pin the blame upon any particular group, whether Norman or Anglo-Saxon.

Despite the later-attested existence of wells supposedly connected with Rumwold, there is no reference to healing waters in *Vita S. Rumwoldi*. A fairly common hagiographical topos is that of a spring spontaneously bursting forth at some significant place, as, for example, in *Vita S. Kenelmi*. If *Vita S. Rumwoldi* were to have been composed with reference to a local cult perpetuated by oral tradition, and if the connection between the various wells and St Rumwold is of any antiquity, then it is perhaps surprising to find no mention of them. In this respect, the text seems only a rather limited, clerically-minded, response to local tradition, when compared with *Vita S. Kenelmi*, but, at the same time, does not appear

---

[119] Cf. e.g. the 'rebellatrix obstinatia' in the preface to *Vita et miracula S. Kenelmi*; the 'obstinatiores' in *Vita S. Wlsini* c. 12 (Talbot, 'St Wulsin', p. 80); and 'temerarios latratus' in the preface to *Vita S. Ethelburge* (Colker, 'Texts', p. 398).

to be at variance with that tradition.[120] Such an observation
bolsters the conjecture that *Vita S. Rumwoldi* was actually composed at some distance from any of the three resting-places,[121] perhaps at a centre which had an interest in recording Anglo-Saxon
saints *per se*. In such circumstances, as already suggested, the story
of the translations may just as well have been a convention
employed in order to cope with the fact that oral tradition associated Rumwold with three separate sites.

The author's vagueness about the identity of Rumwold's parents
may also be pertinent to this point. They are not named, a fact
which invites the suspicion that the pedigree was largely a confec-
tion.[122] It would be as well to consider here the matter of their real
or imagined identities. Rumwold's mother was supposedly King
Penda's daughter. Penda's known offspring are Peada, Wulfhere,
Æthelred, Cyneburh, Cyneswyth (and supposedly Merewalh,
father of Mildburh of Much Wenlock). The only daughter known
to have married a member of the Northumbrian dynasty is Cyneburh, whose marriage to Alhfrith, son of Oswiu, is recorded by
Bede (*HE* iii. 21) as having taken place before that of Peada to
Alhflæd (which occurred in 653). On the death of her husband,
Cyneburh is said to have taken the veil, with her sister Cyneswyth,
at Castor, Northamptonshire, where they were buried, and eventually translated to Peterborough.[123] The claim that Rumwold was a
grandchild of Penda may be compared with the one made for St
Osgyth, in the so-called 'First Essex Life', preserved in Oxford,
Bodleian Library, Bodley 285 (s. xiii) and in abbreviated form in
London, BL, Lansdowne 436 (*BHL* 6352).[124] The Life supplied
Osgyth with a Mercian genealogy, according to which she is the
daughter of Penda's daughter Wilburh, otherwise unknown, who
married a King Fredeswald.[125] The author went on to point out
that Penda's family included many saints. Rumwold was possibly
linked to the same royal 'cousinhood' in order to underpin his

---

[120] Compare the conclusions of Smith, 'Oral and Written', pp. 338, 342–3.

[121] Of course, the popular cult may only have developed in the direction of the
various holy wells after the time when *Vita S. Rumwoldi* was composed; cf. the comments
in § iv above, on the spa at Astrop.

[122] Obviously, the invention need not have been on the part of the hagiographer, but
may belong to the earlier, and largely obscure, development of the cult.

[123] *ASC* 656 *E* and 963 *E*. Cf. the Life in *NLA* ii. 130–2.

[124] See Bethell, 'Lives of St Osyth', and Hohler, 'St Osyth and Aylesbury'.

[125] Possibly 'Frithewoldus subregulus' of Surrey in the early 670s, cf. S 69 = BCS 33
and S 1165 = BCS 34.

claim to sanctity, as another saintly scion of a saintly family.[126] As Christopher Hohler has pointed out, the daughters of Penda proliferate, and may be related to the foundation of minsters.[127] There is no reference in any of the notices of Cyneburh to her having given birth to any child, let alone Rumwold, which is not surprising, because she would have been hindered from joining the ranks of those royal abbesses who, although married, put aside their husbands and remained virgins (for example, Æthelthryth). As Cyneburh attained sanctity in her own right it would in any case make little difference to include the fact that she had borne a saintly son.

Rumwold's father remains equally mysterious; when he is first introduced (c. 1), we are not even told where his kingdom is, let alone his name. Only a little later is he described as 'rex Northanhymbrorum' (c. 3). If Alhfrith, who did marry a daughter of Penda, was intended, there has been some chronological confusion, since he probably only became king, or rather sub-king, of Deira in 655, when his father Oswiu annexed that kingdom to Bernicia. According to Bede, Alhfrith's marriage to Cyneburh had already taken place by that time. Peada was supposedly persuaded to baptism by Alhfrith, which implies that the latter had already been converted. Indeed Alhfrith is described as being a pupil and supporter of Wilfrid.[128] It is therefore surprising to find Rumwold's father described as pagan. The identification of the Northumbrian king in *Vita S. Rumwoldi* with Alhfrith has recently been challenged by R. H. Hagerty, apparently on the grounds that it is too obvious, and that if Cyneburh had given birth to Rumwold, she would have been recorded as the mother of a saint.[129] He suggests instead Æthelwald, son of Oswald, but is unable to produce a wife from Penda's, or any other, family. The hagiographer would, however, surely have thought fit to mention that Rumwold was grandson of the saintly Oswald.[130]

The author's total silence regarding the names of Rumwold's

---

[126] See commentary on c. 1, below. Cf. Campbell, 'Twelfth-century views', pp. 218–19.

[127] 'St Osyth and Aylesbury', p. 63 n. 15.

[128] See Bede, *HE* iii. 25.

[129] 'Buckinghamshire saints', pp. 106–8. As already mentioned, Cyneburh seems to have had a claim to sanctity in her own right.

[130] Cf. the complex 'saintly' genealogies in Goscelin's *Vita S. Mildrethe* c. 4 (Rollason, *Mildrith*, p. 114) and *Vita S. Werburge* cc. 1–3 (*PL* clv. 97–100).

parents ultimately suggests either that by the eleventh century they had been forgotten, or that the saint's genealogy was a fabrication. The latter may have been thought necessary in order to place an essentially local, perhaps orally perpetuated, story in an acceptable historical or hagiographical framework. In that case, any debate about which Northumbrian king or sub-king fathered Rumwold becomes, in effect, meaningless. The inclusion of the story of the marriage of Rumwold's parents may even have been an attempt to fill out what promised to be an exceedingly short *Vita*.[131]

(ix) *The Latinity of* Vita Sancti Rumwoldi *and its Sources*

The overall impression to be gained from the vocabulary of *Vita S. Rumwoldi* is one of modest pretension to grandeur. This is particularly the case in the prologue, where we may note the use of Grecisms such as 'apocripha', 'sc⟨h⟩ema', and 'didascalos'; the compound verb 'floccipendimus'; and the non-classical neologism 'notamen'.[132] None of these is too unusual, and parallels may be cited from other Anglo-Latin texts, but they do suggest at least that, to a small extent, the author was aiming at technical sophistication. The rest of the text is less inflated in style, though in the same vein as the prologue are 'limpha' (c. 5), 'celique machina' (c. 8), 'plasma' (c. 8), and 'almo flamine' (c. 13). The use of the obscure proper noun 'Ididias' (c. 8), exemplifies the same desire for a semblance of erudition.[133]

The use of this type of vocabulary might conceivably provide an approximate date for the composition of *Vita S. Rumwoldi*, since such stylistic pretensions call to mind the hermeneutic style, practised at certain centres in England in the late tenth century.[134] However, the relatively sparse distribution of 'hermeneutic' words should sound a note of caution. The author could have been writing over half a century earlier than the oldest surviving witness to *Vita S. Rumwoldi*, CCCC 9. But alternatively, he might have been trained at a time when (and a place where) the hermeneutic style was popular, and continued to practise it to a limited extent throughout his life, and could thus have composed the *Vita* at any time during the first half of the eleventh century, possibly even

---

[131] Cf. the comments below (pp. clxvii–clxviii) on the motifs employed by the author.
[132] See commentary, p. 92.   [133] See commentary, p. 106.
[134] See Lapidge, 'The hermeneutic style'; esp. pp. 102–3 on *Vita S. Rumwoldi*.

later. The use of such vocabulary may at least be an indication that the text was not composed by a Norman writer, who would almost certainly have eschewed such quaint embellishments. On the other hand, a recognized characteristic of the prose of Goscelin is his fondness for exotic vocabulary, including some Graecisms, and many more neologisms. Although the particular examples found in *Vita S. Rumwoldi* have not been detected as occurring in Goscelin's known writings,[135] the general point remains that it may be unwise to push the dating of *Vita S. Rumwoldi* too far towards the beginning of the eleventh century on grounds of vocabulary alone.

The syntax of *Vita S. Rumwoldi* is generally intelligible, but just occasionally the author seems either to have aimed deliberately at contortion, or else, through stylistic over-ambition, to have got into difficulties of expression which give rise to clumsiness. Sometimes it seems hard to distinguish between peculiarities deriving from early corruption of the text (particularly in the case of the earliest surviving manuscript), and those which may actually have been perpetrated by the author, by pure incompetence or the pursuit of sophistication. An example, in the prologue, is the long period beginning 'Et quia plurima eorum'. The conditional clause 'si a modernis scribuntur' and the qualifying phrase 'olim a Deo ... notamine' intrude into a construction of indirect statement, separating the impersonal main verb far enough from the subject and infinitive of the indirect clause, to obscure the sense. Matters are not helped by the separation of 'equum' from its noun, 'animum'. Another example of syntactical awkwardness occurs in c. 5. The degree of variation between manuscripts may indicate that the original was at fault, although it is difficult to tell how badly. The alternatives are, 'At illi ducentes plenumque aqua in medio ... ponerent, sanctus Rumwoldus ... ait' (**C**), where the first clause has no finite verb and the present participle 'ducentes' is left to do the work, and has no object (assumed from the previous sentence); 'At illi eum ducentes plenumque aqua cum in medio ponerent' (**R**), is a slight improvement for the inclusion of 'eum', although the 'cum' is oddly placed;[136] the redaction represented by

---

[135] At least, not with the same intended meaning; see commentary below, p. 93, for an example of 'schema' in Goscelin.

[136] Cf. also 'cum uxore pregnante cum carperet iter ...' (c. 3), where the jingling 'cum ... cum' may have been ironed out in the 'Canterbury' recension of the *Vita* (see critical apparatus). A similar overuse of 'cum' occurs in 'cum suis ... cum diuersis ... cum iam foret ...' (c. 1).

AW, 'At illi euntes cum plenum aqua in medio . . . ponerent', seems to have solved the problem by making the first participle intransitive and removing the odd '-que'. Syntactical laxness may also be noted in 'Penitentiam quippe agere est',[137] and the string of infinitives which follows (c. 10).[138] Note also the use of present participles with an auxiliary verb in 'erant seruientes . . . colentes' (c. 1).

Apart from the prologue, the story of St Rumwold is told simply, with few departures from straightforward narrative progression, and certainly no embellishing digressions of the kind found, for example, in *Vita S. Birini*. The only real digression, if such it be, is Rumwold's sermon (cc. 7–11), not strictly essential for the progress of the tale (except perhaps firmly to establish the infant saint's credentials as a confessor), but seemingly the only way to prevent the narrative from turning out to be extremely brief, since the life of a 3-day-old saint will necessarily have rather few events in it.

A certain amount of mostly monosyllabic rhyme occurs within sentences, and it seems likely that particular rhythmical cadences were also sought after.[139] Naturally, the desire for these effects influenced sentence structure. Such arrangements were not always contrived very successfully, and the resultant periods are sometimes rather stilted. For example, 'in manibus superborum . . . excipi diuitum' (c. 4), where the two parallel nouns in the genitive are widely separated from one another for the sake of a rhyme. Other rhetorical adornments to be noted are the frequent use of alliteration,[140] and simple hyperbaton or interlace, separating noun from adjective or qualifier.[141]

When we turn to the question of the sources used by the author of *Vita S. Rumwoldi*, the Bible looms largest. It has proved difficult to detect borrowings from many other direct sources, although the suspicion remains that part, or all, of Rumwold's sermon could have been drawn from some untraceable homily. It is possible that

---

[137] See commentary to c. 10.

[138] Cf. also c. 11 which consists entirely of infinitive verbs, dependent upon 'satagite' and 'studeat'.

[139] *Planus*: 32%, *velox*: 15%, *tardus*: 13%, *trispondiacus*: 9%, including by-forms.

[140] 'Carnali commixtione copulari' (c. 2); 'pauper . . . propheta precursor atque baptista' (c. 4); 'parum proderit peccatori a peccato cessare' (c. 10).

[141] E.g. 'multis sunt credentibus'; 'equum non habentibus animum'; 'falso talium detractionis sibilo'; 'humanum sibi adquirant fauorem' (prol.); 'longa trahit prudens sponsa suspiria' (c. 2); 'debita decreto tempore obsequia' (c. 6); 'post finita missarum sollemnia' (c. 7); 'misericordem animarum corporumque medicum' (c. 11).

a couple of phrases were gleaned from Isidore's *Etymologiae*, or from Augustine on the Psalms, but the similarities are perhaps too fleeting to indicate definite citation.

There are, however, various parallels for the motifs used in *Vita S. Rumwoldi*, which could have influenced the author (though this is often hard to demonstrate with certainty). At the very least, such parallels demonstrate the existence of common narrative patterns. For example, a convention found in other Lives is that employed to describe the marriage of Rumwold's parents. The story of the wedding-night (c. 2) has some similarities with accounts of women saints who, although forced into a marriage, yet desire to preserve their chastity (of course, in this case, the birth of Rumwold is not actually compatible with virginity). An interesting parallel is provided by *Vita S. Cuthburge*, the fullest surviving version of which is to be found in London, BL, Lansdowne 436, fos. 38ᵛ–41ᵛ, hitherto unprinted.[142] Aldfrith, king of Northumbria, sends a legation to Cuthburh's brother Ine, king of the West Saxons, asking for her hand in marriage. To please her brother, Cuthburh consents to marry, secretly trusting in God nevertheless to preserve her chastity.

Euoluto igitur non longo temporis interuallo adest dies determinatus nupciarum, et desponsatur beata uirgo Cudburga regi Northamhimbrorum. Cumque nupcie regio more celebrarentur et omnes prouincie illius optimates tante festiuitati interessent, et congratularentur, beata uirgo Cudburga secreto sola cubicularem ingressa thalamum talem dicitur orationem fudisse ad Dominum: 'Domine Iesu, Dominator uniuerse creature, inclina pias aures ad preces ancille tue; Domine Iesu, dominator castitatis, sanctificator uirginitatis, intende, queso, orationi mee paruitatis, et ascendat deprecatio mea in conspectu tue maiestatis. Te solum, Domine, in sponsum mihi elegi, Tibi me totam a iuuentute mea donaui, Tu mihi super omnia complacuisti. Custode, Domine, quod tuum est; conserua tibi partem tuam, et dignare me uocare sponsam tuam. Non sinas corpus meum, quod templum tuum est, aliqua carnis corruptione contaminari, nec aliquod candide uirginitatis mihi detrimentum inferri. Fac, Domine ... ut in corde sponsi mei scilicet huius regis terreni spiritum infundas gratie salutaris, quatinus, despectis seculi huius uanitatibus et carnalibus illecebris, mihi in castitatis proposito consentiat, ut ad Te, qui omnium bonorum dispensator es, recto itinere perueniat.'

Interea uero rex et omnis familia in aula regia cum magna exultatione

---

[142] Cf. the abbreviation in *NLA* i. 244–6, and *ActaS*, Aug. vi. 699–700.

et hillaritate conuiuabant et totius prouincie primates cum senibus et iunioribus pari assensu et uoluntate tante solempnitati festiue et iocunde congaudebant. . . . Et cum essent in cubiculo soli, beata Cudberta [*sic*] opportunum sibi considerans tempus loquendi talibus fertur uerbis regem et sponsum suum affari . . .   (Lansdowne 436, fo. 39ʳ)

Little can be discovered about the date of the composition of this text, but the similarities with *Vita S. Rumwoldi* are noteworthy. In the anonymous *Vita S. Eanswithe*, St Eanswyth was also said to have been courted by an unnamed Northumbrian king (or prince), evidently pagan.[143] She would only consent to marry him if he could, through the power of his pagan god, make a wooden beam, intended for the building of her oratory but found to be too short, grow three feet longer. Her prayers for his failure were answered and her virginity preserved. Also comparable is Wulfhild's flight from the amorous Eadgar in Goscelin's *Vita et miracula Wlfilde*. She, while sitting at the feast next to her admirer 'de sola cogitat fuga et alto silentio alta ad Christum ut eripiatur attolit suspiria'.[144]

Central to any consideration of the composition and sources of *Vita S. Rumwoldi* must be an enquiry into the very idea of writing the Life of a 3-day-old saint. This question is, of course, inextricably linked to that concerning the origins of Rumwold's cult, which, as has already been stated, seem now to be almost totally irretrievable. In order to proceed here, we must build upon certain assumptions about the task which lay before the anonymous hagiographer. One construction of events could be that the author was called upon to commemorate a saint Rumwold about whom very little was known apart from the basic hagiographical co-ordinates (resting-places, feast-day) and the fact that he died relatively young.[145] He sought to render his largely fabricated saint as exceptional and striking as possible by depicting him as the youngest confessor ever.[146] Such a view begs a good many questions about audience and intention. An alternative, and perhaps

---

[143] *Vita* preserved only in *NLA* i. 296–9.

[144] Colker, 'Texts', pp. 418–31, at 421.

[145] It is, after all, worth recalling that of the earliest surviving references to St Rumwold noted above, none actually records that this confessor was 'infans' or 'puer'.

[146] This interpretation of the genesis of *Vita S. Rumwoldi* is to some extent implied by the brief analysis given in E. Giannarelli, 'Infanzia e santità: un problema della biografia cristiana antica', in *Bambini santi. Rappresentazioni dell'infanzia e modelli agiografici*, ed. A. Benvenuti Papi and E. Giannarelli (Turin, 1991), pp. 25–58, at 49.

more convincing hypothesis, already discussed above, is that the author's business was to explain and justify the veneration of a saint who, according to local (oral?) tradition, had miraculously spoken at birth and then died while still in his white baptismal gown.[147] In either case, it is to be wondered which models or literary conventions, if any, can have informed the hagiographer's work. Three types of account could have served him equally well—demonstrations of precocity in the first years of a saint's life, infants (saintly or otherwise) speaking miraculously, and young children meeting an early death but nevertheless attaining to sanctity.

For hagiographers, describing a saint's infancy was fraught with difficulty, because of its proximity to the ritual uncleanness of physical birth, and on account of the doctrine of original sin, which, as expounded, for example, by Augustine, held that even a one-day-old baby is stained with the sin of Adam; indeed the self-centred and greedy wailings of a new-born child are an especially noxious manifestation of its fallen state.[148] The narrative solutions to this difficulty were either silently to pass over a saint's infancy altogether, or to fall back on the literary topos known as 'puer senex' or 'puer maior sua aetate'.[149] Thus a fairly common feature of hagiography is that the young saint is made to spurn the toys and games of his peers, as an early display of detachment from the world and its ways. For instance, the young St Nicholas was said to have abstained from his mother's milk on Wednesdays and Fridays.[150] Among examples of this topos, *Vita S. Rumwoldi* is the *pièce de résistance*, because, with only three days to live, Rumwold must establish his saintly credentials more swiftly than most.[151]

A concomitant figure is that of the speaking 'infans', a miraculous contradiction in terms, enacting the biblical text, 'out of the mouth of babes and sucklings thou hast perfected praise'.[152] There are many variations upon this theme,[153] one of the best known

---

[147] Cf. Bede, *HE* ii. 14 (two of the offspring of Edwin and Æthelburh 'albati adhuc rapti sunt de hac uita').   [148] Augustine, *Confessiones* i. 7 (*PL* xxxii. 665).

[149] As described by E. R. Curtius, *European Literature and the Latin Middle Ages*, trans. W. R. Trask (London, 1979), pp. 98–101.

[150] *Vita S. Nicholai* in CCCC 9, pp. 26–53, at 28. Cf. Loomis, *White Magic*, p. 23.

[151] Cf. Giannarelli, in *Bambini*, pp. 45–9, where *Vita S. Rumwoldi* is cited as the topos at its most extreme.   [152] Ps. 8: 3; Matt. 21: 16.

[153] Although hitherto no Anglo-Saxon vernacular examples have come to light, the folk-motif of the speaking infant is widely attested and seems to have been quite universal—cf. Thompson, *Motif Index*, T575 (from within the womb) and T585. Of the

being the child who is supposed to have cried out 'Ambrose for bishop'.[154] It is worthwhile at least considering examples which bear some similarity to the story of Rumwold. For instance, in the Merovingian *Vita S. Goaris* c. 7, a 3-day-old infant is induced by the saint to supply the names of his unknown parents.[155] The undated *Vita S. Peregrini eremite* c. 2 recounts that the saint, as a baby, responded with 'Amen' to the Lord's Prayer which the priest said at his baptism, and then proceeded to repeat the prayer, followed by the creed, 'ac si fuisset uiginti annorum'.[156] A comparable story is told in *Vita S. Sigiberti* c. 5, about the baptism of the infant Sigibert by St Amand: 'Cumque finita benedictione nemo ex circumstantibus respondisset, Amen; aperuit Deus os infantis, atque cunctis audientibus clara uoce respondit, Amen.'[157] Strikingly similar to the story of Rumwold's preaching is an incident from *Passio S. Maximi martyris* (c. 9), in which the saint instructs his persecutor Fabrian to fetch a 3-month-old infant who will preach the Gospel to him:[158]

Maximus dixit infantulo, 'Tibi dico, infans, per Dei sapientiam te obtestor, qui aperuit os mutum et linguas infantium fecit disertas, ut loquaris ad praesidem omnem ueritatem de Christi fide et de idolorum cultura.' Tunc respondit infans et dixit, 'Audi, praeses, uerba mea, et noli aliquid de me dubitare, cum sim infans. Deus omnipotens loquitur per os meum . . . Nunc ergo, audi me, et crede in Christum, qui michi dedit fiduciam loquendi, ne forte cum diis tuis demergaris in infernum.'

Unfortunately, it cannot securely be demonstrated that any of these texts would have been known to the author of *Vita S. Rumwoldi*, and therefore have influenced his work directly. They do at least provide evidence of the general currency of the motif in hagiography. Such an inference is borne out by a striking analogue

examples collected there, it is difficult to distinguish any which might relate specifically to *Vita S. Rumwoldi*.

[154] Paulinus, *Vita S. Ambrosii* (*PL* xiv. 27–46, at col. 29); cf. P. Courcelle, 'L'Enfant et les "sorts bibliques"', *Vigiliae Christianae*, vii (1953), 194–220.

[155] *BHL* 3565; *MGH*, SRM iv. 411–23, at 417–18. This is similar to a story told by Gregory of Tours, *Historia Francorum* ii. 1.

[156] *BHL* 6630; *ActaS*, Aug. i. 77–80, at 77. Not preserved in any surviving English legendaries.

[157] *BHL* 7712; *ActaS*, Feb. i. 227–30, at 228; composed by Sigibert of Gembloux in the mid-11th cent.

[158] *BHL* 5845 (cf. *BHL* 584; *ActaS*, Oct. xiii. 319–24, at 321–2) possibly datable to the 10th cent. A similar story is told much earlier on, of St Romanus, by Prudentius, *Peristephanon* x. 656–85.

from a milieu much closer to that of our text, namely the account of an unusual infant in *Vita S. Fremundi*, ascribed to one Burghard.[159] This child, the son of Algar and Thova, subjects of Offa, on his third day spoke 'contra nature modum Dei uoluntate', and prophesied that Offa, in old age, would beget a son, who would be a saint (i.e. Freomund). 'Quo dicto, in sancte trinitatis confessione baptismum petiit, et optinuit, et predicto quod prefatus puer Freemundus uocaretur, statim ut baptizatus fuit, paruulus obiit.'[160] Whether this story is to be taken as the accurate reflection of local tradition or merely a literary elaboration by the author, it offers an interesting parallel to *Vita S. Rumwoldi*. The cult of Freomund seems to have been connected with places in the south-west midlands not too distant from King's Sutton and Buckingham.[161] Although *Vita S. Freomundi*, as preserved, is probably a twelfth-century production, it may have been based upon an earlier account which has not survived, or upon locally circulated traditions.

A search for saints specifically stated to have died in very early childhood has proved only a little less disappointingly inconclusive. Starting with the New Testament story of the innocents slain at the behest of Herod, there are many accounts of young children who made their mute profession of faith simply by suffering a martyr's death.[162] Sometimes these martyrs are said to have given oral testimony as well, as, for example, in the record of the martyrdom, at Caesarea, of Julitta and her 3-year-old son Cyriacus. Some versions of their Passion recount that Cyriacus, having been brought before the governor Alexander, was asked his name, and supposedly replied: 'christianus sum', a phrase found also on the lips of Rumwold.[163] The *Acta* of Cyriacus and Julitta were probably available in England by the eleventh century,[164] and it is

---

[159] *BHL* 3144b, ed. from Dublin, Trinity College, B. 2. 7, in *NLA* ii. 689–98. An abbreviated version occurs in London, BL, Lansdowne 436, fos. 32ʳ–43ᵛ.

[160] *NLA* ii. 690. Cf. Merevin, son of Domneva and brother to Mildburh, Mildreth and Mildgyth, 'qui ad sanctos innocentes a baptismate raptus et paruulus'; Goscelin, *Vita S. Werburge*, PL clv. 101A.

[161] Offchurch and Cropredy are named in the text as the places where Freomund rested (*NLA* ii. 694 and 697).

[162] Cf. F. Scorza Barcellona, 'Infanzia e martirio: la testimonianza della più antica letteratura cristiana' in *Bambini*, pp. 59–83.

[163] Cf. e.g. *Epistula Theodori de eorum passione* (*BHL* 1801), c. 7, *ActaS*, Iunii, iii. 23–4, at 24; and the *Acta apocrypha* (*BHL* 1802) c. 2, loc. cit. pp. 28–33, at 29A.

[164] Their shared feast on 16 June is marked in several eleventh-century liturgical calendars; Wormald, *English Kalendars*, nos. 2, 3, 6, 8, 11–13, 16, 17. Arnold-Forster,

interesting to note that a copy is included, immediately following *Vita S. Rumwoldi*, among the additions to the Worcester legendary.[165] This text could just conceivably have influenced the author's formulation of Rumwold's own first utterance. So far as can be ascertained, however, *Vita S. Rumwoldi* is unique, at least among Latin saints' Lives of the medieval West, in offering a detailed account of a baby confessor. Almost by definition, a confessor must surely be shown to have made a 'professio fidei' in order to achieve credibility as a saint. The Hieronymian martyrology preserves the commemoration of an infant saint (confessor), Lusor, or Ludre, of Bourges, who died while still in his baptismal robes, on 1 November.[166] There seems to be no record that Lusor is believed to have spoken, and it is not entirely clear whether the author of *Vita S. Rumwoldi* could have encountered this cult. Similar to Ludre, but closer to home, is Merefin, brother of SS. Mildreth and Mildburh. The Old English tract (probably datable to the early eleventh century) known as the Kentish royal legend, or *þa halgan*, calls him 'sancte Merefynn',[167] and Goscelin, in his *Vita S. Mildrethe*, wrote of him 'Christus paruulum suscipiens paradisi floribus addidit'.[168] Similarly, *Vita S. Werburge* c. 3, probably also by Goscelin, contains the statement 'Merefin filius . . . ad sanctos innocentes a baptismate raptus est paruulus'.[169] Nothing more is known about this child. His claim to sanctity seems almost to be a foregone conclusion from the fact that he was a scion of that particular family.

Another example of a home-grown baby saint is also supplied by Goscelin. In his *Vita et miracula S. Ethelburge*, he recounted how a

Church Dedications, i. 170–1, listed eight early dedications to either Cyriacus, Julitta or both. Relics had reached Auxerre as early as the 4th cent.

[165] See below p. clxxiv. This copy does not correspond exactly to any of the versions listed in *BHL*, but certainly contains Cyriacus's profession of faith in the form 'Christianus sum' (CCCC 9, p. 59).

[166] See 'Commentarium in Martyrologio Hieronymiano', in *ActaS*, Nov. ii (2). 581, 'In Gallia territorio beturico nuncupato Dolos uico desposito S. Lusoris pueri et confessoris', for 1 Nov. Cf. Gregory of Tours, *In gloria confessorum*, c. 90 (*MGH*, SRM i. 805–6), 'In Dolense autem Biturigi terminum uico beatus Lusor, Leucadi quondam senatoris filius, requiescit, qui fertur in albis migrasse a saeculo.' In the liturgical books of Bourges, Ludre was, however, commemorated on 4 and 16 Nov.; cf. M. de Langardière, *L'Église de Bourges avant Charlemagne* (Bourges, 1951), pp. 24–7.

[167] Ed. Liebermann, *Heilige*, pp. 1–10, at 3.

[168] Ed. Rollason, *Mildrith Legend*, p. 115. It is quite likely that Goscelin was familiar with *þa halgan* in some form.

[169] *PL* clv. 101.

3-year-old infant, named Esica, with his dying breath thrice cried out the name of a member of the community at Barking, who also died later the same day.[170] St Esica was commemorated at 19 March in the Barking calendar,[171] but there is no surviving evidence to indicate that he was venerated further afield.

In conclusion, there appears to be no way of determining whether the composition of *Vita S. Rumwoldi* was actually directly influenced by any of the parallels assembled here. Their significance resides in the fact that, while on the one hand they serve to underline the uniqueness of that particular narrative, on the other, they testify to the existence of a mentality which did not apparently find the concept of a baby saint to be entirely preposterous.

(x) *The Manuscripts of* Vita Sancti Rumwoldi

Vita S. Rumwoldi is preserved in five manuscripts, three complete, two fragmentary. The complete manuscripts are as follows:

A = London, British Library, Arundel 91, fos. 195^v–198^r. This manuscript contains fifty-four saints' Lives for the latter part of September, October, and the beginning of November, and once formed part of a multi-volume legendary.[172] The volume which followed this one in the set, containing the Lives for the rest of November, and those for December, is now preserved in Oxford, Bodleian Library, Fell 2.[173] Profusely illuminated in the Canterbury style,[174] the legendary was probably written at St Augustine's Canterbury, to judge not only from the style of the script, but also from the fact that Eadmer's Life of St Peter, the first abbot of St Augustine's, was added to the end of Fell 2 in a slightly later hand.[175] Two script types may be discerned in the manuscript; firstly, the 'prickly' Canterbury type,[176] which began to be used at Christ Church Canterbury from the second half of the eleventh century, was subsequently adopted also at St Augustine's, and at

---

[170] Colker, 'Texts', pp. 405–6.

[171] Ed. Tolhurst, *Ordinale*, i. 3.

[172] Page measurement: 334 mm. × 230 mm.; written area: 260 mm. × 170 mm.; 229 fos.; 37 lines in double columns.

[173] See Ker, *Medieval Libraries*, p. 42. Cf. p. xxv above.

[174] See C. R. Dodwell, *The Canterbury School of Illumination, 1066–1200* (Cambridge, 1954), esp. p. 26, and p. 123, where the MS is given a date between 1100 and 1130.

[175] *BHL* 6702m, probably composed between 1124 and 1130, see Southern, *St Anselm*, pp. 370–1.

[176] See James, *Ancient Libraries*, p. xxx for this definition.

Rochester, and remained in use until about the middle of the twelfth century. Secondly, an anglicized version of the same can be seen.[177] A date in the first third of the twelfth century seems probable for the legendary as a whole.[178]

C = Cambridge, Corpus Christi College, 9, pp. 53–8.[179] This manuscript and London, BL, Cotton Nero E. i, parts 1 and 2, are companion volumes which have a complicated history. At the core is a two-volume legendary, known as the Cotton-Corpus legendary,[180] copied by a single scribe, very probably at Worcester during the third quarter of the eleventh century. Volume 1 contained Lives for January to September and is now Nero E. i, part 1, fos. 55–208 + Nero E. i, part 2, fos. 1–155, with a list of contents on fo. 55^{r-v} of part 1. The rest of the year was covered in volume 2, which is now preserved as CCCC 9, pp. 61–458 + Nero E. i, part 2, fos. 166–80, with a list of contents at p. 61 of CCCC 9.[181]

Only a very short time after the core legendary had been compiled or copied, further items began to be added to both volumes. Computistical material has been bound in at the beginning of the Corpus volume (pp. 1–16), including a liturgical calendar,[182] and Easter tables for 1032–62 and 1063–94, from which it is reasonable to posit a date in the mid-eleventh century for the copying of this section of the codex.[183] Pages 17–60 are slightly later additions, of the third, or possibly the last, quarter of the eleventh century, containing several saints' Lives,[184] written in hands similar to those found in Oxford Bodleian, Hatton 113, 114, Junius 121, and in other Worcester manuscripts.[185]

[177] See Ker, *English Manuscripts*, p. 26, where the 'prickly' script is called the 'Christ Church' type.

[178] Cf. p. lxxxi above.

[179] Page measurement: 401 mm. × 297 mm.; written area: 330 mm. × 210 mm.; 229 + 2 fos.; 36 lines in double columns.

[180] The Cotton-Corpus legendary is discussed at length above, pp. xviii–xxi.

[181] See the list in Jackson and Lapidge, 'The Contents of the Cotton-Corpus Legendary'.

[182] Pages 3–14, printed in Wormald, *English Kalendars*, no. 18.

[183] Cf. James, *Descriptive Catalogue of the Manuscripts in the Library of Corpus Christi College*, i. 21–30. Cf. Dumville, *Liturgy*, p. 52, where the date 1061 is assigned to CCCC 9, on the grounds that two red dots were marked against that year in the table.

[184] pp. 17–26, *Vita S. Saluii*, pp. 26–53, *Vita et miracula S. Nicholai* (pp. 41–52 appear to be a later insertion, written during the 12th cent.), *Vita S. Rumwoldi* and pp. 59–60, *Passio SS. Ciryci et Iulitte*.

[185] See Ker, *Catalogue*, nos. 29, 331, 338.

Vita S. Rumwoldi was copied by two different scribes, the second of whom wrote short stints at p. 54, cols. b and at p. 56 col. b, p. 57 col. a and b, and was apparently more careless or less experienced than the first, in that he perpetrated a considerably higher proportion of errors. The formation of his letters is at times rather awkward. The copy of *Vita S. Rumwoldi* in **C** has at some point (probably not by the original scribes) been marked out as if for three lections, with crosses in the margin signifying the place where each section should begin. This could be interpreted as providing evidence that the text was, at some time, used liturgically at Worcester. None of the other surviving witnesses has been similarly divided.

R = London, British Library, Royal 13. A. x, fos. 55ᵛ–61ᵛ. A composite codex, with three distinct parts.[186] Part 1 (fos. 1–62) is written by two hands successively, datable to the first half of the twelfth century, the first ending at fo. 56ʳ and the second beginning on the verso. The contents are as follows: 1ʳ–53ʳ, Leontius of Cyprus (translated into Latin by Anastasius Bibliothecarius), *Vita S. Iohannis Archiepiscopi Alexandrini*;[187] 53ʳ–55ᵛ, *Passio S. Albani*;[188] 55ᵛ–61ᵛ, *Vita S. Rumwoldi*.

Part 2 (fos. 63–103) contains a copy of Bili's *Vita S. Machuti* and a homily for the feast of the same saint, in a hand dated to the second half of the tenth century.[189] Part 3 (fos. 104–7) is a fragment of Eutropius, copied in the later twelfth or thirteenth century.

Nothing is known about the origin of the three parts of this codex, even whether all derive from the same scriptorium, nor yet quite when or where they were bound together in one codicological unit. Latterly, the codex belonged to John, Lord Lumley (1534–1609), until it entered the Royal library in 1609.[190]

It is difficult even to begin to suggest where part 1, which contains *Vita S. Rumwoldi*, might have been copied. There is no obvious connection between the three saints represented in the manuscript—St John the Almsgiver, St Alban, and St Rumwold. The rounded script of part 1 is reminiscent of that found in manuscripts

---

[186] Page measurement: 228 mm. × 160 mm.; written area 170 mm. × 110 mm.; 107 fos.; 23 lines in a single column.

[187] *BHL* 4388; John the Almsgiver.

[188] Taken from Bede, *HE* i. 7.

[189] *BHL* 5116; see Gneuss, 'List', no. 482.

[190] See G. Warner and J. P. Gilson, *Catalogue of Western Manuscripts in the Old Royal and King's Collection*, 2 vols. (London, 1921), ii. 79.

known to have come from St Albans, for example, Cambridge, King's College, 19 (s. xii[in]), particularly in the formation of the compendium for '-orum'.[191] The same Life of John the Almsgiver is preserved in New York, Pierpont Morgan Library, 926 (s. xi/xii), along with hymns to St Alban, an Office and a mass of St Alban,[192] but in the absence of any further evidence for interest in St Rumwold at St Albans, the origin of this manuscript must, for the time being, remain uncertain.

The two fragmentary manuscripts are as follows: **E** = Canterbury Christ Church Cathedral, Lit. E. 42, fo. 54[r].[193] The fragments Canterbury, Cathedral Library, Lit. E. 42, fos. 1–68, 75–81 + Maidstone, Kent County Archives Office, S/Rm Fae. 2 (2 fos.) were recovered in 1888 from the bindings of business books of the archdeacon's court at Canterbury Cathedral, where they had been employed since the second half of the sixteenth century.[194] These folios are the remains of a seven-volume legendary containing Lives for the entire liturgical year, which was recorded in the catalogue of the library at Christ Church, compiled for Henry of Eastry, prior from 1284 to 1331.[195] Where the survival of the manuscripts permits comparison, this Christ Church legendary contains a collection of Lives very similar to the St Augustine's legendary described above, and both are related indirectly to the Cotton-Corpus compilation.[196]

The legendary was for the most part the work of two scribes, who wrote the narrow, 'prickly' Christ Church, Canterbury type of script mentioned above, and this fact confines the date of the compilation reasonably to the first half of the twelfth century.[197] Richard Southern put forward the idea that the compilation of the Christ Church legendary may have been supervised by Eadmer,

[191] Cf. Thomson, *Manuscripts from St Albans*, ii, plate 31, penultimate line (and i. 84).

[192] Ibid., p. 115, and Hartzell, 'A St Albans miscellany'.

[193] Page measurement: 390 mm. × 275 mm. (dimensions after cutting down); written area: 277 mm. × 190 mm.; 77 fos., 39 lines in double columns.

[194] The fragments are described and their contents listed by Ker, *Medieval Manuscripts*, ii. 289–96.

[195] Henry's catalogue has been printed by James, *Ancient Libraries*, p. 52; the volumes of the legendary are items 359, 361–6.

[196] These and other fragments of the Christ Church legendary are described by Ker, 'Membra disiecta', pp. 83–5. See p. xxiv above.

[197] Several of the surviving initials in these fragments are elaborately decorated, and have been discussed by Dodwell, *The Canterbury School*, pp. 66, 70, 75, 78, and plate 42d.

who was precentor of the Cathedral from about 1121.[198] He suggested *c.*1125 as the date for the planning and execution of the legendary, partly because it includes Eadmer's *Vita S. Anselmi* (Harley 315, fos. 16–39), completed shortly after 1123. It should be noted, however, that Eadmer's text is in a slightly later hand than other parts of the legendary, and probably represents a subsequent addition.[199] Nevertheless, it seems in keeping with the styles of script employed in the copying of Lit. E. 42, to propose a date somewhere in the first quarter of the twelfth century for the legendary as a whole.

Only the last part of *Vita S. Rumwoldi*, from 'universe carnis' (c. 12), to the end of the closing doxology, occurs at fo. 54ʳ, col. a of **E**, and was originally part of the sixth volume of the Christ Church legendary, listed in the fourteenth-century catalogue as 'Passionale Sancti Mathei viᵐ'.

W = Oxford, Worcester College 273. This single leaf, cut into three pieces,[200] was removed in 1949 from a printed copy of the works of A. Montanus (Antwerp 1572), and identified by Neil Ker as being in the same script and format as London, BL, Royal 5. D. III, from Rochester Cathedral Priory. The script is of the same 'prickly' Canterbury type as has already been described, practised in a slightly modified form in Rochester, which had fairly close links with Canterbury, especially in the first quarter of the twelfth century.[201] The fragment may well have come from one of the 'Passionalia in quatuor uoluminibus' recorded in the catalogue of Rochester Cathedral library included (at fos. 224–30) in part B of the so-called 'Textus Roffensis'.[202] Since both parts of the 'Textus

---

[198] Southern, *St Anselm*, p. 238.

[199] Cf. Ker, 'Membra disiecta', p. 84.

[200] Page measurement: 318 mm. × 190 mm. (maximum width); written area: 274 mm. × 190 mm.; 38 lines in double columns.

[201] Ker, *English Manuscripts*, p. 14. On this relationship, see M. P. Richards, *Texts and their Traditions in the Medieval Library of Rochester Cathedral Priory*, Transactions of the American Philosophical Society lxxviii (3) (Philadelphia, PA, 1988), esp. pp. 3–5.

[202] Printed by R. P. Coates, 'A catalogue of the Library of the Priory of St Andrew, Rochester, from the Textus Roffensis', *Archaeologia Cantiana*, vi (1866), 120–8 (no. 56). The same legendary is also listed as 'Passyonaria IIII' in a later catalogue or 'scrutinium' of the Rochester library copied on to leaves at the beginning of London, BL, Royal 5. B. XII, and datable to 1202; see B. Rye, 'A catalogue of the library of the Priory of St Andrew, Rochester, A.D. 1202', *Archaeologia Cantiana*, iii (1860), 47–64, at p. 55. These catalogues are also reproduced in Richards, *Texts and their Traditions*, Table 1, although the possible identification of this fragment of the Passional is not mentioned there.

Roffensis' are thought almost certainly to have been compiled during the episcopacy of Ernulf (1115–24),[203] a mention in this particular catalogue provides a date (i.e. 1124) before which the legendary containing this copy of *Vita S. Rumwoldi* must have been copied.

On the verso of the fragment is written the name Thomas Willoughbey, with the remains of another inscription in the same sixteenth-century hand. This could well be the man of that name who was a canon of Christ Church, Canterbury until 1574, when he left to become dean of Rochester. He may have used the leaf to cover one of his own books, before it was cut into strips for use by the binder of the Montanus volume.[204] This additional evidence lends some weight to the hypothesis that the manuscript to which this leaf belonged was originally at Rochester.

The portions of the *Vita* preserved in this fragment are 'corpus meum pollui . . . responderunt duo' (cc. 2–3) and 'a Widerino presbitero, ac suscipitur . . . ut ad illam declinent quia eam' (cc. 6–7), which are both complete columns of text. The section 'teneri ad presignaculum fidei . . . sanctificatur in eo fons sancti baptismatis' (cc. 3–6) is present in very fragmentary form.

(xi) *Abbreviated Versions of* Vita Sancti Rumwoldi

A copy of *Vita S. Rumwoldi* is to be found in a collection of saints' Lives in Dublin, Trinity College, 172 (B. 2. 7), of the mid-fourteenth century [= **T**].[205] For some time, the manuscript was mistakenly attributed to St Peter's, Westminster, on the basis of a misreading of an inscription on the first page, which actually reads 'Petri Whalley', but had been taken as 'S. Petr. Westm.'[206] Colker, however, suggests that this manuscript may instead be associated with the Northampton area, since St Ragener, the only known copy of whose Life is preserved in TCD 172, is connected with

---

[203] See Ker, *Catalogue*, no. 373, for a description of the contents of the Textus Roffensis, and on the dating of the MS.

[204] See Watson, *Catalogue of Dated and Dateable Manuscripts*, i. 148, and plate 42.

[205] Described in M. L. Colker, *Trinity College Library, Dublin, Descriptive Catalogue of Medieval and Renaissance Latin Manuscripts*, 2 vols. (Dublin, 1991), i. 310–20. Cf. T. K. Abbott, *Catalogue of the Manuscripts in the Library of Trinity College, Dublin* (Dublin and London, 1900), no. 172.

[206] Colker, *Catalogue*, i. 319, cf. Abbott, no. 172. Ker, *Medieval Libraries*, p. 197 (347), had already rejected this attribution, without suggesting an alternative.

Northampton, and the name Whalley is apparently a local Northampton name.[207] The manuscript also contains the fullest surviving copy of *Vita S. Fremundi*, which refers to places in the same south-west midlands region.[208] *Vita S. Rumwoldi*, considering the saint's Northamptonshire connections, fits well into such a context.

The text of *Vita S. Rumwoldi* is a slightly abbreviated version, omitting a section of Rumwold's homily: 'Nam hec est illa sapientia ... redemptio mundi' (cc. 7–8), as well as certain other discursive sections which could be regarded as extraneous to the narrative, for example, 'In ea quippe impletum est ... fidelem' (c. 2); the explanation of why Rumwold's parents should go to see King Penda: 'quo simul ... letarentur' (c. 3), the account of John the Baptist 'factus inter homines ... uitiorum' (c. 4), and the account of the nature of Rumwold's birth-place 'In eodem prato ... redolent' (c. 6).

The prologue is, however, retained in full, although with numerous unique errors, such as *proparare* for *propalare*, *sibi* for *sibilo*, *oppendimus* for *floccipendimus*, and the insertion of *iuste* in the phrase *iniusta redargutione iuste redarguuntur*. Similar errors are to be found in the rest of the *Vita*, as well as variations which may well have come about through the redactor's efforts to rationalize what he felt to be ambiguous features in his exemplar. For example, *insula maioris Britannie* for *insula maiori Britannia* (c. 1); *tertio* for *tertia* and *domumque reuersus* for *demumque* (c. 2); *tegebatur* for *degebat* (c. 4); *ualliculo* for *uallicule* (c. 5).

A more thoroughly abridged version of *Vita S. Rumwoldi* exists in a compilation of English saints' Lives found in London, BL, Lansdowne 436 (s. xiv) [= **L**], written at or for the nunnery at Romsey in Hampshire.[209] In this copy of *Vita S. Rumwoldi*, the prologue has been wholly rewritten, as also has c. 1, and almost all the lengthy utterances of Rumwold have been cut out (cc. 4, 7–11). General 'pruning' activity leaves only the bare bones of the account of Rumwold's already brief life.

The third abbreviated version of *Vita S. Rumwoldi* occurs in John of Tynemouth's *Sanctilogium*, made in the first half of the fourteenth century [= **S**].[210] In his account of Rumwold, John omitted

[207] *Catalogue*, i. 318.

[208] *NLA* i. 689–98.

[209] See p. lxxxii above for a description.

[210] See p. lxxiii above.

the prologue, but retained a fuller form (although rewritten in some places) of the remainder of the text than in either of the two abbreviations mentioned above (the only sentences omitted completely are c. 1, 'Cuius uoto ... debebant'; c. 12, 'Vocatur ... quoque Buccingham').[211] Evidence for another copy of *Vita S. Rumwoldi*, now lost, was supplied by the antiquary John Leland. He gave a brief summary of Rumwold's Life from a version he had come across at Exeter Cathedral, and which he ascribes to the mid-fourteenth-century bishop of Exeter, John Grandisson.[212] Leland's account contains only the bald facts about Rumwold's life, adding nothing new, and certainly not betraying the nature of the source, and is thus of little use in reconstructing the history of the transmission of *Vita S. Rumwoldi*.

Nicholas Roscarrock, a prominent Roman Catholic and poet (*c.*1549–1634),[213] made a large compilation of British saints' Lives, now preserved in Cambridge, UL, Addit. 3041. When discussing St Rumwold, Roscarrock mentioned not only Tynemouth and Lambarde, but also 'an ancient manuscript', which he claimed to have, containing details of the saint's life corresponding roughly to *Vita S. Rumwoldi*. Much work on the materials used by Roscarrock remains to be done. His manuscript may have been one of those just described, or a now-lost copy, but it is impossible to tell.

(xii) *The Relationship of the Manuscripts*

Although **C** is demonstrably the oldest surviving manuscript of *Vita S. Rumwoldi*, it can claim priority in no other respect. The considerable number of unique scribal errors or variants displayed by this witness precludes the possibility that any other manuscript can have been copied directly from it. For example, c. 2, *alienata* for *alienato*; c. 3, omission of *rex*; c. 4, *uirtute* for *uirtutem*; c. 5, *iter* for *a terra*; c. 9, *sapienti* for *sapientia*; c. 10, *exuterat operatur* for *exstiterat operator* and omission of *post*; c. 11, *indesinent* for *indesinenter*; c. 12, *uitam* for *in tam*; c. 13, *prelibanum* for *prelibatum*; and the omission of an entire phrase by homoeoteleuton, *inscrutabilia sunt iudicia eius et in-*, leaving the rather improbable *uestigabiles* (c. 7).

In a similar way, **R** cannot have served as the exemplar for any other surviving manuscript. Of the three complete manuscript

[211] *NLA*, ii. 345–50.
[212] *Itinerary*, ed. Toulmin-Smith, i. 229, and ii. 37.
[213] See *Dictionary of National Biography*, xlix (London, 1897), pp. 220–1.

witnesses to the *Vita*, **R** alone preserves several scribal errors, such as c. 3, *tempus* for *tempore*; c. 5, omission of *uelociter*; c. 6, omission of *infans*; c. 10, *quos* for *quomodo*, and *sequentibus* for *sequendo*. Furthermore, there are a good many places where **R** preserves independent variations in word order, apparently supplied, in many cases, in an effort to lend the syntax greater clarity, or for aesthetic reasons. For example, c. 1, *donis atque honoribus*; c. 2, *eleuans ad ethera*; c. 4, *ac huius mundi diuitum de regeneratione sancti baptismatis excipi, dei exemplum imitari*; c. 5, *indice ostendit* and *iussum illius*; c. 7, *bonitatis honestate*, and *diuine legis preceptis*; c. 8, *uera summaque sapientia est*, and *inenarrabili syderum pulchritudine*; c. 9, *est filius* and *est in filio*.

Simplification or 'rationalization' by the scribe of **R** might also be seen in the reading *undaque munda* for the more unusual *nitidaque limpha* (c. 5), and in the abbreviation of the lengthy and unusual doxology at the end of the *Vita* (c. 13). Similar activity may have given rise to readings such as addition of *et dicit* (c. 3); c. 8, *creauit* for *condidit*, *finis* for *initium*, and addition of *sum*; and possibly, c. 11, *periurium* for *periuriam*.

At this point it seems appropriate to consider briefly the evidence supplied by the abbreviated *Vita S. Rumwoldi* in **T**. This witness follows **R** very closely, not only in a couple of its errors (c. 10, *quos* for *quomodo*; *sequentibus* for *sequendo*), but also in the majority of the variations listed above. The possibility that **T** was copied directly from **R** is, however, almost certainly excluded by the following: Prologue, *scemate* for *themate* of **R**; c. 3, *tempus* in **R**; c. 3, *Merciorum* for *excertitium* of **R**; c. 5, *nitidaque limpha* where **R** has *undaque munda*; and omission of *uelociter* from **R** alone. The evidence suggests that **R** and **T** may have had a common exemplar, the conjectural hyparchetype δ, now lost, which contained all the alterations named above, and the errors shared by **R** and **T**. We should bear in mind that **T** is an abbreviated version of the text, and therefore cannot be used to support every reading of **R**. It might also conceivably be the case that **T** represents a conflation of **R** (or δ) with another manuscript.[214]

From inspection of the critical apparatus it is evident that in

---

[214] Such a possibility may be indicated by certain readings which **T** shares with other MSS, esp. **A**, against **R**; for example, c. 1, *eodem* and *ac*; c. 2, *et unum*; c. 3, addition of *suum*, and *Merciorum*; c. 6, inclusion of *sibi*; c. 7, omission of *eius*; c. 10, *quomodo* for *quo*; and c. 11, *uicino*.

several respects **C** and **R** are very similar (leaving aside **T** for one moment). Examples of the readings shared by these two witnesses are: c. 1, *coniunctione* for *coniunctionem*; c. 3, *Northumbrorum* for *Northanhymbrorum* where it can be seen that the reading of **R** was subsequently altered from that of **C** to that of the other witnesses; c. 3, *citim*, altered subsequently in **R** to *citatim*; c. 6, omission of *sibi*; c. 11, *uicinum* for *uicino*. At the simplest level of hypothesis, we might from this evidence suppose **C** and **R** to have been copied from a common exemplar (β) now lost, which displayed the errors just listed, as well as the other variants shared by **C** and **R** alone against **AEW**. While the scribe, or rather, scribes of **C** very frequently erred in the copying of their exemplar, the scribe of **R** seems to have intentionally altered or simplified the text as he copied it.

Needless to say, one or several more stages of transmission may well have intervened between **CR** and the hypothetical hyparchetype β, that is to say, both the errors of **C** and the alterations of **R** could actually have been made by the scribes of copies which served as the exemplars for **C** and **R**, but which are now lost, rather than by the scribes of **C** and **R** themselves. This is where the observations made above about **R** and **T** come in. It should be noted that **T** shares two of the variants common to **C** and **R**, namely c. 1, *coniunctione*, and c. 5, *prodente*. Thus an alternative configuration of events is that the hypothetical δ and **C** have a common exemplar, namely the conjectural hyparchetype β.

L, although heavily abbreviated, has some similarities with **C**, **R**, and **T**, for example c. 3, *cum uxore . . . cum carperet* for *dum cum uxore . . . carperet*; c. 5, *prodente* for *prouidente*; c. 7, *deque uera* where **AW** has *de ueraque*; c. 12, *nota* where **AE** has *notata*; and c. 13, *ibique* for *ubi* (*nunc*). Thus it cannot have been copied from **A**, **E**, or **W**, or any (now lost) witness similar to them. On the other hand, neither **C** nor **R** can have served as the direct source for **L**, since each has variant readings which **L** does not share, as demonstrated at the beginning, for example, c. 3, *At post hec* against *Ad hec* of **C**; addition of *et dicit* in **R**; c. 5, *ostendit indice*; *iter* in **C**; c. 6, omission of *infans* in **R**, and of *sibi* in **CR**; *odor gratissimus* in **R**; *nec* in **R**; c. 7, *bonitatis honestate* in **R**; c. 12, addition of *hac* in **R**; c. 13, *prelibanum* in **C**; addition of *etenim* in **R**. It may be that **L** was copied from the same (hypothetical) exemplar as that of **C** and **R** (and **T**), that is, β or δ, either directly or through the mediation of a descendant of that group, a now lost copy of *Vita S. Rumwoldi*.

A close relationship can be established for the two Canterbury manuscripts and the Rochester fragment. There is known to have been co-operation of some sort between the scriptoria of Canterbury, and that of Rochester, particularly in the early part of the twelfth century, and pairs of similar manuscripts have been discovered.[215] The fragmentary text of **W** corresponds extremely closely to **A**, fos. 196 (col. a, line 20)–197 (col. a, line 28), and hence the question immediately arises whether **W** could have been copied directly from **A**, or vice versa. It must be stressed that the fragmentary nature of **W** only permits a highly conjectural reconstruction of the relationship. In the majority of cases where **A** differs from the other witnesses, **W**, where present, follows; the only differences between the two copies are four instances of unique variation in **W**, namely, omission of *me* (c. 2, note i); c. 3, *ita* for *itaque*; c. 6, *susceperit* for *susceperat*; and c. 7, *fluentibus* for *fluctibus*. These readings suggest that **A** cannot have been copied from **W**. There are also five places where **A** shows a unique reading, each of them an 'addition' to the text as found in the other witnesses, for example, c. 2, addition of *diuine gratie*, and of *Paulum*; c. 6, addition of *seruus Dei* and, c. 7, of *uidelicet*. Although the evidence is only slight, if one were to suppose that **W** had been copied directly from **A**, it would seem a strange coincidence that in exactly the places where the scribe of **A** (or of its exemplar) had made additions, the scribe of **W** should subsequently make omissions. Such variations could be better explained in terms of a common exemplar for **A** and **W**.

When we come to consider the relationship between **A** and the fragmentary witness **E**, two kinds of evidence are available. First of all, it has already been noted that there is a close similarity between the contents of volume 6 of the Christ Church legendary (Lit. E. 42) and those of the St Augustine's legendary (Arundel 91/ Fell 2).[216] Ker was firmly of the opinion that the former cannot be derived from the latter, judging from their respective copies of *Passio S. Firmini*, where Arundel has an omission not paralleled in

[215] See Ker, *English Manuscripts*, p. 14, for a list of these pairs.
[216] Cf. Ker, *Medieval Manuscripts*, ii. 294.

Lit. E. 42.[217] In other words, even if it proved impossible to determine the relationship between **A** and **E** in *Vita S. Rumwoldi*, it may in theory be possible to determine it by comparing the text of other saints' Lives common to both legendaries. Ker's assertions must now be compared with the evidence available from *Vita S. Rumwoldi*.

What little remains of the text of *Vita S. Rumwoldi* in **E** is identical with that in **A**, fo. 198 (col. a, lines 7 onwards), except for a single addition in **A**: *ubi nunc requiescit*, where **E** has *ubi requiescit* (c. 13). It is striking that both witnesses originally shared the error *curriculam* for *curricula* (c. 12), subsequently corrected in **A** by erasure of the 'm'. This evidence, taken alone, could probably indicate a relationship in either direction: the scribe of **E** could, when copying from **A**, have omitted 'nunc', and the 'm' could have been erased from **A** *after* **E** had been copied from it. Alternatively, the scribe of **A**, using **E** as an exemplar, may have added *nunc*, and at first copied *curriculam*.[218] In fact, the reading *nunc* in **A** is not paralleled in any other witness, and as we saw from a comparison of **A** and **W**, addition of words and small phrases seems to be characteristic of the work of the scribe of **A**. Hence, there is little to contradict the hypothesis that **A** was copied from **E**. However, with this small quantity of evidence, the alternative possibility cannot be excluded that **A** and **E** (and hence also **W**) have a common exemplar (γ).

Unfortunately, there is no point at which the portions of *Vita S. Rumwoldi* preserved in **E** and **W** correspond, so that no certain conclusions can be drawn about their relationship. Having put forward the possibility that **A** and **W** have a common exemplar, and that **A** might have been copied from **E**, we must infer that **W** could also have been copied from **E**. This would effectively remove the necessity for including the unique variants of **A** and **W** in the critical apparatus, if it were not for the fact that **E** and **W** are only fragments of the text. It would not even be safe to attempt a reconstruction of **E** from **A** (bearing in mind the tendency of **A** to add to its exemplar), since in one case, both **A** and **W** preserve additions

---

[217] Ibid. ii. 295 n. 1. In a letter kept with **W**, Ker stated his opinion more strongly that Arundel 91 is 'almost certainly a copy of Christ Church, Canterbury *Passionale Sancti Matthei*' (i.e. Lit. E. 42).

[218] The 'm' could have been erased at any time, from the stage of 'official correction' onwards, either by knowledge of the gender of 'curriculum', or possibly during comparison of **A** with another copy of *Vita S. Rumwoldi*.

not found in any other witness (namely in c. 3, addition of *mutuo*). In other words, it would be difficult, when considering those portions of text where **A** is the only representative of the Canterbury recension, to distinguish between an addition made by the scribe of **E**, and an addition peculiar to **A**. Consequently, the only secure way to treat this Canterbury recension of *Vita S. Rumwoldi* seems to be to report all the readings of **A**, and of **E** and **W** where present, and to note every instance of agreement between them.

The abridgement of *Vita S. Rumwoldi* provided by John of Tynemouth (**S**) is somewhat fuller than that in **L** and **T**. Horstmann suggested that John had used **A**.[219] Certainly the majority of the variant readings of **A(EW)** are preserved by **S** (such that it cannot have been copied from either **C** or **R**), for example c. 2, *et unum* for *unumque*; c. 3, *dum cum* for *cum*, and omission of *ameno*; c. 4, omission of *namque*; *accipiant* for *excipiant* and addition of *est*, *fieri* for *effici*; c. 10, *debeatis* for *debetis*; c. 11, *scientia* for *conscientia*, and so on. But although undoubtedly **S** follows **A** very closely, there are enough instances where it does not share **A**'s unique variants, to cast some doubt upon the directness of the relationship between these two witnesses; for example, in the places where **A** alone adds a word or phrase, as in c. 2, c. 6, and c. 7, and one unique error in **A** (c. 11, *alicubi* for *alicui*). It is noteworthy that several of the additions in **A** not followed by **S** are also not shared by **W** (as noted above). However, it is not likely that **S** was copied from **W** either, since none of **W**'s three unique variants appear in **S**. Unless it be assumed that John, in producing his redaction of the *Vita S. Rumwoldi*, by coincidence removed all that had previously been added in his exemplar **A**, and corrected the one error, the only way to describe the relationship of **S** to **AW** is to suppose that they were all copied from the same hyparchetype, **E**, either directly, or indirectly, through the mediation of another copy of *Vita S. Rumwoldi* now lost. If this were the case, then the readings of **S** could be used as a control to determine the extent to which **A** is representative of **E** (where **E** and **W** are missing), so that the unique errors of **A**, **S**, and **W** would not need to be included in the critical apparatus. This is precluded by the fact that, particularly at the beginning of the text, **S** is an abbreviation (and also by the possibility that **S** may actually represent a conflation of **A** with one or more other witnesses).

[219] *NLA* i. 34 n. 3.

Conjectural *stemma codicum*

It can be seen that the surviving witnesses (full, fragmentary, and abbreviated) to *Vita S. Rumwoldi* fall into two groups or recensions, characterized by certain common errors or variants. The task of tracing the relationship further back, that is, of discerning the nature of the archetype, is rather more difficult. Possible clues may be the following. The obscure name which occurs in **R** as *Ydidas*, and as *Ididias* in **C**, has been altered in **A** from the latter reading to *Ididas* by erasure of the extra *i* (**S** has *Ydidas*). Also, in c. 11, where **R** and **T** have *periurium*, **C** has *periuriam*; the scribe of **A** had also originally written *periuriam*, which was subsequently altered to *periuria* by erasure of the 'm'. Where a decision has been required between the reading of **CR(T)** and **A(EW)**, the former has most frequently been selected for inclusion in the text. The reasoning is simply that, just as the impression from the unique variants of **R** is that they are the work of a later redactor, so also one senses that **AEW** may represent an early twelfth-century 'Canterbury' recension of the text. As already noted, the authority of **C**, as the witness standing closest in date to the composition of the *Vita*, is undermined by its many obvious textual flaws, but may perhaps be trusted when supported by other witnesses. A further complicating factor in the establishing of the text is the inescapable suspicion that the author of *Vita S. Rumwoldi* did not always write perfect Latin.

(xiii) *Previous Editions of* Vita Sancti Rumwoldi

The only previous edition of *Vita S. Rumwoldi* is in the Bollandists'
Acta Sanctorum.[220] The manuscripts used were **R** (= 1), **C** (= 2), **A**
(= 3) and **L** (= 4), with **R** as a base text. The readings of both **C**
and **R** are poorly reported and the Bollandists were not aware of
the existence of **E**, **T**, or **W**. Parallel to the main text, under the
heading *EIVSDEM VITAE EPITOME*, they printed the version of
the *Vita* in John of Tynemouth's *Sanctilogium* (**S**).

[220] Nov. i (1887) 682–90.

THE LATIN TEXTS:
EDITORIAL PROCEDURES

EXCEPT in the case of *Vita S. Birini*, where some manuscripts provide headings, all divisions of the texts into chapters are editorial, and have been made for ease of reference. The punctuation is also editorial, and follows modern principles. As regards the orthography of these three editions, the following general practices have been observed. Where *ae* would be required in classical Latin, all the witnesses have either *e* or *e*-caudata with varying frequency, as is normal in manuscripts from the late eleventh century onwards. Consequently *e* has been supplied in every case. Since a reconstruction of authorial orthography would be virtually impossible, that of the majority of the witnesses, or of the earliest witness, has generally been chosen for the texts, in order to avoid enumeration in the critical apparatus of the very many variations of the type 'c' for 't', '-mpn-' for '-mn-' or '-nn-', 'con' and 'com', 'y' for 'i'.

In the English translations, where the Vulgate text of the Bible has been cited verbatim in the Latin, the equivalent has been supplied from the Douai-Rheims version as revised by Richard Challoner (1749–50).

The following are further comments particular to each of the three texts.

(i) Vita S. Birini

As already stated above, the variant readings of all the direct manuscript witnesses have been reported except those of the abbreviated versions **B** and **F**. In the case of these two witnesses, only variants shared with one or more other witnesses have been noted. The chapter-headings are those found in **A, C,** and **D**.

(ii) Vita et miracula S. Kenelmi

The text provided here follows **D** most closely, because, besides being the earliest witness (a fact which in itself cannot guarantee priority) it offers the fewest unique errors. There would perhaps have been more interest in an attempted reconstruction of one or all of the hypothetical hyparchetypes posited in the foregoing description of the relationship of manuscripts, but, because of the relatively small number of witnesses, and the very tentative nature of the *stemma*, this would in reality lead only to the creation of a whole new set of witnesses of dubious authority.

As far as personal and place-names are concerned, the only variation which has not been reported is between *uu* and *w*—in every case the orthography of **D**, as the witness closest in time to date of composition, has been reproduced. In the other manuscripts there is some degree of inconsistency—as to 'Wigornensis', 'Oswald(us)' and 'Æthelwold(us)' only **D** uses *Vu* and *uu*; all manuscripts use *W* for 'Winc(h)elcumbe', and, in those witnesses which contain the name, for 'Wlfred(us)'. In this respect, **B** is the most inconsistent, reading *Vuluuinus* (Preface) and *iuuentuna* (c. 18), but *Vulwenne* (c. 3) and *Godwinus* (c. 18). **G** never uses *uu*, neither does **L**—hardly surprising by the fourteenth century. **H** uses *uu* only once, in the name of the abbot Godwin (c. 12). **J**, like **H**, has *uu* only once, in 'Vulfuuin(us)' (preface). Except for the name 'Oswald(us)', **P** is consistent in using -*uu*- medially, and *W* initially.

(iii) Vita S. Rumwoldi

In the critical apparatus, all variant readings of the full witnesses have been reported, as well as those of the fragmentary witnesses, where present. As regards the later abbreviated versions of the text, it has seemed best (for the sake of clarity) only to report variant readings which in some way follow or support those of the other witnesses and thus contribute towards defining the relationship of the manuscripts. The many unique variants of the abbreviated versions, often arising from the very activity of abridgement, are not strictly relevant to a reconstruction of the earlier transmissional history of the text.

The orthography of personal names has been standardized. There is some inconsistency in the manuscripts in the spelling of *Rumwold(us)* and *Eadwald(us)*. In the case of the five earliest manuscripts the use of *uu*, *w* or the Anglo-Saxon runic character wynn (*ρ*), needs also to be noted. In the critical apparatus, only divergence from the following norms will be reported:

(a) **C** almost always has *Rumold(us)*, except for the rubric (incipit), where it has *RVMWALDI*,[1] and the second occurrence of the name in the *Vita*, where the name appears as *Rumpoldi*. **R** has *Rumwold(us)* on every occasion except two, when it has *Rumold(us)*. All other manuscripts have *Rumwold(us)* consistently, except **L**, which always uses the form *Rumold(us)*.

(b) **C** always has *Eadwold(us)*. **R** has *Eadwald(us)*, on every occasion but one, where it has *Eadwold(us)*. **A** reads *Eadwald(us)* four times and *Eadwold(us)* twice. In the fragments **E** and **W** only the form *Eadwald(us)* is found. **S** and **T** consistently have *Edwold(us)*, and **L** always *Edwald(us)*.

(c) The scribes of **C** were extremely inconsistent in their use of *uu*, *w* and *p* in personal names: *Widerin(us)* occurs three times with *W*, twice with *Vu* and once with *p*; *Eadwold(us)* occurs twice with *w*, once with *uu* and three times with *p*, and *Rumwold(us)* occurs just once with *p*.[2] **A** always uses *uu* in *Rumuuold(us)* and *Eaduuald(us)*, and in four out of six cases for *Vuiderinus* (the other two are *W*-). In what remains of **E**, *uu* is used in every case, and in **W** always *w*. **R** also uses *w* throughout.[3]

---

[1] 'Rumwald(us)' is the form of the name found in the majority of the surviving liturgical calendars which include the saint, and in the earlier of the two MSS of the Old English resting-place list, *Secgan* (cf. Lieberman, *Heilige*, p. 13).

[2] It should be noted that this variation occurs within the work of both scribes.

[3] Ker, *Catalogue*, p. xxxii, notes that *u*, *uu* and *w* occur in place of *p* in 12th-cent. MSS, as is the case here; thus **C** can be seen to have been written during a transitional phase in scribal practice.

VITA SANCTI BIRINI

SIGLA OF MANUSCRIPTS

A Oxford, Bodleian Library, Digby 39, fos. 57^r–74^v (s. xii^{in})
B Oxford, Bodleian Library, Bodley 509, fos. 135^v–138^v (s. xiii^{in})
C London, BL, Cotton Caligula A. VIII, fos. 121^r–124^v (s. xii^{in})
D Oxford, Bodleian Library, Digby 112, fos. 5^v–17^r (s. xii^{in})
F Oxford, Bodleian Library, Fell 2, pp. 263–8 (s. xii$^{1/3}$)
G Gotha, Forschungsbibliothek, I. 81, fos. 113^r–118^v (s. xiv^2)
H Hereford Cathedral Library, P. VII. 6, fos. 134^v–139^r (s. xii^{med})
T London, BL, Cotton Tiberius D. IV, pt. 2, fos. 105^v–110^v (s. xii^{in})

§ 1. *INCIPIT VITA BEATISSIMI BYRINI EPISCOPI ANG-LORVM APOSTOLI.* *ᵇVBI ORTVS ET NVTRITVS.ᵇ* Beatis-simus igitur Birinus, magnificus pater, pastor egregius oriturᶜ Rome, futurus ciuis ciuitatis eterne. Oritur autem Rome, ut eum loci leuaret dignitas, quem uite spiritualis aliquando commendaret auctoritas. Diuina prouidentia natiuitati illius preparauit locum in quo totius sancte ecclesieᵈ uoluit esse primatum. Genuit eumᵉ Roma natiuitate carnis, quem postea paritura erat ad regulam catholice ueritatis. Protulit ᶠergo eumᶠ Roma ad ortum carnis et fidei, non adhucᵍ erroris discipula, sed iam in omnibus gentibus magistra ueritatis[1] effecta. Ecce, O beatissimi apostoli, uera mundi lumina, duo ante Deum lucentia candelabra,[2] ecce de radice fidei uestre, de pinguedine sanctitatis uestre palmes religiosusʰ exiliit,ⁱ oliua fructifera in domo Domini.[3] Ecce de luce et claritateʲ sapientie uestre futurus in basilica regis eterni lucerna emicuit; de fir-mitate et constantia uestra columna[4] excisa est, que intrabit in domum Domini, lapis qui non reprobabitur[5] ab edificio ecclesias-tice ciuitatis. Genuistis eum ad fidem, parturistis eum ad chris-tianam religionem, quatinus successor idoneus preco ueritatis[6] effectus pro uobis fungeretur legatione, non metuens nomen Domini et fidei sacramento et operis testimonio ubique portare.

§ 2. *ᵏDE GENERE ILLIVS ET CONVERSATIONE SANCTA.ᵏ* Nascitur itaque ingenuus puer illustris quidem familia, illustrior uirtute et gratia, qui quanto se humilius diuinis obsequiis mancipauit, tanto sullimius sibi gloriam et honorem de

ᵃ⁻ᵃ C; *om. AD*; INCIPIT VITA BEATI BIRINI EPISCOPI ET CONFESSORIS .III. NONAS DECEMBRIS *G*; ET CONFESSORIS .III. NONAS DECEMBRIS *add. H*; INCIPIT VITA SANCTI BYRINI EPISCOPI *T*   ᵇ⁻ᵇ VBI ORTVS SIT ET NVTRITVS *D*; *om. CGHT*   ᶜ ortus est *BH*   ᵈ *om. G* ᵉ enim *C*   ᶠ⁻ᶠ eum ergo *H*   ᵍ ad huc *D*   ʰ religiosius *C*   ⁱ ex-siliuit *G*   ʲ caritate *T*   ᵏ⁻ᵏ *om. GHT*

---

[1] The epithets 'erroris discipula' and 'magistra ueritatis' are adapted from Leo the Great, *Sermo* lxxxii, ed. A. Chavasse, *Sancti Leonis Magni Romani Pontificis Tractatus septem et nonaginta*, 2 vols., *CCSL* cxxxviii and cxxxviii A (1973), ii. 508–9. The version used by the author of the *Vita* corresponded to the 'β-recension' in Chavasse's edition. Material from the same sermon is used elsewhere in the *Vita* (cc. 7 and 8): *Isti enim sunt uiri per quos tibi Euangelium Christi, Roma, resplenduit, et quae eras magistra erroris, facta es discipula ueritatis. Isti sunt sancti patres tui uerique pastores, qui te regnis coelestibus inserendam multo melius multoque felicius condiderunt . . . Isti sunt qui te ad hanc gloriam prouexer-unt, ut gens sancta multis aucta uictoriis ius imperii tui terra marique protuleris, minus*

§ 1. HERE BEGINS THE LIFE OF ST BIRINUS, BISHOP. WHERE HE WAS BORN AND BROUGHT UP. The blessed Birinus, great father and eminent pastor, was born in Rome, a future citizen of the eternal city. And he was born in Rome so that the dignity of the place might elevate him whom the authority of the spiritual life would finally commend. Divine providence prepared a place for his nativity, in which He desired that the primacy of the entire holy church should be. Rome gave birth to him in the nativity of the flesh, whom subsequently she would bring forth to the rule of universal truth. Therefore Rome brought him forth in the birth of flesh and of faith, not now a disciple of error, but already made a teacher of truth to all peoples.[1] Behold, O blessed apostles, true lights of the world, two candelabra shining before God,[2] behold from the root of your faith, from the fullness of your sanctity, a religious vine-shoot springs forth, a fruitful olive tree in the house of the Lord.[3] Behold from the light and clarity of your wisdom, one who will be a lamp in the temple of the eternal king, has shone forth; from your steadfastness and constancy a column has been hewn,[4] which will enter into the house of the Lord, a stone which will not be rejected[5] from the building of the ecclesiastical city. You bore him for faith, you gave birth to him for Christian religion, to the end that, made a suitable successor, a herald of truth,[6] he might function as an ambassador for you, not fearing to carry everywhere the name of the Lord, by the sacrament of faith and the testimony of works.

§ 2. ABOUT HIS ORIGIN AND HOLY WAY OF LIFE. So the noble boy was born, distinguished as to family, yet more distinguished in virtue and grace. The more humbly he subjected himself to divine obedience, the more sublimely he acquired for himself glory and honour from his servitude. For to serve the Lord

---

tamen est quod tibi bellicus labor subdidit quam quod pax Christiana subiecit (CCSL cxxxviii A. 508–9). See p. liv on the hagiographer's knowledge of a homiliary containing Sermo lxxxii.

[2] Rev. 11: 4 ('Hi sunt duae oliuae et duo candelabra in conspectu Domini terrae stantes').

[3] Ps. 51(52): 10 ('Ego autem, sicut oliua fructifera in domo Dei').

[4] Cf. Rev. 3: 12 ('Qui uicerit, faciam illum columnam in templo Dei mei').

[5] Ps. 117(118): 22 ('lapis quem reprobauerunt aedificantes').

[6] Cf. Paschasius Radbertus, Expositio in Matheo Libri xii ii. 2612 and 2917; iii. 1034, and vi. 741 ('preco ueritatis') [of an Apostle], ed. B. Paulus, 3 vols., CCCM lvi–lvi B (1984), i. 195, 205, and 266, and ii. 578.

seruitute comparauit. Seruire enim Domino regnare est,[1] et eius deseruire uoluntati summa ingenuitas est. Deuote ergo et sine crimine Deo seruire erat sibi nobilitatis lumen insigne. Nec de parentum laude superbiens, gloriam sibi exigebat, sed pie et religiose moralitatis ornamenta querebat. Erat enim placidus uultu, mansuetus affectu,[a] promptus obsequio, benignus eloquio. Parcus sibi, ad pauperes largus, non thesaurum ubi[b] demolitur tinea et ubi fures effodiunt et furantur,[2] sed thesaurum bonorum operum indeficienter sibi thesaurizabat, et in celum[c] sudores suos officiose et strenuo comportabat. Accinxit se cingulo[d] continentie, firmauit se uigore pudicitie, amauit titulum castitatis, subneruauit in se uniuersum carnalis[e] impetum uoluptatis. Erat omnibus uirtutis[f] scola,[3] boni operis forma, magisterium uite,[4] ordo iustitie, firmissima fidei disciplina, seueritatis[g] exemplar, speculum honestatis, religionis liber, pagina sanctitatis. In corde ipsius sanctitatis et fidei magnitudo, in ore illius legis euangelice plenitudo,[5] et ex eo quod eum gratia sancti spiritus debriabat, auditoribus suis pia uite pocula ructuabat.[6] Qui iuxta illum erat iuxta cellam erat uinariam,[7] de qua bonus odor concipitur, qui ducit ad uitam. Sapientia enim Dei sibi eum in spiritualem cellam consecrauit, quam uniuersorum pigmentorum suorum bonorum uidelicet morum iocunda suauitate ditauit. Ordinauit in illo caritatem[8] ut bene posito fundamento structura que superedificanda erat[9] non moueretur uel deficeret, sed ad omnes assultus grassantis malitie firma consisteret.

§ 3. [h]QVOD CRESCENTE ODORE OPINIONIS SANCTE AD GRADVM SACERDOTII EVECTVS SIT.[h] Crescebat

[a] affectus *D*   [b] om. *T*   [c] eelum *D*   [d] singulo *G*   [e] carnis *D*
[f] uirtutibus *G*   [g] se ueritatis *G*   [h-h] om. *GHT*

[1] Cf. 'Deus auctor pacis et amator quem nosse uiuere, cui seruire regnare est' from the postcommunion prayer for the 'Missa pro pace' which formed part of the *Gelasian Sacramentary*, ed. H. A. Wilson (Oxford, 1894), p. 272; see also the 'Missal of Robert of Jumièges' (ed. Wilson, p. 265), for the occurrence of the same prayer in a sacramentary closer in date to that of the composition of *Vita S. Birini*.

[2] Matt. 6: 19–20 ('Nolite thesaurizare uobis thesauros in terra: ubi aerugo, et tinea demolitur: et ubi fures effodiunt et furantur. Thesaurizate autem uobis thesauros in caelo').

[3] This sentence is probably based upon Peter Chrysologus, *Sermo* cxxvii (*De natale S. Iohannis Baptistae*): 'Iohannes, uirtutum schola, magisterium uitae, sanctitatis forma, norma morum, uirginitatis speculum, pudicitiae titulus, castitatis exemplum, poenitentiae uia, peccatorum uenia, fidei disciplina', ed. A. Olivar, 3 vols., *CCSL* xxiv–xxiv B (1975–82), iii. 782. Paul the Deacon included this sermon in his homiliary (Olivar, i. xxviii–xxix; Grégoire, *Homéliaires*, p. 466); cf. p. liv above.

is to reign,[1] and to be subject to his will is the highest nobility. Therefore, to serve God devotedly and without sin was to him the glorious light of nobility. He did not take pride in his parents' renown or claim glory for himself, but piously and religiously sought the adornments of morality. For he was placid of mien, mild in disposition, quick to obey and gentle of speech. Sparing with himself, generous to the poor, he unfailingly laid up for himself not the hoard which the worm demolishes, and which thieves dig up and steal,[2] but the treasure of good works, and carried with him to heaven the fruits of his toil dutifully and strenuously. He girt himself with the girdle of continence, strengthened himself with the vigour of modesty, he loved the name of chastity, and inwardly undermined the general onslaught of fleshly pleasure. He was a school of virtue to all,[3] a pattern of good work, an instruction for life,[4] and a good order of justice, the strictest teaching of faith, exemplar of severity, a mirror of honesty, book of religion, and page of sanctity. In his heart was a breadth of sanctity and faith, on his lips the fullness of the evangelical law,[5] and that which the grace of the Holy Spirit intoxicated him with, he poured forth into the holy cups of life for his listeners.[6] Whoever was near him was near a wine cellar,[7] from which a fine fragrance rises, which leads to life. For the wisdom of God consecrated him as a spiritual cellar, which He has enriched with the lovely sweetness of all His spices, to wit, righteous ways. He [God] ordained love in him[8] so that the structure which was to be built upon,[9] being placed well on its foundations, should not subside or weaken, but should stand firm against all the assaults of encroaching malice.

§ 3. THAT WITH THE INCREASING ODOUR OF HOLY REPUTATION HE WAS RAISED TO THE RANK OF THE PRIESTHOOD. He grew every day in the practice of virtue, a

---

[4] Cf. *Vita S. Swithuni* c. 2, 'ordinem morum magisterium uite' (Sauvage, p. 375).

[5] Cf. Rom. 13: 10 ('plenitudo ergo legis est dilectio').

[6] Cf. Alcuin, *Epist.* ccxiii, 'instructus reuelatione celesti ac sancti spiritus gratia debriatus', ed. E. Duemmler, *MGH, Epistolae*, iv (Berlin, 1865), p. 355. This is also reminiscent of a metaphor which Augustine applied several times to John the Evangelist, for example, *Sermo* cxix, 'hoc enim principium euangelii sancti Iohannis ructuauit, quia de pectore Domini bibit' (*PL* xxxviii. 673)—also *Sermo* cxx (col. 676), cxxxiii (col. 741), cxxxv (col. 750), and cxliii (col. 786).

[7] S. of S. 2: 4 ('Introduxit me in cellam uinariam; ordinauit in me charitatem').

[8] See previous note.

[9] Cf. 1 Cor. 3: 11–12 ('Fundamentum enim aliud nemo potest ponere praeter id quod positum est, quod est Christus Iesus. Siquis autem superaedificat super fundamentum hoc').

cotidie in usum*a* uirtutis miles expromptus*b* militia christiana fortis audacia, sagitta ad transfodiendum cetum*c* Sathane de faretra dominice prouisionis¹ intenta.*d* Satagebat unus esse de sexaginta fortibus de fortissimis Israhel, qui ambiunt*e* lectulum*f* Salomonis, omnes tenentes gladios et ad bella doctissimi. Vniuscuiusque ensis super femur *g*suum propter timores nocturnos.² Habebat autem gladium super femur*g* quia*h* discretione uersatili omnes mundane occupationis premebat affectus, cauens sibi ad occursum hostis nocturni—hostis quidem illius qui in nocte est et tenebras diligit, qui in circuitu totus est et circuit tanquam leo querens quem deuoret.³ Preliabatur in amplitudine cordis bella dominica, aduersus tyrannidem uitiorum certamen legitimum concertabat; carnem edomans, spiritum roborabat. Sciebat enim quia coronari non habet nisi qui*i* legitime certauerit.⁴ Pugnabat pro patria, sciensque se non habere hic manentem ciuitatem, futuram fortiter inquirebat.⁵ Celesti discipline adeo se perfecte contradidit, ut ab ipsis pueritie annis aliquem cotidie gradum crescendi et ascendendi perciperet,*j* et in carne degens, tanquam nichil de carnea mole gestaret. Vnde non nomine sed uirtute sullimis, insignis non gradu sed merito, non iam clericus putabatur⁶ *k*ab omnibus sed sacerdos.*k* Electus enim a Domino ante merebatur esse quam fieret, et quasi quadam lingua uirtutum uaticinabatur iam in ecclesia Dei sacerdotem procul dubio se esse futurum. Sacrificabat enim se sedulo in hostiam exultationis, in odorem suauitatis,⁷ se in cruce compunctionis configens, et in ara confessionis totum se Deo

---

a unum *G*   *b* et promptus *H*; promptus *GT*   *c* ortum *G*   *d* in tenta *T*   *e* ambiant *G*   *f* lectum *G (and D before correction in margin)*   *g-g om. G by homoeoteleuton*   *h* que *G*   *i om. D*   *j* prepararet *T*   *k-k* sed sacerdos ab omnibus *H*

---

¹ Cf. Isa. 49: 2 ('Et posuit me sicut sagittam electam, in pharetra sua abscondit me').

² S. of S. 3: 7 ('En lectulum Salomonis sexaginta fortes ambiunt ex fortissimis Israel, omnes tenentes gladios, et ad bella doctissimi, uniuscuiusque ensis super femur suum propter timores nocturnos'). The Christian allegorical interpretation of the Song of Songs goes back as far as Gregory of Nyssa and Origen, but an influential text for Western exegesis was Bede's *In Cantica Canticorum allegorica expositio*, ed. D. Hurst, *Bedae Venerabilis Opera, Pars II: Opera Exegetica*, CCSL cxix B (1983), pp. 167–375. Almost all subsequent expositions are, to some extent, indebted to Bede's work; see H. Riedlinger, *Die Makellosigkeit der Kirche in den lateinischen Hohenliedkommentaren des Mittelalters* (Freiburg, 1956); and F. Ohly, *Hohelied-Studien; Grundzüge einer Geschichte der Hoheliedauslegung des Abendlandes bis zum 1200* (Wiesbaden, 1958). No extant exegesis of the Song of Songs has yet been found which matches the interpretation of the sixty strong men of Israel offered in *Vita S. Birini* so closely as to be regarded as the direct source. The

soldier ready at hand in the Christian campaign, strong in courage, with an arrow from the quiver provided by the Lord,[1] aimed to transfix the sea-monster of Satan. He was eager to be one of the three-score strong men out of the strongest of Israel, who surround Solomon's couch, all holding their swords, and skilled in battle. Each has his sword on his thigh on account of fears in the night.[2] He had his sword on his thigh because he was keeping in check all the passions of worldly occupation with circumspect discernment, guarding himself against the attack of the night-enemy—indeed, of that enemy who exists in the night and loves the shadows, who spends his time entirely in prowling, and prowls about as a lion, seeking whom he may devour.[3] He fought the Lord's battles in greatness of heart, he contended in the just struggle against the tyranny of the vices; taming the flesh, he strengthened the spirit. For he knew that only he who battles justly gains the crown.[4] He fought for his native land, and knowing that he had here no lasting city, boldly sought the one to come.[5] He so perfectly delivered himself up to heavenly discipline, that from the very years of his boyhood he attained every day a step in the direction of growth and ascent, and although living in the flesh, yet he bore nothing of the fleshly burden. Whence, not lofty by name but by virtue, outstanding not by rank but desert, he was no longer regarded by all as a minor cleric, but as a priest.[6] For he had earned the right to be chosen by the Lord before he was chosen, and as if by the speaking tongue of his virtues, he already prophesied that he would without doubt be a priest in the church of God. For he gave himself eagerly as the sacrificial victim of exultation, in the odour of sweetness,[7] crucifying himself upon the cross of remorse, and setting himself

hagiographer might simply have been providing his own version of the standard interpretation. Compare Bede, *In Cantica Canticorum* (Hurst, p. 238): 'quia et praesentem ecclesiae quietem ac pacem praedicatores sancti contra hereticorum tuentur incursus . . . Ensem uero super femur habent milites Christi cum motum carnalium uoluptatum spiritalis uerbi districtione comprimunt et hoc propter timores nocturnos, id est ne eos insidiae temptatoris antiqui si securos inermesque reppererint sternant.'

[3] 1 Pet. 5: 8 ('aduersarius uester diabolus tanquam leo rugiens circuit, quaerens quem deuoret').

[4] 2 Tim. 2: 5 ('Nam et qui certat in agone, non coronatur nisi legitime certauerit').

[5] Heb. 13: 14 ('Non enim habemus hic manentem ciuitatem, sed futuram inquirimus').

[6] Cf. Sulpicius Severus, *Vita S. Martini* ii. 7 ('ut iam illo tempore non miles sed monachus putaretur'), ed. J. Fontaine, *Sulpice Sévère, Vie de Saint Martin*, 3 vols., Sources Chrétiennes cxxxiii–cxxxv (Paris, 1967), i. 256.

[7] Cf. Eph. 5: 2 ('et hostiam Deo in odorem suauitatis').

deuote succendens. Sacrificium enim Domino spiritus humilia-
tionis,[1] et odor incensi uirtus assidue orationis.[2] Crescebat autem
in seruo quod accipiebat seruus a Domino. Augmentabatur de die
in diem in milite*a* quod miles se suscepisse credebat a rege. Non
enim meritum suum pensabat, sed Dei uirtutem; non naturam
attendebat humanam, sed gratiam in spiritum operantem. Succedente autem tempore ordinem*b* suscepit *c*quod opere dicebatur,*c*
et ut misteria diuina tractaret ad culmen sacerdotalis honoris
euectus*d* est. Factus autem presbiter, qualis quantusque in hoc
ministerio effulserit non est nostre facultatis euoluere,[3] cum iam
uita presens altitudinis sue dignitate eam quam primitus duxit
uideretur obtegere.

§ 4. *c*QVOD SVMMO PONTIFICI PRESENTATVS SIT ET
QVIA EVM IN BRITANNIAM PAPA LEGAVERIT.*e* Suauis-
sime igitur opinionis illius*f* odor[4] longe lateque uiritim*g* et publice
Deo ordinante cepit emanare*h* ad auditum totius Romani conuentus, quasi de horto liliorum suauiter*i* effraglare.*j* Nec patiebatur
diutius in eo munera sua Dominus abscondi, quia que illi confere-
bat uidebat eum humiliter suscipere[5] fideliterque complecti.*k* Sed
neque ciuitas in monte posita absconditur et*l* lucerna imponitur
candelabro, ut qui in domo sunt in luce sint*m* et de luce letentur.[6]
Peruenit ergo rumor ille sanctissimus ad solium summi pontificis,
ad sedem Romani antistitis, qui nomine Honorius[7] beate sue con-
uersationis honore*n* honorem cumulabat sancte uniuersalis ecclesie. Inuitatur itaque beatus Birinus a summo pontifice, *o*etiam
illius*o* presentatur optutibus, quem multa et sapienti indagatione
perlustrans,[8] quod auditu conceperat iam ex effectu*p* tenebat.
Cognouit in eo esse simplicitatem columbinam et nullatenus sibi

---

a militem *G*   *b* *CG*; ordine *ADH (and T before correction by later hand)*
c–c quem opere dicebatur implesse *T (later alteration over erasure)*   *d* effectus *C*
e–e *om. GHT*   *f* istius *H*   *g* interim *FG*   *h* et *add. H*   *i* suauitate
D   *j* *AC*; efflaglare *D*; effragrare *GT*; efflagrare *H*   *k* completi *G*
l set *G*   *m* *om. FG*   *n* *om. D*   *o–o* et illius iam *D*   *p* effecto *AC*
(and D before correction of o *to* u*)*

---

[1] Cf. Ps. 50(51): 19 ('Sacrificium Deo spiritus contribulatus; cor contritum et humili-
atum, Deus, non despicies').
[2] Cf. Rev. 8: 4 ('Et ascendit fumus incensorum de orationibus sanctorum').
[3] Cf. Sulpicius Severus, *Vita S. Martini* x. 1, 'Iam uero, sumpto episcopatu qualem se
quantumque praestiterit, non est nostrae facultatis euoluere' (Fontaine, i. 272).
[4] Cf. *Vita S. Swithuni* c. 3, 'factum est ut opinionis suauissime odor de prato sanctitatis ipsius emanans regi supradicto innotuerit' (Sauvage, p. 375).

wholly and devotedly alight on the altar of confession to God. The sacrifice to the Lord was the spirit of humility,[1] and the odour of incense was the assiduous power of prayer.[2] There grew in the servant that which the servant received from the Lord. There increased day by day in the soldier that which the soldier believed he had received from the King. For he did not weigh his own desert, but the might of God; he did not look to human nature, but grace, working on the spirit. With the passage of time, he took up the rank which was devoted to good works, and, so that he might perform the divine mysteries, he was raised to the height of priestly honour. Having been made a priest, it is not within our capabilities to unfold in what way and how greatly he shone in this ministry,[3] since now his present life by the grandeur of its loftiness seems to hide the nature of the one which he formerly led.

§ 4. HOW HE WAS PRESENTED TO THE HIGH PON-TIFF, AND THAT THE POPE SENT HIM TO BRITAIN. Therefore, the odour of his sweet reputation[4] began to spread far and wide, privately and publicly, as God ordained, to the hearing of the whole Roman community, as if wafting fragrantly from a garden of lilies. Nor did the Lord allow His gifts to lie hidden in him any longer, because He saw that what He had conferred upon him, he humbly accepted[5] and faithfully embraced. But a city situated upon a mountain is not hidden, and a lamp is placed upon a lamp-stand so that those in the house may be in the light and rejoice in the light.[6] And thus the holy rumour reached the throne of the high priest, to the seat of the bishop of Rome, who, by name Honorius,[7] increased the honour of the holy and universal church by the honour of his own blessed life. Therefore, St Birinus was invited by the high priest, indeed was presented before his gaze; he, examining with much and wise investigation,[8] now perceived in effect, that which he had only heard about. He saw that there was in him a dove-like simplicity, and that the cunning of a serpent was

---

[5] Cf. *Vita S. Swithuni* c. 1, 'susceptum humiliter uiriliterque portauit' (Sauvage, p. 375).

[6] Matt. 5: 14–15 ('Non potest ciuitas abscondi supra montem posita, neque accendunt lucernam, et ponunt eam sub modio, sed super candelabrum, ut luceat omnibus qui in domo sunt').

[7] The only 7th-cent. pope named Honorius was Honorius I, who was consecrated on 27 Oct. 625, and died on 12 Oct. 638—see *Liber Pontificalis (Pars Prior)*, ed. T. Mommsen, *MGH*, Gesta Pontificum Romanorum, i (1) (Berlin, 1898), pp. 170–4.

[8] Cf. *Vita S. Swithuni* c. 3, 'quem rex euocatum multimoda indagatione perlustrans' (Sauvage, p. 376).

deesse serpentis astutiam,[1] *ᵃ*ut astutia*ᵃ* simplicitatem igniret, et astutiam simplicitas*ᵇ* temperaret. Cognouit eum puritate uite simplicem,*ᶜ* sed emulatione et sapientia moderata discretione feruentem. Intellexit eum et uite merito precellere, et prerogatiua sapientie idoneum predicationi posse seruire. Intellexit quia bene posset eum ordinare episcopum, quem et uite sanctitas informabat, et doctrine dignitas exornabat. Sciebat enim quia tam doctrina quam uita radiare debet pastor in ecclesia.[2] Doctrina enim absque uita arrogantem, uita sine doctrina parit inutilem. Sciebat quia uectibus aureis archa testimonii*ᵈ* portabatur et sancta ecclesia a bonis doctoribus sustentatur. Et *ᵉ*bene dictum*ᵉ* est 'aureis', ut cum alios sermone instruant,*ᶠ* ipsi uite splendore fulgescant.[3] Sciebat quia regimen honoris non meretur suscipere qui nescit subditos sibi tramite uite melioris antecedere.*ᵍ*

§ 5. Perscrutatus*ʰ* igitur*ⁱ* beatissimus pater beatissimi*ʲ* filii sui uitam*ᵏ* fidei et scientie qualitatem,*ˡ* per Asterium[4] qui tunc sibi aderat Genuensem episcopum, eum ad episcopatus euexit officium.[5] Tunc beato Birino episcopali gradu honorifice sullimato[6] uenerandus papa mandatum dat, ut sibi Britanniam*ᵐ* que adhuc maxima*ⁿ* ex*ᵒ* parte paganissimis tenebatur erroribus, prouinciam legat, quam et fidei uerbo et uite confirmet exemplo. Imperat illum ibi esse *ᵖ*euangelium predicaturum,*ᵖ* ubi nondum nominatus est Christus, ne super alienum fundamentum edificet, sed sicut scriptum est 'quibus non est annuntiatum de eo uidebunt et qui non

ᵃ⁻ᵃ om. D; que T   *ᵇ* simplitatas D   *ᶜ* simplicita D   *ᵈ* testamenti H
ᵉ⁻ᵉ benedictum ACD   *ᶠ* instruunt T   *ᵍ* ante cedere ACD; C breaks off after this word, and resumes at c. 11 Vestigando consilium . . .   *ʰ* Perscrutatis T
ⁱ itaque FG   *ʲ* beati T   *ᵏ* uita T   *ˡ* qualitate T   *ᵐ* Britannia G; Brittaniam H   *ⁿ* magna FG   *ᵒ* om. H   *ᵖ⁻ᵖ* euangelii predicatorem T

[1] Cf. Matt. 10: 16 ('Estote ergo prudentes sicut serpentes et simplices sicut columbae'). Compare Gregory the Great, *Homiliarum xl in Euangelia libri II*, ii. 30. 5, 'quatenus et columbe simplicitatem astutia serpentis accenderet, et serpentis astutiam columbe simplicitas temperaret' (*PL* lxxvi. 1224).

[2] This sentence and the one following are a paraphrase of Isidore, *Sent*. iii. 36 (*De doctrina et exemplis praepositorum*), 'Tam doctrina quam uita clarere debet ecclesiasticus doctor. Nam doctrina sine uita arrogantem reddit, uita sine doctrina inutilem facit' (*PL* lxxxiii. 707).

[3] The biblical text behind this is Exod. 25: 13 ('Facies quoque uectes de lignis setim et operies eos auro'). The author of the *Vita* supplied the standard exegesis of that text,

by no means lacking,[1] so that the cunning might set alight the simplicity, and the simplicity temper the cunning. He saw that he was artless in the purity of life, but burning with zeal to excel, and with wisdom moderated by discrimination. He understood that he was both outstanding in the worthiness of his life, and also capable of subjecting himself to the prerogative of wisdom, ideal for preaching. He understood that he could well ordain him a bishop, him whom both sanctity of life moulded, and dignity of doctrine adorned. For he knew that a pastor in the church ought to shine as much in his teaching as in his life.[2] For doctrine without good life produces an arrogant priest, good life without doctrine a useless one. He knew that the ark of the covenant was carried on golden poles and the Holy Church is supported by good teachers. And 'golden' is the right word, since whilst they instruct others by their words, they themselves glitter with the excellence of their life.[3] He knew that he who does not know how to go before his subjects on the path of better life, does not deserve to receive honourable rule.

§ 5. Therefore, having thoroughly inspected the life of faith and the quality of the knowledge of his blessed son, the blessed father elevated him to the office of bishop, through Asterius,[4] the Genoese bishop, who was then with him.[5] Then, when Birinus had been honorably exalted to the rank of bishop,[6] the venerable pope commanded him to take as his province Britain, which was still for the most part possessed by pagan errors, so that he might strengthen it with the word of faith and by the example of his life. He commanded him to go to preach the gospel there, where Christ has not yet been named, lest he should build upon another man's foundations, but as it is written, 'those to whom it has not been announced

---

possibly here deriving ultimately from Gregory the Great, *Regula Pastoralis*: 'Vectibus quippe arcam portare, est bonis doctoribus sanctam Ecclesiam ad rudes infidelium mentes praedicando deducere. Qui auro quoque iubentur operiri, ut dum sermone aliis insonant, ipsi etiam uitae splendore fulgescant' (*PL* lxxvii. 49).

[4] P. B. Gams, *Series Episcoporum Ecclesiae Catholicae* (Ratisbon, 1873), p. 795, dated the episcopacy of Asterius at Milan to *c.*630–640, while in *Dictionnaire d'histoire et de géographie ecclésiastiques*, ed. A. Baudrillart *et al.*, i– (Paris, 1912–), under 'Asterius', the dates given are 27 Feb. 629 to 4 July 639. Asterius, and at least three of his predecessors, resided, in flight from the Arian Lombards, at Genoa, where the bishops of Milan had a palace. Cf. G. Cappelletti, *Le Chiese d'Italia dalla loro origine fino ai nostri giorni*, 21 vols. (Venice, 1844–70), xi. 132 (which gives the dates 630–40).

[5] The source for this is Bede, *HE* iii. 7. Occasionally, the author of *Vita S. Birini* borrows verbatim from Bede's account of Birinus' mission (in cc. 17, 18, 20, and 21).

[6] Cf. *Vita S. Swithuni* c. 5, 'honore pontificali honorifice sullimatus' (Sauvage, p. 377).

audierunt intelligent.'¹ Secutusᵃ uidelicet apostolum dicentem
'non in aliena regula in his que preparata sunt gloriantes, non ᵇin
immensumᵇ in alienis laboribus, sed secundum mensuram regule
quam nobis mensus est Deus.'²

§ 6. ᶜVBI EGREDITVR DE VRBE, TENDENS IN BRITAN-
NIAM.ᶜ Beatus ueroᵈ Birinus quia sciebat ex precepto apostoli
omnem animam potestatibus sullimioribus esse subdendam, et
quia qui potestatiᵉ resistit Dei ordinationi resistit,³ profitetur
obedientiam, suscipit iussionem, opus iniunctum libenter inire
promittit. Benedictione denique suscepta,⁴ parato comitatu,
sumptis uiaticis, quod sibi mandatum est, confisus de misericordia
Dei, implere festinat. Romanus ciuis Roma egreditur, patriam
parentesque dum relinquit, exultat.ᶠ Exultat, inquam, dum egreditur, dum exulatᵍ gaudet, dum se egenum facit, exultat.⁵ Nec de
ciuium affinitate relicta merebat, ʰqui Deum inhabitantem in ciuitate mentis habebat.ʰ Nec de ciuitate multitudinis exiens turba-
batur, qui de unius Dei inhabitatione interius letabatur. Quam
pulchrum quamque Deo dignum commercium, distracta multitudine unitatem adquiri! In multitudine enim confunderis, in
unitate firmaris. Dicit sermo diuinus quia 'ad multa sollicitus es,
turbaris erga plurima, unum autem est necessarium.'⁶ 'Vnam petii
a Domino', dicit propheta, 'hanc requiram ⁱut inhabitemⁱ in domo
Domini,⁷ ut habitemʲ in eo⁸ et ipse ᵏhabitet in me.'ᵏ Beatus autem
Birinus unam petiit, quia optimamˡ partem elegit, ut inhabitet in
Deo, ut mereatur inhabitari a Domino. Exiuit itaque de domo sua,

---

ᵃ secus *D*   ᵇ⁻ᵇ inmensum *DG (and H before correction)*   ᶜ⁻ᶜ *om. GHT*
ᵈ ergo *H*   ᵉ potest *G*   ᶠ exulat *D*   ᵍ exultat *G*   ʰ⁻ʰ *om. G (perhaps by homoeoteleuton)*   ⁱ⁻ⁱ et in habitem *G*   ʲ inhabitem *H*   ᵏ⁻ᵏ in me
habitet *G*   ˡ meliorem *H*

---

¹ Rom. 15: 20–1 ('Sic autem praedicaui Euangelium hoc, non ubi nominatus est
Christus, ne super alienum fundamentum aedificarem: sed sicut scriptum est: Quibus
non est annuntiatum de eo uidebunt, et qui non audierunt, intelligent').
² 2 Cor. 10: 13 ('Nos autem non in immensum gloriabimur, sed secundum mensuram
regulae, qua mensus est nobis Deus, mensuram pertingendi usque ad uos') and 10: 15–
16 ('Non in immensum gloriantes in alienis laboribus; spem autem habentes crescentis
fidei uestrae, in uobis magnificari secundum regulam nostram in abundantiam, etiam in
illa, que ultra uos sunt, euangelizare, non in aliena regula in iis quae praeparata sunt
gloriari').

will see and let those who have not heard understand.'[1] To wit, according to the apostle, 'glory not in the sphere of another man, in things which are to hand, nor in the work of other men beyond us, but according to the measure of the rule which God has measured out for us.'[2]

§ 6. IN WHICH HE LEAVES THE CITY ON THE WAY TO BRITAIN. Indeed St Birinus, because he knew from the teaching of the apostle that every soul should be subject to higher powers, and that he who resists power resists the ordinance of God,[3] professes obedience, accepts his orders, and promises to enter willingly upon the task enjoined on him. When at length a blessing has been given,[4] the company prepared, and provision for the journey taken up, he hastens to fulfil what has been entrusted to him, trusting in the mercy of God. The Roman citizen sets forth from Rome; as he leaves his homeland and parents he exults. He exults, I say, as he goes away, he rejoices as he exiles himself, he exults whilst he makes himself needy.[5] He, who had God dwelling in the city of his mind, did not grieve at relinquishing contact with the citizens [of his homeland]. Nor was he, who rejoiced at the inward habitation of the one God, disturbed at leaving the city of multitudes. How beautiful and how worthy of God is that communing, to seek the unity, having put aside the multitude. For in the multitude you are confounded, in unity you are strengthened. The Divine word says that 'you are troubled as to many things, you are disturbed about many things, but one thing is necessary.'[6] 'One thing I have sought of the Lord,' says the prophet, 'this I require, that I may dwell in the house of the Lord, that I may dwell in Him[7] and that he may dwell in me.' St Birinus desired one thing, because he chose the best part,[8] that he might dwell in God, so that he might deserve to have God dwelling in him. Therefore he left his

---

[3] Rom. 13: 1–2 ('Omnis anima potestatibus sublimioribus subdita sit: non est enim potestas nisi a Deo: quae autem sunt, a Deo ordinatae sunt. Itaque qui resistit potestati, Dei ordinationi resistit').

[4] Cf. *Vita S. Swithuni* c. 5, 'Suscepta denique benedictione' (Sauvage, p. 377).

[5] Note the play upon the words 'exulto' and 'exulo'.

[6] Luke 10: 41–2 ('Martha, Martha, sollicita es et turbaris erga plurima. Porro unum est necessarium. Maria optimam partem elegit, quae non auferetur ab ea').

[7] Ps. 26(27): 4 ('Vnam petii a Domino, hanc requiram, ut inhabitem in domo Domini').

[8] Cf. 1 John 3: 24 ('Et qui seruat mandata eius, in illo manet, et ipse in eo'); and 1 John 4: 15 ('Quisquis confessus fuerit quoniam Iesus est Filius Dei, Deus in eo manet, et ipse in Deo').

egressus est de cognatione sua.¹ Exiuit autem per presentiam corporis, qui dudum exierat per desiderium mentis. Exiuit ab urbe, ut orbem ᵃintraret. Exiuit ab urbe, ut orbemᵃ perlustrans, eum pro illa doceret. Exiuit de unius ciuitatis angustia, quia iam sibi preparabatur a Domino seruitura prouincia. Egressus igitur emetitur iter, uiam peragit, ut et qui preceptum dedit et cui preceptum est, de peracta iussione letentur.

§ 7. Iste est beatissimus uir ille² per quem tibi euangelium Christi, Britannia, resplendeat,ᵇ ut que dedita eras idolorum spurcitiis, ad honorem christiane religionis Deo miserante peruenias. Iste est sanctissimus pater tuus pastorque magnificus, qui pie et sancte te preparet Deo regnis inserendamᶜ celestibus. Iste est qui ᵈhac gloria teᵈ ditauit, et ditatam cumulauit, ut sis gens sancta, populus adquisitionis,³ ciuitas regis magni.⁴ Iam iam respexit te oriens ex alto⁵ stella matutina⁶ de celo. Ecce aurora tibi orta est,⁷ que fugatis tenebris diem adesse denuntiet.ᵉ Iam iam lucifer oritur⁸ tibi qui noctem ignorat, qui nescit occasum, lucifer ille qui ascendit super occasum, et Dominus nomen est illi.⁹ Ecce sol iustitie¹⁰ illuxit tibi et radium sue illustrationis tibi luminosum aperuit. De occulto celorum tibi cometa¹¹ dirigitur, que interitum imperii tui et commutationemᶠ fideliter preconetur. Aquilonaris enim rex qui frigidus est et frigidos facit, rex uenti et turbinis qui habet potestatem aerem commouendi, dominabatur tibi a principio, dum seruiebasᵍ idolis, dum demonumʰ famulabaris imperio. Et ecce iste fortis armatus predicante Birino

---

ᵃ⁻ᵃ om. G by homoeoteleuton   ᵇ resplenduit GT   ᶜ miserandam G
ᵈ⁻ᵈ te hac gloria H   ᵉ denuntiat T   ᶠ commutatio A; commutatione H
ᵍ seruibas A   ʰ demonium D

---

¹ Gen. 12: 1 ('Egredere de terra tua, et de cognatione tua, et de domo patris tui'). Cf. Goscelin, *Historia maior de aduentu Sancti Augustini* c. 3 (on Augustine's departure from Rome), 'Exiuit de senatoria cognatione sua' (*PL* lxxx. 52 B).
² The source for the greater part of these first three sentences, up to 'gens sancta', is Leo the Great, *Sermo* lxxxii; see note on c. 1, p. 2.
³ 1 Pet. 2: 9 ('Vos autem . . . gens sancta, populus adquisitionis').
⁴ Matt. 5: 35 ('per Hierosolymam, quia ciuitas est magni regis').
⁵ Luke 1: 78 ('In quibus uisitauit uos, oriens ex alto').
⁶ Rev. 2: 28 ('et dabo illi stellam matutinam').
⁷ S. of S. 6: 9 ('quae est ista quae progreditur quasi aurora consurgens').
⁸ Cf. 2 Pet. 1: 19 ('et lucifer oriatur in cordibus uestris').
⁹ Cf. Ps. 67(68): 5 ('Iter facite ei qui ascendit super occasum. Dominus nomen illi').
¹⁰ Mal. 4: 2 ('Et orietur uobis timentibus nomen meus sol Iustitiae').

home, and departed from his kindred.[1] He departed in the physical presence of the body, but in the desire of the mind he had long since set out. He left the city that he might enter into the world. He left the city, so that, wandering through the world, he might teach it, on her [i.e. Rome's] behalf. He left the confines of one community, because now a province that would serve Him was already being prepared by the Lord. Having set forth, he passes through the journey, travels along the road, so that He who gave the command, and he who received it, might rejoice in the completion of the task.

§ 7. This is the blessed man,[2] through whom the gospel of Christ is to shine brightly for you, Britain, so that you who were given over to the filthiness of idols, might attain to the honour of the Christian religion, by the mercy of God. This man is your holy father and noble pastor, who is to prepare you in pious and holy fashion to be grafted into the heavenly kingdom by God. This is he who enriched you with this glory, and having enriched you heaped on more, so that you might be a holy race, a people of increase,[3] the nation of a great king.[4] Already now the morning star[6] rising from the depths[5] has looked down upon you from the sky. Behold, your dawn has come,[7] which, when the shadows are put to flight, will announce that day is approaching. Already now the morning star rises over you[8]—he who never sees night, who knows no setting, that morning star which ascends upon the west—and the Lord is his name.[9] Behold the sun of righteousness[10] has risen upon you and has revealed the luminous ray of his brightness to you. From the hidden depth of the heavens a comet[11] is aimed at you which will faithfully herald the destruction and transformation of your kingdom. For the king of the north who is chill and makes men chill, the king of wind and hurricane, who has the power to stir the weather, he dominated you from the beginning, as long as you were enslaved to idols, while you waited upon the command of demons. And behold, this armed warrior will be defeated by the preaching of

---

[11] Cf. Tiberius Claudius Donatus *Interpretationes Vergilianae* on Vergil, *Aen.* x. 275, 'conparantur his sidera cometes et Sirius, quae, cum oriuntur, morbos ferunt hominibus et interitum plurimorum, haec dicuntur et imperii commutationem portendere', ed. H. George, 2 vols. (Leipzig, 1905–6). It remains an open question whether the author of *Vita S. Birini* could have known Donatus's commentary, since no MSS of the work are known to have survived from Anglo-Saxon England—see *Texts and Transmission: A Survey of the Latin Classics*, ed. L. D. Reynolds (Oxford, 1983), pp. 157–8. He may have found the above cited in some other source.

debellabitur.[a] Rex autem ille qui calore spiritus sancti gelu peccatorum euacuat regnaturus inducitur. Venit ecce aduersum te—immo pro te—miles fortissimus, non armis quidem sed precibus pugnaturus. Procedit in pugnam non manu non hasta, sed lingua et fide bellaturus.[b] Ecce sacerdotalis[c] debellat humilitas, quam nec Romanorum potentia preualuit,[1] nec cesariana uesania. Plus ualuit lingua sacerdotis, quam manus exerta imperatoris. Tela militaria omnis armorum apparatus milia populorum, non ualuerunt efficere, quod deuotio, quod caritas mentis in uno potuit sacerdote perficere.

§ 8. Mira res, Cesar reicitur, et sacerdos recipitur. Venit Romanus imperator, uincitur et fugatur; uenit sacerdos humilis, uincit et honoratur. Reuertitur denuo collecto exercitu Cesar et uincit, sed quod [d]a Deo[d] non habebat, diu habere non[e] potuit. Venit semel humilis presbiter, uicit[f] predicando et quia non sibi sed Deo uicit, possidet [g]eam in perpetuum, immo Deus in sacerdote suo possidet[g] eam in eternum. Cesar de morte sua illam perdidit, Birinus de morte uiuens melius eam[h] habere iam cepit. Moritur moriente Cesare, Roma, imperium tuum in Britannia, sed quod in eo amittis, in sacerdote recuperas. Multis quidem uictoriis[i] aucta imperium et dominatum tuum terra[j] marique[k] protulisti,[2] minus tamen est quod[l] tibi bellicus labor subdidit, quam quod pax christiana subiecit.[m] De pace creuit[n] imperium tuum, et permanet, quia iam seruis illi, qui pacem amat et cui in pace sunt cuncta que possidet.[3] De imperio[o] minuebatur imperium tuum, et ecce de seruitute crescit imperium tuum. Imperas ergo et deficis,[p] seruis et crescis. Seruis iam Deo non diis, non demonibus, ideoque[q] tibi subicitur mundus. De[r] [s]pluralitate deorum[s] quos uenerabaris [t]incurrebas defectum,[t] de cultura unius comparas[u] incrementum.[4] Dii multi,

[a] debellabatur *G* [b] bellatur *GH* [c] socerdotalis *G* [d–d] adeo *G* [e] *om. G* [f] uincit *H* [g–g] *om. D, by homoeoteleuton* [h] *om. G* [i] uictoriosis *G* [j] terre *T* [k] mari que *G* [l] quam *T* [m] subegit *H* [n] uenit *A* [o] imperium *D* [p] deficit *T* [q] ideo que *G* [r] dum *A* [s–s] pluritate dierum *G* [t–t] de fectum *T* [u] comperas *AD*

[1] The allusion here, and in the following peroration of c. 8, is to the attempts made by Gaius Julius Caesar, in 55 and 54 BC, to invade Britain. The rhetorical force of the lengthy comparison of 'conquests' lies first in the fact that Caesar's initial invasion was a failure, and only on the second expedition ('Reuertitur denuo collecto exercitu') did he find victory. The second point is that Birinus's lone 'conquest' was more successful

Birinus. And the King, who melts away the ice of sins with the heat of the Holy Spirit, is brought in to reign. Behold, a mighty warrior comes to fight against you—nay rather on your behalf—not with weapons but with prayers. He proceeds to fight in battle not with hand or spear, but with speech and faith. Lo, priestly humility vanquishes that over which neither the might of the Romans prevailed,[1] nor the raging of Caesar. The tongue of a priest has more strength than the general's thrust-out fist. Warlike weapons, all the battle gear, thousands of men, could not achieve what devotion, and charity of mind in one priest were able to bring about.

§ 8. Miraculously, Caesar is driven back, and the priest is accepted. The Roman emperor comes, is conquered and put to flight; a humble priest comes, conquers, and is honoured. Having gathered together his army, Caesar returns again, and conquers, but that which he did not receive from God, he was not able to possess for long. A humble priest came once, conquered by preaching, and because he conquered not for himself, but for God, he has possession in perpetuity. Or rather, God through His priest possesses the land for eternity. Caesar lost it at his death; Birinus, gaining life from death, has now taken better possession of it. At Caesar's death, your rule in Britain dies, Rome, but what you lose in him, you regain in a priest. Indeed, strengthened by many victories, you have extended your rule and domination by land and sea;[2] however, that which warlike toil brought under your power is a lesser thing than that which Christian peace has made subject to you. Through peace your rule increased, and it endures, because now you serve Him who loves peace and with Whom all things in His possession are at peace.[3] Through domination, your rule was diminished, and behold, out of servitude your rule increases. So you govern and fail, you serve and increase. Now you serve God not gods, not demons, and so the world is subject to you. Whereas you suffered loss from the plurality of gods whom you venerated, from the worship of one God you receive increase.[4] The many

because more lasting. Britain was not really gained for Rome fully until the later invasion of Claudius in AD 43, so Caesar's victory was transitory, whereas Holy Rome, through her ambassador, Birinus, gained Britain permanently.

[2] This and the phrases following are derived from Leo the Great, *Sermo* lxxxii; see note on c. 1, p. 2.

[3] Cf. Luke 11: 21 ('cum fortis armatus custodit atrium suum, in pace sunt ea quae possidet').

[4] Cf. 1 Cor. 3: 6 ('Deus incrementum dedit').

quibus inclinabas caput tuum, non prestiterunt tibi[a] quod unus a quo per superbiam recedebas prestare[b] preualuit.

§ 9. [c]VBI PERVENIT AD MARE.[c] [d]Decursis igitur[d] multis diuersarum terrarum spatiis peruenit beatus Birinus ad mare, quo transacto [e]fines debeat intrare[e] Britannie. Opponit sibi mare [f]natura;[1] situs loci[f] ne intret mari interiecto repugnat.[g] Pugnat mare pro terra, euomit terra mare, ut in uenientem deseuiat. Offert mare fluctus marinos [h]sales[2] equoreos,[h] representat scopulos infames,[i] animalia predicat monstruosa.[3] Hostes marini ad mentem occurrunt, sed uincuntur hec omnia, dum a transitu mari sacerdotem Dei deturbare contendunt. Periculum timor non dissuasit, quod caritas uehemens in cordis aure persuasit. Neque poterant eum a transeundo diuertere, quem gentis asperitas, barbara lingua, mores inuersi, ritus inordinatus non preualebant a predicando repellere. Iam in se quidem furor maris populi furorem figurabat, sed miles Dei prepotens tam de maris quam de gentis subiectione gloriam sibi a Deo humiliter expectabat. Interea nauim ascensurus gloriosus antistes diuina celebrat misteria, sibi suisque uiaticum parans; offert Deo hostie salutaris pia libamina. Quibus rite peractis, urgente[j] et instante nauigationis articulo ad nauim festine deducitur, quo ascendente tolluntur armamenta, naturam arte oppugnant,[k] nauticus clamor[4] in immensum porrigitur. Flat aura, uentus insurgit, deseuit mare, nauis unda tumultuante[l] succutitur. Insistunt naute remigio, portus[m] in uoto est, illum uultu manu sermone requirunt, periculum dampnum mortem se declinare contendunt.

§ 10. Dum autem nauis illa multo labore multoque sudore nautarum alta sulcaret pelagi, reminiscitur beatus Birinus se quod carius quod pretiosius sibi erat amisisse seque a negotio nauigationis correptum et nautis urgentibus[n] conclamantibusque prepeditum in littore unde ascenderat reliquisse. Dederat siquidem ei

---

[a] om. G   [b] preparare G   [c-c] om. GHT   [d-d] Igitur decursis G   [e-e] insula insisteretur B; insula sisteretur FG   [f-f] naturam locus loco G   [g] propugnat G   [h-h] ales equoreas G   [i] in fames D   [j] urguente A   [k] oppugnat A   [l] tumultu ante G   [m] postus G   [n] urguentibus A

---

[1] Cf. Lucan, *Pharsalia* ii. 619–20, 'Hinc illinc montes scopulosae rupis aperto | Opposuit natura mari flatusque remouit'.

[2] Cf. Lucan, *Pharsalia* x. 257, 'sales aequorei'.

[3] Cf. Horace, *Carmen* i. 3. 18–20, 'qui siccis oculis monstra natantia | qui uidit mare turbidum et | infamis scopulos Acroceraunia?'

gods, to whom you bowed your head, did not provide for you that which the one God, from whom you retreated through pride, has been able to provide.

§ 9. IN WHICH HE REACHES THE SEA. Having crossed many distances in diverse lands, the blessed Birinus reaches the sea, by the crossing of which he should enter the bounds of Britain. Nature puts the sea in his way,[1] the position of the place resists his entry by casting the ocean between. The sea fights on behalf of the land, the land spews forth the sea, so that it rages furiously at him who approaches. The sea proffers marine billows, ocean brine,[2] displays infamously dangerous rocks, vaunts monstrous animals.[3] Marine foes rush to mind, but all these are overcome even as they strive to beat back the priest of God from crossing the sea. Fear did not dissuade him from that peril, which vehement love, whispering in the ear of his heart, persuaded him of. They could not turn him aside from crossing, whom the fierceness of the people, the barbarian tongue, the perverted morals, and unorthodox ritual could not manage to hold back from preaching. Now indeed the raging of the sea prefigured in itself the raging of the people, but the doughty soldier of God humbly looked for glory for himself from God as much from the subduing of the sea as from the subduing of the people. Meanwhile, as he is about to ascend the ship, the glorious bishop celebrates the divine mysteries, preparing the viaticum for himself and for his men; he offers to God the holy libations of the saving victim. When these things were duly completed, as the moment of sailing is urgent and immediate, he is led hastily to the ship; upon his entering, the ship's tackle is raised up, they wage war with nature by skill, and the sailor's cry[4] echoes out endlessly. The breeze blows, the wind rises, the sea rages, the ship is tossed up on the stormy wave. The sailors apply themselves to the rowing, the port is their desire, they aim at it with countenance, hand and speech, and strive to avert from themselves danger, disaster or death.

§ 10. But while that ship, by much toil and sweat on the part of the sailors, ploughs the depths of the sea, St Birinus remembers that he has lost what was very dear and precious to him, and that he, carried away by the business of the embarkation and hindered by the urging and bawling sailors, has left it on the shore from which he had embarked. For indeed, Pope Honorius had given to

[4] Cf. Vergil, *Aen.* iii. 128, 'nauticus exoritur uario certamine clamor'.

Honorius papa pallam[1] super quam corpus Christi consecrabat corpusque Dominicum in eadem inuolutum, quod collo suspensum semper secum portabat, et inter sacranda sacrosancta misteria super sanctum altare ponere consueuerat. Notandum est autem tantum pontificem admodum sagacem, [a]prudentem adeo,[a] non ex negligentia uel insipientia sic peccasse, sed quia dispositionis[b] erat diuine, ut seruus Dei qui[c] adhuc celabatur, per hoc factum communi traderetur notitie. Proditur[d] enim seruus Dei euidenti miraculo, signo celesti Dei amicus declaratur. Vilitas eius transit in gloriam, in honorem humilitas, de contemptu celebritatem accepit. Nesciebant naute quem uehebant quia et eum a quo mittebatur ignorabant. Ignorabant seruum, quia illius nesciebant Dominum. Ignorato Domino, ignorabatur et seruus, et nulla reuerentia eum suscipiebant, cuius meritum nullatenus attendebant. Erant nempe gentiles, eumque de simili sorte putabant.[e] Seruitores erant idolorum et eum [f]de eadem[f] cultura esse credebant. Venitur ergo ad uirtutem miraculi ut de nocte in qua erant eruerentur, ut perditus in eis repararetur intuitus,[g] ut ab erroris illusione recederent, et ad uiam[h] ueritatis se omnino conuerterent, ut Deum et seruum illius agnoscere preualerent.

§ 11. [i]VBI SVPRA MARE REVERSVS EST AD LITTVS.[i] Cepit interea beatus antistes contristari et dolere, attendit, obseruat si quod amisit aliqua posset ratione recipere. Cupit reuerti, sed uirtus nature non temeranda resistit. Consulit nautas, artem remigandi rimatur, multa promittit, plurima pollicetur. Denegatur sibi omne humanum auxilium, timet experiri diuinum.[2] Nec desperatione timet, sed humilitate. Nec diffidentia, sed

---

[a-a] et prudentem a deo G   [b] disposionis D   [c] quia D   [d] proditor D   [e] putantes H   [f-f] deadem D   [g] in tuitus G   [h] uitam G [i-i] om. GHT

---

[1] What seems to be intended here is a corporal with a Host wrapped in it. In Western liturgical use, from about the 4th cent., the 'palla corporalis' was a large linen cloth, spread on the altar so that the bread and wine could be consecrated over it. The cloth was large enough to be lifted up over the top of the chalice. See DACL iii. 2986–7, and J. Braun, Die liturgische Paramente in Gegenwart und Vergangenheit (Munich, 1924), pp. 205–9. In a review of L. Blouet's Le Chrismale de Mortain (Bion, 1954), in AB lxxiii (1955), 278–9, P. Grosjean listed Birinus's 'palla' among examples in Insular texts of the use of the chrismal, a small pyx-like box in which a consecrated Host was kept, and which was apparently sometimes worn around the neck. Examples of such a use are to be found in Columban's Regula Coenobialis, c. 4, ed. G. S. M. Walker, S. Columbani Opera, Scriptores Latini Hiberniae, ii (Dublin, 1970), p. 148; and Vita S. Comgalli, c. 2, ed. C. Plummer,

him a corporal,[1] over which he used to consecrate the body of Christ, and had wrapped the host in it—this he carried with him always, hung around his neck, and while celebrating the sacrosanct mysteries he was wont to place it on the holy altar. It should be noted, however, that such a great bishop, wholly wise, also prudent, had not thus sinned out of negligence or foolishness, but because it was part of God's plan that the servant of God, who had been hitherto in obscurity, might by this deed be brought to popular notice. For the servant of God is proclaimed by a clear miracle, by a heavenly sign the friend of God is declared. His baseness has been transformed into glory, his humility into honour, from contempt he has received renown. The sailors did not know whom they were transporting, because they were also ignorant of the One by whom he was sent. They were ignorant of the servant, because they did not know his master. Since the master was unknown, so too was the servant, and they did not receive him with any reverence, whose merits they were by no means aware of. They were of course gentiles, and imagined him to be of the same sort. They were the worshippers of idols and believed him to be of the same religion. Therefore, it fell to the power of a miracle that they might be plucked from their benighted state, so that understanding, once lost, might be restored in them, and that they might desist from the deception of error, and turn completely to the way of truth, in order to be able to acknowledge God and His servant.

§ 11. IN WHICH HE RETURNED OVER THE WATER TO THE SHORE. The blessed bishop begins meanwhile to grieve and be sorrowful; he applies his mind and looks to see whether he could in any way regain that which he has lost. He longs to return, but the power of nature, not to be scorned, resists. He consults the sailors, he investigates the art of rowing, he vows many things, promises much. All human aid is denied him, and he is afraid to try divine aid.[2] He does not fear in desperation but in humility. He is

---

Vitae Sanctorum Hiberniae, 2 vols. (Oxford, 1910), ii. 11; and also no. lv (*De crismali*) of Aldhelm's *Enigmata*, ed. R. Ehwald, *MGH*, AA, xv (Berlin, 1919), p. 122. Cf. *DACL*, iii. 1478–81, and J. Braun, *Das Christliche Altargerät in seinem Sein und in seiner Entwicklung* (1932; reprinted Hildesheim, 1973), p. 287. It seems mistaken, however, to regard Birinus's 'palla' as being the equivalent of a chrismal, since it was evidently not any kind of box, but a corporal, left behind on the altar when Birinus was dragged straight from Mass to the ship, 'urgente et instante nauigationis articulo', as the text makes quite clear. The 'palla' containing the Host could, however, have been carried in a chrismal.

[2] Cf. Bede, *HE* ii. 7 ('confidens episcopus in diuinum ubi humanum deerat auxilium').

equanimitate formidat.ᵃ Via nulla ad littus, quia hominibus uia per
mare denegatur. Redimere tempus non iudicabat idoneum, quia
omnis mora uidebatur esse dispendium. Dum igitur cogitat, dum
consilia stipulatur, recedit terra, mare magis ac magis intratur.
Vestigandoᵇ consilium, consilii differtur effectum.ᶜ Iam consilium
contra se est, ratio dum inquiritur uacuatur.ᵈ Quid multa? fide
armatus in mare descendit, naturam terre experitur in mari.
Prestat mare soliditatisᵉ obsequium quem fidei soliditas uehebat
ad Dominum. Stupet mare nouum et inusitatum iter, sed ad
iubentis imperium prestat et gaudet. Natura maris se gaudet
exemptam, quia obtemperabat ei, qui creauerat eam. Nec deplorat
dampnum sed gaudet quasi de cremento,ᶠ dum Deo commutanteᵍ
terre fungitur officio. Viam mirabatur humanam sed diuinam
attendebat potentiam. Natura elementi leuis et mobilis ut Dei
seruo seruiret, facta est fortis et stabilis. Vadit per mare, mare non
timens beatus antistes. Materiam timoris uis amoris extinxit.[1] Ecce
impletum est in beato uiro quod a Salomone de caritate ecclesie
dictum est: 'Aque multe non poteruntʰ extinguere caritatem tuam
et flumina non obruent illam.'[2] Exhausit omne periculum qui intus
ardebat. Ignis mentis impetus aque uincebat. Tantum cogitabat
seruus de Domino et ideo de nature non desperabatⁱ seruitio.
Placaueratʲ sibi iras maris, qui sibi eum assumpsit in seruum, qui
de mari huius seculi leuaturus eumᵏ erat in celum. Magna erat
fides tua, beate Birine, magna et immensa fides tibi pro naui est,
pro remigio fortitudo mentis est.ˡ In naui sedens, mare timebas,
per mare incedens, mare non times. In naui positus, periculum
metuebas, dum de nauis remigio, de nautarum arte pendebas. Sed
iam per mare remigem Deum non hominem habens non metuis,
Deum ductoremᵐ habens, securus incedis.ⁿ Ecce quod olimᵒ
operabatur Dominus in Petro,[3] operatur modo in Petri uicario.
Quod olim exhibuit in magistro, iterare uoluit in discipulo. Petrus

---

ᵃ formidet *G*   ᵇ *C resumes with this word*   ᶜ effectus *H*   ᵈ euacuatur
H   ᵉ solidatis *G*   ᶠ incremento *T*   ᵍ comitante *G*   ʰ potuerunt *A*   ⁱ de *add. C*   ʲ Placuerat *DG*   ᵏ eam *C*   ˡ *om. G*
ᵐ auctorem *BG*   ⁿ in celis *A*   ᵒ *om. G*

---

[1] Cf. Leo the Great, *Sermo* lxxxii (addressed to St Peter), 'Vincebat ergo materiam
formidinis uis amoris' (*CCSL* cxxxviii. 513, line 98).
[2] S. of S. 8: 7 ('Aquae multae non potuerunt extinguere charitatem, nec flumina
obruent illam').
[3] See Matt. 14: 28–9.

fearful not for want of faith, but with equanimity. There is no way
to the shore, because to walk through the sea is denied to men. He
did not consider it suitable to bide his time, because all delay
seemed to be waste. While he thus meditates, while he insists upon
strategies, the land recedes, the sea intervenes further and further.
By searching for a plan, the accomplishment of any plan is delayed.
Now counsel is against itself; while a means is sought it is at the
same time being rendered ineffectual. What more needs to be said?
Armed with faith, he descends on to the sea, and experiences the
quality of dry land in the sea. The sea renders the service of solidity
to him whom solidity of faith was carrying to the Lord. The sea is
brought to a standstill in amazement at the new and unfamiliar
passage over it, but responds to and rejoices in the command of
Him giving the order. The true nature of the sea rejoices to be put
aside, because it was complying with Him Who had created it. Nor
does it lament the loss but rejoices as if over an increase, while,
upon God's bringing about a change, it performs the function of
dry land. It marvelled at the passage of the human but gave heed to
the power of God. The element's light and mobile property, in
order to serve God's servant, is made strong and stable. The
blessed bishop walks through the sea, without fearing it. The
strength of love consumed the substance of fear.[1] Behold, that
which was said by Solomon about love of the church is fulfilled in
the blessed man: 'Many waters will not be able to quench your love
and the floods will not drown it.'[2] He who burned within consumed all danger. The fire of the mind conquered the assault of the
water. The servant thought only of God, and thus he did not
despair of the service rendered by nature. He had soothed for him
the ragings of the sea, Who has taken him to Himself as a servant,
and Who was to lift him from the sea of this world up into heaven.
Great was your faith, St Birinus; great and immeasurable faith is
your ship, and strength of mind is your oars. Seated in the ship you
feared the sea, but walking through the sea you do not fear it.
Placed in the ship you trembled at the danger, while you depended
upon the skill of the sailors for the rowing of the ship. But now
since you have God and not man as oarsman through the ocean
you are not afraid, with God as the guide you walk confidently.
Behold, that which the Lord once effected in Peter,[3] He now
brings about in Peter's vicar. That which once He displayed in the
master, He chose to repeat in the disciple. Peter, strengthened by

fidei petra firmatus pedibus super mare peruenit ad petram, ad eum qui participium nominis sui[1] contulerat ei, quia[a] super eum edificaturus erat ecclesiam.[2] A petra enim Petrus nomen accepit, 'petra autem erat Christus,'[3] secundum uerbum apostoli. Cucurrit ille ad Dominum incessu[b] fidei, passibus caritatis; cucurrit et iste eisdem passibus fidei et amoris. Cucurrerunt ambo non de merito suo sed de gratia confisi diuina, de Deo presumentes non de uirtute humana.[4] Peruenit autem beatus Birinus fide remigante ad littus receptoque quod reliquerat, ad nauim reuertitur.

§ 12. [c]VBI REVERSVS EST AD NAVIM.[c] Reuersus sanctissimus pater reperit[d] nauim stantem, quam ante reliquerat per amfractus maris, per uada marina uolantem. Stabat autem nauis quia quem emiserat expectabat. [e]Stabat nauis quia uectorem suum humiliter expectabat.[e] Stabat, inquam, nauis a uentis inpacta seruo Dei letabunda prestans obsequia. Tenduntur carbasa, antenne[f] curuantur, concutiuntur remi, omnia nauis armamenta laborant. Miratur magister nauis, naute mirantur et stupent, nec Dei agnoscunt uirtutem. Mirantur uentos mare artem nauigandi suam omnia perdidisse naturam, nec Dei attendunt esse potentiam. Intrauit itaque uenerabilis pontifex et inuentus[g] est in uestimento suo nec unam habere stillicidii guttam. Deus enim qui populo Israhel diuisit mare,[5] ut secure per terram in mari ambularet, ipse huic uero[h] Israhelite concessit, ut per uoraginem maris illibatus incederet. Expauere qui in naui erant miraculum, procidunt ad pedes eius, cultorem Dei esse fatentur, eumque adorant ut deum.[6] Mirantur quia de naui egressus iuit per mare securus, mirantur quia exiens de mari nullum in ueste uestigium stille alicuius ostendit. Mirantur et nauim dum uoluit retentam esse et ex placito illius iterum cucurrisse. Iam in corde suo Deum quem nesciebant adorabant, uenerabantur et ore publico predicabant. 'Verus', inquiunt, 'Deus cui homo iste famulatur, qui

---

[a] qui *H*   [b] in cessu *G*   [c-c] *om. GHT*   [d] recepit *D*; repperit *H*; reperit *altered to* repperit *in T*   [e-e] *om. G by homoeoteleuton*   [f] antemne *H*   [g] in uentus *G*   [h] *om. G*

---

[1] Cf. Mark 3: 16 ('et inposuit Simoni nomen Petrus').

[2] Matt. 16: 18 ('Et ego dico tibi, quia tu es Petrus, et super hanc petram aedificabo ecclesiam meam').

[3] 1 Cor. 10: 4 ('petra autem erat Christus').

[4] Cf. Judith 6: 15 ('non derelinquis praesumentes de te: et praesumentes de se, et de sua uirtute gloriantes, humilias').

the rock of faith, walked upon the sea towards the rock, towards Him who had conferred upon him the partaking of His name,[1] because He intended to build the Church upon him.[2] For from the rock Peter received his name, 'but the rock was Christ',[3] according to the words of the apostle. Peter ran towards the Lord with the acceleration of faith, with the steps of charity; and this man too ran with the same steps of faith and love. Both were enabled to run, trusting not in their own desert, but in divine grace, having confidence in God and not in human power.[4] So St Birinus with the oar-strokes of faith reaches the shore, and having collected that which he had left behind, returns to the ship.

§ 12. IN WHICH HE RETURNED TO THE SHIP. Returning, the most holy father found the ship at a standstill, although he had previously left it speeding through the whirling of the sea, through the marine depths. But the ship was standing still because it was awaiting the one it had sent forth. The ship was standing still because it humbly awaited its passenger. It stood still, I tell you, that ship battered by the winds, offering joyful obedience to the servant of God. The sails are unfurled, the sail-yards are bowed, the oars crash together, all the ship's tackle strains. The master of the ship marvels, the sailors marvel and are stunned, but they do not recognize the power of God. They marvel that the winds, the sea, and the art of sailing have all lost their quality, but they do not consider that it is the might of God. And so the venerable bishop entered and he was discovered to have not one drop of moisture on his clothing. For the same God who divided the sea for the people of Israel, so that they might safely walk on dry land in the sea,[5] granted to this true Israelite to pass through the whirl of the sea unharmed. Those who were in the ship were sorely afraid of the miracle and fall prostrate at his feet, they say that he must be a worshipper of God, and even adore him as a god.[6] They marvel that he, going out of the ship, walked through the sea safely, and they marvel that, upon climbing out of the sea, he showed no sign of any wetness on his clothing. They marvel also that the ship was held back, as long as he desired, and then hastened onwards again at his pleasure. Now they adored in their hearts the God whom they did not know, venerated Him and proclaimed Him aloud. 'It is', they say, 'the true God, Whom this man serves, Who saves by

[5] See Exod. 14: 15–30.
[6] Cf. Acts 28: 6 (and Acts 14: 10).

saluat in mari et terra sperantes in se,[1] cui seruiunt omnia iura nature.'

§ 13. Iam iam deos suos uilipendunt,[a] iam uituperant, iam[b] in agnitione ueri Dei falsos eos appellant. Iam iam recognoscunt figmenta hominum, contemplantur et reperiunt opera manuum hominum. Iam humiliantur seruo cuius Dominum admirabantur, exhibent seruo reuerentiam dum per eum Domino suo [c]se conplacere[c] festinant. Aduoluuntur pedibus eius, osculantur[d] pedes illius,[e] satagunt de salute sua inquirere, precepta [f]requirunt salutis[f] et uite. Tunc beatus Birinus intelligens illos a spiritu sancto uisitatos interius euangelizauit illis catholicam fidem, semitam iustitie,[2] ecclesiasticam[g] ueritatem. Nec mora, adquieuerunt idolatre, se credere confitentur, quod preceperit[h] se perficere[i] pollicentur. Benedixit denique aquam, respersit super eos et baptizati sunt, fidem sancte trinitatis ore et corde confitentes, Deum in mirabilibus suis laudantes et benedicentes. Diuinitus autem sopore inmisso omnes obdormierunt[j] nec unus superfuit preter beatum pontificem, qui de tanta multitudine uigilaret.[3] Dormientibus illis ad portum quem petebant nauis deducitur nec potuit naufragium pati, que diuino ducimonio[4] ducebatur. Ascendit interim beatus Birinus in locum magistri, peritus nauis [k]de recenti[k] effectus, ut inter undas maris nauim regeret corporaliter, qui inter fluctus mundi et turbines recturus erat ecclesiam spiritualiter. Intrante autem naui in portum, euigilantes naute custodem salutis sue Dominum et seruum eius beatum Birinum dignis ut preualent preconiorum laudibus accumulant.

§ 14. [l]DE PREDICATIONE ILLIVS VBI PRIMVM APPLI-CVIT.[l] Factum est autem ut maneret in eodem loco beatus Birinus per tres dies.[m] Bene autem per tres dies inducitur commorari,[n] quia sancte trinitatis seruus predicabat illis misterium sancte et indiuidue trinitatis. Merito etiam[o] dies inducuntur non noctes quia

---

[a] ubi pendunt *G*   [b] iam *add. H*   [c-c] conplacere se *G*   [d] oculantur *T*   [e] eius *D*   [f-f] salutis requirunt *H*   [g] euuangelicam *T* [h] precepit *G*   [i] per fidem *T*   [j] ordormierunt *G*   [k-k] derecenti *DT* [l-l] *om. GHT*   [m] praedicans ibi diem a quo omnis dies *add. FG*   [n] cummorari *C*   [o] et *G*

---

[1] Cf. Dan. 13: 60.
[2] Isa. 40: 14 ('Et docuit eum semitam iustitiae').
[3] Cf. Gregory of Tours, *Historia Francorum*, i. 48 ('Denique nocte media omnes Pectaua somno falanga conprimitur, nec ullus superfuit, qui ex hac multitudine uigilaret'), ed. W. Arndt and B. Krusch, *MGH*, SRM, i (Hanover, 1885), p. 56.

land and sea those who put their trust in Him,[1] to whom all the laws of nature are subject.'

§ 13. Already now they despise their gods, now they disparage them, now they call them false in recognition of the true God. Already now they call to mind the idols of men, contemplate them and find them to be the works of men's hands. Now they are humbled before the servant whose Lord they were astonished at, they show the servant reverence, and at the same time hasten through him to make themselves pleasing to their Lord. They fall down at his feet and kiss them, they are intent upon searching out the means of their salvation, they seek the ordinances of salvation and life. Then St Birinus, understanding that they were visited within by the Holy Spirit, preached to them the catholic faith, the path of righteousness,[2] the truth of the Church. Without delay, the idolaters assented, they confess that they believe, and promise that they will carry out that which he will decree. At length he blessed some water, sprinkled it over them and they were baptized, confessing the faith of the Holy Trinity with their lips and in their hearts, praising and blessing God in his marvellous works. A drowsiness was sent down from heaven, they all fell asleep, and none was left to keep watch, out of such a multitude,[3] except the blessed bishop. While they are sleeping, the ship is carried to the harbour they were heading for, and since it was borne by divine guidance[4] it could not suffer shipwreck. Meanwhile St Birinus climbed up to the captain's post, having recently become skilled in sailing, so that he might physically guide the ship through the waves of the sea, just as he was to guide the Church spiritually through the floods and whirlwinds of the world. As the ship enters the harbour, the sailors awake, and heap upon the Lord, the guardian of their safety, and His servant, St Birinus, worthy praises of proclamation, as best they are able.

§ 14. ABOUT HIS PREACHING WHEN HE FIRST CAME TO SHORE. It happened that St Birinus was to remain in the same place for three days. But it is good that he is moved to stay for *three* days, because the servant of the Holy Trinity preached to them the mystery of the Holy and Undivided Trinity. Rightly the days are occupied and not the nights, because the servant of the

---

[4] 'Ducimonium' seems to have been coined by the author; it is not to be found in either *DMLBS*, *OLD*, or *TLL*.

seruus diei*a* tenebrarum inimicus[1] docebat eos noctem declinare,
diem uero diligere et seruare.[2] In die quippe erat et diem predicabat. In die erat quia secundum apostolum in omni bonitate et iustitia et ueritate[3] Deo fideliter seruiebat.*b* Predicabat autem diem a
quo omnis dies et de quo omne bonum, qui*c* erat lux uera, illumi-
nans omnem hominem uenientem in hunc mundum.[4] Noctem
uero increpabat et dampnabat, dum non communicare infructuosis operibus tenebrarum, sed surgere de sopore, a mortuis exur-
gere[5] uerbo et opere predicabat. Erant autem ex his qui audiebant
multi ad catholicam et apostolicam fidem iam conuersi, per predicationem beatissimi Augustini ecclesie Dorobernensis archiepiscopi.[6] Ruebant igitur populi cateruatim audire beatum antistitem
et illa salutaria monita, quibus os illius admodum affluebat, non
tam aure corporis quam cordis humiliter*d* amplectebantur. Vacuantur urbes, oppida solantur, fit ingens concursus et letus ab
omnibus celebratur auditus. Currunt omnes ad medicum tam corporum quam animarum, salutem sitientes. Currunt ad apostoli-
cum uirum uerbum uite et salutis eterne ab eo deuote querentes.
In tanto et tam leto spectaculo confundebatur gentilitas, idolatria
erubescit, exultat fides, uictoriosa coronatur Christiana deuotio.
Cadunt idola, fana sternuntur, franguntur simulachra, omnis
eorum cultus aut minuitur aut dampnatur. Silent theatra, templo-
rum dolent pontifices, sua lucra sibi surrepta deplorant. *e*Surgunt
ecclesie,*e* grata Deo parantur hospitia, leuatur crux, uictoria
Christi predicatur ab omnibus. Gemit hostis, inimicus dolet, arma
illius rapiuntur et ab his quos possidebat extruditur. Letatur uenerabilis pontifex quia hiems*f* et gelu infidelitatis a cordibus*g* eorum
pertransiit,[7] quia torpor opturationis mortifere abiit et recessit.

---

a Dei *DT*   *b* seruibat *A*   *c* quia *D*   *d* om. *H*   *e–e* Surgit
ecclesia *T*   *f* hiemi *AD*   *g* cordis *G*

---

[1] Cf. 1 Thess. 5: 5 ('Omnes enim uos filii lucis estis et filii diei; non sumus noctis,
neque tenebrarum').
[2] This section shows the hagiographer at his most desperate in the face of a parlous
lack of material. Having been told that Birinus lingered for three days, we are treated to
an almost absurd kind of exegesis on the text, 'it was good that he stayed *three* days,
because . . .', 'it was right that he stayed three *days* and not nights (!), because . . .'.
[3] Eph. 5: 9 ('fructus enim lucis est in omni bonitate, et iustitia et ueritate').
[4] John 1: 9 ('Erat lux uera quae inluminat omnem hominem uenientem in hunc
mundum').
[5] Eph. 5: 11 ('et nolite communicare operibus infructuosis tenebrarum, magis autem
redarguite') and 14 ('Propter quod dicit: Surge qui dormis, et exsurge a mortuis, et
illuminabit te Christus').

day, the enemy of darkness,[1] taught them to avoid the night, but to love and preserve the daylight.[2] Certainly he was in the daylight and preached the Day. He was in the daylight because, according to the apostle, he served God faithfully in all goodness, righteousness, and truth.[3] He preached the Day, by whom every day is made and from whom every good thing comes, who was the true light, illuminating every man who comes into this world.[4] But he rebuked and condemned the night, whilst he preached by word and deed that we should not commune with the fruitless works of the shadows but arise from slumber, and rise up from the dead.[5] There were amongst those who were listening many already converted to the catholic and apostolic faith, by the preaching of the blessed Augustine, the archbishop of the church at Canterbury.[6] Therefore the people rushed in crowds to hear the blessed bishop, and humbly embraced not so much with the ears of the body as of the heart the teachings of salvation, with which his lips were fully abounding. The cities are emptied, the towns deserted, there is a flocking together, and the joyful message is celebrated by all. They all hasten towards the physician of bodies as much as of souls, thirsting for salvation. They hasten towards the apostle, devotedly seeking from him the word of life and of eternal salvation. Paganism was confounded in such a great and joyful spectacle, idolatry blushes, faith rejoices, victorious Christian devotion is crowned. The idols crumble, the temples are flattened, the images are smashed, all their cult is either diminished or condemned. The theatres are silent, the temple priests grieve and lament their wealth being dragged away from them. Churches spring up, hostels pleasing to God are prepared, a cross is raised up, the victory of Christ is proclaimed by all. The enemy groans, the foe grieves, his weapons are snatched away and he is thrust out by those whom he once possessed. The venerable bishop rejoices because the winter and ice of unbelief has passed away from their hearts,[7] because the torpor of deathly deafness has departed and

---

[6] The hagiographer apparently envisaged that Birinus had landed in Kent, and to judge from the description which follows, 'Cadunt idola, fana sternuntur', first dealt, in three days, with all those who remained unconverted there before moving on to the territory of the Gewisse. It is noticeable that Birinus is not here (or in Bede's account) said to have had any contact with the authorities at Canterbury on arrival. Cf. the comments on Birinus's apparent independence as a possible sign of the relative insignificance of Canterbury at the time, in N. Brooks, *The Early History of the Church of Canterbury* (Leicester, 1984), p. 65.

[7] Cf. S. of S. 2: 11 ('Iam enim hiems transiit').

Letatur quia tempus aduenit amputandi sarmenta[a] iniquitatis sterilia,[1] quia flores iustitie et fidei apparuerunt in terra.[2] Exultat et gaudet quia euangelicus populus antiqui hostis raptum diffugiens, in cauerna macerie,[3] in custodia uirtutis et gratie delitescit, quia in foraminibus petre[4] [b]in Christi piis[b] uulneribus[5] per bona opera nidificare contendit. Exultat et gaudet quia terra salsuginis[6] conuersa est in conuallem frumenti, quia de terra deserta et sterili multa [c]bonorum filiorum[c] messis excrescit.

§ 15. [d]QVOD MVLIER CECA ET SVRDA CVRATA SIT.[d] Non [e]est autem[e] pretereundum silentio quod ad laudem serui sui in eodem loco Dominus operari dignatus est. Erat quidem[f] in eadem prouincia mulier quedam annosa,[g] quam iam per multum tempus calamitas geminata uastabat.[7] Nam gemine orbitatis dampno percussa, nec uidere quid nec auditu[h] capere preualebat. Inimicus quippe humani generis duas illas portas sentiendi graui opturatione obstruxit,[i] sed unde illam misere perdidit et construit, inde seruo Dei occasionem[j] miraculi inuitus ministrauit. Quiescenti [k]etenim illi[k] anicule mulieri de nocte in lecto suo per uisum significatum est, ut ad beatum antistitem ire celeriter debeat, quia ille sanaturus est eam,[l] quia ipse sibi erit medicina. Quid plura? surgit muliercula senex de lecto, parat ducem qui gressus eius [m]regat,[8] ad seruum Dei ire contendit. Sistitur optutibus eius,[m] rogat nesciens quem precatur precibus inmurmurat, uoce[n] immugit[o] et quia se non attendit, uoce confunditur, clamore colliditur. Intentio quidem supplicantis et deprecantis erat sed[p] horrorem comminantis uox exhibet. Nec ut impetraret orata lenocinatur[q] blanditiis, sed tanquam ui precipientis extorquet.

---

[a] sacramenta G   [b-b] in piis Christi CG; Christi in piis T   [c-c] filiorum bonorum T   [d-d] om. GHT   [e-e] est k A, which suggests scribal misinterpretation of the insular compendium for autem used in the exemplar; autem est G   [f] siquidem G   [g] om. G   [h] auditum H   [i] obstrusit CG   [j] occasione G   [k-k] ergo FG   [l] illam G   [m-m] om. G, by homoeoteleuton   [n] C ends with this word   [o] iniungit G   [p] et add. G   [q] lenocinantur D

---

[1] Cf. Gregory the Great, *Homiliae in Hiezechihelem Prophetam*, ii. 2. 429 ('In potatione quippe sarmenta sterilia reciduntur'), ed. M. Adriaen, *CCSL* cxlii (1971), p. 269 (repeated verbatim in Bede, *In Cantica Canticorum*, vi. 178, ed. Hurst, *CCSL* cxix B. 363).
[2] S. of S. 2: 12 ('Flores apparuerunt in terra nostra').
[3] S. of S. 2: 14 ('Columba mea, in foraminibus petrae, in cauerna maceriae').
[4] See previous note.

gone. He rejoices because the time has come for cutting off the sterile boughs of iniquity,[1] since the flowers of justice and faith have appeared in the land.[2] He exults and rejoices because the evangelical people, escaping the grasp of the ancient enemy, has hidden away in a hollow in the wall,[3] in the guardianship of virtue and grace, and because it is striving to nest in the chinks in the rock,[4] in the holy wounds of Christ,[5] through good works. He exults and rejoices that the land of brackishness[6] has been turned into a valley of corn, and that a great harvest of good sons is growing from a desert and barren land.

§ **15.** THAT A BLIND AND DEAF WOMAN WAS CURED. We should not pass over in silence that which God deigned to bring about to the praise of his servant in that same place. For there was in the same province an old woman, whom a double calamity had already for a long time afflicted.[7] Smitten by the harm of a double deprivation, she could neither see nor hear anything. For the enemy of the human race obstructed those two portals of sensation with a severe obstruction, but by that with which he destroyed and confounded the poor woman, he also involuntarily gave an opportunity for a miracle to the servant of God. For truly, while the old woman was resting at night in her bed, it was indicated to her in a vision, that she should go quickly to the blessed bishop, because he was going to heal her, since he would himself be her medicine. What more need be said? The little old woman rises from her bed, gets for herself a guide to direct her steps,[8] and hastens to the servant of God. Coming in his sight she asks, not knowing whom she beseeches, she mumbles prayers, she bellows out, and because she cannot hear herself, she is jumbled up in her speech, and is at variance with her shouting. Indeed her intention was supplication and prayer, but her voice gives the terrifying impression of someone making threats. In order to obtain her desires, she does not wheedle with flatteries, but she extorts them, as it were, with the violence of one giving orders. The

---

[5] Compare Bede's exegesis of this text: 'Si iuxta expositionem apostoli "petra erat Christus", quae sunt foramina Petrae nisi uulnera que pro nostra salute suscepit Christus? In quibus profecto foraminibus columba residet ac nidificat' (*In Cantica Canticorum*, ed. Hurst, *CCSL* cxix B. 224). See note on c. 3, p. 6.

[6] Jer. 17: 6 ('in terra salsuginis et inhabitabili').

[7] Cf. Goscelin, *Historia translationis S. Augustini* i. 3, 'Femina hic surda, muta et clauda, a trina scilicet calamitate est mutata' (*ActaS*, Maii, vi. 414).

[8] Cf. *Miracula S. Swithuni* c. 6 ('adducens ducem qui regat illas et ducat').

Sonus uocis et intellectus mentis in diuersa contendunt, ut sermo oris distincte non personet aures officiunt.

§ 16. Intellexit uir Deo plenus desiderium mulieris: non uerbo sed cordi respondet,[a] pietate motus, dexteram leuat, auribus et oculis signum crucis opponit. Nec mora, dissoluitur cecitas, redditur uisus, uitio surditatis eliso subitus reparatur auditus. Transit senex in adolescentem, annosa in iuuenem, acuit oculos ad radium solis, aquilinum[1] lumen se comprehendisse letatur. Miratur [b]in gemino[b] sensu annos pubertatis sue reuersos, quibus si sua sibi natura intemerata consisteret, hoc tempore forsitan etate consumpta deficeret. Iam incipit uidere medicum suum, intueri curatorem[c] suum. Intuetur eum ad ipsum conuersa, quem[d] paulo ante non uidens precabatur auersa. Aduoluitur pedibus eius, gratias reddit,[e] et que deprecando prius furialiter intonabat, iam audiens se iam sibi contemperans, strepitum interim[f] uocemque modificat. Auris placidi est magistra sermonis; aure correcta[g] sermo moderatus incessit. Audit cum populo assistente salutis uerbum, anime medicinam, et non iam adeo letatur quia infirmitatem euasit quia sibi [h]reddita est, quantum[h] quia monita et precepta beati antistitis audire iam potest. Mirantur omnes et gaudent, exultant uniuersi et stupent, magnalia Dei predicant, seruum Dei ueneratione attollunt.[2] Stupebant autem miraculum hoc uniuersi exhibitum corporaliter, qui non attendebant tamen in milibus ipsius populi impletum spiritualiter. Vere beati huius pontificis meritum magnificum et magnifice uenerandum, qui imitatus Dominum suum—immo operatus per Dominum suum—dixit et factum est,[3] uoluit et [i]operatus est.[i] Manus illius ueloces ad faciendum fuerunt et tornatiles,[4] non autem quia ipsius, sed quia Deus in eo est. Neque ipse quidem presumebat[5] de se tanquam operaretur a se, sed[j] totum dans Deo

---

[a] respondit H   [b-b] ingenio G   [c] creatorem G   [d] que T
[e] reddidit G (and A before correction)   [f] inter ADH; interim added above the line by later hand in T   [g] correpta H   [h-h] sanitas reddita est, quantum F; reddita est sanitas, sed T (added in a later hand over erasure)   [i-i] operatum est A; operatus G
[j] set add. G

---

[1] 'Aquilinum', literally, eagle-like (from 'aquila'), hence sharp, seems slightly odd as an adjective to describe light, but could in this context be interpreted as 'piercing' or 'brilliant'. The adjective may also have been intended as a transferred epithet, referring to the keenness of restored sight (cf. Isidore, Etym. xii. 7. 10, 'Aquila ab acumine oculorum uocata').
[2] Cf. Acts 2: 11–12 ('audiuimus eos loquentes nostris linguis magnalia Dei. Stupebant autem omnes, et mirabantur adinuicem').

sound of her voice and the understanding of her mind strive in opposite directions, her ears hinder the speech of her mouth from sounding out distinctly.

§ 16. The man filled with God understood the woman's desire, responds not to the word but to the heart; moved by piety, he lifts his right hand and makes the sign of the cross upon her ears and eyes. Without delay, the blindness is dissolved, sight is restored, and with the defect of deafness removed, she suddenly regains her hearing. Old woman turns into young girl, aged woman into youthful one, her eyesight sharpens to the sun's ray, and she rejoices to have seen the brilliant light.[1] She marvels with double sensation at the years of her youth returned, in which, if her state had remained unaltered, at this time perhaps she would have died of old age. Now she begins to see her physician, to look upon the one who cured her. She looks upon him, turned towards the same one, whom, a little while before, not seeing, she besought while turned away. She falls at his feet, gives thanks, and she who just before thundered furiously in her petitions, now able to hear herself, now in control of herself, moderates in the meantime the sound of her voice. Of calmed hearing she is mistress of her speech; with normal hearing, moderate speech has come to her. She listens, along with the people present, to the word of salvation, the medicine of the soul, and now she rejoices not so much that she has escaped disability and is returned to herself, as that she is now able to hear the teachings and precepts of the blessed bishop. Everyone marvels and rejoices, all exult and are awestruck, they proclaim the wonderful works of God, and raise aloft the servant of God in veneration.[2] They were all amazed at this miracle shown physically, whilst however they did not heed the miracle fulfilled spiritually in thousands of that very people. Truly, the worth of this blessed priest is marvellous and marvellously to be venerated, who, imitating his Lord—or rather working through his Lord—spoke and it was done,[3] willed and carried it out. His hands were swift and well wrought for action,[4] not because they were his, but because God is in him. Nor did he trust in his own power[5] as though he were acting from his own resources, but gave all to God

[3] Cf. Gen. 1: 9 (*et passim*), 'Dixit uero Deus . . . Et factum est ita', and Ps. 32(33): 9 and 148: 5 ('Quoniam ipse dixit, et facta sunt; ipse mandauit et creata sunt').

[4] S. of S. 5: 14 ('Manus illius tornatiles').

[5] See note on c. 11, p. 24.

et nichil sibi, seruum non preceptorem se esse dicebat, ministrum se profitebatur non operatorem.

§ 17. *^a*VBI CONVERTIT REGEM AD FIDEM.*^a* Per triduum itaque commoratus beatus Birinus in loco quo applicuerat ualedicens fratribus profectus est, et quo amplius gentilitatis insaniam feruere cognouit, illuc intrepidus*^b* calore fidei et predicandi ardore succensus ire contendit. Ac primum sicut uenerabilis presbiter Beda refert,[1] Geuissorum terram ingrediens, cum omnes ibidem paganissimis obuolutos erroribus inueniret, utilius esse ratus est inibi uerbum Dei predicare quam ultra progrediens alios quibus predicare deberet inquirere. Tempore illo Cynegilsus rex arcem possidebat imperii, adhuc furorem gentilitatis anhelans, et ritu superstitionis deseuiens.*^c* Aduersus hanc crudelem bestiam,*^d* aduersus hunc ferocem leonem miles Dei ex uerbo apostoli doctus, qui dicit 'secundum hominem ad bestias pugnaui*^e* Ephesi'[2] lorica sanctitatis[3] indutus occurrit, accinctus gladio spiritus qui est uerbum Dei.[4] Procedit aduersum*^f* regem presbiter, fide armatus non ferro, diuino non humano concertat auxilio.[5] Pugnat aduersum*^g* regem sed salutem regis inquirit. Exerit uires, fortitudine dimicat, sed de illius salute*^h* contendit. Vt eum debellet, init duellum, pugnat non odio sed amore, hostem pace non crudelitate rimatur. Quam beata et quam pia certantis hostilitas, ubi non odit qui pugnat, ubi qui percutit amat! Quam gloriosa et quam utilis pugna, ubi qui percutit curat, qui uulnerat sanat, ubi*ⁱ* qui occidit uiuificat! Quam sanctus quamque magnificus iste conflictus ubi de uulnere nascitur salus, uita de morte egreditur, ubi qui uincitur coronatur! Gloriosa lucta est, ubi qui uincit et qui uincitur uictor est. Gloriosa pugna est, ubi qui uincit non extollitur, qui uincitur nulla humiliatione confunditur. Quam bonum luctamen est ubi etsi dissideatur in principio, in fine*^j* tamen concordia est, ubi uota concordant, postquam*^k* ad euentum*^l* uentum est. Insonuit preco ueritatis euangelii tubam[6]

---

^{a–a} om. *GHT*   *^b* et *add. H*   *^c* deseruiens *T*   *^d* hostiam *T*
^e pugnandi *D*   *^f* aduersus *G*   *^g* aduersus *G*   *^h* laude *G*   *ⁱ* om.
G   *^j* fide *T*   *^k* priusquam *AG*   *^l* effectum *G*

---

[1] Bede, *HE* iii. 7.
[2] 1 Cor. 15: 32 ('Si secundum hominem ad bestias pugnaui Ephesi, quid mihi prodest?').
[3] Cf. 1 Thess. 5: 8 ('induti loricam fidei et charitatis'), and Eph. 6: 14 ('et induti loricam iusititiae').
[4] Eph. 6: 17 ('gladium spiritus quod est uerbum Dei').

and none to himself, said that he was a servant and not a ruler, professed himself a minister and not a worker.

§ 17. IN WHICH HE CONVERTED THE KING TO THE FAITH. And so St Birinus stayed for three days in the place where he had come to shore, and then, saying farewell to his brothers, he set out, and identified a place where the madness of paganism burned more widely, and intrepidly strove to go there, stirred by the heat of faith and the fire of preaching. And first, as the venerable priest Bede reports,[1] upon entering the land of the Gewissae [West Saxons], since he found all there enveloped in pagan errors, he considered it to be more useful to preach the word of God there, than, proceeding further, to seek out others to preach to. At that time King Cynegils held the citadel of government, still breathing out the fury of heathenism, and raging in the ritual of superstition. Against this cruel beast, against this ferocious lion, the soldier of God, learned in the word of the apostle who says 'after the manner of men I fought with beasts at Ephesus',[2] putting on the breastplate of sanctity,[3] advanced, girt with the sword of the spirit, namely the word of God.[4] The priest goes forth against the king, armed with faith and not the sword; with divine not human help he enters combat.[5] He battles against the king but seeks the salvation of the king. He makes use of might, fights with fortitude, but strives for the other man's salvation. So that he might defeat him, he enters battle, fights not with hatred but with love, overturns the enemy with peace not cruelty. What blessed and holy hostility in a warrior, where he who fights does not hate, where he who smites loves! What a glorious and useful battle, where he who strikes cures, who wounds heals, where he who kills brings to life! How holy and magnificent that conflict, where deliverance is begotten of wounding, where life comes from death, where he who is vanquished is crowned! It is a glorious struggle where he who conquers and he who is conquered are victors. It is a glorious fight, where he who conquers is not exalted, he who is conquered is not confounded by any humiliation. What a good contest it is where, even if in the beginning there is dissension, yet in the end there is harmony, where desires are in harmony after the outcome is reached. The herald of truth sounded the trumpet of the gospel[6]

---

[5] Cf. note on c. 11, p. 21.

[6] Cf. Jerome, *Contra Iohannem Hierusolymitanum* c. 10, 'ubi electionis uas, tuba euangelii, rugitus leonis nostri' (*PL* xxiii. 379).

et salutarem anime predicat medicinam.[1] Dicebat regi presbiter quod erat legis, quod fidei, quod morum erat, quod salutis, quod uite, fideli sermone referebat, misterium quidem sancte trinitatis fideli interpretatione annuntians, culturam idolorum firmissimis[a] argumentis euacuans.

§ 18. Quid multa? Vicit regem sacerdos, quia non solus erat, sed erat Deus cum eo. Vicit sacerdos regem, immo Deus hominem superauit, rex regem. Vicit qui non apparebat, quia unde sacerdos uinceret, in spiritu edocebat. Ostendebat ictus, artem pugnandi monstrabat, qualiter instanti occurreret et cedentem sequeretur, interius inspirabat. Quam sancta quamque sine fraude dolositas, ubi in uno duo pugnant, aduersus unum in duello duo concertant! Sed hoc ad laudem et honorem regis factum est, ut iam non presbitero soli, sed regi imputare rex debeat quod uictus est. Foris erat qui suscipit[b] bellum, sed intus est, qui belli[c] operatur euentum. Neque tantum sacerdoti aderat, ut uincere edoceret, sed et regi[d] intus adest, ut uinci non dubitet. Inspirat regi homini rex Deus, ut sacerdotem quem uidet audiat, quatinus sibi quem non uidet seruiturus obediat. Inspirat ei ut seipsum superet, malam conuersationem[e] suam deuincat, ut cultum[f] idolatrie reiciens, fidem religionis incunctanter admittat. Vicit rex Deus in sacerdote suo hominem regem, et licet ipse debellauerit, tamen a munere suum non priuat sacerdotem. O magna dulcedo, misericordia inmensa: Dominus preliatur et presbiter muneratur! Dominus dimicat et merces de prelio presbitero repensatur. Superat Dominus et presbiter de uictoria coronatur. Credidit igitur idolatra, ad baptismum deducitur, fidei sacramenta suscepit. Humiliatur sub manu sacerdotis, humiliatus benedici promeruit, et qui prius superbus incedebat fastu seculari, ecce humiliter fungitur militia[g] sui saluatoris. De rege factus est seruus, immo de seruo liber et rex factus est. Seruiebat[h] quidem diabolo et pompis eius uniuersis,[2] nunc illis

---

[a] firmissis G   [b] suscepit G   [c] om. D   [d] reri D   [e] conuersionem G   [f] cultrum D   [g] miliciam G   [h] seruibat A

---

[1] Cf. Cassiodorus, *Expositio Psalmorum*, xxxi. 170 ('O medicina salutaris! contra morbos omnium peccatorum'), ed. M. Adriaen, 2 vols., *CCSL* xcvii–xcviii (1958), i. 278; and also xxxvii. 40, 305, and 394 (id. i. 343, 350 and 352).

[2] 'The Devil and all his pomps' is an echo of the triple renunciation which formed part of the rite of Christian initiation from the second century onwards (the phrase derives ultimately from Tertullian, *De baptismate*), 'Abrenuntias Satane? Abrenuntio. Et omnibus operibus eius? Abrenuntio. Et omnibus pompis eius? Abrenuntio.' See e.g. *Ordo ad cati-*

and is proclaiming the saving medicine of the soul.[1] The priest told the king that which pertained to the law, and that which pertained to faith, he told with faithful words of morals, of salvation, and of life, announcing the mystery of the Holy Trinity with faithful interpretation, making the cult of idols void with strong arguments.

§ 18. What more needs to be said? The priest overcame the king, because he was not alone, but God was with him. The priest conquered the king—or rather, God overcame man, King overcame king. He who could not be seen, conquered, because He taught, in the spirit, from what the priest was to conquer. He showed where to lay the blows, demonstrated the art of fighting; He gave inward inspiration how to meet the threatening enemy, and how to pursue the enemy in retreat. What holy and what guileless deceit, where two fight in one, two enter battle against one! But this was done to the praise and honour of the king so that now the king ought to ascribe the fact that he has been conquered not to the priest alone, but to the King. He who takes up the battle was on the outside, but within is He who brings about the outcome. And He was not only present in the priest, so as to show him how to win, but He is also within the king, so that he does not hesitate to be conquered. God the King inspires the human king, to listen to the priest, whom he can see, to the end that he may obediently serve Him, Whom he cannot see. He inspires him to overcome himself, conquer his evil way of life, so that, casting aside the worship of idolatry, he may without delay let in the faith of religion. God the King conquered the human king through His priest, and although He Himself fought out the battle, He does not, however, deprive the priest of his reward. O great sweetness, immeasurable mercy: the Lord battles, and the priest is rewarded. The Lord fights and the priest is paid the reward for the battle. The Lord overcomes and the priest is crowned for victory. Therefore the idolater has believed, is brought to baptism, and received the sacraments of faith. He is humbled at the hand of the priest, and being made humble, he deserved blessing, and he who first proudly stalked with secular contempt, behold, serves humbly in the army of his saviour. Out of a king a servant was made—or rather, out of a servant was made a free man and a king. Indeed he used to serve the devil and all his pomps,[2] now, they being emptied out, he has been

cuminum faciendum, in the early 11th-cent. sacramentary, the 'Missal of Robert of Jumièges' (ed. Wilson, p. 97), for a form of baptismal rite which would probably have been familiar to the author of *Vita S. Birini*.

uacuatis sub potenti manu Dei humiliatus[1] et confractus, definito consilio Deo seruire constituit. Scriptum est autem quia seruire Deo regnare est.[2] Regnat igitur rex factus e[a] seruo, fidem seruans, religionem amplexans.[b] Contigit[3] autem disponente gratia Dei tunc temporis sanctissimum ac uictoriosissimum regem Northanymbrorum[c] Oswaldum[d] affuisse eumque de aqua lauachri ascendentem suscepisse, ac sic[4] pulcherrimo et Deo digno consortio, cuius filiam erat accepturus in coniugem, ipsum prius misterio regenerationis Deo dicatum sibi accepit in filium.

§ 19. [e]QVOD BAPTIZATO REGE TOTA PROVINCIA BAPTIZATVR.[e] Baptizato autem rege, baptizatur et eius familia, uetus homo exuitur et noua induitur creatura,[5] succedente nouitate delitescit uetustas et demonica seruitute supplosa prodit Christiana libertas. Ecce serui regis facti sunt reges, et regenerati quique pari cum eo conditione ditantur. Magna est domus illa et omni admiratione suscipienda, ubi reges seruiunt et ubi[f] de seruitute reges sunt; ubi qui seruit liber est,[g] qui se liberum facit seruus est.[6] Baptizatur itaque rex et eius familia, baptizatur etiam cum eo gens imperii sui, uniuersa prouincia. Videre erat magnum miraculum, inusitatum quidem sed letum spectaculum, non unam personam, non familiam unam, sed gentem[h] unam prouinciam totam cum rege una suscepisse baptismum. Omnis etas, uterque sexus, uniuersa conditio,[7] Dei corripiunt[i] militiam, et omnes eos in unam parit ecclesia[j] mater infantiam. Sterilis surculus uernat in palmitem, marcens etas reparatur in iuuenem, constitutus in hora undecima[8] de sua conuersionis nouitate letatur. Ecce impletum est tibi, beate Birine, quod in Canticis Canticorum in quibusdam membris suis dicitur ecclesie: 'Veni, coronaberis de capite Amana, de uertice Sanir, de cubilibus

---

[a] est D   [b] amplectens FGH   [c] AFT; nordanhimbrorum B; noruuanymbrorum D; northumbrorum G; norðanymbrorum H   [d] DGT; Oswoldum A; Osuualdum FH   [e-e] om. GHT   [f] om. A   [g] et add. G
[h] gententem D   [i] arripiunt G   [j] ecclesiam D

---

[1] 1 Pet. 5: 6 ('Humiliamini igitur sub potenti manu Dei').
[2] See note on c. 2, p. 4.
[3] From Bede, HE iii. 7.
[4] 'ac sic pulcherrimo' is a variant reading, supplied by Colgrave and Mynors, Bede's Ecclesiastical History, p. 232, note a, of their c2 recension, which was the most widely current in England; cf. C. Plummer, ed., Venerabilis Baedae Opera Historica, 2 vols. (Oxford, 1896), i. 139 n. 6.

humbled and broken under the mighty hand of God,[1] and has, in no uncertain terms, determined to serve God. It is written that to serve God is to reign.[2] Therefore he reigns, made a king from a slave, keeping the faith, embracing religion. And it so happened,[3] by the grace of God, that at that time the holy and victorious king of Northumbria, Oswald, was present to receive him as he rose up from the cleansing water [i.e. of baptism], and thus,[4] in an alliance beautiful and acceptable in the sight of God, he accepted him, newly dedicated to God in the mystery of rebirth, as son, and then his daughter as wife.

§ 19. IN WHICH, WITH THE KING BAPTIZED, THE ENTIRE PROVINCE IS BAPTIZED. After the baptism of the king, his family is also baptized, the old man is put off and the new creature put on,[5] the new takes the place of the old, which lies hidden, and, with slavery to the devil trodden underfoot, Christian liberty comes forth. Behold, the king's servants are made kings, and each, being regenerate, is endowed with a status equal to his. Great is that household, and worthy of all admiration, where kings serve, and where from servitude come kings; where he who serves is free, he who makes himself free is a slave.[6] Therefore the king and his family are baptized, and with him also the people of his kingdom is baptized, the entire province. A great miracle was to be seen, an unfamiliar, indeed, but joyful spectacle, that not one person, not one family, but one people, a whole province, together with its king, received baptism. All ages, both sexes, every estate,[7] take up the military service of God, and all these the mother Church bears in one single infancy. The barren shoot blooms into a young bough, withered old age is restored to youth, set aright at the eleventh hour[8] it rejoices in the newness of its conversion. Behold, in you, blessed Birinus, what is said to certain members of the Church in the Song of Songs is fulfilled: 'Come, you will be crowned from the top of Amana, from the peak of Sanir, from the

---

[5] Cf. Eph. 4: 22 ('deponere uos secundum pristinam conuersationem ueterem hominem'), and 24 ('et induite nouum hominem'); and 2 Cor. 5: 17 ('Si qua ergo in Christo noua creatura, uetera transierunt').

[6] Cf. 1 Cor. 7: 22 ('Qui enim in Domino uocatus est seruus, libertus est Domini, similiter qui liber uocatus est seruus est Christi').

[7] Cf. *Vita S. Swithuni* c. 4, 'omnis etas, omnis sexus, uniuersa conditio, clerus ac populus Wentane ciuitatis, eadem uoluntate, pari consilio petierunt a rege' (Sauvage, p. 376).

[8] Cf. Matt. 20: 9 ('Cum uenissent ergo qui circa undecimam horam uenerant').

leonum, de montibus pardorum.'[1] Coronatur[a] etenim predicator de latere montis, quando per predicationem suam humiliat superbiam populi non credentis. Coronatur autem de monte uel de uertice montis, quando reges, quando principes debellat et uincit. Qui bene accipiuntur Amana[b] uel Sanir, quia inuigilant ut lanient, quia sunt aues nocturne, tenebras diligentes et noctem.[2] Qui etiam̃ cubilia uel montes leonum uel pardorum sunt, quia tanquam montes in superbia extolluntur et malignis spiritibus cubilia prebent.[3] In neutro ergo tibi, pater beatissime, corona deest, quia de rege, de principibus, quia de populo tibi data et aucta est. Manus tue sonuerunt coram eis correctionis et discipline psalterium, cuius pia et suaui melodia auribus eorum insonante, spiritus malus fugit, et spiritu sancto donati sunt. Temperasti ante eos legis et euangelii consonantiam, qua interius delectati omnes satagunt de salute et tendunt ad uitam.

§ 20. [c]DE SEDE ILLIVS ET CONVERSATIONE SANCTA. DE MORTE ET TRANSLATIONE IPSIVS.[c] Donauerunt autem supradicti reges beato Birino ciuitatem que Dorcacester[d] uocatur, ad faciendam inibi sedem episcopalem.[4] Sublimatus igitur in sede beatus antistes parat ecclesias, altaria ponit, simulachra dissipat, fana subuertit. Legit[e] homines quos uita et scientia idoneos probat, sueque attitulatos matri ecclesie leuat ad ordines

---

[a] coronantur G   [b] Amanam T   [c-c] om. GHT   [d] H; Dorkinga AFG; Dorcascester D; Dorchacester T   [e] Elegit G

[1] S. of S. 4: 8 ('Veni de Libano, ueni, coronaberis; de capite Amana, de uertice Sanir et Hermon, de cubilibus leonum, de montibus pardorum'). The interpretation of chap. 4, v. 8 given here is the standard one; compare Bede, In Cantica Canticorum: 'Cum ergo uulgus ignobile ad Dominum ecclesia conuertit coronam de lateribus montium in quibus bestiae latuerant consequitur qua praemium de saluatione populi contradictoris accipit; at cum ipsos malitiae principes cum persecutores publicos ad uiam uitae perduxerit de capite nimirum ac uertice coronatur montium quia cum labore certaminis crescit palma retributionis' (CCSL cxix B. 255). As before (c. 3) it has not been possible to find any extant version of the exegesis of this passage from which the hagiographer can have copied verbatim—he may have conflated several sources. There are some similarities with Haymo of Auxerre, Enarratio in Canticum Canticorum: 'per hos autem montes, saeculi potestates, reges uidelicet et principes intelliguntur, qui ueluti montes in superbia extolluntur, et malignis spiritibus quasi leonibus et pardis cubilia praebent' (PL cxvii. 319).

[2] The standard interpretations of Amana and Sanir make no reference to 'aues nocturne'; see M. Thiel, Grundlagen und Gestalt der Hebräischkenntnisse des frühen Mittelalters (Spoleto, 1973), pp. 235 and 406. The only other occurrences of this interpretation discovered hitherto are in Alan of Lille (d. 1203), Elucidatio in Cantica Canticorum, PL ccx. 51–110, at col. 80, 'Sanir nocturna auis interpretatur', and Rupert of Deutz, Commentaria in Canticum Canticorum (completed in 1117), iii, line 685, 'de capite Amana

lions' dens, from the mountains of the leopards.'[1] For truly, the preacher is crowned from the mountain side, when by his preaching he humbles the pride of an unbelieving people. He is crowned from the mountain, or the top of the mountain, when he defeats and conquers kings and princes. These are well interpreted as Amana and Sanir, because they keep watch, to rend in pieces, because they are night birds, loving the shadows and the night.[2] They are also the dens or mountains of lions or leopards, because they are raised high as mountains in pride and offer dens to malignant spirits.[3] In neither of these, therefore, do you lack a crown, blessed father, because from the king, from princes, and from the people it has been given and increased unto you. Your hands have sounded in their presence the psaltery of correction and discipline, by whose holy and sweet melody, sounding in their ears, the evil spirit is put to flight, and they are presented with the Holy Spirit. Before them you have regulated the harmony of the law and the gospel, in which all delight inwardly so that they seek after salvation and turn to true life.

§ 20. ABOUT HIS SEE AND HIS HOLY LIFE. ABOUT HIS DEATH AND TRANSLATION. The aforementioned kings gave to St Birinus a city called Dorchester, to create there an episcopal see.[4] Accordingly, elevated to a see, the blessed bishop builds churches, sets up altars, scatters effigies, overturns heathen temples. He chooses men whom good life and knowledge show to be suitable, and, having ordained them to his mother church,

quod interpretatur nocturna auis', ed. H. Haacke, *CCCM* xxvi (1974), p. 78. Of course, both of these works are too late to have been used by the author of *Vita S. Birini*, but, since both Alan and Rupert drew heavily upon earlier, known, exegesis of the Song of Songs, it is likely that the interpretation of 'Sanir' also came from an (as yet unidentified) earlier source, which was also available to our author.

[3] See n. 1 above.

[4] Cited from Bede, *HE* iii. 7. There, the name of the see is given as 'Dorcic' (although in *HE* iv. 23, it occurs as 'Dorciccaestrae'). The variant reading offered by **A**, **F**, and **G**, of 'Dorkinga/Dorkynga' must be an error, perhaps derived from an exemplar which preserved Bede's 'Dorcic', since the place-name Dorchester is never attested in any form approximating to 'Dorking'. Possibly the variant came about through confusion with Dorking, Surrey—cf. *DB, Surrey* 1. 13 (i. 30c), 'Dorchinges'. See M. Gelling and D. M. Stenton, *The Place-Names of Oxfordshire*, 2 vols., EPNS xxiii–xxiv (1953–4), i. 152. In *ASC* (s.a. 635 and 639), the name is preserved as 'Dorkeceastre' or 'Dorceceastre'; but by the time of Domesday Book, had reached the form 'Dorchecestre' (*DB, Oxfordshire*, 6. 1a, fo. 155a), more closely approximating to that found in the 12th-cent. witnesses **D**, **H**, and **T**. Cf. also the forms 'Dorcacestrie' or 'Dorcacestra', found in the late 12th-cent. *Eynsham Cartulary*, ed. H. E. Salter, 2 vols., Oxford Historical Society, xlix and li (1906–8), i. 69 and 109.

sanctos, gradibus eos sublimat canonicis. Quod ordinis diuini, quod regule clericalis, quod discipline canonice didicerat,[a] in eis et inter eos primus exercet. Ipse pater eorum et seruus est, socius eorum est et magister. Nouit melius esse subuenire illis et prodesse, quam dominari et praeesse. Districtio illius regularis non de[b] tirannide, non de crudelitate, sed de misericordia, de caritate pendebat. Imperatoris et militis, domini et serui officium circa eos sapienti discretione gerebat. Bene uiuentes ut in melius crescerent uerbo et exemplo hortabatur, peccantes ut peccare desinerent, paterno non furioso puniebat affectu. Nec de commissa sibi dominatione in subditos furit,[c] sed alis misericordie uir columbinus ex mansuetudine ferit. Sepe etenim iracundi doctores rabie furoris accensi discipline ministerium in immanitatem crudelitatis conuertunt, et unde emendare subditos[d] poterant, inde peius sauciant et uulnerant.[1] Mens etenim que catena caritatis non astringitur male ad omnem occasionem commouetur. Vbi autem commotio mentis est, discretionis oculus esse non potest. Predicabat autem Dei seruus uerbum Dei ad populum non remisse, instabat secundum apostolum opportune et importune.[2] Opus faciebat euangeliste, ministerium[e] suum studio bono studebat implere. Curabat sollicite seipsum probabilem exhibere Deo operarium inconfusibilem,[f] recte tractantem uerbum ueritatis.[3] Erat autem abstinentie uigore fortis in elemosinis profusus, in oratione peruigil, lectionis[g] studiosus, et quod de prato pagine diuine deflorabat, in armarium cordis ut in actum usque deduceret,[h] fideliter collocabat. In humilitate, in mansuetudine, in continentia, in castitate, ita perfecte uiuebat, ut non humanam sed uitam agere crederetur angelicam. His et aliis uirtutum ornamentis adeo refulsit in terris, ut iam a communi conuersatione subtractus, uersari ab omnibus putaretur in celis. Iste est, Britannia, propugnaculum tuum,[4] pater et pastor tuus, uir apostolicus, preco

---

^a didicant T   ^b om. A   ^c fuerit T   ^d om. D   ^e misterium G
^f in confusibilem G   ^g lectione G; lectioni HT   ^h deducens T

---

¹ For this and the following sentence, see Isidore, *Sent*. iii. 40 (*De iracundis doctoribus*), 'Iracundi doctores per rabiem furoris disciplinae modum ad immanitatem crudelitatis conuertunt, et unde emendare subditos poterant, inde potius uulnerant ... Mens enim soluta in diuersis catena charitatis non astringitur, sed male laxata, male ad omnem occasionem mouetur' (*PL* lxxxiii. 710).
² 2 Tim. 4: 2 ('praedica uerbum, insta opportune, importune').
³ 2 Tim. 2: 15 ('Sollicite cura teipsum probabilem exhibere Deo, operarium inconfusibilem recte tractantem uerbum ueritatis').

raises them to holy orders, elevates them by the canonical degrees. That which he had learnt of divine order, clerical rule and canonical discipline, he practises towards them and as first among them. He is their very father and servant, he is their companion and master. He knows that it is better to help and benefit them than to dominate and rule over them. His strictness in the rule depended not on tyranny, not on cruelty, but on mercy and love. He carried out the office of general and soldier, master and servant in their company with wise discretion. He encouraged by word and example those living in the right way to grow to something better and those who sinned to cease from sin, and meted out punishment with fatherly feeling and not angrily. Nor does he rage against those subject to him because of the power entrusted to him, but, being a dovelike man, beats with wings of mercy, out of gentleness. For truly, angry teachers, inflamed with mad anger, often change the administering of discipline into the savageness of cruelty, and with that by which they could have corrected their subjects, they inflict worse pain and injury on them.[1] For a mind which is not bound by the chain of love is moved to act wrongly on every occasion. Where there is disturbance of mind, there can be no eye of discernment. But the servant of God did not preach the word of God to the people negligently; he pressed it home in season and out of season,[2] according to the apostle. He did the work of an evangelist, and was eager to carry out his ministry with zeal. He was carefully concerned to show himself acceptable to God, as a labourer who need not be ashamed, teaching correctly the word of truth.[3] He was strong in the vigour of his abstinence, generous in almsgiving, ever watchful at prayer, studious in reading, and that which he plucked from the meadow of the divine page, he placed faithfully in the book-cupboard of his heart, so as to bring it into action. In humility, in gentleness, in temperance, in chastity, he lived so perfectly that he was thought to lead not a human but an angelic life. Adorned with these and other virtues he so shone on earth, that now, withdrawn from common life, he is thought by everyone to be in heaven. This is your fortress of defence,[4] Britain, your father and shepherd, an apostle, a herald of

---

[4] Cf. Jerome, *Commentariorum in Esaiam Libri xviii*, xv. 54 ('Qui ergo in disputando fortissimus est et sanctarum scripturarum testimoniis roboratus, iste propugnaculum ecclesiae est'), ed. M. Adriaen, 2 vols., *CCSL* lxxiii–lxxiii A (1963), ii. 612.

ueritatis, tuba euangelica,[1] casti consilii angelus, medicus qui uulnera tua curare paratus est. Iste exturbauit a te idolatriam, gentem peccatorum peruersam, habitatores malos, quibus diabolus caput est, et introduxit in te fidem[a] et omnem bonum iustitie comitatum,[b] habitatores[c] pacificos, quibus [d]Christus caput[d] est.[2] Iste est qui te de miseria erroris reuocans, feritatem tuam adeo permulsit et fregit, ut que prius tantum[e] barbarum frendere[3] consueueras, iam diuinam[f] edocta armoniam, non tam consona uoce, quam mente deuota, laudem Deo cantare[g] leteris.

§ 21. Factis igitur et dedicatis multis ecclesiis, multisque ad Dominum pio eius labore populis aduocatis,[4] nature concedens humane, plenus bonorum operum, spem bonam habens de filiorum propagine, securus migrauit ad Dominum. In eadem autem ciuitate, ubi Deo donante pontificatus ministerium gerebat, corpus eius sepultum est, ubi etiam per multos requieuit annos usque ad tempus beati patris nostri[h] Hedde,[5] qui quintus ei in episcopatu[i] successit. Qui bono zelo ductus indigne ferens tantam tamque pretiosam margaritam loci uilitate fuscari,[6] Deo annuente transtulit illud in Wentam[j] ciuitatem et in ecclesia beatorum apostolorum Petri et Pauli honorifice tumulauit,[7] sapienti usus consilio, ut ciuitas Wentana, que et eiusdem pontificatus arce[k] sullimis, inter ciuitates autem Britannie populosior et diuitiis famosior erat,[8] suo gloriosius et cumulatius celebraretur apostolo.[l] Euoluto autem multo tempore, beatus Athelwoldus,[m] magne religionis et auctoritatis uir,[9] qui et ipse uigesimus[n]

[a] finem D   [b] cominatum T   [c] habitores A   [d-d] caput Christus D
[e] tatum D   [f] diuina G   [g] decantare A   [h] om. FG   [i] episcopat
D   [j] Wentanam FH   [k] est add. FG   [l] a populo AF   [m] Athel-
uuoldus DH   [n] uicesimus FH

---

[1] See note on c. 17, p. 35.

[2] Cf. Leo the Great, *Sermo* lxxxii, 'cui caput est Christus' (*CCSL* cxxxviii A. 517), echoing Eph. 5: 23; and also Bede, *In Tobiam*, vi. 43, 'Sicut autem Dominus noster caput ecclesiae suae . . . ita diabolus caput omnium iniquorum' (*CCSL* cxix B. 9).

[3] Gregory the Great, *Moralia in Iob*, xxvii. 11 ('Ecce lingua Britanniae quae nil aliud nouerat quam barbarum frendere, iam dudum in diuinis laudibus Hebraeum coepit Alleluia resonare'), ed. M. Adriaen, 3 vols., *CCSL* clxiii–clxiii B (1979–85), iii. 1346. This is also cited by Bede, *HE* ii. 1, which is quite as likely to have been the indirect source which the author of the *Vita* had in mind. Compare also the use of 'barbarie frendens' in Wulfstan's abecedarian hymn to Birinus, referred to on p. lxix above.

[4] Bede, *HE* iii. 7.

[5] Bede named Hædde as the fifth Bishop 'Orientalium Saxonum', succeeding Leuthere (*HE* iv. 12), and marked his death as occurring in 705. *ASC* recorded Hædde's succession at 676 (see *MS. A*, ed. Bately).

truth, evangelic trumpet,[1] messenger of chaste counsel, the physician who is ready to heal your wounds. He drove idolatry out from you, a perverse race of sinners, evil inhabitants, with the devil at the head, and has introduced faith and all the good retinue of righteousness into you, peaceful inhabitants, with Christ at the head.[2] He it is who called you back from the misery of error, tamed and broke your wildness to such an extent that, where once you were accustomed to gnash your teeth in barbarous fashion,[3] now instructed in divine harmony, not only with one voice, but with devoted mind, you delight to sing praise to God.

§ 21. Therefore, having built and dedicated many churches, and having summoned many people to the Lord,[4] by his pious toil, yielding to human nature, filled with good works, and having good hope for the posterity of his sons, he passed away to the Lord in all confidence. In the same city where he had, by the gift of God, ministered as bishop, his body was buried, and there also he rested for many years, until the time of our blessed father Hædde,[5] who was the fifth to succeed him in the episcopate. He, led by right zeal, considered it unworthy that such a great and precious pearl should be darkened by the meanness of the place,[6] and, with God's consent, transferred it to the city of Winchester, and entombed it with due honour in the church of the blessed Apostles Peter and Paul,[7] following wise counsel, so that the city of Winchester, which was both exalted by the stronghold of the bishopric, and also, amongst the cities of Britain, more thronged, and more renowned for its riches, might be still more gloriously and copiously celebrated for its apostle.[8] And after the passage of some time, the blessed Æthelwold, a man of great holiness and authority,[9] who himself also was made by God the twenty-sixth successor to the

[6] Cf. *Passio S. Eadwardi*, 'nimis indigne ferens tam pretiosam margaritam in tam uili loco obfuscari' (ed. Fell, *Edward*, p. 8).

[7] Cf. *Miracula S. Swithuni* c. 1, 'referens diuina miseratione prouisum se de ubi iacebat debere leuari intra ecclesiam loco digniori honorificentius tumulandum', and c. 3, 'Athelwoldus ... in animo reuoluebat non decere ut uilitas et humilitas loci humiliaret quem tanta a Deo signorum ac uirtutum sullimitas exaltaret', and 'loco eminentissimo intra ecclesiam honorificentius apponitur collocatum' (ed. Grosjean, 'De codice', pp. 190–3).

[8] Cf. the construction of Goscelin, *Vita S. Yuonis* c. 18, 'ut et ipsa ecclesia ob reuerentiam sanctorum honoratior atque celebrior haberetur, et a populis undique diffusis, praesentium intercessione patronorum, affluentius atque deuotius frequentaretur' (*PL* clv. 81–90, at col. 90 B).

[9] Æthelwold was consecrated bishop of Winchester on 29 Nov. 963, and died 1 Aug. 984.

sextus[1] in honore episcopatus successor a Deo factus est, de loco ubi positum fuerat illud corpus sanctissimum eleuauit, et in eadem ecclesia iuxta maius altare honorificentius collocauit.[2] In quo loco ad laudem sui sacerdotis a Deo multa prestantur beneficia multeque fiunt uirtutes, per filium suum Dominum nostrum, qui cum eo[a] uiuit et regnat in spiritu sancto in secula seculorum, AMEN. [b]EXPLICIT VITA SANCTI BYRINI EPISCOPI.[b]

[a] *After this word, the remainder of T is obliterated*   [b-b] *H; om. A;* ET CONFESSORIS *add. D;* EXPLICIT VITA SANCTI BYRINI CONFESSORIS ET EPISCOPI *G*

[1] The information that Æthelwold was twenty-sixth bishop of Winchester (and that Hædde was fifth Bishop), may have been derived from an episcopal list available to the hagiographer. According to Simon Keynes's list in *HBC*, p. 223, Æthelwold was in fact twenty-seventh bishop of the West Saxons, succeeding Brihthelm. Inspection of surviving Anglo-Saxon episcopal lists is instructive. Of those lists discussed by R. I. Page, 'Anglo-Saxon Episcopal Lists, Part III', *Nottingham Mediaeval Studies*, x (1966), 2–24, CCCC 173, fo. 55[r–v], has a numbered list of *Nomina episcoporum Occidentalium Saxonum*, in which Hædde appears as fifth, and Æthelwold as twenty-sixth, with Briht-

honour of the episcopate,[1] lifted that holy body from the place where it had been laid, and placed it in the same church with greater honour next to the high altar.[2] In this place to the praise of his priest, many benefits are bestowed by God, and many miracles take place, through His Son Our Lord, Who lives and reigns with Him in the Holy Spirit, for ever and ever, AMEN. HERE ENDS THE LIFE OF ST BIRINUS, BISHOP.

helm omitted. The list was probably compiled at Winchester between 984 and 988 (Ker, *Catalogue*, p. 58). An identical list apparently once existed in London, BL, Cotton Otho B. xi. The same list with the same numbering is found in the *Liber Vitae* of Hyde, now London, BL, Stowe 944, ed. W. de Gray Birch, *Register and Martyrology of New Minster and Hyde Abbey, Winchester*, Hampshire Record Society (London and Winchester, 1892), at p. 15. The *Liber Vitae* was written in the first half of the 11th cent., perhaps in 1031, at New Minster, Winchester. It is possible that one of these lists, or a very similar copy, was available to the author of *Vita S. Birini*.

[2] Cf. p. 45 n. 7 above. Cf. also Goscelin, *Vita S. Yuonis* c. 5, 'tam spectabilis Dei famuli membra asportari in ecclesiam et iuxta altare collocari fecit' (*PL* clv. 84 c). In Wulfstan, *Narratio Metrica de S. Swithuno* (ed. Campbell), *Epistola specialis*, 261–2, the resting place of Birinus is referred to as in 'haec ... aula', that is, in the newly constructed Old Minster, 'qua uir apostolicus iacet almus et ille Birinus | has lauacro gentes qui lauit occiduas'.

VITA ET MIRACVLA SANCTI KENELMI

SIGLA OF MANUSCRIPTS

B Oxford, Bodleian Library, Bodley 285, fos. 80^r–83^v (s. xiii^{in})
C Cambridge, Corpus Christi College, 367, fo. 48^r (s. xii^{in})
D Oxford, Bodleian Library, Douce 368, fos. 79^r–83^v (s. xii^2)
G Gotha, Forschungsbibliothek, I. 81, fos. 47^v–50^v (s. xiv$^{3/4}$)
H London, BL, Harley 3037, fos. 157^v–163 (s. xiii^2)
J Oxford, St John's College, 149, fos. 72^v–81^v (s. xiii^1)
L London, BL, Lansdowne 436, fos. 88^r–91^r (s. xiv^{med})
P Gloucester, Cathedral Library, 1, fos. 113^r–115^v (s. xiii^{in})
R Cambridge, UL, Ff. 1. 28, fos. 102^v–107^v (s. xiv)
V Valenciennes, Bibliothèque municipale, 116, fos. 208^v–210^v (s. xii$^{3/4}$)

^aINCIPIT PREFATIO IN VITA SANCTI^b KENELMI REGIS ET MARTYRIS.^a De beato Kenelmo in tota Anglia clarissimum est quod regius ^cfilius fuerit,^c quod patri successurum innocentem emula soror¹ per Askebertum^d extinxerit, quod superno lumine diuersisque miraculis sanctus Dei comprobatus sit. Legitur per totam patriam epistola,² que uiolenter absconditum in Anglia, celitus prodiderit^e in Roma.³ Inter plures ^ftestes etiam^f ueteranos fideles ab antiquioribus deductos, quidam Vuigornensis^g monachus beati Osuualdi Eboracensis archiepiscopi⁴ discipulus nomine Vulfuuinus^h nobisⁱ ^jfide certissima^j reliquit memoranda.⁵ Quem^k sancti patres Dunstanus⁶ et^l Adeluuoldus^m ipseque sacer Osuualdusⁿ ceterique sancti^o patres nunquam celebrassent^p nec coli consensissent, nisi dignum cognouissent.⁷ ^qIpsius quoque passio sacra Parisius⁸ perhibetur haberi descripta.^q Sed et^r ^scantilena⁹ et Anglica scripta^s plura memorant inde probabilia et

^{a–a} INCIPIT PROLOGVS IN VITA BEATI KENELMI REGIS ET MARTYRIS *B*; INCIPIT PROLOGVS IN VITAM ET PASSIONEM SANCTI KENELMI REGIS ET MARTYRIS *H*; INCIPIT PASSIO BEATI KENELMI MARTIRIS *L*; INCIPIT PROLOGVS IN PASSIONE BEATI KENELMI MARTYRIS *P*   ^b BEATI *J*   ^{c–c} fuerit filius *J*   ^d Aschebertum *HP*; procuratorem suum *add. B*   ^e prodidit *B*   ^{f–f} etiam testes *B*   ^g Wigorniensis *HL*; Wigornenssis *J*   ^h uulfuuius *B*; Wuluuinus *J*   ⁱ et Winnoc cognomine. Hec suo ordine a maioribus audita, fratri Alfuuino adhuc superstiti *B*   ^{j–j} certissima fide *J*   ^k *om. B*   ^l *om. H*   ^m Ethelwoldus *H*; æðelwoldus *J*; Athelwoldus *L*; æthelwoldus *P*   ⁿ qui eius reedificauit ecclesiam *add. B*   ^o *om. J*   ^p eius celebrassent festum *B*   ^{q–q} *B, and erased in D*; ipsius quoque passio sacra parisius haberi perhibetur scripta *L*; *om. HJP*   ^r *om. L*   ^{s–s} cantilene in anglia scripte *B*; cantilene scripta anglica *H*; cantilena et angelica scripta *L*

¹ Cf. *Vita breuior* c. 5.
² This may be a reference to the Old English couplet preserved by **G, H, J,** and **P** and purporting to be the content of the letter delivered by the dove (c. 10), which also seems to have circulated independently. See pp. cxvii–cxviii above.
³ The syntax of this terse sentence is so strange as to give the impression that, in fact, all the manuscripts are lacunose: the past participle 'absconditum' has no antecedent, and the whole phrase has to be taken as a noun-clause ('that-which-was-violently-concealed-in-England'). The difficulty seems partly to arise from the author's desire for balancing, rhymed clauses. Cf. note on c. 10, p. 64.
⁴ Oswald, abbot of Ramsey, 966–92 (*Heads*, p. 61), bishop of Worcester from 961 and simultaneously archbishop of York from 971 until his death on 29 Feb. 992 (*HBC*, p. 224).
⁵ On Wulfwine, and Ælfwine named in **B**, see pp. xciv–xcvii above.
⁶ Dunstan, abbot of Glastonbury from 940 to 957 (*Heads*, p. 50), bishop of Worcester in 957, bishop of London in 959, and archbishop of Canterbury from 960 until his death

HERE BEGINS THE PREFACE TO THE LIFE OF ST KENELM KING AND MARTYR. Of St Kenelm it is well known throughout the whole of England that he was an atheling, that, as he, an innocent, was about to succeed his father as king, his jealous sister[1] murdered him through the agency of Æscberht, and that by a light from heaven and various miracles he has been proved to be a saint of God. Throughout the entire land the letter is read,[2] which, sent from heaven, disclosed in Rome that which had been concealed by violent means in England.[3] Amongst the many witnesses, ancient and faithful, who learnt from a yet older generation, a certain monk of Worcester, a disciple of St Oswald, archbishop of York,[4] named Wulfwine, left to us material of most certain trustworthiness.[5] The holy fathers Dunstan and Æthelwold[6] and the venerable Oswald himself, and the other holy fathers, would never have celebrated him (sc. Kenelm) nor consented to his cult, unless they had recognized that he was worthy of it.[7] His holy passion is also said to be preserved in writing in Paris.[8] But also, both a song[9] and writings in English mention many credible things from that time, and the most learned Queen

on 19 May 988 (*HBC*, pp. 214, 224). Æthelwold was bishop of Winchester from 963 until 984 (*HBC*, p. 223).

[7] Cf. Goscelin, *Lectiones de S. Hildelitha* c. 3, 'non solum a modernis sanctis uidelicet Dunstano, Aethelwoldo, Aelfego, digna ueneratione est celebrata uerum etiam a superioribus sanctis' (Colker, 'Texts', p. 456).

[8] 'Parisius', undeclined, was by this time a perfectly acceptable locative, 'at Paris'; cf. Aimoin of Fleury, *Miracula S. Benedicti* (written in 1005), ed. *ActaS*, Mart., iii. 314–32 (3rd edn.), 'Nam Parisius eam ad S. Dionysii sepulcrum . . . perducentes' (p. 332 A) and Goscelin, *Miracula S. Yuonis*, 'Apud sanctum Dionisium Parisius' (Macray, *Chron. Rames.* p. lxvii). See C. Du Cange, *Glossarium Mediae et Infimae Latinitatis*, 10 vols. (Niort, 1883–7), s.v. Hence, the import of this rather allusive sentence seems to be that a copy of Kenelm's *Passio* was said to be preserved somewhere in Paris (perhaps at Saint-Denis). It is a pity that the hagiographer did not supply more detail, or name his source for this information, but presumably the intention was mainly to demonstrate that Kenelm's fame had even reached overseas. That most of the other witnesses do not preserve this sentence, and that it was erased from **D** is hardly surprising, given the obscurity of the reference, yet it seems likely to have been part of the author's original text.

[9] It is not clear whether the 'cantilena' was in the vernacular as well as the other materials named. The reading of **B**, 'cantilene in anglia scripte' (cf. **H**), gives the impression that there were several vernacular songs or poems. Whatever these poems were, they are now lost—cf. pp. cxviii–cxix above. But as well as 'song' or even 'canticle', 'cantilena' can have the meaning, 'oft-repeated saying' or 'refrain' (*OLD*, s.v.), which applies well to the Old English couplet referred to above, and economically avoids the necessity of supposing the existence of now-lost lays of Kenelm.

doctissima regina[1] Eadgyda[a] nobis exposuit que de ipso se legisse dicebat preclara indicia.[2] Nec desunt adhuc uisiones et reuelationes super eo sanctissime. Porro in huius fine textus tam recentia et late nota referemus signa, ut ea calumniari [b]non possit ipsa[b] [c]rebellatrix obstinatia.[c3] Cum itaque iuxta apostolum 'uix pro iusto quis moritur',[4] tua demum paterna diligentia pro hoc iusto et sancto Domini accendatur,[5] quatinus tua fides eius merita efferendo eius patrocinia mereatur que merito perdit, quisquis in ipso uigere salutiferam Christi gratiam credere renuerit.[d] Nec sis hic censor artificii, sed approbator ueri.[e]

§ 1. 'INCIPIT PASSIO SANCTI KENELMI MARTIRIS.[f] Kenulfus[g] gloriosissimus et piissimus rex Merciorum anno[h] Domini octingentesimo nonodecimo,[6] imperii uero sui uicesimo quarto,[i] migrans[j] ad sydereum[k] regnum[7] paterno[l] affectu heredem propositum reliquit [m]filium Kenelmum.[m] Erant Kenelmo regie

[a] Egyda *B*; Eadgitha *HP*; Eadgida *L*; Eadiþa *J*   [b-b] possit ipsam *L*. *After* obstinatia *the rest of the prologue is omitted in L*   [c-c] bellatrix obstinata *B*; rebellatrix obstinatio *P*   [d] renuit *B*   [e] EXPLICIT PROLOGUS *add. BHP*; EXPLICIT PREFATIO *add. J*   [f-f] INCIPIT PASSIO BEATI KENELMI REGIS ET MARTIRIS *BJ*; INCIPIT VITA ET PASSIO SANCTI KENELMI REGIS ET MARTIRIS *H*; INCIPIT PASSIO *P*; *om. GL*   [g] Kenolfus *B*   [h] incarnationis *add. H*   [i] primo *P*   [j] *until this word the order of G is slightly different:* Anno ab incarnatione Domini nostri Iesu Christi octingesimo nono decimo imperii uero sui uicesimo quarto Kenulphus gloriosissimus et piissimus rex merciorum migrans . . .   [k] siderium *GL*   [l] patrono *G*   [m-m] filio Kenelmo *P*

[1] Queen Eadgyth, daughter of Godwine, earl of Essex, was married to Edward the Confessor on 23 Jan. 1045 (*ASC C* 1044, *E* 1043). She died in Dec. 1075 (*ASC D* 1076, *E* 1075), at Winchester, and was buried at Westminster, with her husband. According to the anonymous *Vita Ædwardi regis*, Eadgyth was educated at the monastery at Wilton (ed. Barlow, *Life of King Edward*, p. 23). It was to this place that she retired after the death of Edward in 1066 (ibid. 137–9). William of Malmesbury, *Gesta Regum*, ii. 197 (ed. Stubbs, i. 239) and Osbert of Clare, *Vita S. Edwardi Confessoris* c. 4 (ed. M. Bloch, 'La Vie de S. Edouard le Confesseur par Osbert de Clare', *AB* xli (1923), 5–131) extolled Eadgyth's learning. These writers may well have drawn on the anonymous *Vita S. Edwardi* for such information; the relevant section of that work (c. 2), describing the Queen's character, is now lost in the only remaining MS, but may be recovered from Richard of Cirencester's *Speculum historiale de gestis regum Angliae* (see Barlow, *Life of King Edward*, pp. xxxix and lxv–lxvi).
[2] For the use of the word 'indicia' to refer to evidential information about saints, compare Goscelin, *Historia translationis S. Augustini*, ii. 14, 'nomina eorum et indicia chartulis inscripta' (*ActaS* Maii, vi. 432 C); *Lectiones de S. Hildelitha* c. 4, 'et si nobis . . . ipsius miracula uel scripturarum indicia defecere' (Colker, 'Texts', p. 456); and *Libellus contra usurpatores* c. 5, 'de . . . praeclaris miraculorum indiciis, quae in eius certissimae translationis libro copiose exposuimus' (Colker, 'Polemic', p. 75; cf. also c. 9, p. 77).

Eadgyth[1] has revealed to us the remarkable documents of proof
which she said she had herself read about him.[2] Nor is there any
lack of holy visions and revelations of him. Moreover, at the end of
this text, I shall record miracles so recent and widely known, that
the rebel Obstinacy herself cannot make light of them.[3] Since,
therefore, as the apostle says, 'scarce for a just man will one die',[4]
then may your fatherly diligence be kindled on behalf of this just
saint of the Lord,[5] to the end that your faith, by proclaiming his
merits, may deserve his patronage, which is deservedly lost by
anyone who refuses to believe that the saving grace of Christ is
alive in this saint. And do not be here a critic of the handiwork, but
an approver of the truth.

§ 1. HERE BEGINS THE PASSION OF ST KENELM
THE MARTYR. Coenwulf the most glorious and holy king of
the Mercians, in the eight-hundred and nineteenth year of Our
Lord,[6] and in the twenty-fourth year of his own reign, passed
away to the realm of the stars,[7] and, with fatherly affection, left as
his declared heir his son Kenelm. Kenelm had two royal sisters:

---

[3] The abstract noun is usually 'obstinatio', as the scribe of **P** (or his exemplar)
noticed. That is the only form to be found in *TLL*, though Latham, *Word-List*, records
the '-acia' variant as having been in frequent use between 1173 and 1494. Here the form
was evidently preferred for the sake of rhyme. Of 'rebellatrix' (cf. 'rebellatrix Germania',
Ovid, *Tristia* iii. 12. 47, though unlikely to be the source), it may be worth commenting
that Goscelin seemed fond of both masculine agentive nouns in '-or', and also feminine
ones, such as this (cf. Rollason, 'Translation and miracles', p. 142). Cf. also Goscelin,
Vita S. Wlfhilde prologue, 'rebellis infidelitas' (Colker, 'Texts', p. 418). For use of
'calumniari' (especially in close conjunction with 'obstinatio'), cf. Goscelin, *Vita S.
Wlsini* c. 12, 'Quem ... ne ab hiis qui obstinatiores sunt ad credendum temeritatis forte
calumpniaretur adhuc frequentioribus uirtutum choruscationibus diuina manus ...
declarat' (ed. Talbot, 'St Wulsin', p. 80).

[4] Rom. 5: 7.

[5] The person to whom 'tua ... paterna diligentia' refers, remains unknown, since
the text has no named dedicatee, in contrast, for example, with many of Goscelin's
Lives—compare the prologue of *Historia translationis S. Augustini*, addressed to Anselm,
'tuae paternae celsitudini' (*ActaS*, Maii, vi. 408); and that of the *Vita S. Wlfilde*, dedicated to Maurice, bishop of London, 'tuam paternam excellentiam' (Colker, 'Texts',
p. 418). Perhaps there was originally a dedicatory incipit, not preserved by any of the
surviving manuscripts, but it seems unlikely.

[6] The date supplied here for the death of Coenwulf is two years too early. The
error is quite likely to have derived ultimately from the *Anglo-Saxon Chronicle*, which,
as a result of a dislocation of years between 754 and 845 in all extant vernacular
versions, also recorded Coenwulf's death at 819, rather than 821. See Harrison, *Framework*, p. 106, and *EHD*, p. 124. The length of Coenwulf's reign, however, is correct,
because he succeeded Ecgfrith in 796.

[7] Cf. *Vita brevior* c. 4 ('ad sidereum solium').

germane Quendryda,[a] que postea fraternum sanguinem hausit,[1] et Burgenhylda,[b] que fratrem [c]sororia affectione dilexit.[c] Puer inter candida Anglorum pignora speciosus forma[2] et illustrante superna gratia amabilis[d] Deo et hominibus florebat etatula.[e] Preuentus a Deo spiritu dilectionis ac benignitatis, multis karismatibus gratiarum[3] apparebat filius [f]diuine adoptionis.[f]

§ 2. Hunc euo paruulum sed animo ac pietate magnificum in regem elegerat amor populi sui,[4] iuxta natalicium[g] priuilegium et testamentum patris Kenulfi. At Quendryda,[h] seuo liuore et regnandi ambitione[5] stimulata, insidiabatur[i] illi ut Herodias Iohanni, ut Helie[j] Iezabel, ut Cain[k] Abel.[6] Quem cum ueneno [l]non posset extinguere,[l] eius nutricium et procuratorem intimum nomine Askebertum,[m7] quia non [n]est pernitiosior[n] pestis quam familiaris inimicus,[8] ingentibus premiis et spe consortis imperii armat in fraternum iugulum.[9] Tali modo inuicem consiliati,[o] absconderunt[p]

[a] Quendreda G; Quendritha H   [b] Burkenhilda B; Burgenilda GH
[c-c] sororea affectione dilexit G; affectione sororia dilexit J; sororia dilectione amabat L
[d] amabili H   [e] oracula G   [f-f] adoptionis diuine L   [g] natalium H (and P before addition of ci above the line by a later hand)   [h] Quendreda G; Quendritha H
[i] insidiebatur G   [j] elye L   [k] Chain G; Caim HLP   [l-l] extinguere non posset G   [m] Aschebertum HP   [n-n] est pernisciosior G; pernitiosior est H; est pernicior L   [o] conciliati G   [p] abscondunt L

---

[1] It is possible to piece together the career of Kenelm's 'wicked' sister: the name 'Quoenthryth', or 'Cwoenthryth', is found in several authentic documents of the ninth century. Her earliest certain appearance is as a signatory to a grant of Coenwulf in 811 (S 165 = BCS 339), as 'Quoenðryð filia regis'. By 824, she seems to have become abbess of *Suthmynstre* in Kent (probably Minster-in-Thanet), in which capacity she came into conflict with Wulfred, archbishop of Canterbury (805–32). She and her community were evidently in possession of lands, at *Oesewalum*, which rightly belonged to Wulfred, and a partial settlement of the dispute (S 1434 = BCS 378) was reached at the synod of *Clovesho* in 824. Other lands were similarly in dispute, and final reconciliation was achieved at the synod of *Clovesho* the following year (S 1436 = BCS 384/385, where Cwoenthryth is specifically stated to be Coenwulf's daughter and heiress). See Hartland, 'Legend of St Kenelm', pp. 17–26, and Levison, *England and the Continent*, pp. 251–2, though the suggestion made there that the same woman also appears as abbess of Winchcombe is less secure than the rest (cf. P. Sims-Williams, *Religion and Literature in Western England, 600–800*, Cambridge, 1990, p. 166 n. 107). Burgenhild, on the other hand, is not mentioned in any other source, and it is strange that her name does not begin with 'C' like the rest of her supposed family. Searle, *Onomasticon*, supplies only two examples of a female name in that form: 'Burhhild', in the boundary clause of a 9th-cent. charter (S 354 = BCS 565); and in the *Liber Vitae de Hyda* (ed. W. de Gray Birch, Hampshire Record Society, Winchester, 1892), p. 144, where 'Burhilde' is one of the later additions to a 12th-cent. list of lay-persons. We should probably regard

Cwoenthryth, who afterwards shed her brother's blood,[1] and Burgenhild, who loved her brother with sisterly fondness. The boy at a tender age flourished among the bright offspring of the English, handsome in appearance,[2] and, illumined by heavenly grace, pleasing to God and to men. Being thus early endowed by God in the spirit of love and gentleness with the many gifts of graciousness,[3] he seemed clearly to be a son of divine adoption.

§ 2. This child, little in years, yet eminent in mind and holiness, the love of his people had chosen as king,[4] in accordance with the privilege of his birth and the will of his father Coenwulf. But Cwoenthryth, goaded by savage envy and an ambition to rule,[5] lay in wait for him as Herodias did for John, as Jezebel did for Elijah, as Cain did for Abel.[6] Since she could not kill him with poison, she equipped his tutor and personal steward, named Æscberht[7]—because there is no more baneful pest than an enemy in the home[8]—as her brother's murderer,[9] offering huge bribes and the promise of a share of the rule. Having thus plotted together, they

the character as an invention, to create a foil for the figure of the wicked sister. Indeed, Burgenhild plays no further part in the story.

[2] *Vita brevior* c. 2 ('forma . . . aetatula').

[3] Cf. Goscelin, *Historia translationis S. Augustini*, c. 11, 'Tanta uero gratiarum Christi charismata' (*PL* clv. 18 D). And *Vita S. Sexburge*, 'Inter innumera autem gratiarum Christi charismata' (*NLA* ii. 355–7, at p. 356).

[4] *Vita brevior* c. 3 ('pretendebat eum amor populi sui').

[5] Ibid. c. 4 ('regnandi temptat ambitio').

[6] Ibid. c. 5 ('Omni ergo intentione . . . fraterno sanguine'). For Herodias and John the Baptist, see Matt. 14: 3, Mark 6: 17–29; for Jezebel and Elijah see 3 Kgs. (1 Kgs.) 19: 2; for the account of Cain and Abel see Gen. 4: 8.

[7] The vernacular form of this name would be Æscberht. Searle, *Onomasticon*, gives several instances of its occurrence, the most noteworthy of which is one 'Escberth', a signatory to a copy of a charter by which Coenwulf granted Barham, Kent, to Archbishop Wulfred in 809 (S 164 = BCS 328). This may only be a coincidental correspondence, and nothing more can be discovered about the identity of Kenelm's supposed murderer, or about this otherwise unattested signatory.

[8] The source for this is Boethius, *Philosophiae Consolatio*, iii. 5. 36 ('quae uero pestis efficacior ad nocendum quam familiaris inimicus?'). Note that *Vita brevior* preserves a version closer to the original than that offered in *Vita et miracula*.

[9] A weakness of the narrative is that, although Cwoenthryth is here said to have bribed Æscberht with the promise of a share of her power, we are not told what became of him, especially after the gruesome demise of the queen herself. In his *Itinerary*, ed. L. Toulmin-Smith, 3 vols. (London, 1907–10), iv. 220, John Leland reported on his findings at Clent: 'Averey parson of Dene tolde me that he had redd that Askaperius the murtherer of S. Kenelme was maried to Quindred, sistar to S. Kenelme, and that he reynid a 2 or 3 yeres after Kenelme untyll suche tyme that a kinnesman of Kenelme's put hym downe. But loke bettar for this mattar.'

laqueos, intenderunt*a* arcum, parauerunt sagittas suas in pharetra ut sagittent in obscuro rectum*b* corde.¹

§ 3. Ea tempestate² uidit per somnum*c* *d*claram uisionem*d* Dei hostia Kenelmus, quam cum suspirio retulit nutrici sue³ degenti Wincelcumbe*e* habenti gratiam interpretationis et intelligentie,⁴ nomine Vuluuenne.*f* 'Visum est', *g*inquit, 'mihi,*g* o *h*mater karissima,*h* quod ante cubiculum meum arbor staret altissima usque ad sydera, me uero uidebam stare in eius arduo uertice unde *i*late poteram omnia*i* conspicere. Erat autem *j*arbor pulcherrima*j* *k*et late*k* effusis ramis spatiosa*l* ab imo*m* ad summum omnibus floribus refertissima.⁵ Videbam*n* quoque innumeris luminaribus et lampadibus totam ardere, michi uero*o* tres partes huius terre prona curuari deuotione.⁶ Cumque de tanta specula mirarer uisionem, quidam meorum subter irruentes succiderunt arborem et illa cecidit ingenti ruina. Ego uero protinus efficiebar auicula candida⁷ et libero uolatu *p*penetraui ethera'.*p*

§ 4. Vix elocutus erat*q* iste*r* alter Ioseph⁸ uisionem cum nutrix pectus tundens talem erupit*s* in uocem: 'Heu me', inquit,*t* 'fili mi*u* dulcissime,⁹ heu lactatio et nutrimentum meum suaue, ergone insidie tuorum, ergone maligna consilia*v* sororis et nutricii tui preualebunt aduersum*w* te? Heu, quam timeo arborem illam succisam indolis*x* tue presignare*y* iacturam cum tribus partibus regni

---

a tetendunt *L*   *b* iterum *L*   *c* somnium *B (and D before erasure of the* i *); P originally read* somnum, *which was altered to* somnium *by a later hand*   *d-d* uisionem claram *JL*   *e* Winchelcumbe *BGHJ*; Wynchcombe *L*; Wincelcumbe *P (altered to* Winchelcumbe *by a later hand)*   *f* Wlfwenne *H*; Wluuenna *P*   *g-g* mihi inquit *G*; mihi *L*   *h-h* karissima mater *BG*   *i-i* poteram late *B*; late omnia poteram *J*   *j-j* pulcherrima arbor *B*; arbor puchelrima *J*   *k-k* elate *G*   *l* speciosa *L*   *m* usque *add. J*   *n* Viderem *G*   *o* autem *G; om. L*   *p-p* sydera penetraui *L*   *q* fuerat *JL*   *r* ille *J*   *s* irrupit *G*   *t* in quid *J*   *u* om. *G*   *v* concilia *G*   *w* aduersus *G*   *x* in ydolis *G*   *y* prefigurare *G*

---

¹ This is a conflation of Ps. 63(64): 4–6 ('Intenderunt arcum rem amaram, ut sagittent in occultis immaculatum . . . Narrauerunt ut absconderunt laqueos'); and Ps. 10 (11): 3 ('Quoniam ecce peccatores intenderunt arcum; parauerunt sagittas suas in pharetra, ut sagittent in obscuro rectos corde'). Identical with *Vita brevior*, end of c. 6.

² cc. 3 and 4 are almost identical with *Vita brevior* c. 7.

³ The nurse is not named in *Vita brevior* c. 7. The name Wulfwenne/Wulfwynn is attested in various forms (Searle, *Onomasticon*), as Wuluuen (Birch, *Liber Vitae*, p. 137) and Wulfwyn (ibid. 58, 71) and Wulfwynn (ibid. 62)—the last of these referring to the abbess of Wareham (*ASC C*, s.a. 982).

⁴ Cf. Dan. 1: 17 ('Danieli autem intelligentiam omnium uisionum et somniorum').

⁵ Nabuchodonosor's dream in Dan. 4: 7–11 may have been the model for this: 'Videbam, et ecce arbor in medio terrae, et altitudo eius nimia. Magna arbor, et fortis, et

laid snares, they have bent their bow and they have prepared their arrows in the quiver, to shoot in the dark the upright of heart.[1]

§ 3. At that time Kenelm,[2] the sacrificial victim of God, saw in his sleep a clear vision, which he recounted with a sigh to his nurse,[3] an inhabitant of Winchcombe, named Wulfwynn, who had the power of interpretation and understanding.[4] 'It seemed to me,' he said, 'dear mother, that a tree stood before my bed, so high that it reached right up to the stars, and I saw myself standing in its lofty top, from where I could see everything for miles around. The tree was very beautiful and spreading, with wide-stretched branches, filled from bottom to top with all kinds of flowers.[5] I saw also that the whole thing blazed with countless lights and lamps, and what is more, three parts of this land were bending low in devotion to me.[6] As I marvelled at the view from such a great watch-tower, some of my men rushed up below and cut down the tree and it fell with a great crash. And I was straightway turned into a little white bird and soared into the heavens with easy flight.'[7]

§ 4. Scarcely had this second Joseph[8] told of his vision when the nurse, beating her breast, burst out with these words: 'Woe is me,' she said, 'my sweet son,[9] alas for my milk-bearing, and my sweet nourishment; will the plots of your family, will then the evil schemes of your sister and your tutor prevail against you after all? Alas, how greatly I fear that that felled tree foreshows the loss of your life, because, along with the three parts of the kingdom which

proceritas eius contingens caelum; aspectus illius erat usque ad terminos uniuersae terrae. Folia eius pulcherrima . . . et ecce uigil, et sanctus de caelo descendit, clamauit fortiter, et sic ait: Succidite arborem.' His dream is also interpreted as foreshadowing his downfall, but unlike the martyr, who trusts in God, Nabuchodonosor is afraid (Dan. 4: 2). A comparable dream is that of St Æthelberht of Hereford, described in the eleventh-century *Passio* (c. 5) preserved uniquely in CCCC 308, ed. James, 'Two Lives', p. 239. We are told that Æthelberht saw his royal hall collapsing, a tall beam from which blood flowed, a column of light reaching up to heaven and himself as a bird with golden wings.

[6] The earth was regarded as being divided into four parts (north, south, east, and west). Cf. a charter of Oswald of Worcester, preserved in Heming's cartulary, and dated 985 (S 1351), which begins 'Regnante in perpetuum Domino nostro Ihesu Christo per uniuersa quadriflui orbis climata'. Every element of the dream is carefully made to play a part in the foreshadowing of Kenelm's death. This detail is not included in *Vita brevior* c. 7, which has 'regni regiones et populos cum suis opibus'.

[7] A white dove as the symbol of the ascending soul is a very common hagiographical motif, found as early as Prudentius' *Peristephanon* (iii. 161, of Eulalia) and Gregory's *Dialogi* (for example, ii. 34 and iv. 10), and reflected in early Christian funeral iconography; cf. *DACL* i. 1485 s.v. 'ame', section v, and *DACL* xiii. 2206–7 s.v. 'colombe'.

[8] For Joseph's dream, see Gen. 37: 5–10.

[9] Cf. Tobias 10: 4 ('Flebat mater eius irremediabilibus lacrymis, atque dicebat: Heu heu me, fili mi, ut quid te misimus peregrinari').

subiectis partem sororis[a] habeas[b] aduersam! Verumtamen in
auicula qua [c]penetrabas ethera[c] intelligitur ascensure[d] anime tue
gloria'.[e] Non[f] hec terrebant[g] infantem, quia, ut scriptum est 'qui
ambulat simpliciter, ambulat[h] confidenter'.[1]

§ 5. Tandem Askebertus[i] ut ille alter Scarioth[j] proditor Domini
sui, rapta occasione sceleris maturandi, Kenelmum abducit[k] in
siluam gratia[l] uenandi,[2] quasi oblectandum amore studii paterni.
Ille imitator[m] Domini ut agnus ductus ad uictimam[3] presaga[n]
mente[4] cruentum hostem comitabatur ad corone gloriam. Septem
circiter annorum tunc puer fuisse[o] describitur. Vbi uero silue
approximarunt,[p] tenellus pusio[q] somno pregrauante equo delabi-
tur, ibique[r] recubans[s] securus malorum totus soporatur.

§ 6. Tunc cruentissimus nutricius pro [t]cunis et[t] lectulo fossam
parat, in qua eum citius obruat. Verum ubi[u] puer expergiscens
consilium preuenit laniste,[5] fertur[v] prophetica mente sapientiam
paruulis prestante[6] Domino[w] dixisse, 'Frustra [x]hanc molitus es
mihi[x] speluncam; non enim[y] hic, ut cogitas, sed remotiori[z] loco ubi
[aa]Deus prouidit[aa] occumbam. Vnde tibi [bb]certum dabit signum hec
uirga'[bb]—nam [cc]uirgam manu[cc] gestabat et terre affixerat—'si modo
plantata frondeat.'[dd] Hec eo pronuntiante[ee] statim radicata uirga
cepit frondescere, unde adhuc ingens fraxinus ostenditur, que in
memoriam[ff] beati[gg] Kenelmi celebris habetur.[7]

§ 7. Hinc seuissimus carnifex, percussus[hh] et[ii] uoce ueridica et
dira conscientia, longius puerum abducit[jj] obturata fouea. Est[kk]

---

[a] sorore J; sororem P   [b] habetis L   [c-c] penetrabis etheria L
[d] accensure G   [e] glorie J; in D there is an insertion mark after this word and sed credimus is supplied in the margin by a later hand   [f] Nec G   [g] terrebat G
[h] ambula L   [i] Aschebertus HP   [j] Scarioht D; Scharioth G; Acharioth L
[k] adducit L   [l] ire add. B   [m] inuitator G   [n] presagia L   [o] esse
B   [p] approximant G   [q] pusillo L   [r] inter aprica frondium ac herb-
arum add. B; ibi H   [s] recumbans L   [t-t] om. B   [u] ut B; etiam ubi H
[v] om. B   [w] fertur add. B   [x-x] hanc mihi molitus es B; mihi hanc molitus es
L   [y] om. B   [z] in remotiori G   [aa-aa] Dominus prouiderit G
[bb-bb] dabit certum hec uirga signa L   [cc-cc] manu uirgam J   [dd] fronderat L
[ee] proferente B; dicente G; cogitante pronuntiante H, with the first word marked for deletion
by underpointing   [ff] memoria B   [gg] Sancti G   [hh] perculsus H
[ii] om. B   [jj] adducit L   [kk] En G

---

[1] Prov. 10: 9.
[2] Vita brevior c. 8 ('Tandem ergo . . . oblectationem'). Cf. Passio S. Eadwardi (ed. Fell,
p. 4), 'die quadam cum canibus et equitibus uenandi gratia in siluam accessit'.

are your loyal subjects, you have the hostile (fourth) part which is your sister's. However, the bird in the form of which you entered the heavens is to be interpreted as the glory of your ascending soul.' These things did not frighten the child, since as it is written, 'He that walketh sincerely walketh confidently.'[1]

§ 5. At length, Æscberht, like that other Iscariot, the betrayer of his lord, seizing the opportunity to bring his crime to fruition, carried off Kenelm into a wood to go hunting,[2] as if to delight him with a love of his father's favourite occupation. He, emulating the Lord, like a lamb led to the slaughter[3] with foreboding mind,[4] followed the bloodthirsty foe to a crown of glory. The boy is described as being about 7 years old at that time. When they have come to the wood the tender little lad slides from his horse with heavy weariness, and lying down just there, careless of all evils, falls deeply asleep.

§ 6. Then the bloodthirsty tutor instead of a cot and cradle prepares a grave, in which to bury him quickly. But when the boy, waking up, anticipated the plan of the evil-doer,[5] it is told that with prophetic mind, the Lord granting to his little ones wisdom,[6] he said: 'In vain have you laboured over this tomb for me, for I shall not lie here as you suppose, but in a more distant place, which God has provided. This staff will give you a sure sign of it'—for he was carrying in his hand a staff, and had stuck it in the ground—'if now, being planted, it becomes green.' As he said these words, immediately the staff took root and began to grow leaves, and from it grew a huge ash-tree, still visible now, which is honoured in memory of St Kenelm.[7]

§ 7. At this the savage butcher, smitten both by the voice of truth and by fearful conscience, drags the boy further away, having filled

---

[3] Cf. Jer. 11: 19 ('Et ego quasi agnus mansuetus, qui portatur ad uictimam'). Cf. *Vita brevior* c. 8 ('Cum . . . agniculus').

[4] Cf. Vergil, *Aen*. x. 843 ('praesaga mali mens').

[5] 'Lanista' in Classical Latin referred specifically to a gladiator, or trainer of gladiators, but cf. Isidore, *Etym*. x. 159 ('lanista, gladiator, id est carnifex'), and Abbo, *Passio S. Eadmundi* c. 10 ('Cumque nec sic Hinguar furcifer eum lanistis assensum prebere conspiceret') of the Vikings (ed. Winterbottom, *Three Lives*, p. 79).

[6] Cf. Ps. 18 (19): 8 ('Testimonium Domini fidele, sapientiam praestans paruulis').

[7] The flowering staff is a common motif in hagiography, taking its origin probably from the story of Aaron's rod (Num. 17: 8), which grew into a tree and produced almonds. A good many examples are listed by Loomis, *White Magic*, p. 205 n. 1. Cf. e.g. the flowering 'uirga' where St Æthelbert pitched his tent, in Gerald, *Vita S. Ethelberti regis et martyris* c. 15 (ed. James, 'Two Lives', pp. 233-4).

profunda[a] uallis inter duos montes abdita in ipsa silua, Clento[b] dicta.[1] Iam[c] herentem hostem et diuersa petentem secreta mente[2] furiata[d] sic [e]increpare martyr uidebatur[e] ex[f] uoce dominica, 'Quod facis, fac citius'.[3] Ibi[g] igitur[h] sub arbore spinea[i4] caput Kenelmi lacteum septennis, ut dictum est, paruuli[j] absciditur, quod[k] ipse [l]protinus extensis[l] palmulis excepisse memoratur,[5] quo[m] uelut lilium aut demessa[n] rosa gratificatur, ut in conspectu Domini pretiosa[o] mors sancti sui[6] commendetur. Hinc et lactea columba aureis pennis transuolasse ethera[p] merito creditur, qualis ipse [q]sibi auicula[q] in superiori[r] uisione uidebatur.

§ 8. Asseritur etiam quod iam decollandus[s] sacrum ymnum 'Te Deum laudamus, te Dominum confitemur', inceperit,[t] atque in illo uersu 'Te martyrum candidatus laudat exercitus', iugulatus[u] occubuerit.[7] Ilico autem impius percussor cesum innocentem terra obruit, [v]nequicquam ratus[v] quod illa deserti uastitas scelus[w] suum

---

[a] om. L [b] Clentho D, Clentheo L [c] Iamque B [d] furia L [e-e] martyr uidebatur increpare G [f] om. B [g] Vbi BL [h] autem L [i] spine B [j] om. B. L [k] om. L [l-l] extensis protinus B [m] quod JL [n] de messa B [o] om. L [p] om. P [q-q] auicula sibi P [r] superiore G; predicta L [s] decollandum G; decolandus J [t] incepit P [u] in gloriatus G [v-v] frustra estimatus B; nec quicquam ratus GP; ne quiquam ratus J; nequaquam ratus L [w] scesus L

---

[1] This is a fairly accurate description of the Clent hills, in northern Worcestershire. In about 1016, Clent, along with Tardebigge and Kingswinford, had been granted by King Æthelred to Æthelsige (Ægelsige), dean or prior of St Mary's, Worcester, for 200 pounds of silver, for the perpetual possession of the monastery. However, once the aforementioned dean had died, the sheriff of Staffordshire, Æfic, wrongfully seized the estates. See *Hemingi Cartularium Ecclesiae Wigornensis*, ed. T. Hearne (Oxford, 1723), i. 276–7; cf. J. Amphlett, *A Short History of Clent* (London, 1890), p. 11. They must subsequently have reverted to royal possession, since William held Clent in 1086, as the Confessor had before him (*DB, Worcs.* 1: 6; i. 172c). Although the chapel of Kenelm is now in Halesowen parish, it may well have been part of the land at Clent which was acquired by St Mary's, Worcester (see commentary on c. 13).

[2] Cf. 'furiata mente', Vergil, *Aen.* ii. 407 and 588.

[3] John 13: 27. Cf. *Vita brevior* c. 8.

[4] *Vita brevior* c. 8 ('sub arbore spinea . . .', and 'Abscisum est . . . sancti sui').

[5] Cf. with this Goscelin's brief account of the death of St Juthwara: 'decollata fratre memoratur post caput abscisum trunco corpore cucurrisse et illud utrisque palmulis in collem, unde deciderat reuexisse' (*Vita S. Wlsini* c. 21, Talbot, p. 84). Similar accounts of the catching-up of a decapitated head occur in many saints' Lives, and the earliest Passion of St Denis of Paris have been thought to have been the origin of the motif—see P. Saintyves, 'Les Saints céphalophores. Étude de folklore hagiographique', *Revue d'Histoire des Religions*, xcix (1929), 156–231 (including a list of 120 cephalophoric saints, pp. 225–31), and H. Moretus Plantin, *Les Passions de Saint Lucien et leurs dérivés céphalophoriques* (Namur, 1953), esp. pp. 46–61. It has also been suggested that the topos

in the pit. There is a deep valley hidden between two mountains in that wood called Clent.[1] Now as the foe stood perplexed and hunted for secluded spots in different places with maddened mind,[2] the martyr seemed with the voice of the Lord to rebuke him saying: 'That which thou dost, do quickly.'[3] And so there under a thorn-tree[4] the milky-white head of Kenelm, a little lad, as has been said, of 7 years, is cut off. He himself is said to have caught it straightway with outstretched hands,[5] in order that, just as a lily or a plucked rose gives pleasure, so in the sight of the Lord the precious death of His saint[6] may be commended. Hence also a milk-white dove is rightly thought to have flown through the heavens on golden wings—just the kind of bird Kenelm saw himself as in the vision recounted above.

§ 8. It is also stated that, at the very moment he was to be beheaded, he began to sing the sacred hymn 'Te Deum laudamus, Te Dominum confitemur', and when he got to the verse: 'Te martyrum candidatus laudat exercitus', he fell down dead.[7] Right there the wicked murderer buried the dead innocent in the ground, thinking in vain that the vast expanse of that deserted place would

derives from early iconographical representations of beheaded martyrs carrying their heads as a token of their victory; see J. Gessler, 'De HH. Cefaloforen', *Revue Belge d'archéologie et d'histoire de l'art*, xi (1941), 193–211, and C. Cahier, *Caractéristiques des saints dans l'art populaire*, 2 vols. (Paris, 1867), pp. 761–5. More recently, it has been proposed by A. Simonetti, 'Santi cefalofori altomedievali', *Studi Medievali*, xxviii (1987), 67–121, that the roots of the motif of cephalophory, particularly when associated with springs and trees, might lie in the 'substratum' of pagan Celtic superstition. Kenelm fits in with such a hypothesis insofar as a healing spring was said to have emerged in the place where his head and body were first buried (c. 13). The other English cephalophoric saints are Osgyth (see Bethell, 'Lives of St Osyth', pp. 113, 115); Juthwara (*NLA* ii. 98–9); and Freomund (Burghard's *Vita S. Fremundi*, ed. *NLA* ii. 689–98, at 694). According to Moretus Plantin's terminology (p. 55), the present example of the motif is 'static', since Kenelm does not walk anywhere with his head, unlike Denis, for example (Hilduin, *Vita S. Dionysii*, c. 32; *PL* cvi. 47), or Osgyth. In this respect, Kenelm is similar to St Just, who was said to have picked up his head and placed it in his lap, and then to have spoken. Just's Passion is discussed as the possible origin of the motif by M. Coens, 'Aux origines de la céphalophorie: un fragment retrouvé d'une ancienne passion de S. Just, martyr de Beauvais', *AB* lxxiv (1956), 86–115. The purpose of the topos of the head actually being carried away from the site of martyrdom was that the saint should appear to be making an unambiguous choice of resting-place. In the case of Kenelm, the 'static' motif does not seem to serve such a specific purpose, but may have been included by the hagiographer to heighten the drama and wonder of his account.

[6] Ps. 115: 5 (116: 13) ('pretiosa in conspectu Domini mors sanctorum eius').

[7] The rhythmical hymn 'Te Deum laudamus', on which see A. E. Burns, *The Hymn 'Te Deum' and its Author* (London, 1926), was prescribed by the Rule of Benedict for use on Sundays and feast days, after the twelfth and last respond at nocturns (cf. Tolhurst, *Monastic Breviary*, vi. 9).

absconderet,[a] cum ueritas clamet, 'nichil[1] opertum[b] quod non reueletur'.[c] Denique qui celo teste erat martyrizatus, celo teste est[d] declaratus,[2] quatinus fulgida lucis columna[3] ab ethereis[e] arcibus[4] [f]sepe uideretur super eum[f] effusa. Quem[g] etiam ab humana notitia abscidere[h] nitebatur inhumanitas beluina,[i] illum prodebat hominibus pecualis[j] diligentia.[5]

§ 9. Nam[k] candida bos[l] [m]cuiusdam (ut fertur) uidue[m] relicta[n] [o]publica pascua,[o] ab alto monte ad infimum sepulti monumentum [p]decurrit ibique[p] inseparabilis adhesit, mira uidelicet oblectatione diuinitus attracta et allecta[q] ut nullius inde auelli [r]posset instantia,[r] siue inuenta, siue ignota.[6] Quotiens uero nota [s]stabula domi[s] repetisset plena, totum armentum duplo lactis superabat copia, tam salubri circa sanctam[t] glebam [u]pascebatur herba[u] et gratia. Miroque modo, quod[v] uesperi[w] detonsum erat, recrescente[x] uirore mane habundantius inueniebat.[y] Hinc autem[z] locus idem 'uacce uallis'[7] appellari assueuit.[aa]

§ 10. At[bb] Quendryda[cc] empto per fratricidium regno potita, tali edicto omnes terruit, ut si quis Kenelmum requireret[dd] uel

---

[a] absconderit B   [b] est add. G   [c] reuelabitur B   [d] erat J
[e] etheris BHL   [f-f] super eum sepe uideretur H   [g] Quam B; The twelfth-century addition [= C] to the Vita brevior lections begins with this word, preceded by martirem suum which completed the last sentence of the eighth lection   [h] abscondere G; om. L
[i] abscondere add. L   [j] spiritualis L   [k] In D a space was left for a coloured initial N which was never supplied, or else has faded completely   [l] uos L   [m-m] ut fertur cuiusdam uidue B; cuiusdam uidue ut fertur CH; cuiusdam uidue G   [n] relinquens ut dicitur L   [o-o] pascua publica B   [p-p] decurrens ibi H   [q] illecta L   [r-r] instantia posset B   [s-s] pabula L   [t] stantem L
[u-u] herba pascebatur H   [v] om. G   [w] uespere H   [x] recente B; crescente G   [y] ueniebat L   [z] om. L   [aa] solet B; consueuit L   [bb] Et B   [cc] Quendritha BH; Quendreda G   [dd] quereret L

---

[1] Luke 12: 2.
[2] Vita brevior c. 8 ('Sed qui solo . . . reuelatus').
[3] This is an extremely common hagiographical motif; compare, for example, Passio S. Eadwardi, 'circa locum ipsum ubi occultatum fuerat, columna instar ignis desuper emissa apparuit, quae lucis suae radiis locum undique frequenter irradiare uisa est' (ed. Fell, p. 7), and Goscelin, Historia translationis S. Augustini ii. 21, of Jaenberht, 'sepe effusa desuper etheree lucis columna celesti honore sanctorum probauit dignum' (ActaS, Maii, vi. 434 E); cf. also Vita S. Wistani, ed. Macray, Chron. Evesham, p. 331; Passio SS. Ethelredi atque Ethelbricti, ed. Rollason, Mildrith Legend, p. 95; and the two versions of Passio S. Ethelberti c. 10 (in both cases), ed. James, 'Two Lives', pp. 229 and 242.
[4] Cf. Caelius Sedulius, Carmen Paschale i. 31 ('Arcibus aethereis'); and Aldhelm, Carmen de Virginitate, line 1762.
[5] Cf. Vita S. Werburge c. 11, 'Bene ergo illi pecualis creatura parebat . . .' (PL clv. 105).

conceal his crime, since truth will cry out: 'There is nothing covered that shall not be revealed.'[1] In fact, he who was martyred with heaven as witness, is proclaimed by the witness of heaven,[2] in that a bright column of light[3] from the heights of heaven[4] was often seen to be pouring forth upon him. While bestial inhumanity sought to cut him off from human attention, the loving care of animals made him known to men.[5]

§ 9. For a white cow (so it is said) belonging to a certain widow, abandoning the common pasture-land, ran all the way down from the high mountain to the low-lying site of the burial, and kept inseparably close to that place, divinely drawn and attracted, evidently by a miraculous delight, so that the perseverance of no person, whether known to her or not,[6] could tear her away from there. Whenever she returned home to the familiar stall with udders full, the supply of her milk was twice that of the entire herd, so healthful was the grass and the grace she grazed upon around the holy sod. Miraculously, that which had been cropped by evening time, she found growing again more abundantly and with increased verdure in the morning. Hence that place has come to be called Cow-valley.[7]

§ 10. Cwoenthryth, having taken control of the kingdom gained by fratricide, terrorized everyone with the edict that if anybody were to look for Kenelm or show where he was, or even mention

And also *Passio S. Eadwardi*, 'sacrum corpus more beluino per pedes abstrahunt . . .' (ed. Fell, p. 6).

[6] A comparable miracle is told in the *Vita S. Coemgeni abbatis*, ed. C. Plummer, *Vitae Sanctorum Hiberniae* (Oxford, 1910), i. 237, in which a cow licked the saint's clothing, 'illa uacca habundanciam lactis incredibiliter habebat de tactu uestis uiri Dei'. It is, however, somewhat unlikely that the author of *Vita et miracula S. Kenelmi* can have known the *Vita S. Coemgeni*, since few Irish saints' Lives seem to have circulated widely in England.

[7] No 'Cow-valley' or 'Cowbatch' is to be found in A. Mawer and F. M. Stenton, *The Place-Names of Worcestershire*, EPNS iv (Cambridge, 1927), or on any available maps of the area, and the name does not seem to have survived to modern times. However, J. Humphreys, 'The Story of St Kenelm and St Kenelm's Church, Romsley', *Studies in Worcestershire History* (Birmingham, 1938), pp. 209–16, referred to 'the wild Cowbach Valley between Clent and Romsley Hills' (p. 210), which perhaps reflects local knowledge. John Leland, in his *Itinerary* (ed. Toulmin-Smith, iv. 220), recorded his visit to Clent: 'Clinte in Cowbage, wher S. Kenelme was martirid, is a. 2 miles from Hales Priorie'. Mawer and Stenton, *Place-Names of Worcestershire*, list several names which include 'bæc', meaning 'stream-valley', for example Foxbatch and Hawkbatch (p. 367), and note that such forms are particularly common in Worcestershire, Herefordshire and Shropshire (p. 377). Humphreys's Cowbach seems to fit into this pattern, and matches the form found in the Old English Kenelm couplet, variously, 'cubeche' (**H**), 'coubeche' (**G**), and 'qu becche' (see above, p. cxvii).

indicaret, uel etiam^a nomen^b loqueretur, sine dilatione capite plec-
teretur.^{1} Hinc^c quod^d de celo ^{c}indicabant clara luminaria^e et in terris
quodam modo muta ^{f}loquebantur animalia,^{f} nec mutire^2 audebat^g
humana ignauia, et gemitum ^{h}extincti domini^h premebant ^{i}ab indic-
tione^i terrifica. Verum prefulgida lucerna que obfuscabatur in Anglica patria, ^{j}clarius emicuit^j in arce mundi Roma,^{k} quatinus latius
diffunderet^l illa excellentia, quod claudebat angusta inuidia.^{3} Nam
cum ^{m}Leo papa^4 iunior^m missarum solemnia innumerabili populo
astante celebraret, ecce columba^n super niuem candida desuper
^{o}palam omnibus^o apparuit, que niueam menbranam aureis litteris
anglice inscriptam^p blando rostro ferens super altare beati Petri
deposuit,^{5} sicque in altum sublata disparuit.

§ 11. At sacer apostolicus cum tremore respiciens ^{q}nouam
scedulam,^{q} ignotis uerbis ac litteris editam,^{6} populum diuersarum
nationum ad beatum Petrum confluum^r obtestatur,^{s} quatinus

^{a} om. HL ^{b} nomine G ^{c} est add. B ^{d} om. P $^{e-e}$ clara luminaria indicabant B; micabant clara luminaria P $^{f-f}$ animalia loquebantur C
^{g} audebant C $^{h-h}$ deum extincti G $^{i-i}$ ab indignatione B; ex indicione L
$^{j-j}$ clarius enituit G; claruit L ^{k} Romana L ^{l} et add. G; diffunderetur P
$^{m-m}$ iunior Siluester papa BGL; quidam sanctus apostolicus P *(a later hand has supplied
Leo secundus in the margin)* ^{n} omnibus add. G $^{o-o}$ omnibus palam B;
palam G ^{p} scriptam B $^{q-q}$ ad nouam cedulam atque B; nouam cedulam
GL ^{r} confluentium B; confluxum C; confluum *altered above the line by later hand to*
confluentium J ^{s} contestatur P

---

^{1} Cf. *Passio S. Eadwardi* (ed. Fell, *Edward King and Martyr*, p. 7), where Queen
Ælfthryth, after the death of Edward is described as giving out an 'edictum quo nil
inclementius proposuit, ne quis de interitu eius gemeret aut omnino loqueretur'.
^{2} Properly, 'muttire'. Note the play on the words 'mutus' and 'muttire'.
^{3} The syntax here makes for some confusion: without imputing to the author a
serious grammatical error, 'illa excellentia' cannot strictly speaking be taken as the
antecedent of 'quod', since we should expect 'quam'; i.e. 'so that that excellence, which
narrow envy was concealing, might pour forth more abundantly'. Another way to
approach the clause would be to take 'illa excellentia' as referring to Rome, and to allow
the antecedent of 'quod' to be understood: 'so that that excellence (Rome) might pour
forth more abundantly that which (= 'quod') base envy was stifling'. Cf. note on the
preface, p. 50.
^{4} There was evidently some confusion about which pope should be included here.
The Pope Leo whose dates fall closest to the supposed death of Coenwulf in 819 (recte
821) would be Leo III (795–816)—see Kelly, *Oxford Dictionary of Popes*, p. 97. This is the
pope whose privilege (dated 811), confirming the possessions of Coenwulf, is preserved
in fragmentary form in the Winchcombe *Landboc* (ed. Royce, i. 21–2). He is there called
'Leo papa iunior'. According to the *Liber Pontificalis*, Leo II (682–3), was known as 'Leo
iunior' (Mommsen, p. 200). The alternative reading of 'iunior Siluester', offered by
BGL, is even more anachronistic, since Silvester the Younger, Silvester II, was pope
from 999 to 1003 (Kelly, pp. 136–7). One may suppose that the intention here in naming
a pope was to lend some sort of credibility to the account, regardless of strict chrono-

the name, he would without delay be executed.[1] Hence that which bright lights from heaven made known, and on earth mute animals, as it were, spoke of, human cowardice did not dare to mutter,[2] and they suppressed all open lamentation for their dead lord because of the terrifying edict. But the brilliant light which was obscured in its homeland of England, shone yet more brightly in the citadel of the world, Rome, so that that excellence [scil. Rome] might spread abroad more widely the thing which base envy was stifling.[3] For as Pope Leo the Younger[4] was celebrating the rites of mass in the presence of a multitude of people, behold a dove whiter than snow appeared from above in the sight of everyone, and it carried in its gentle beak a snow-white parchment inscribed with golden letters in English, which it put down on the altar of St Peter,[5] and then disappeared high into the sky.

§ 11. The holy and apostolic father looks with trembling at the strange crisp sheet written all over with unfamiliar words and letters,[6] and implores the throng of diverse nations flocking together to St Peter, to indicate whether anyone among them

logy (not in any case an essential of hagiography). To choose Silvester was probably a stab in the dark. If we are correct in supposing that the reading in **BGL** might preserve an earlier state of the text than **D** and the other witnesses, then 'Leo papa iunior' would have been an early emendation, itself inaccurate, to cover up a particularly glaring anachronism; see p. cxxxii above.

[5] Cf. the incident in the *Passio S. Aegidii*: 'Proxima namque die Dominica, dum Vir sanctus [scil. Aegidius] missam de more celebrans, pro iam dicto rege Dominum in canone deprecaretur, apparuit ei angelus Domini, super altare scedulam ponens, in qua descriptum erat ordine et ipsum regis peccatum . . .' (*ActaS*, Sept. i. 301–4, at 302). There are many other examples of this motif; cf. H. Günter, *Die christliche Legenden des Abendlandes* (Heidelberg, 1910), pp. 91–2. Probably the best-known letter from heaven was that purporting to have been written by Christ, encouraging rigorous sabbatarianism, see R. Priebsch, *Letter from Heaven on the Observance of the Lord's Day*, ed. W. E. Collinson and A. Closs (Oxford, 1936). A version of Christ's letter was known in Anglo-Saxon England, by at least the 11th cent., since several vernacular translations survive (see Priebsch, pp. 10–11; Ker, *Catalogue*, nos. 68, art. 2; 178, art. 2; 186, art. 17; 283, artt. 4, 5), and it may have influenced the formulation of the legend about the Kenelm letter. The principal MSS of the letter and surviving Old English versions are conveniently listed, with bibliographical details, by C. A. Lees, 'The "Sunday Letter" and the "Sunday lists"', *ASE* xiv (1985), 129–51. One might also compare the introduction to an Anglo-Saxon charm in London, BL, Cotton Caligula A. xv, fo. 140, which claims that the charm was deposited at St Peter's, Rome, by an angel: see Ker, *Catalogue*, no. 139; and T. O. Cockayne, *Leechdoms, Wortcunning and Starcraft of Early England*, 3 vols., RS xxxv (1864–6), iii. 288. No other account of a heavenly missive delivered by a bird has yet come to light, however.

[6] 'schedula' or 'scedula' is the earlier form of this diminutive (not a Classical word, to judge from Lewis and Short, which gives only an example from Jerome, *In Rufinum* iii. 2, and *OLD*, which does not include the word at all); 'cedula', the variant given by **BGL**, is, according to Latham, *Word-List*, found from *c.*1160 onwards.

indicarent siquis inter eos aliquid huius epistolaris[a] relationis cognouisset.[b] Intererant tot terrarum conuentibus plerique Angli atque Mercii,[c] siue in [d]Anglica scola[d] a superioribus Anglorum regibus Rome ordinata[1] constituti siue ab ipsa Anglia recenter[e] aduenticii. Ab his recitatur[f] sacra epistola[g] cuius interpretatio est ista: 'In Clento[h] [i]uacce ualli[i] Kenelmus regius natus iacet [j]sub spino[j] capite[k] truncatus.'[l] Tum[m] uero obnixius[n] papa insistente, postposito feminearum minarum terrore, Angligene ciues omnia suo ordine et signa super eum[o] uisa exposuere.

§ 12. Dehinc memoratus papa mittit cum Anglis fidelibus legatos cardinales cum litteris et potestate apostolica ad archipresulem[2] Wlfredum[p] Dorobernie[q] ceterosque pontifices Anglorum. Ipsum quoque celitus allate epistole mittit indicium, quatinus de indigno latibulo in ecclesiam Deo placitam probabilem Dei martyrem transferrent[r] Kenelmum,[3] in patrocinium uidelicet multorum uenerandum.[s] Itaque ad auctoritatem apostolicam et archipresulis potentem gratiam, tota plebe Merciorum atque Anglorum conspirante,[t] excipitur sacrum corpus Kenelmi cum[u] superna laude, quatinus transferretur ad beatum genitorem suum[v] Wincelcumbe,[w] ubi idem [x]Deo amabilis rex[x] requiescit in templo quod ipse Dei genitrici regaliter condidit, ac regiis opibus [y]extulit, cum ibi firmauerit[y] oppidum[4] muro cinctum.[z]

[a] epistolare G; epistolate L   [b] cognouissent B; agnouisset P   [c] merchii L   [d-d] Anglia L   [e] om. B   [f] recitata est P   [g] ita continens In Klent Koubeche Kenelm kunebearn liy under yorne heaved bereved G; what follows is then made a new sentence Cuius . . .   [h] Clentho BD   [i-i] uacceuallis B   [j-j] supino B; sub spina GJLP   [k] capina L   [l] truncato P; Quod anglice dicitur Ine clent cubeche Kenelm kine bern lid under thorne hefdes bireaved add. H; Kenelm kinebern inne clenc⟨o⟩ dene under þa þorne liŏ hefd⟨es⟩ bereved added in the outer margin of J, partly trimmed off   [m] Tunc L   [n] obnixius J   [o] om. C   [p] om. BGL; Wulfredum J; in P, the name was originally omitted and has been supplied above the line by the later hand   [q] Derobernie G   [r] om. L   [s] transferret add. L   [t] conueniente B   [u] om. G   [v] om. J   [w] Winchelcumbe BHJ; Winchelcoumbe G; Winchecombe L   [x-x] amabilis Deo rex B; Deo rex amabilis C; Deo amabilis L   [y-y] ornauit, ibique firmauit B; expulit cum ibi confirmauerit P   [z] C ends with this word, adding the closing phrase: Asseritur quod cum decollandus esset beatus Kenelmus, sacrum ymnum 'Te Deum laudamus', inceperit, atque in illo uersu 'Te martirum candidatus laudat excercitus' occubuerit, ad laudem et gloriam Dei patris omnipotentis, qui uiuit et regnat per omnia secula seculorum, Amen.

---

[1] The 'anglica scola' was not, as the name might suggest, an educational establishment, but rather a hostelry set up in the Trastevere for the many pilgrims who went to Rome from England—similar establishments existed for other foreign pilgrims. Known as the 'Schola Saxonum', or in Old English 'Angelcynnes scole' (ASC 817 and 885), it is variously said to have been set up by Ine of Wessex (Roger of Wendover, Flores

might understand anything of the text of this letter. There were, among the assembly of so many lands, a good number of Englishmen, even Mercians, either staying at the English school in Rome set up by former kings of the English people,[1] or just recently arrived from England. By them the holy letter is read out, and its interpretation is as follows: 'In Clent Cow-valley, Kenelm king's son lies under a thorn-bush deprived of his head.' Then at the strenuous insistence of the Pope, putting aside the terror of the woman's threats, the English citizens revealed all the events in order, and the signs which had been seen concerning him.

§ 12. After that, the aforementioned pope sends, in company with the English faithful, cardinal legates bearing letters and apostolic authority to Wulfred, archbishop of Canterbury,[2] and the other English bishops. He sends the very proof of the letter delivered from heaven, so that they might translate the proven martyr of God, Kenelm,[3] from his unworthy hiding-place into a church pleasing to God, namely to be venerated as the patron of many. Therefore upon papal authority and the powerful grace of the archbishop, the whole race of the Mercians, indeed of the English, being of one accord, the holy body of Kenelm is with heavenly praise gathered up, so as to be taken to his blessed father at Winchcombe, where that king beloved of God rests in the church he himself founded and dedicated in kingly fashion to the mother of God, and adorned with royal treasures, when he established there a walled town.[4]

Historiarum, ed. Coxe, i. 215–16) or Offa of Mercia (William of Malmesbury, *Gesta Regum*, ed. Stubbs, i. 109), presumably the 'superioribus anglorum regibus' referred to here, and funded by the collection of Peter's Pence or 'Romescot'. Cf. Barlow, *English Church, 1000–1066*, p. 290, *Asser's Life of King Alfred*, ed. W. H. Stevenson (Oxford, 1904), p. 243, and S. Keynes and M. Lapidge, *Alfred the Great* (Harmondsworth, 1983), p. 244.

[2] Wulfred was consecrated archbishop of Canterbury in 805 (*ASC* 803) and died in 832 (*ASC* 829).

[3] Cf. Goscelin, *Vita S. Werburge* c. 17, 'quatenus sacrosancta ipsius gleba de tumulo eleuaretur, clamantibus cunctis indignum esse, ut tanta lux multorum sub modio terre absconderetur' (*PL* clv. 107 B).

[4] See Leland's *Itinerary* (ed. Toulmin-Smith, iv. 221): 'He [Averey, parson of Dene] saythe that it aperithe by S. Kenelme's legend that Winchelcumbe was oppidum muro cinctum. And he saythe that the towne buyldinge was muche toward Sudeley Castell, and that ther yet remayne sum tokens of a diche and the foundation of a wall, and that ther be tokens of an othar way up a praty way beyonde the highe strete above the churche where the farme of Cornedene is: so that of old tyme it was a mighty large towne.' The archaeological evidence for the site of Coenwulf and Kenelm's burials is discussed by S. Bassett, 'A Probable Mercian Royal Mausoleum at Winchcombe, Gloucestershire', *The Antiquaries Journal*, lxv (1985), 82–100.

§ 13. In assumptione autem*[a]* almiflue[1] glebe ab ipsa eius spelunca arente, fons*[b]* sacer emersit[2] qui hactenus*[c]* in riuum effluit et multis inde gustantibus salutem impendit.[3] Cum ergo efferretur*[d]* e*[e]* silua confluente *[f]*cum patribus*[f]* maxima multitudine detentus est in itinere ubi plurima turba*[g]* cecorum *[h]*surdorum claudorum*[h]* diuersorumque languorum*[i] [j]*undique annitens*[j]* curata est.[4]

§ 14. Cum autem asportaretur a populo prouincie Glauecestre,*[k]* occurrit *[l]*armatus populus*[l]* Wigornensis*[m]* prouincie, obstititque ad uadum[5] Pyriford,*[n]* quatinus illum pretiosissimum thesaurum a Glauescestrensibus*[o]* nisi ultro cederent,*[p]* in castrum*[q]* Wigornense*[r]* auferrent.*[s]* Altercantibus autem utrisque*[t]* partibus*[u]* sicut quondam Turonicis et Pictauis pro beati Martini corpore,[6] complacuit

---

[a] om. B; uero L   *[b]* fonte fons L   *[c]* attentius L   *[d]* effereretur G
[e] de B   *[f–f]* om. B; cum partibus H   *[g]* multitudo L   *[h–h]* claudorum surdorum B   *[i]* languidorum BL; in D a later hand has added do above the line to be inserted between the u and o   *[j–j]* adueniens undique B; undique amittens G; undique L   *[k]* Glaucestrie B; Glauescestrie GH; Glancestrie L; Gloecestrie P   *[l–l]* populus armatus GH   *[m]* Wigorniensis HL   *[n]* Priuorde B; Pirifort G; Piriford H; Pyriuord J (and D before correction by substitution of f for u); Piriuord L   *[o]* Glauestrensibus BG; corrected from Glauestensibus by addition of ces in the margin, and an r above the line, by the slightly later corrector in D; Glauescensibus J; Glaucestrensibus L; Gloecestrensibus P   *[p]* concederent L   *[q]* castro L   *[r]* Wigorniense H; Wygorniesium L   *[s]* ui transferrent B; ferrent L   *[t]* utriusque GL   *[u]* populis P

---

[1] 'Almifluus' is a fairly rare word, possibly coined in the late 10th cent. (Latham, *Word-List*, gives a citation dated 970). It is not listed in *OLD* or *TLL*, but Goscelin used the word quite frequently; cf. *Vita S. Yuonis* c. 16, 'tumba almiflua' (*PL* clv. 89), and 'almiflui Deusdedit' in *Historia translationis S. Augustini* c. 21 (*ActaS*, Maii, vi. 413 E), cited in *DMLBS*. 'Gleba' is a fairly common name for corporeal remains, used very often by Goscelin, for example *Vita S. Werburge* c. 17, 'quatenus sacrosancta ipsius gleba de tumulo eleuaretur' (*PL* clv. 107 B), and *Historia maior de miraculis S. Augustini* c. 39 (*ActaS*, Maii, vi. 403 C), 'salutiferam glebam'.

[2] For some time this spring remained one of the centres of Kenelm's cult. *Vita brevior* already indicated the existence of an 'oratorium' at Clent (c. 8). A mile and a quarter north-west of Romsley village, a 12th-cent. chapel survives to the present day, built precariously at the head of the steep ravine which constitutes the boundary of Clent parish. The earliest portion of the building is the south doorway, datable to about 1150. Outside, high up on the south wall, there is a small stone figure of a saint, which Pevsner (*Worcs.*, p. 254), dates to the 12th cent. According to the present parish boundaries, the chapel falls within the parish of Halesowen rather than Clent. Formerly, a stream flowed from the east end of the chapel down into the ravine. An undercroft may still be seen below the east end of the church, which had housed the holy spring. During the restoration of the chapel in 1848, the water was diverted and there is now, a few yards north of the building, a spring which does actually rise within the modern parish of Clent. See Amphlett, *Short History*, pp. 7–8; E. Dent, *Annals of Winchcombe and Sudeley* (London, 1877), pp. 45–6; and Humphreys, 'Story of St Kenelm', p. 212. A hamlet, Kenelmstowe (see Mawer and Stenton, *Place-Names of Worcestershire*, p. 301), grew up around the chapel, and it is recorded that in 1253, Roger de Somery, lord of Dudley

§ 13. As the holy and gracious sod[1] was lifted up, right from his dusty grave a holy spring burst forth,[2] which to this day flows into the stream and gives healing to the many who drink from it.[3] When he was being carried out of the wood, a great multitude assembled along with the holy fathers, and he was detained on the way, where a great crowd of blind, dumb, lame and divers sick persons, pressing in on every side, were cured.[4]

§ 14. As he was being borne away by the people of the province of Gloucester, the people of the province of Worcester came running up to meet them armed with weapons and blocked the way by the ford at Perryford,[5] intending to take away from the men of Gloucester that precious treasure into the fortress at Worcester, unless they surrendered it voluntarily. Both sides wrangled, as once the peoples of Tours and Poitiers did over the body of St Martin.[6]

Castle, obtained from Henry III permission to hold a fair there on the eve and day of St Kenelm and for two days following. Kenelmstowe has now disappeared, presumably because the shrine, which was dismantled in the sixteenth century, was the main livelihood of those who dwelt there. A fair 'of an attenuated nature' continued to take place until the mid-nineteenth century, when it was eventually suppressed (Amphlett, p. 26; Dent, pp. 45–6). Kenelm's head, encased in silver and gold, was at some time purported to have been preserved at the chapel at Clent: see *Collectanea Anglo-Praemonstratensia*, ed. F. A. Gasquet, 3 vols., Camden 3rd Series, vi, x, xii (London, 1904–6), ii. 265.

[3] Cf. *Vita brevior* c. 8 ('ibi fons . . . inpendit').

[4] Cf. *Passio S. Eadwardi*, 'Fons etiam in loco in quo prius iacuerat, dulces et perspicuas aquas ex eo tempore usque hodie emanare cernitur . . . ubi infirmis multa cotidie . . . praestantur beneficia' (ed. Fell, p. 8).

[5] Probably Perryford, a river-crossing now lost, which lay on the common boundaries of Cropthorne and Bricklehampton where they meet the Avon (see Mawer and Stenton, *Place-Names of Worcestershire*, p. 120). The reference to this crossing gives a hint as to the nature of the route which the author envisaged the bearers of Kenelm's relics as having taken. A network of ancient tracks, known as saltways, and radiating in every direction from Droitwich, from at least Roman times the only salt-producing centre in the Midlands, can be traced from place-name and charter evidence (ibid. pp. 4–9). Perryford was situated where one of these saltways crossed over the Avon. That particular saltway (ibid. p. 5, 'A') may be traced from Droitwich, via Martin Hussingtree, Perryford, Toddington, Stanway, and Hailes, to Salter's hill, just east of Winchcombe, whence it passed on southwards. In the light of other references in *Vita et miracula*, such a route could well have been followed on a journey from Clent to Winchcombe. Among the possessions confirmed to Winchcombe abbey by a 12th-cent. bull of Pope Alexander III, dated 1175 (ed. Royce, *Landboc*, i. 25–9), salt-rights at Droitwich were included, which the abbey may have had for some time (although there is no record of any rights in *DB*). Thus the saltway in that direction may have been a journey familiar to the members of the community.

[6] The dispute between the peoples of Tours and Poitiers is not recounted in Sulpicius Severus, *Vita S. Martini*. The incident is, however, described by Gregory of Tours, *Historia Francorum*, i. 48, ed. Krusch, *MGH*, *SRM*, i. 55–6. Cf. also a more elaborate example of the same topos in *Vita S. Erkenwaldi* (ed. Whatley, *Saint of London*, pp. 91–5).

tandem ut populus qui in crepusculo sequentis diei[a] prior euigilasset sacratissimum Kenelmum[b] quasi diuinitus [c]datum sibi[c] auferret.

§ 15. Itaque Glauescestrenses[d] uigilantiores iam quinque miliariis cum sacra gleba euasere, antequam Wigornenses[e] possent expergiscere. Tum[f] uero [g]accensi ira[g] et rubore, insecuntur[h] tota[i] celeritate.[1] Quos ubi eminus respexere fugitiui, inuocato suffragio ducis Kenelmi per angustam semitam inter frutecta protegentia[j] excurrere[k] anheli.[l] Iamque[m] in conspectu monasterii Wincelcumbensis[n] fuga labore sitique grauissima defessi,[o] subsederunt cum sancta gleba respiraturi. Nec prodire ausi poscebant se tanti patroni presentia remediari. Continuo uero fons erupit[p] sub quadam[q] petra, qua ablata totus cetus salutem[r] bibit et processit. Fons autem hactenus in amnem decurrit.[2]

§ 16. Stabat[s] tunc Quendryda[t] in solario occidentalis[u] ecclesie beati Petri, quam uie spatium dirimit ab atrio monasterii.[3] Que respiciens a monte decurrentem[v] multitudinem cum triumpho fraterne glorie ira[w] indignatione[x] felle[4] cepit tabescere. Arreptoque psalterio[y] quodam prestigio studuit non cantare pro illo, sed [z]incantare contra illum[z] centesimum octauum psalmum,[5] quatinus[aa]

---

[a] om. L   [b] corpus L   [c-c] sibi donatum B; datum L   [d] Glauestrenses B; Glauenses GJ (and D before correction); Glaucestrenses L; Gloecestrensses P   [e] Wigornienses H   [f] Tunc G   [g-g] accensura G   [h] insequuntur B; insequitur L   [i] om. L   [j] tegentia B   [k] excurrerunt H; excurcere L   [l] anibeli L   [m] Iam B   [n] Winchelcumbensis BGHJ; Wyncheconbensis L   [o] defossi G   [p] erupuit L   [q] aqua J   [r] salubriter BG   [s] igitur add. G   [t] Quendritha BH; Quendreda G   [u] occidentis G; occidentali L   [v] decurrente G   [w] irata L   [x] indignationis B   [y] salterio cum G   [z-z] contra illum incantare G   [aa] et add. B

---

[1] Cf. the story of the theft of St Neot's relics, and the subsequent pursuit by the angry inhabitants of 'Neotestoc', told in *Vita Prima S. Neoti*, cc. 18–19, ed. Lapidge, pp. 134–7.

[2] There were, according to the Middle English version of the Life of Kenelm, a healing well and a chapel on the side of Salter's Hill, 2,000 yards east of Winchcombe Abbey (Bennett and Smithers, p. 106, lines 251–6). On the well, see R. C. S. Walters, *The Ancient Wells, Springs, and Holy Wells of Gloucestershire* (Bristol, 1928), pp. 9–11. The chapel, dedicated to Kenelm, was demolished in 1850 (see Verey, *Glos.*, p. 441). Hence Salter's Hill is presumably the incline down which Cwoenthryth is said to have espied the triumphant party running (c. 16). Although this seems, at first sight, to be a strange route for a party coming from Clent to have taken, involving a considerable detour to the east of Winchcombe, there are indications that the author imagined their journey to have followed one of the ancient saltways (see above, p. 69).

[3] This account of the layout of the church and monastery at Winchcombe has been analysed in the context of the archaeological evidence by Bassett, 'A Probable Mercian Royal Mausoleum'. The present (15th-cent. and later) parish church of St Peter lies

At length it was agreed that the people who woke up first in the dawn of the following day should take away the most holy Kenelm, as if granted to them from Heaven.

§ 15. And so it was that the more watchful men of Gloucester had already got five miles away with the holy sod, before the men of Worcester could rouse themselves. But then they, fired with anger and shame, pursue with all speed.[1] Those in flight saw them back in the distance, called upon the help of their lord Kenelm and rushed breathlessly along a narrow path through the protecting undergrowth. Now in sight of the monastery of Winchcombe, worn out by the flight, the effort, and a burning thirst, they collapsed, with the holy sod, to catch their breath. Not daring to advance, they prayed that they might be refreshed by the presence of such a great patron. And immediately a spring burst forth under a rock, which they lifted up, and the whole company drank healthfully before moving on. The spring runs into the river to this day.[2]

§ 16. At that moment Cwoenthryth was standing in the upper room of the western church of St Peter, which is separated from the forecourt of the monastery by a road.[3] When she saw the multitude running down the hill with the triumphal procession of her brother's glory, she began to be consumed with anger, indignation, and bitterness.[4] Snatching up her psalter, by some kind of witchcraft she set about singing not for him, but rather, chanting against him the one hundred and eighth psalm[5] so that, in perversely

directly to the west of the site of the abbey church, and a north–south track still separates them. The description in this text was clearly written by someone familiar with the layout of Winchcombe.

[4] Note the use here of asyndeton in a tricolon: 'ira indignatione felle'.

[5] Ps. 108 (109) is numbered among the so-called 'imprecatory psalms' (see F. L. Cross and E. A. Livingstone, eds., *The Oxford Dictionary of the Christian Church*, 2nd edn. (Oxford, 1988), p. 695) in which the wrath of God is called to work upon the wicked man (since 1928 they have been omitted from recitation as being contrary to the spirit of Christianity). The 'cursing' portion of psalm 108 is from v. 5 to v. 19. It is perhaps significant that Cwoenthryth was stopped in her backwards recitation at verse 20; thus she did not get a chance to say the specifically imprecatory verses. The reasoning behind the back-to-front reading was presumably to reverse the force of the imprecation, turning white, as it were, to black: cf. H. Bächtold-Stäubli, ed., *Handwörterbuch des deutschen Aberglaubens*, 10 vols. (Berlin and Leipzig, 1927–42), i. 1225 and viii. 845; and S. Thompson, *Motif-Index of Folk-Literature*, 6 vols., 2nd edn. (Copenhagen, 1955–8) D1985. 2 and G257. 2 (cf. D1812. 2. 1 and G224. 8 and Q473. 5. 2). The phrase 'uerum in ipsam redundauit maledictum suum' recalls the spirit of verse 18 of the psalm: 'Et dilexit maledictionem, et ueniet ei; et noluit benedictionem et elongabitur ab eo.' The alliteration used in the description of this incident is striking: 'fraterne felicitati efficeret' and 'uersum ore uolueret uenefico'.

a fine ad caput, ab ultimo uersu ad primum peruertendo eum, fraterne felicitati*a* efficeret pernitiosum.[1] Verum in ipsam*b* redundauit*c* maledictum suum. Cum enim a fine ascendendo hunc uersum *d*ore uolueret uenefico:*d* 'hoc opus eorum qui detrahunt mihi apud Dominum*e* et qui locuntur mala aduersus animam meam', continuo sibi utrique oculi suis sedibus extirpati decidere*f* super ipsam*g* quam legebat paginam.[2] Adhuc autem ipsum psalterium*h* argento paratum, huius *i*correptionis prebet*i* indicium, in eadem serie lapsorum orbium cruore maculatum.[3] Ipsa uero infelix post paululum interiit, quam ferunt nec in ecclesia nec in atrio nec in campo sepultam posse teneri, sed quendam infantem lucidissimum apparentem*j* cuidam iussisseque*k* in quodam profundo semoto*l* proici.[4]

§ 17. Regius uero martyr Kenelmus paterno*m* monasterio Wincelcumbe*n* cum altisonis laudibus infertur, ubi ipsum patris*o* monumentum sancta memoria celebratur, et ipse filius innumeris ibi signis tunc et deinceps exhibitis hostia cognoscitur sanctitatis. Quibus ab antiquitate celo reconsignatis, exequamur pauca ex*p* multis moderni et nostri temporis.*q*

§ 18. Sub rege[5] Cnuto*r* uir*s* prediues *t*Osgotus[6] cognomine Digera*t* Danus natione, partem terre adiacentem ruri beati Kenelmi

---

a felicitatis *G*   *b* ipsa *BL*   *c* redundat *G*   *d-d* uolueret ore uenifico *G*; ore uoluerit uenifico *L*; ore uolueret uenenifico *P*   *e* Deum *G*   *f* cecidere *G*   *g* om. *J*   *h* spalterium *J*   *i-i* correctionis seruat *G*; correctionis prebet *L*   *j* apparere *B*; apparuisse *H*   *k* iussisse eam *B*; iussisse *GL*   *l* semito *G*; semoto loco *L*   *m* patrono *G*   *n* Winchelcumbe *BHJ*; Wynchelcoumbe *G*; Wynchecombe *L*   *o* patri *L*   *p* de *H*   *q* EXPLICIT VITA ET PASSIO SANCTI KENELMI REGIS ET MARTYRIS. INCIPIVNT MIRACVLA EIVSDEM *add. H*; EXPLICIT PASSIO BEATI KENELMI. INCIPIVNT MIRACVLA POST OBITVM EIVS OSTENSA *add. P*   *r* Cnutho *B*; Knuto *G*; Chunto *J*; Canudo *L*; Cunuto *P (and D before erasure of the first* u *)*   *s* quidam *add. H*   *t-t* Osgorus cognomine Digera et *G*; Osgodus nomine *L*

---

[1] Cf. *Vita breuior* c. 5 ('fraterna felicitate').

[2] Perhaps the best-known instance of this punishment, an outward token of the inner blindness of unbelief, is St Alban's executioner, whose eyes are said to have fallen to the ground with Alban's head (cf. Bede, *HE* i. 7).

[3] Although in the miracles appended to the *Vita* no further mention is made of Cwoenthryth's psalter, Gerald of Wales, *Itinerarium Kambriae* i. 2, ed. J. F. Dimock, *Giraldi Cambrensis Opera*, 8 vols., RS xxi (1861–91), vi. 25, uniquely records a miracle attached to this grisly relic. A monk at Winchcombe committed fornication on the eve of St Kenelm's day. The following day, he presumed to carry the venerable psalter in procession, but found when he came to put the book down that it was stuck fast to his hands, and he was only freed on confessing his sin. Gerald went on to give his own version of Cwoenthryth's demise: 'Liber autem ille ideo in ueneratione magna ibi tenetur, quia cum corpus Kenelmi exanime deferretur, et clamarunt turbae: "Martyr

saying it back to front—from end to beginning, from the last verse to the first—she might make it harmful to her brother's happy state.[1] But her own curse turned back on her. For, working upwards from the bottom, as this verse rolled off her venomous lips: 'This is the work of them who detract me before the Lord: and who speak evils against my soul', straightway both her eyes, rooted out from their sockets, dropped upon the very page she was reading.[2] That same psalter, adorned with silver, still shows the proof of this chastisement, stained on the same sentence with the blood of the fallen eye-balls.[3] That wretched woman died shortly afterwards, and they say she could not stay buried in either the church or the fore-court nor in the cemetery, but that a brilliantly shining child appeared to a certain man, and gave instructions that she should be thrown into some remote gully.[4]

§ 17. Meanwhile, the kingly martyr Kenelm is brought into his father's monastery at Winchcombe with loud-resounding praises, where the tomb of his father is held in blessed memory, and the son himself is recognized as a sacrificial victim of sanctity, by the countless miraculous signs revealed then and afterwards. Having recounted afresh these things of old sent from heaven, let us describe a few of the many miracles of modern times and of our own time.

§ 18. In the reign of King Cnut,[5] a very rich man, Osgot, sur-named Digera,[6] a Dane by race, made efforts to annex to his own

Dei est, est uere; martyr Dei est", respondit Quendreda, fratricidii rea et conscia, "Adeo uere martyr est, sicut uerum est quod oculi mei super psalterium istud eruti iacent"; ea enim hora psalterium forte legebat. Et statim oculi eius ambo a capite diuinitus auulsi in librum apertum, ubi et uestigia sanguinis adhuc apparent, ceciderunt.' This version does not appear to derive directly from *Vita et miracula*, but may represent Gerald's rather free embellishment of what he had heard or read. William of Malmesbury, *Gesta Regum*, ii. 211 (ed. Stubbs, i. 263), gives a slightly different version again of the story of Cwoenthryth's punishment, though probably based on the *Vita*, and adds that the marks are still on the psalter in his own day: 'Cruoris signa exstant hodie, immanitatem mulierculae et Dei ultionem spirantia.'

[4] It seems unlikely that this can be a true record of the demise of Cwoenthryth—see note, p. 54 above.

[5] Cnut's reign as king of all England began in Nov. 1016 (*ASC* 1017 *CDE*), and he died on 12 Nov. 1035 (*ASC CD* 1035, *E* 1036).

[6] Osgot Digera is not known elsewhere. The name Osgot or Osgod derives from the Old Norse, 'Ásgautr' (Old Danish, 'Asgut', Old Swedish, 'Asgot'), on which see O. von Feilitzen, *The Pre-Conquest Personal Names of Domesday Book*, Nomina Germanica (Uppsala, 1937), pp. 165–6. The *cognomen* 'Digera', 'the stout' (or 'fatty', depending on the point of view), Old West Scandinavian 'Digri' from the adjective 'digr', was given to Siward, Earl of Northumbria (ob. 1055, *ASC CDE*, at York)—William of Malmesbury, *Gesta Regum*, iii. 253 (ed. Stubbs, ii. 311–12): 'filius Siwardi magnificentissimi comitis,

[a]in Neuuentona,[a] sue possessioni [b]ad Tudintun[b] moliebatur adiungere.[1] Vbi collecto prouincialium[c] placito Goduuinus[d] [e]tunc abbas[e] beatum Kenelmum medium intulit iudicio.[2] Iudicatur[f] ergo ut ille prepotens cum uiginti quatuor [g]paribus optimatibus[g] suum ius probet[h] sacramento super sanctum presentis [i]Kenelmi corpus[i] iurando. Cumque ille in abbatem probrosus ad iusiurandum sese proriperet, subito clara Dei uirtute repulsus, retrogradus abscessit,[j] et quasi uasto[k] ictu obrutus supinus concidit.[3] Tunc [l]omnis ille[l] conuentus coram sacro feretro humi affusus, ueniam flagitauit,[m] ipsique[n] suam partem incunctanter adiudicauit.[o] Aduersarius uero ut amens domum deductus non diu superuixit, et qui unam [p]sancti possessiunculam[p] inique auferre temptauit, omnia possessa cum [q]seculo iure[q] perdidit.

§ 19. Item quidam notissimus nomine Godricus,[4] cum de collecto censu plebis calumniaretur in placito[r] prouinciali[s] habito, iurauit per sanctum Kenelmum se nunquam inde quicquam[t] uel ad quattuor nummos defraudasse, statimque[u] mutus factus, [v]reatum suum[v] tacendo prodidit, quem loquendo defenderat,[w] totaque plebs silentio cognitum fraudatorem corripuit.

[a-a] in iuuentuna B; in Niwentuna G; in Neowentona H; om. L; in Niuuentuna P (and D before alteration to Neuuentona)   [b-b] ad Tuditun B; adtudintune H; om. L   [c] prouinciali B   [d] Goduinus D (before correction)   [e-e] abbas tunc B   [f] Indicatur L   [g-g] partibus opimatibus L   [h] prebet L   [i-i] corpus Kenelmi J   [j] abcessit H   [k] ualido H   [l-l] ille omnis B   [m] flagitant L   [n] ibique B   [o] adiudicant L   [p-p] possessiunculam B; possessiunculam sancti L   [q-q] suo rure B   [r] palatio P   [s] Wincelcumbensi add. B   [t] om. L   [u] statim B   [v-v] suum reatum B   [w] celauerat H

quem Digera Danico uocabulo, id est fortem cognominabant' (cf. *Vita Ædwardi regis*, 'Siwardus . . . Danica lingua "Digara", hoc est fortis, nuncupatus'; ed. Barlow, p. 34); see G. Tengvik, *Old-English Bynames*, Nomina Germanica, iv (Uppsala, 1938), p. 310. It is possible that the author of *Vita et miracula* confused Siward Digera with Osgod Clapa, a Danish noble who was outlawed by King Edward in 1046 (*ASC C* 1046; *ASC D* 1047; *ASC E* 1044). Their deaths are reported by *ASC* in consecutive years. If the same Osgod is intended, the weak link in the chronology of the miracle would be that *ASC* (*C* and *D*) gives the death of Osgod Clapa in 1054, and not 'sub rege Cnuto'. Perhaps the hagiographer seized upon a roughly contemporary figure of some notoriety in order to increase the credibility and interest of his text. Osgod Clapa appears elsewhere in hagiography as a malefactor, namely in Herman, *Liber de Miraculis Sancti Eadmundi* (late 11th-cent.), c. 21 (ed. T. Arnold, *Memorials of St Edmund's Abbey*, 3 vols., RS xcvi (1890–6), i. 54–5), where the insolent pride of the Dane is punished.

[1] Although there are several possible Nauntons, this is probably present-day Naunton in Toddington, a hamlet just over three miles north of Winchcombe. Naunton ('Niwetone') is included amongst the possessions of the church of Winchcombe in *DB*,

property at Toddington a piece of the land adjacent to St Kenelm's land in Naunton.[1] When the county court was assembled Godwin, the abbot of the time brought St Kenelm there to arbitrate in the judgement.[2] It is decided that the landowner shall, in company with twenty-four of his noble peers, prove his right by an oath, to be sworn over the holy body of Kenelm, there present. And when that shameful man rushed at the abbot to swear the oath, suddenly repulsed by the manifest might of God, he retreated backwards and, as if overwhelmed by a massive blow, tumbled over on to his back.[3] Then all the present gathering prostrated themselves on the ground before the holy bier, begged forgiveness, and without hesitation adjudged to the saint his portion of land. The antagonist meanwhile, seemingly out of his mind, was taken home, and did not survive for long afterwards, and he who attempted unjustly to take away one little possession of the saint has rightly lost all his possessions along with this life.

§ 19. On another occasion a notorious man named Godric,[4] when he was telling a lie at the assembled county court about the rent collected from the people, swore by St Kenelm that he had never defrauded them of anything, not even four farthings or less. But immediately he was struck dumb, and by keeping quiet betrayed the guilt which he had by speaking defended, and all the people, recognizing from his silence that he was a cheat, fell upon him.

Glos. 11.6 (i. 165d). The place appears several times in Landboc as 'Niwetone', 'Newinton(a)' and 'Newentona' (ed. Royce, i. 24, 74, and 76); cf. A. Mawer and F. M. Stenton, Place-Names of Gloucestershire, 4 vols., EPNS xxxviii–xli (1927), ii. 34 and iv. 68. 'Tudintun' is likely to be Toddington, which lies about a mile west of Naunton, and was held at Domesday ('Todintun', DB, Glos. 61. 2; i. 169b) by Harold, son of Ralph the Timid (Earl of Herefordshire from about 1053 to 1057), and previously by Ralph himself.

[2] Godwin became abbot of Winchcombe in 1042, and died Oct. 1053 (Heads, p. 79).

[3] Miracles of this kind are fairly common. See e.g. one of the miracles of St Ecgwine of Evesham, recorded by Byrhtferth (Vita S. Ecgwini, iv. 10), in which it is told of a certain 'rusticus' of the neighbourhood, 'exarsit illi animus ad inuadendam iuris ecclesiae beati praesulis Ecgwini terrulam.' It was adjudged that the malefactor must stand on the disputed land and swear by the relics of Ecgwine that the land was his (cf. also the example among Goscelin's Miracula S. Mildrethe, ed. Rollason, 'Translation', pp. 201–2). The dispute with Osgot is noted by P. Wormald, 'A handlist of Anglo-Saxon lawsuits', ASE xvii (1988), 247–81, no. 166.

[4] This Godric could possibly be Godric, sheriff of Berkshire and Buckinghamshire, who was killed at Hastings in 1066; see Green, English Sheriffs, pp. 26 and 28, and F. Harmer, Anglo-Saxon Writs, 2nd edn. (Stamford, 1989), p. 561. Cf. Wormald, 'Lawsuits', no. 167.

§ 20. Ea tempestate iusserat ex more sacerdos[1] in Peyletona[a] festum beati[b] Kenelmi intermissis operibus celebrari.[2] Quod cum audisset eidem[c] uille presidens matrona uti[d] recumbebat ad prandium in ipso[e] die festo, typo[f] superbie refutauit,[3] atque indignantia uerba in sanctum intorsit, nec quicquam operis intermitti tumido fastu imperauit.[g] 'Pro Kenelmo', inquit, 'nescio quo[h] fructum diei perderemus.'[i] Vix elocuta erat et utrique oculi supra mensam cecidere[j] excussi, ut supra indigne martyris sorori.[k] Tum uero sera penitentia cum luctu et ululatu inclamat sanctum Kenelmum eiusque cum omni reuerentia feriari rogauit[l] diem festiuum.[m] Merito autem omnium dierum respectum perdidit,[n] que[o] unum diem [p]Dei dilecti[p] despexit.[4] Porro boues ipsius[5] qui eo[q] die iugabantur ad uehicula omnia lora et iuga excutientes[r] ita dispersi sunt ut deinceps inueniri non possent.[s]

§ 21. Celeberrimum quoque est in Hereforda[t] quomodo fabro in eiusdem solemnio proterue operanti inheserit malleus dextro, et forceps sinistro palmo, uel [u]molam rotanti[u] ministro ad acuendam[v] falcem ita ligno incluso manus coaluerit,[w] ut solui cuneis et malleis impellentibus nequiuerit,[x] magisque teneretur quam teneret.[6] Votis

---

[a] Peiletuna *BJP*; Perletona *G*; Peylentona *H*; Puletuna *L*; *in D, the letter* o *is a later alteration for* u   [b] sancti *G*   [c] eiusdem *L*   [d] ut *J*   [e] *om. B*   [f] stipo *G*   [g] imperaum *H*   [h] cur *L*   [i] perdemus *B*; proderemus *L*   [j] a capite *add. B*   [k] sororis *L*   [l] rogat *H*   [m] festum *G*   [n] perdit *G*; perdiderit *L*   [o] qui *B*   [p-p] dilecti Dei *BHP*   [q] eodem *J*   [r] excuscientes *G*   [s] possunt *G*   [t] Herefordia *BGP*; Herfordia *L*   [u-u] mola rotandi *J*   [v] tuendam *G*   [w] maluerit *G*; coaluerunt *L*   [x] nequiuerint *L*

---

[1] Cf. Goscelin, *Vita S. Wulsini* c. 15, 'Iusserat hoc sacerdos ex more digna celebritate feriari. Parent omnes et opera rerum intermittunt' (Talbot, p. 81).

[2] Identification of this place has proved difficult. One possibility is Pailton in Warwickshire, which appears variously as 'Pailintona', 'Payl(l)inton', and 'Peilinton'— see J. E. B. Gover, A. Mawer, and F. M. Stenton, *The Place-Names of Warwickshire*, EPNS xiii (1936), p. 118. The fact that Pailton was only a hamlet within the parish of Monks Kirby, and perhaps not likely to have had a 'sacerdos', may count against this conjecture. There are a couple of less closely comparable place-names in Somerset: Paulton, for which see E. Ekwall, *The Concise Oxford Dictionary of English Place-Names*, 4th edn. (Oxford, 1987), where the name is recorded as taking the form 'Pealton' in 1194 (no study of Somerset place-names has yet been published), and Pilton, recorded in *DB, Somerset*, 8. 20, as 'Piltone', among the possessions of St Mary's, Glastonbury. There seems to be no way of adjudicating between these alternatives, and the possibility cannot be excluded that the name refers to a now lost village.

[3] 'Typhus' (from Gk. τυφός) is a late Latin word, meaning 'pride, arrogance'; used frequently by Goscelin, for example, *Historia maior de miraculis S. Augustini* c. 53, 'typo indignationis' (*ActaS*, Maii, vi. 406 B) and c. 54, 'typo exprobationis' (p. 406 D).

§ 20. At that time the priest in Pailton,[1] as was the custom,[2] directed that the feast of St Kenelm should be celebrated by a break from work. When the lady who presided over that village heard this, as she reclined at dinner on that very feast-day, she refuted it with arrogant pride,[3] hurled impatient words at the saint, and commanded with haughty contempt that no work should be interrupted. 'Just because of Kenelm', she said, 'I don't know why we should lose a day's profit.' Scarcely had she spoken when both her eyes shot out on to the table, as had happened above to the unworthy sister of the martyr. Now indeed in late repentance she calls on St Kenelm with grief and wailing, and begged that his feast day be celebrated with all reverence. Rightly she who despised the one special day of God's beloved, ceased to care about all days.[4] Furthermore her oxen, which were that day yoked up to carts, shook off all their reins and yokes and scattered so that they could not afterwards be found.[5]

§ 21. The story is also famous of how in Hereford a blacksmith was shamelessly working on that same feast day when his hammer stuck to his right hand, and the tongs to his left hand, and as his assistant was turning the grind-stone to sharpen a scythe his hand became embedded in the wood it was gripping, so that it could not be freed by striking it with chisels and hammers, and he was more himself held than holding.[6] It is said that when beseeching prayers

---

[4] Cf. Andrew of Fleury, *Miracula S. Benedicti* vi. 10, where a rich man who refused to acknowledge St Benedict's feast-day was punished, 'Ac ita qui unius diei cultor fore erubuit, nolens et inuitus cum maximo detrimento sui, totius anni ferias Benedicto patri exhibuit'; ed. E. de Certain, *Les Miracles de Saint Benoît* (Paris, 1858), pp. 232–3.

[5] It is intriguing to note the record of a miracle almost identical to this one, involving a man at Sapperton ('in Glawornae ciuitatis prouincia') who ploughed on St Dunstan's day (to whom Sapperton church was apparently dedicated—this dedication to Dunstan does not seem to be recorded elsewhere), spoke of the saint with contempt, and as he did so, felt one eye fall out of its socket. He nearly lost his oxen, and another man doing the same the following year lost half of his team. This is told by Eadmer, *Miracula S. Dunstani* c. 24 (Stubbs, *Memorials*, pp. 247–8), reworking the same story included only in certain MSS of Osbern's *Miracula* (ibid. pp. 144–5, in the footnotes). Their account could have been influenced by the miracle of Kenelm, either at the writing-up stage (though there is no textual similarity), or possibly at the level of the presumed Gloucestershire source for the story. It has not yet proved possible to discover whether this Sapperton was actually the same as the Sapperton (Glos.) which now has a church dedicated to St Kenelm (see p. cxix), let alone whether the two churches are one and the same, and that the dedication was altered at some stage.

[6] Miracles of adhesion, punishing work on both Sundays and feast days, occur in numerous saints' Lives. Cf. e.g. Goscelin, *Vita S. Wulsini* c. 15, where a woman who insisted upon spinning on St Wulfsige's day was said to have been stuck to her seat and her distaff: 'ita miro modo ipso opere quod ante inreuerenter tenebat iam inextricabili

uero factis*a* requirendo sancto retinacula quidem cessisse,*b* sed clausos*c* pugnos artius impressis*d* ungulis palme donec ad sanctum *e*medicum ueniretur*e* perdurasse. Conspexere*f* inde presentes*g* fratres impactis digitis *h*manum contractam*h* iamque luminaribus oblatis*i* sancto Kenelmo integre reparatam.*j*

§ 22. Item in ipsius natalicio cum ex tota Anglia ad eius festa annuo usu confluerent, cecus natus Lifsius*k* nomine[1] ibidem sancti martyris suffragia postulabat, cum ecce raptus in extasi coram ipso corruit, totoque uolutabatur et impingebatur uestibulo, anhelis*l* uocibus clamitando 'Sancte Kenelme parce mihi,*m* quid *n*me sic crucias?'*n* Interea contemplatur*o* puerum (ut postea referebat) speciosissimum *p*ac splendidissimum sibi assistere,*p* duo sydera prefulgida manu gestantem,*q* et ea*r* oculorum sedibus sibi*s* imprimentem. Nec mora, reuersus ad se reseratis*t* oculis profluente sanguine hausit diem,*u* mirabatur ignotas rerum species, mundi amplitudinem, lucis nitorem,[2] pro quo abbas*v* Goduuinus[3] cum fratribus grates *w*Deo immolat*w* excelsis laudibus.*x*

§ 23. Similiter alius aduenerat mutus a natiuitate altor canum et assecla[4] uenationum*y* Alfrici*z* uiri clarissimi, qui in uico *aa*ad Stertel*aa* mansitabat.[5] Hic quoque eodem die decidens in excessum mentis uidit fulgido decore paruulum cum cereo flagrante sibi

---

a de add. *L*   *b* stessisse *G*   *c* clanos *G*   *d* in ipsis *L*
e–e ueniretur medicum *L*   *f* consperere *L*   *g* perentes *L*   *h–h* manus contractas *B*   *i* cum prece add. *B*   *j* reparatas *B*   *k* Lefsius *BH*; Lissius *GL*; Leofsius *J*; Leoffius *P*   *l* hanelis *G*   *m* et add. *G*   *n–n* sic crucias me *B*   *o* contemplabatur *P*   *p–p* sibi assistere ac splendidissimum *G*   *q* tenentem *B*   *s* om. *P*   *s* om. *H*   *t* reserans *G*   *u* et add. *J*   *v* om. *B*   *w–w* Deo immolauit *H*; immolat Deo *J*; Deo immolabat (altered from immolat by later hand) *P*   *x* laudis uocibus. Explicit de sancto Kenelmo rege et martire *L* (ends here)   *y* nationum *P*   *z* Alurici *H*   *aa–aa* ad Stercel *G*; adstertel *P*

---

tenebatur' (Talbot, p. 81); cf. also Magnobod's *Vita S. Maurilii* c. 16 (*ActaS*, Sept. iv. 72–5, at 74 B); *Vita tertia S. Audomari* c. 41 (*ActaS*, Sept. iii. 406–15, at 415); *Miracula S. Bauonis* c. 30 (*ActaS*, Oct. i. 293–303, at 299); and *Miracula S. Gudwali* c. 71 (*ActaS*, Iun., i. 743–8, at 746–7).

[1] Lifsius/Lefsius is the Latinization of Leofsige, a name widely attested in Anglo-Saxon sources, though this particular Leofsige seems impossible to identify—see Searle, *Onomasticon*, and Von Feilitzen, *Pre-Conquest Personal Names*, p. 315.

[2] Cf. Goscelin, *Historia maior de miraculis S. Augustini* c. 49, 'noua luce infusa haurit lumen ubique diffusum. Miratur lucis candorem, mundi decorem, tam diuersas rerum formas et species' (*ActaS*, Maii, vi. 405 D), and c. 51, 'primo reseratis oculis ceco lux

were offered up to the saint the bonds were loosed, but the fists stayed clenched up with the nails ever more tightly pressed into the palm until they came before the holy physician. Thereupon the brothers who were present saw the contracted hand with its clenched fingers restored to wholeness, at the very moment when lamps had been offered up to St Kenelm.

§ 22. Again, on his birthday, as people flocked together from the whole of England for his feast, as was the yearly custom, a man born blind, named Leofsige,[1] implored the aid of the holy martyr. He fell to the ground in a fit in the presence of the saint, and rolled around and dashed himself against the entrance, crying out breathlessly: 'St Kenelm, have mercy upon me; why do you torture me in this way?' During this (as he later reported), he sees a most beautiful shining boy come to his aid, holding in his hand two incredibly bright stars, which he presses into the sockets of the blind eyes. Straightway, he came to himself, and with unclosed eyes flowing with blood, drank in the daylight, marvelled at the unfamiliar aspect of objects, the wideness of the world, and the brightness of the light.[2] For this Abbot Godwin[3] and all the brothers give thanks to God with high praises.

§ 23. Likewise another man, mute from birth, came—he was the kennelman and hunt-steward[4] of Ælfric, a nobleman, who lived in the village of *Stertel*.[5] On the same feast day he also, falling down in a seizure, saw a small child of bright beauty approach him with a

---

infunditur' (p. 406 B); also *Historia maior de aduentu S. Augustini* c. 36, 'resilientibus oculorum palpebris clarum diem hausit' (*PL* lxxx. 79 D).

[3] On Abbot Godwine, see p. 75 above.

[4] Cf. the frequent use of this word, though in a figurative sense, by Goscelin (*DMLBS*, s.v.); e.g. *Historia maior de miraculis S. Augustini* c. 34, 'summi clauigeri Augustinus assecla' (*ActaS*, May, vi. 402 B); and *Vita S. Ethelburge* c. 7, 'Christi asseclam' (Colker, 'Texts', p. 407).

[5] It has proved difficult to determine for certain where 'Stertel' might be, since placenames of a comparable form, from the Old English 'steort' (a promontory or tongue of land), are fairly common. Furthermore, the personal name 'Ælfric' was even commoner. A couple of possibilities present themselves; first, Sturthill in Dorset, which appears as 'Sterte' in *DB, Dorset*, 55: 19 (i. 83d), held by one 'Aluric' under the Confessor. Secondly, in Wiltshire, there is Stert, also held by an 'Aluric' during the reign of Edward; see *DB, Wilts.*, 27: 3 (i. 70d). There seems to be no way of deciding between these—the latter is slightly preferable in being just a little closer to Winchcombe geographically, though early recorded forms of Sturthill are most similar to our 'Stertel'. If *Vita et miracula* could confidently be associated with Goscelin, the record of a miracle in Wiltshire would be less surprising, given that he was, at the time, active in the diocese of Sherborne.

aduenire atque ita ardentem in os sibi patulum[a] impingere, sicque exiliens loquebatur recte. Queque prius [b]tantum poterat[b] audire iam ualebat[c] referre. Testabatur autem[d] dominus suus qui eum a paruulo norat,[e] quod nunquam antea locutus sit, et quod canes in uenando ad sui oris sonitum licet inconditum[f] assuefecerit.[g]

§ 24. Alius nichilominus mutus ad gradus presbiterii uelut amens hac illac iactabatur,[1] et miserabiliter sanctum Kenelmum inclamabat[h] ut sibi misereretur.[i] Isque[j] redditus loquele coram predicto abbate et fratribus turbisque frequentibus in laudem Dei omnes compulit qui in sanctis suis[k] gloriosus existit.[l] Interrogatus [m]autem ab ipso monasterii patre[m] quid angustie sibi fuisset cur ita uolutatus succlamasset,[n] iurabat se nichil sensisse, nichil prorsus scire, nisi quod excitatus a quiete redditus sit facundie.

§ 25. Debilem quoque repentem per humum quis digne referet[o] erectum? O erumnam[p] et necessitatem humanam![2] Ligneas soleas cauatis truncis alligauerat genibus[q] pro coturnis pedalibus, et calciatis[r] ligno poplitibus, nitebatur pro gressibus.[s] Scabellula pro [t]bacillis suppeditabant[t] manibus et egre[u] sustentabant labile[v] corpus. Videres hominem ad celestia contemplanda sublimatum, peccati conditione in reptile[w] conuersum.[3] Is igitur coram beato Kenelmo tota die [x]uniformiter genuflexus aut genu progressus[x] implorabat multis compertum salutis munus. Verum transacta solenni die cum iam sequenti diluculo pararet [y]discedere desperando,[y] subito corripitur miraculo. Rumpuntur fortia[z] lora lignorum,[4] excutiuntur hinc inde lignee conche genuum, surgit de trunco uir procerus in statum suum,[5] unde omnes cantant Domino in [aa]sancto suo[aa] laudis hymnum.

---

[a] paulatim B   [b-b] tamen B; tamen poterat GHP   [c] uolebat P
[d] om. B   [e] nouerat H   [f] mirabiliter add. B   [g] assuesserit G
[h] inclamitabat B   [i] miseretur G   [j] Ilico P   [k] om. G   [l] extitit P
[m-m] a patre monasterii B   [n] succlamasse G   [o] referret GP; referat H
[p] corumpnam G   [q] et add. J   [r] caluatis G   [s] gressus B
[t-t] baculis suppeditabat B   [u] egrum B   [v] labia B; debile P   [w] reptibile B   [x-x] informiter genuflexo B   [y-y] desperando discedere B
[z] fortiora B   [aa-aa] sanctis suis G

---

[1] 'Hac illac' is a relatively rare abverbial phrase—generally occurring as 'hac et illac', or 'hac illacque', as for example in Terence, *Eunuchus* i. 2. 25 ('hac atque illac perfluo'); but cf. id., *Heautontimorumenos* iii. 2. 1 ('hac illac circumcursa'). Cf. also Augustine, *Confessiones* x. 17. 11 ('per haec omnia discurro et uolito hac illac'), ed. L. Verheijen, *CCSL* xxvii (1981), p. 168; and id., *Enarrationes in Psalmos* cxxxii. 3. 17 ('solent ire hac illac'), ed. E. Dekkers and J. Fraipont, *CCSL* xxxviii–xl (1966), iii. 1928.

lighted candle, and stick it, thus burning, into his open mouth, and then, leaping up, the dumb man spoke clearly. Those things which previously he had only been able to hear he could now express in words. His master, who had known him from childhood, testified that he had never spoken before, and that he had accustomed the dogs in the hunt to the sound of his voice although it was incomprehensible.

§ 24. Another man, no less dumb, at the steps of the presbytery was dashed this way and that as if mad,[1] and cried out wretchedly to St Kenelm to have mercy on him. He, restored to speech in the sight of the aforenamed abbot and the brothers and the assembled crowds, urged everyone to praise God, who is glorious in his saints. When asked by the same abbot of the monastery what distress had come upon him that he should have thus rolled on the ground and cried out, he swore that he had felt nothing, and knew of nothing whatsoever except that, stirred from sleep, he was restored to fluent speech.

§ 25. Also, who can properly restore to uprightness a crippled man who crawls through the dust? O tribulation and human need![2] He had bound wooden soles to his hollow disfigured knees in place of shoes, and, his knees shod with wood, he struggled forwards instead of walking. Little stools in his hands served as walking sticks and scarcely held up his limp body. Here you may see a human being who had been raised up to contemplate heaven, turned by his sinful state into a crawling creature.[3] The whole day he knelt or walked always in the same way on his knees before St Kenelm, begging for the gift of healing which has been granted to many. But when the feast-day was over, as he was already preparing to depart in despair at dawn the next day, he is seized by a sudden miracle. The stout thongs binding the wood snap[4] and the wooden shells on his knees are hurled away on each side, and from the mutilated wreck a man tall in stature rises up to full height,[5] at which all sing a hymn of praise to God working in His saint.

---

[2] Cf. Goscelin, *Historia translationis S. Augustini* i. 3, 'O miserandam cladis humanae conditionem! Non poterat hec . . . suas erumnas proloqui' (*ActaS*, Maii, vi. 414 B).

[3] On parallels for this account, see above pp. xcix–c.

[4] Cf. Goscelin, *Historia maior de miraculis S. Augustini* c. 36, 'franguntur et dissiliunt fortia lignorum robora' (*ActaS*, Maii, vi. 402 D).

[5] Cf. ibid. c. 6, 'Nec mora in statum suum erigitur' (*ActaS*, Maii, vi. 395 D); and *Miracula S. Edithe* c. 18, 'is apud apostolorum alumnam in statum suum de trunco erectus est' (Wilmart, 'La légende', p. 293).

§ 26. Alio tempore uenerat huc quidam Saxonicus[a] ferro uentrem[b] accinctus per uisum de tam longinquo in Angliam ad beatum Kenelmum ut ipse referebat uenire iussus, nimirum apud ipsum soluendus.[1] Quindecim autem diebus anticipauerat eius natalitiam sollennitatem, postulans speratam ipsius absolutionem. Iam uero instantem celebritatem attentioribus uigiliis et orationibus exercebat, utpote qui hanc sibi maxime remediabilem expectabat. Sed expectandus est Dominus donec misereatur, qui non nostro sed suo qui nos fecit arbitrio nobis salutem operatur. Itaque finita illa luce sollenni, obtenebrescere[c] cepit in aduena lux presumpte[d] fidei. Mane[e] cum discedere salute iam desperata pararet,[f] ualedicens [g]cum alto clamabat suspirio[g] 'O beate Kenelme, celitus mihi reuelate [h]et in liberationem promissam[h] de tam longinquo quesite, quomodo tandem mihi inuente[i] et expectate[j] derelinquis me, ut sine spe remedii cogar abscedere?' Tali modo eo conquerente statim ferreus nexus eius confractus dissiliit,[k] et absolutus reus cum uenia peccatorum in gratiarum actionem se saluatori prostrauit. Cui[l] exesum et liuentem uterum molli cera abbatis refouit benignitas, donec rediret[m] sanitas.[2]

[a] om. J   [b] om. B   [c] obtenebrascere P   [d] presentis B   [e] ergo add. G   [f] parararet J   [g-g] clamabat cum suspirio B   [h-h] pro liberatione promissa B   [i] inuentus H   [j] expectatus H   [k] desiliit G; dissiliut J   [l] cuius P   [m] redderetur B; ad integrum add. H

---

[1] Miracles of this kind follow a common narrative thread: a murderer (often a parricide) is condemned by the local bishop to exile in penitential chains or a bond made of the murder weapon; he drags himself from shrine to shrine in vain, seeking divine absolution, until finally told in a dream to go to England (usually to a specific shrine), where, after vigils and prayer, the chains are released, with some violence; sometimes the sores caused by the bonds are also miraculously healed. The motivation for the inclusion of these stories in the saint's 'repertoire' was presumably to demonstrate the extent to which he shared the apostles' power to bind and to loose, to emphasize how widely his reputation had spread, and to highlight his superiority over those whose shrines had been visited in vain. Goscelin described several such incidents: in *Miracula S. Yuonis*, a Venetian who had murdered his sister; three parricidal brothers ('saxones'); and a man from Cologne (Macray, *Chron. Rames.*, pp. lxvii–lxviii); in *Historia maior de miraculis S. Augustini*, cc. 34–6 (*ActaS*, Maii, vi. 402), and cc. 50–1 (p. 405), involving a 'gentis Germanicae uir'; and *Miracula S. Edithe* c. 18 (ed. Wilmart, p. 293). Cf. also Lantfred, *Translatio et miracula S. Swithuni* c. 24, on the penitent 'de transmarinis partibus'; Eadmer, *Miracula S. Oswaldi* c. 2 (Raine, *HCY* ii. 44–5) describing the release of one 'natione Saxonicus', whose lesions were also miraculously healed; and *Passio S. Eadwardi*, ed. Fell, p. 15. Also comparable is Byrhtferth's story of how St Ecgwine bound his own feet 'uinculis ferreis', and threw the key into the river (*Vita*, i. 13); and of the man shackled with nine chains, who was miraculously freed at Evesham (ibid., iv. 7). For a witness to the age of this practice, see Gregory of Tours, *De gloria confessorum* c. 85, 'Quidam fratricida pro enormitate criminis, ferreis circulis alligatus, praeceptum habuit

§ 26. On another occasion, a Saxon came here with his belly all bound up in iron, commanded in a vision, as he himself related, to come from that long distance to England, to St Kenelm, to receive sure release from him.[1] He had come fifteen days in advance of the feast of the saint's birth, seeking his much hoped-for absolution. Already he was observing the imminent feast with more attentive vigils and prayers, seeing that he expected it especially to bring healing for him. But we must wait upon the Lord until He has mercy, since He who created us brings us salvation not according to our bidding but according to His own. Therefore, that day of celebration being ended, the light of supposed faith began to grow dim in the foreigner. In the morning, as he was preparing to depart despairing of any cure, he cried out his farewell with a deep sigh: 'O blessed Kenelm, revealed to me from heaven, and sought from such a long distance as promised deliverance, how can you, whom I have at last found and long waited for, leave me, so that I am forced to depart without hope of a cure?' As he thus lamented, immediately his iron fetter sprang away all shattered in pieces, and the guilty man now pardoned, his sins forgiven, prostrated himself in thanksgiving to his saviour. The kindly abbot soothed his abraded and bruised belly with soft wax, until his health returned.[2]

ut septem annis loca sanctorum peragrando circuiret', ed. W. Arndt and B. Krusch, *MGH*, SRM i (Hanover, 1885), p. 803; and *De vitis patrum* viii. 6, describing the sight of broken fetters and chains hung up around a particular shrine (*MGH*, SRM i. 697). Chained penitents must have become quite a familiar sight at medieval shrines; cf. C. Vogel, *La Discipline pénitentielle en Gaule des origines à la fin du VIIᵉ siècle* (Paris, 1952), pp. 162–3. Surviving medieval handbooks of penitence seem, however, only to specify the first part of this particular penance, namely the exile (generally for seven years), and not the second part which plays such an important role in these miracles; but H. J. Schmitz, *Die Bussbücher und die Bussdisciplin der Kirche* (Mainz, 1883), pp. 152–3, describes a kind of penance for murder (especially of blood relations) by enforced exile, sometimes with the iron of the murder-weapon forged into a band of some kind. Cf. also the detailed discussion by A. J. Binterim, *Die vorzüglichsten Denkwürdigkeiten der Christkatholischen Kirche*, 7 vols. in 12 parts (Mainz, 1825–41), v (3). 133–59; where it is noted that this very public penance became widespread in the 10th cent., and remained current longest in France and Germany (p. 157). Almost all the above examples describe the penitents as foreigners (in a way, stating the obvious of an exile), often specifically 'saxonici' or 'saxones'. The present example differs little from others, except that the cause for penitence is not mentioned. An unusual feature is that the abbot of Winchcombe himself is said to have applied a salve to the penitent's lesions (only the case of the young Venetian is comparable; see next note).

[2] Cf. Goscelin, *Miracula S. Yuonis*, 'gratias abbati et fratribus refuderit, maxime quod egrotantem tanta benignitate refouerint' (Macray, *Chron. Rames.*, p. lxviii). A somewhat later instance of the use of warm wax to heal sores is described by Adam of Eynsham in his *Magna Vita S. Hugonis*, ii. 10; ed. D. H. Farmer and D. L. Douie, 2 vols., NMT (1961–2); OMT (1985).

Excusso etiam ferro ab alterius brachio medietas circuli supra chorum fratrum euolauit,[a] reliqua uero medietas inueniri non potuit.

§ 27. Sed[b] quia lux tanto clarius quanto uicinius conspicitur,
oculis et[c] manu fidei proximius attrectentur nuper patrata miracula.
De proxima uilla[1] Sudham[d] ante altare beati Kenelmi pater illatum
proiecit filium ita contractum ut calcanei natibus infixi et manus
hinc inde hererent lateri, nec poterat nisi portando moueri loco. Is
ergo[e] abbate proximo[f] Godrico[2] uespertinam[g] antiphonam in euangelio incipiente, absolutus subita uirtute cunctis aspicientibus
supra pedes stetit et manus in gratiarum actionem Deo extendit.[h]

§ 28. Anno autem preterito complacuit presenti patri monasterii
et fratribus quatinus ad antiquum sue passionis locum reuisendum
deferretur[i] beatus Kenelmus.[3] Cumque[j] hospitarentur[k] in oppido[4]
Wic,[l] illustrissimi uiri[5] Osberni[m] filius sursum uersis oculorum
pupillis uisibusque latentibus sub palpebris uelut in[n] nube stellis
cecus aderat. Qui orans ibi ad sanctum Kenelmum utraque acie in
rectum conuersa protinus attigit[o] lucis gaudia.

§ 29. Ipsa uero nocte [p]omnibus somno[p] oppressis candela ardens
super altare coram apposito[q] sancti corpore de candelabro cecidit,
diuque[r] super pallia[s] et lintheamina altaris acsi super siccum
lapidem arsit.[6] Cumque monachi ceterique[t] ministri expergefacti ad

[a] euolat G	[b] Et B	[c] om. B	[d] Sutham B	[e] igitur H
[f] om. H; presente P	[g] uespertinamque P		[h] ostendit H	[i] deferretur
in D was later altered to deferretur by the addition of an e above the line				[j] Cum B
[k] hospitaretur BH	[l] Wich B; Wicc P		[m] Osberti G	[n] sub B
[o] optinuit H	[p-p] somno omnibus B		[q] apposita G	[r] denumque B
[s] pallam B	[t] et ceteri B			

[1] This is probably present-day Southam Delabere, Glos., about four miles WSW of
Winchcombe (Smith, *Place-Names of Gloucestershire*, p. 89). Held at Domesday by St
Mary's, Worcester (*DB, Glos.* 3. 7; i. 165a), as it was already in the late tenth century (S
1308 = BCS 1166 and 1167).
[2] Godric became abbot of Winchcombe in 1054, but was subsequently deposed by
William the Conqueror, probably in 1066, as an opponent of the Conquest (*Heads*,
p. 79).
[3] Presumably a trip to Clent.
[4] Since Wick is a fairly common place-name, it is not easy to distinguish the modern
equivalent of this 'Wic'. In view of the context, two possibilities present themselves:
Droitwich, Worcs., and Wick, a hamlet near Pershore, both of which might have been
on the supposed route taken by the monks carrying Kenelm to Clent (see pp. 69 and 70
above). In *DB, Worcs.* (*passim*), Droitwich appears as 'Wich', and variously as 'Wic' and
'Wich' from about the 9th cent. to the 13th (see Mawer and Stenton, *Place-Names of
Worcestershire*, p. 285). As the only place in the Midlands where salt was produced, it
must have been a large town by the eleventh century, and more worthy of the designation 'oppidum' than Wick near Pershore. Cf. E. Gee, 'A miracle of St Kenelm in MS.
Douce 368', *Notes and Queries*, ccxxxi (1986), 149–54.

When the iron was hurled from the arm of another man, half of the ring flew up over the monks' choir, and the other half could not even be found.

§ 27. But because a light is brighter the closer at hand it is seen, miracles recently brought about are more closely groped for by the searching eyes and fumbling hand of faith. From the neighbouring village of Southam[1] a father brought his son and cast him before the altar of St Kenelm. He was so crookedly deformed that his heels dug into his buttocks and both his hands pressed into his sides, and he could not stir from the spot except by being carried. And so, as the next abbot, Godric,[2] was beginning the evening antiphon to the gospel reading, this boy was released by a sudden miraculous power and, in the sight of all, stood on his feet and stretched out his hands in thanksgiving to God.

§ 28. Last year, the present abbot of the monastery, and the brothers, decided to take St Kenelm to revisit the ancient site of his passion.[3] When they were staying in the town of Wick,[4] the son of a nobleman, Osbern, was present.[5] His eye-balls were turned upwards and the pupils hidden under the eye-lids like stars behind a cloud, so that he was blind. As he prayed there to St Kenelm, each pupil was forthwith returned to its correct position, and he attained the joys of the daylight.

§ 29. That same night, when all were overcome with sleep, a candle burning on the altar, right next to where the body of the saint had been placed, fell from the candlestick, and for a long time burnt on the altar-cloths and linen as if on dry stone.[6] When the monks and other servants, awaking to their great negligence,

---

[5] This could be Osbern, son of Richard fitz Scrob, a Norman who had settled in Herefordshire at the time of the Confessor, and continued to hold land after the Conquest. Osbern was lord of Richard's castle in Herefordshire, succeeded his father in his estates, and is recorded in *DB* as holding substantial amounts of land in Worcestershire, including Clifton-on-Teme (*DB*, *Worcs*. 19: 3; i. 176d), and also in Gloucestershire. See Harmer, *Writs*, p. 569. Alternatively, he could be Osbern Giffard who held estates in Gloucestershire, as well as a salt-house in Droitwich (*DB*, *Glos*. 50: 1; i. 168c).

[6] Cf. Wulfstan, *Vita S. Æthelwoldi* c. 36 (ed. Lapidge and Winterbottom, *Wulfstan*, p. 54), on the candle which fell on a book. And especially compare Goscelin, *Historia translationis S. Augustini episcopi* i. 7, where a very similar incident is described, 'candela oblata, candelabro negligenter affixa, super tumulum sancti linteis et palliis solemniter ornatum decidit, ibique trium pedum tractum signante fauilla (aberant enim custodes) exarsit. Tandem superuentum est, candela ablata, fauilla excussa, lintea et pallia prorsus intacta fulsere' (*ActaS*, Maii, vi. 410 B). Cf. also *Historia translationis* i. 38 (ibid. 419 C); and *Visio de S. Ethelburga* c. 3, 'lintheamina et pallia' (Colker, 'Texts', p. 454).

tantam negligentiam suam exilissent, inuenerunt candelam ad mensuram ulne *ªfauilla signanteª* conflagratam, raptimque*ᵇ* leuantes candelam, excussa fauilla uiderunt omnia illesa, nullam*ᶜ* prorsus incendii uel cerei fluoris maculam habentia. Quis tunc in tanto populo*ᵈ* tacere Dei preconia poterat in martyre suo? § **30.** In Clentum*ᵉ* uero delatus locum monumenti sui tertio miraculo celebrat.*ᶠ* Nam ibi puellam terretenus inclinatam, gratia saluatoris erexit,*ᵍ* secundum illam uidelicet curuam in euangelio¹ restitutam.*ʰ*

§ **31.** Quidam miserabiliter a natiuitate contractus erat talos *ⁱuidelicet natibusⁱ* habens impressos manusque retortas, adeo ut digiti retrorsum brachiis inhererent. Hunc frater suus carnalis sanitatis gratia, per plerasque deportauerat ecclesias, sanctorum requirens suffragia. Summo tandem cum labore peruenit Romam, sancti Petri cum lacrimis expetens beneficia. Nec ei cessit in uacuum, tanti itineris perrexisse*ʲ* spacium. Edocetur enim per sompnium ut in patriam cito redeat, *ᵏlocum uocabuloᵏ* Wincelcumbam*ˡ* adeat, et a sancto martyre Kenelmo fratris sui salutem obtineat.² Quod gratanter accipiens, laboremque spe salutis paruipendens, debilem fratrem huc a Roma detulit, et ante altare deposuit. Cumque summa cordis intentione*ᵐ* sanctum martyrem uterque deposceret, debilis sopore depressus puerum speciosissimum de altari uidit descendere aureaque uirga quam manu gestabat se tangere, et ut surgeret imperare. Ilico mirum in modum qui nisi manibus alienis nunquam loco motus est supra pedes suos stetit, cursuque ueloci brachiis extentis altari super incumbens, *ⁿinfantem predictumⁿ* sanatorem suum ut ipse postea retulit nisus*ᵒ* est apprehendere. Postquam enim uirga salutis eum tetigerat, uisus est illi uelociter altare conscendere, scriniumque quo sacra

ᵃ⁻ᵃ fauillam signanter *B*   *ᵇ* raptim *B*   *ᶜ* nullamque *P*   *ᵈ om. G*
ᵉ Clenthun *B*; Clento *G*   *ᶠ* celebrauit *B*   *ᵍ* erigit *H*   *ʰ* His aliisque
quam plurimis uirtutibus in sancto suo Kenelmo Dei lucent magnalia, deuotis fidelibus
salutifera, cuius intercessio sancta nobis obtineat ueniam et eterna gaudia per regis et
saluatoris gratiam regnantis in secula, AMEN *add. B*; His aliisque quam plurimis
uirtutibus lucent in sancto suo Kenelmo Dei magnalia, deuotis fidelibus salutifera,
cuius intercessio sancta nobis obtineat ueniam et eterna gaudia per gratiam saluatoris
regnantis in secula, AMEN *add. G*   *ⁱ⁻ⁱ* natibus uidelicet *J*   *ʲ* transmeasse
H   *ᵏ⁻ᵏ* uocabulo locum *H*   *ˡ* Wilchelcumbam *H*; Winchelcumba *J*; Wincelcumba *P*   *ᵐ* deuotione *P*   *ⁿ⁻ⁿ* predictum infantem *P*   *ᵒ* uisus *P*

---

¹ Luke 13: 11–13.
² Cf. Lantfred, *Translatio et miracula S. Swithuni* c. 16, for a similar miracle in which a

leapt up, they found the candle burnt the length of an ell, as the embers showed. Quickly lifting up the candle and shaking off the ashes they saw that everything was unharmed, with not a single mark from the fire or the melted wax. Who then amongst such a great throng of people could keep silent the praises of God in His martyr?

§ 30. When he was taken to Clent he celebrated the place of his burial with a third miracle. For there, by the grace of the Saviour, he raised upright a girl, who had been stooped down to the ground, just like that crooked woman restored in the Gospel.[1]

§ 31. A certain man was from birth wretchedly crippled, so that his heels pressed into his buttocks, and his hands were bent back in such a way that his fingers stuck into his arms. His brother, for the sake of bodily healing, had carried him through many churches and sought the help of the saints. At length, with the utmost labour he reached Rome, imploring tearfully the aid of St Peter. Nor did it happen to be in vain that he had come on such a long journey. For it was shown him in a dream that he should return quickly to his native land, go to the place called Winchcombe and obtain healing for his brother from the holy martyr Kenelm.[2] Accepting this with gratitude, and, in the hope of a cure, counting the labour as nothing, he carried his crippled brother hither from Rome, and placed him before the altar. When both of them were beseeching the holy martyr with intense concentration of mind, the cripple was overcome by sleep and saw a beautiful boy descend from the altar, touch him with the golden staff which he held in his hand and tell him to get up. There and then in a miraculous way he who had never moved an inch, except in the hands of another person, stood on his own two feet, and with swift steps and outstretched arms he leaned over the altar and struggled to grasp the child who had been his healer, as he himself later recounted. For after the healing staff had touched him, it seemed to him that the child quickly climbed up on to the altar and entered the shrine where the

'caecatus' went to Rome and was there informed about the curative powers of St Swithun. Cf. Goscelin, *Translatio S. Mildrethe cum miraculorum attestatione* c. 24, 'manus pugilis digitos contorte palme insertos acsi clauos gemebat infixos; nodosum genu se in terga curuauerat: pes calcaneum ex talibus affixerat, et caro carni concreta uelut brachium humero inoleuerat' (Rollason, 'Translation', pp. 190–1). The invalid there described goes first to St Albans, then Westminster where he is told in a vision to go to Thanet for a cure. Cf. also Goscelin, *Historia maior de miraculis S. Augustini* c. 3 (*ActaS*, Maii, vi. 394).

eius ossa requiescunt intrare. Qua de re ualde letantes qui aderant, Deum in sanctis suis mirabilem collaudabant.[1] Vir autem ille omnium membrorum plenissime uigore percepto plurimis hic[a] postea mansit annis, habens semper cicatrices patulas in natibus, ubi calcaneos infixos habuerat.[b]

[a] *om.* P   [b] ad laudem et gloriam Domini nostri Iesu Christi, qui cum patre et spiritu sancto uiuit et regnat Deus per omnia secula seculorum, AMEN. *add. H.* Multis quidem et aliis uirtutibus sanctum martirem suum Kenelmum diuina miraficauit potentia, que per ueterum incuriam uel historiographorum paucitatem nostre subtrahuntur memorie. Nos itaque uirtutem omnium operatori Deo cum ymnis et laudibus gratias referentes ipsius imploremus clementiam ut per huius sancti sui intercessionem ad

holy bones rested. Those who were present rejoiced greatly at this happening, and praised God who is wonderful in His saints.[1] That man, having received the full strength of all his limbs, stayed here afterwards for many years, always bearing the clear scars on his buttocks, where his heels had dug in.

electorum suorum nos perducat consortium, qui in trinitate perfecta uiuit et regnat Deus per omnia seculorum secula, AMEN. EXPLICIT PASSIO BEATI KENELMI REGIS ET MARTYRIS *add. J.* per omnia benedictus Deus, AMEN *add. P*

---

[1] Ps. 67(68): 36 ('mirabilis Deus in sanctis suis').

VITA SANCTI RVMWOLDI

SIGLA OF MANUSCRIPTS

A London, BL, Arundel 91, fos. 195^v–198^r (s. xii$^{1/3}$)

C Cambridge, Corpus Christi College, 9, pp. 53–8 (s. xi$^{3/4}$)

E Canterbury, Cathedral Library, E. 42, fo. 54^r (s. xii^{in})

L London, BL, Lansdowne 436, fos. 104^r–105^v (s. xiv^{med})

R London, BL, Royal 13. A. x, fos. 55^v–61^v (s. xii^1)

S John of Tynemouth, *Sanctilogium Angliae, Walliae, Scotiae et Hiberniae* (s. xiv^1)

T Dublin, Trinity College Library, 172 (B. 2. 7), pp. 239–43 (s. xiv^{med})

W Oxford, Worcester College, 273 (s. xii^{in})

^aINCIPIT PROLOGVS IN VITAM SANCTI RVMWOLDI.^a
Legitur Christi magnalia enarrare que in sanctis gloriose superno
nutu effulsere atque eorumdem sanctorum preclara merita ad Dei
gloriam propalare, nil aliud est quam Christum solum regem cum
patre sanctoque spiritu super omnia regnantem colendumque suis
fidelibus predicare.[1] Et quia plurima eorum eximia opera multis
sunt credentibus incognita, siue propter eruditorum^b precedentium
neglegentiam,[2] seu rudium insipientiam, aliquibus equum non
habentibus animum[3] estimatur si a modernis scribuntur olim a Deo
suisque famulis aliqua preclaro notamine facta esse apochripha uel
stolido scemate^c compta,[4] unde a falso talium detractionis sibilo
blasphemantur, eorumque iniusta redargutione^d redarguuntur.[5] Et
hoc non ob aliud agunt nisi ut ab hominibus humanum^e sibi
adquirant fauorem, perhibentes se esse didascalos in plebe, uel quia
agitantur stimulis[6] inuidie.^f Nos itaque, qui cogimur exhortationi-
bus precibusque fidelium diuinum pandere eloquium, floccipendimus[7] eorum ambages, quoniam in illo confidimus qui dixit:

^{a–a} VITA SANCTI RVMWALDI CONFESSORIS C   ^b erudiatorum C
^c stemate C; themate R   ^d reprehensione C   ^e inanum C
^f inuide C

[1] 'Legitur' suggests that the author was citing a particular text, but hitherto none has
come to light which corresponds to this introductory flourish. With what follows compare Gregory of Tours' preface to *Liber de Miraculis Beati Andreae apostoli*, ed. M. Bonnet,
MGH, SRM, i (Hanover, 1885), pp. 821–46, at 827: 'repperi librum de uirtutibus sancti
Andreae apostoli, qui propter nimiam uerbositatem a nonnullis apocrifus dicebatur; de
quo placuit . . . admiranda miracula clauderentur, quod ei legentibus praestaret gratiam
et detrahentium auferret inuidiam.' There is no dedicatee or addressee for the prologue
of *Vita S. Rumwoldi*, which might have helped to identify the exact place and time of
composition.
[2] The negligence of predecessors was a common hagiographical complaint, tendered
partly as an excuse for a dearth of material. Compare Ælfric's comments on Swithun,
referred to above, p. xxxv, and Whatley, *Saint of London*, p. 212, on a similar use of the
topos in Arcoid's *Miracula S. Erkenwaldi* (composed 1141).
[3] Note the way in which 'equum' and 'animum' have been interlaced with the
pronoun 'aliquis' and its participle, presumably as a stylistic affectation. Compare the
separation of 'falso' and 'sibilo' which follows.
[4] The grecisms 'apocrifa', 'scemate', and 'didascalos' were evidently used in an effort
to imbue the prologue with a certain erudite loftiness of tone. None of them is, however,
particularly obscure; 'apoc(h)ryphus' may be found quite widely in Christian latinity,
either referring specifically to apocryphal texts, or more generally with the meaning
'obscure' or 'hidden' (cf. *TLL* and *DMLBS* s.v.); 'didascalus' or '-ulus' (from Greek
διδάσκαλος) occurs several times in the prose and verse of Aldhelm (for example, *De
uirginitate*, Ehwald, p. 280. 12; *Carmen de uirginitate* 2154), and also in Lantfred (preface
to *Translatio et miracula*). With the use here of 'scema', one might compare the sense of

HERE BEGINS THE PROLOGUE TO THE LIFE OF ST RUMWOLD. We are taught that to expound the great works of Christ which have by heavenly assent gloriously shone forth in the saints, and to divulge the distinguished merits of those same saints to the glory of God, is nothing other than to preach that Christ is the sole King, Who, with the Father and the Holy Spirit, rules over all things, and that He is to be worshipped by His faithful people.[1] A large number of the excellent works of the saints are unknown to many believers, either because of the negligence of the scholars of the past[2] or because of the folly of ignorant men. Consequently it is thought by some, who have no goodwill,[3] that, if any acts of outstanding note performed in the past by God and by His servants are written down by contemporary men, they are spurious, or composed in a coarse style,[4] and are therefore blasphemed with the false hissing of slander by such people, and mocked with unjust mockery.[5] But they do this for no other reason than to gain human favour for themselves from men, calling themselves teachers of the populace, or because they are pricked by the goads of envy.[6] I therefore, driven by the exhortations and prayers of the faithful to disclose divine eloquence, account their circumlocutions of little value,[7] since I trust in Him Who said:

Vita S. Dunstani by 'B', c. 1 (prologus), 'crisidineo schemate ... disserere gestiebam' (Stubbs, p. 4); a much earlier parallel is Aldhelm, *Epistola ad Acircium'* c. 4, 'Romanis concatenato scemate scribens' (Ehwald, p. 74. 15) describing a Pauline epistle (Aldhelm more frequently used 'schemata' as a technical term in *De metris*). The word subsequently seems to have taken on the meaning 'garb' or 'habit'; cf. Goscelin, *Historia translationis S. Augustini* c. 54 (Augustine appears in dream), 'pontificali affulsit schemate' (*ActaS*, May, vi. 426 c). Part of the same inflated style of writing is the non-Classical neologism 'notamen' (not in *OLD* or *TLL*), which is to be found as synonym for 'nomen' in various grammatical handbooks, deriving ultimately from Priscian, *Institutiones*, ii. 22, 'nomen quasi notamen', ed. M. Hertz, 2 vols., H. Keil, Grammatici Latini, ii–iii (Leipzig, 1855–8), i. 57. The hagiographer may have encountered the word in Isidore, *Etym.* i. 7. 1, 'nomen dictum est notamen'. Similarly, 'floccipendimus' derives ultimately from Terence (e.g. *Eunuchus* iii. 1. 21), but is found frequently in Anglo-Latin authors from the 10th cent. onwards, for example in Oda of Canterbury (preface to Frithegod's *Breuiloquium*, ed. Campbell, pp. 1–3), and Lantfred (*Translatio et miracula*, cc. 3, 10, 36). On the use here of such vocabulary, see Lapidge, 'Hermeneutic style', pp. 102–3; and cf. pp. clxiv–clxv on the author's stylistic affectations.

[5] The syntax of this long period is sufficiently contorted to hamper comprehension. The parenthetical clause 'si a modernis ... facta' intrudes into the construction of indirect statement 'estimatur ... esse apochrifa'. Cf. the comments on p. clxv above.

[6] Cf. 'antiqui hostis millenos inuidiae stimulos' in the preface to Stephen of Ripon's *Vita S. Wilfridi*, ed. Levison, *MGH*, SRM, vi. 193.

[7] See n. 4 above.

'Aperi os tuum et ego implebo illud.'[1] Et nos quidem os nostrum aperimus de uita et meritis beati Rumwoldi confessoris, quem Deus sua dispositione*a* in ortu illius secundum carnem loqui mirabiliter fecit, ac huic mundo ad suam gloriam manifestauit. *b*EXPLICIT PROLOGVS.*b*

§ 1. *c*INCIPIT VITA SANCTI RVMWOLDI.*c* Fuit namque*d* in insula maiori Britannia quidam rex *e*nomine Penda*e* *f*clarus potentia*f* honestate elegans,[2] qui sacri baptismatis unda perfusus[3] Christique crismate linitus*g* copulauit sibi uxorem,[4] ex qua genuit filiam, que post perceptionem sacre fidei, in ipsa tenera etate cepit Deum timere eiusque mandatis inherere.[5] Eodemque*h* tempore in predicta insula plurimi reges regnabant ex quibus aliqui erant idolis seruientes, aliqui uero *i*Deum uerum*i* colentes. Inter quos unus extitit rex potens atque*j* strenuus, quamuis nostre fidei ignarus,[6] qui filiam Pende regis diligens petiit eam a parentibus sibi dari in coniugium. Cuius uoto*k* annuens *l*rex Penda*l* cum suis magnatibus uel propinquis, cum diuersis *m*honoribus ac donis*m* tradidit illi dilectam filiam in coniunctione*n* legitimi coniugii,[7] cum iam foret in adulta etate, eo uidelicet tenore ut illi liceret Deum patrem omnipotentem eiusque filium unicum Dominum nostrum Iesum Christum cum sancto spiritu colere, suisque legibus sanctis parere. Hoc itaque pacto cum concessa esset puella uiro, ibat idem sponsus cum sua sponsa festino gressu ad propria, quo celebres

a dispotione *R*   *b-b* om. *C*   *c-c* om. *C*; CONFESSORIS .III. NONAS NOVEMBRIS add. *A*   *d* om. *AS*   *e-e* Penda nomine *A*   *f-f* potentia clarus *R*   *g* litus *A*   *h* Eodem *AT*   *i-i* uerum Deum *RT*   *j* ac *AT*   *k* uota *A*   *l-l* Penda rex *C*   *m-m* donis atque honoribus *RT* *n* coniunctionem *A*

---

[1] Ps. 80 (81): 11 ('Dilata os tuum et implebo illud').

[2] The accession of Penda of Mercia (son of Pybba) is dated by *ASC* to 626; he is stated to have been 50 at the time, and to have reigned for thirty years. Yet the way Bede describes Penda's involvement with King Cadwallon in the war against Edwin in 633, gives the impression that he was not king then (*HE* ii. 20): 'Penda uiro strenuissimo . . ., qui et ipse ex eo tempore gentis eiusdem regno annis XX et IIbus uaria sorte praefuit'. Penda was killed in 655, at the battle of Winwæd against Oswiu (*ASC* s.a., and Bede, *HE* iii. 24).

[3] There is no mention by Bede, or any other source, of Penda ever having been baptized; he is portrayed, on the contrary, as an inveterate pagan: 'Penda cum omni Merciorum gente idolis deditus, et Christiani erat nominis ignarus' (*HE* ii. 20). But his stance seems to have been one of indifference, 'Nec prohibuit Penda rex, quin etiam in sua, hoc est Merciorum, natione uerbum, siqui uellent audire, praedicaretur' (*HE* iii. 21). The baptism of Penda's son Peada is reported in the same chapter; cf. Wallace-Hadrill, *Historical Commentary*, p. 116.

[4] Presumably Queen Cynwisse, referred to only once, by Bede, *HE* iii. 24.

'Open thy mouth and I will fill it.'[1] And so I open my mouth to speak of the life and merits of St Rumwold the confessor, whom God by His own direction caused miraculously to speak at the moment of his coming forth into flesh, and whom He showed clearly to this world, in glorification of Himself. HERE ENDS THE PROLOGUE.

§ 1. HERE BEGINS THE LIFE OF ST RUMWOLD. There was in the greater island of Britain a certain king named Penda, renowned for his power and excellent in integrity,[2] who, when he had been sprinkled with the water of holy baptism[3] and had received the anointing of Christ, took to himself a wife.[4] She bore him a daughter, who, on receiving the holy faith, began at an early age to fear God and keep to His commandments.[5] At the same time there were ruling in that island many kings, some of whom were enslaved to idols, while others worshipped the true God. Among these was one king who was powerful and vigorous, though ignorant of our faith.[6] He loved King Penda's daughter, and asked her parents to give her to him in marriage. King Penda, assenting, together with his nobles and kinsmen, to this wish, handed over his beloved daughter, along with various honours and gifts, to this man in the union of lawful marriage,[7] since she was now of age. He made the condition that she should be allowed to worship God the Almighty Father and His only Son, our Lord Jesus Christ, with the Holy Ghost, and to obey His holy laws. When this had been agreed upon and the girl had been granted to him, that husband went

---

[5] The identity of this daughter is uncertain. See the discussion above, p. clxii.

[6] It is not obvious who this 'rex' is meant to be; we are not even told which is his king-dom until c. 3. See above pp. clxi–clxiii.

[7] The betrothal and marriage of Rumwold's parents is more likely to reflect the customs with which the 11th-cent. hagiographer was familiar, than the circumstances of a real or supposed 7th-cent. arrangement (unless he was making a conscious effort to archaize). It is possible to gain some idea of the workings of betrothal and marriage in late Anglo-Saxon England from the tract entitled 'Be wifmannes beweddunge' (written perhaps between about 970 and 1060) found in the early 12th-cent. 'Textus Roffensis', fos. 94ᵛ–95, and under the rubric 'Hu man mæden weddian sceal 7 swylce forewarde þær aghon to beonne', in CCCC 383, pp. 84–6, and also in the Latin *Quadripartitus*, under the title 'de sponsalibus', ed. F. Liebermann, *Die Gesetze der Angelsachsen*, 3 vols. (Halle, 1903–16), i. 442–5. See *EHD*, no. 50; and D. Whitelock, M. Brett and C. N. L. Brooke (eds.), *Councils and Synods with other Documents relating to the English Church, I: 871–1204*, 2 vols. (Oxford, 1981), i no. 58. As is pointed out in *Councils and Synods* (p. 427), the tract concerned itself principally with marriage of persons of humbler status than Rumwold's parents, although the arrangements seem to differ very little. Two early 11th-cent. marriage agreements survive of persons of higher status (*Councils and Synods*, i. 427–8).

ualeret preparare nuptias, quoniam proci illarum nuptiarum nobiles*a* proceres patrie erant, qui*b* in illo apparatu interesse debebant.[1]

§ 2. Igitur cum in contuberniis nuptiarum iuxta morem uescentes letarentur, cogitabat puella—quin*c* et sponsa—quomodo posset ad uiri thorum ingredi ipsique carnali commixtione copulari qui nondum signo Christi erat insignitus, nec sacri fontis lauacro ablutus, ipsaque esset omnipotenti Deo subdita et ab idolorum cultura aliena. Ad hec ex interno cordis pectore longa trahit prudens sponsa suspiria, oculosque *d*ad ethera eleuans,*d* Christum regem atque omnia moderantem inuocat, taliterque*e* cum lacrimis exorat: *f*'Domine', inquiens,*f* 'creator redemptorque omnium, ne sinas corpus*g* meum pollui cum uiro a te alienato*h* sed conuerte cor eius ad amorem tuum, et illumina illud splendore uultus tui, daque illi intelligentiam ut te intelligere ualeat, et gratiam tui baptismi percipiat.'[2] Et hec orans ilico cum sponso intrat ad thalamum illumque ita affatur: 'Scias', ait, 'nunquam me*i* intraturam tuum thorum priusquam baptismum*j* accipias, Deumque trinum unumque*k* ex toto corde confitearis abiectis ydolorum culturis.'[3] Cumque hec*l* dixisset, gratum atque acceptabile Deo uolente fuit suo*m* sponso uerbum salutis, sicque suscepto ieiunio tertia die baptizatus est, demumque iuxta ritum Christianorum coniugi sue coniunctus est. Concepit ergo mulier ex eo filium, fuitque pregnans. In ea quippe impletum est, quod per apostolum*n* dictum est: 'Saluabitur uir infidelis per mulierem fidelem.'[4]

§ 3. Itaque*o* adpropinquante tempore*p* pariendi misit rex Penda ad generum suum et ad eius coniugem ut pariter ad eum uenirent, quo simul *q*publicas res*q* ciuiles equo discrimine constituerent,[5] atque in amore*r* letarentur. Denique rex*s*

---

a nobilissimi *A*; nobili *C*; nobiliores *T*	*b* quoniam *C*	*c* que *A*
d-d eleuans ad ethera *RT*; ad ethera leuans *LS*	*e* eum *add. A*	*f-f* inquiens
Domine *RT* *g* *W begins with* corpus	*h* alienata *C*	*i* *om. W*
j diuine gratie *add. A* *k* et unum *ALSTW*	*l* hoc *ASW*; *om. C*	*m* *om.*
ASW *n* Paulum *add. A* *o* Ita *W*	*p* tempus *R*	*q-q* res
publicas *R* *r* mutuo *add. ASW* *s* *om. C*		

---

[1] Cf. the 'proci' in Bede, *HE* ii. 9.

[2] Cf. *Vita S. Cuthburge* (see above, pp. clxvii–clxviii).

[3] This is reminiscent of the stipulation made by Oswiu, king of the Northumbrians, that Peada could only marry his daughter Alhflæd if he accepted the Christian faith and was baptized (Bede, *HE* iii. 21). Compare also the arrangement between Edwin and

hastily home with his wife, there to prepare the wedding festivities, since the suitors for that marriage were the chief nobles of the land, who were to take part in the preparations.[1]

§ 2. While they were at the wedding party making merry and feasting, as was the custom, the girl, or indeed rather, the bride, was meditating how she could enter her husband's bed and have intercourse with him, who was not yet signed with the emblem of Christ, nor cleansed with the washing of the holy spring, and herself remain subject to Almighty God and hostile to the worship of idols. At these thoughts the wise bride heaved long sighs from the depths of her heart, and, lifting her eyes heavenwards, called upon Christ the King and ruler of all, tearfully beseeching Him with these words: 'O Lord,' she said, 'the creator and redeemer of all, do not allow my body to be polluted by a man estranged from You, but turn his heart to love of You, and enlighten it with the brightness of Your face. Grant to him the intelligence to understand You, and to receive the grace of Your baptism.'[2] With this prayer, she straightway entered the bridal chamber with her husband and addressed him thus: 'You know', she said, 'that I shall never enter your bed until you receive baptism, and confess God the three in one with all your heart, and cast aside the worship of idols.'[3] When she had spoken these things, the word of salvation was pleasing and acceptable to her husband, by the will of God; thus, he took to fasting, and was baptized on the third day. Only then was he joined to his wife in marriage, according to the custom of Christians. As a result, the woman conceived a son by him, and was pregnant. Indeed, in her is fulfilled what the apostle said: 'An unbelieving man will be saved by a believing woman.'[4]

§ 3. When the time for the birth was approaching, King Penda sent a message to his son-in-law and his wife, to say that they should both go to him, where they might together establish civil administration by a fair division,[5] and rejoice in mutual love. Thereupon the

Æthelburh (Tate), daughter of King Æthelberht of Kent, described in very similar terms by Bede (HE ii. 9). Also comparable is the account of the marriage of Æthelberht himself, to Bertha (HE i. 25).

[4] 1 Cor. 7: 14 ('Sanctificatus est enim uir infidelis per mulierem fidelem').

[5] Some sort of treaty or agreement between Mercia and Northumbria is implied here, but the hagiographer is characteristically vague about historical detail. The summons may have been a narrative contrivance to bring Rumwold's parents to the right part of the country. It is thought that, at some point, there was co-operation between Penda and Alhfrith in opposition to Oswiu, as very briefly referred to by Bede (HE iii. 14). Perhaps this is the 'equo discrimine', if indeed the identification of

Northanhymbrorum[a1] cum[b] uxore pregnante cum[c] carperet iter ad socerum[d] Pendam regem Merciorum,[e2] cogebat partus mulierem parere, sicque in quodam ameno[f] prato liliis rosisque referto extendunt famuli militesque certatim[g] papiliones atque tentoria, moxque regina peperit filium a multis optatum et a Deo sanctificatum. Cumque infans natus fuisset, statim clara uoce clamauit dicens: 'Christianus sum, christianus sum, christianus sum.'[3] [h]Ad hanc uocem responderunt [i]presbyteri duo[i] Widerinus[4] et Eadwaldus[j] dicentes 'Deo gratias.'[h] [k]At post hec[k] subsequitur infans,[l] 'Trinum et unum Deum colo, confiteor, adoro patrem et filium et spiritum sanctum.' At[m] presbyteri et parentes et omnes qui aderant mirantes ceperunt cantare 'Te Deum laudamus'.[5] [n]Enimuero finito ymno[n] rogat se infans catecuminum ab Widerino[o] sacerdote fieri[6] et ab Eadwaldo[p] teneri ad presignaculum fidei et Rumwoldum[q] uocari.[7]

§ 4. Perfecto namque[r] presignaculo aiunt parentes adinuicem: 'Mittamus ad conuicinos reges ac duces ut nostrum excipiant[s]

---

[a] Northumbrorum C (and R before alteration to Nortanhimbrorum); Northamhimbrorum T   [b] dum cum ASW   [c] om. ASW   [d] suum add. AT   [e] mercenorum C; excertitium R; om. LS   [f] om. ASW   [g] citim C (and R before correction to citatim by insertion of ta above the line); festinantes L; om. ST   [h-h] Added in margin R (official correction)   [i-i] duo presbyteri ALW; after this W is either very fragmentary or completely lost until §6, but consistently agrees with A where present, as indicated   [j] Eaduuoldus AC   [k-k] Ad hec C; Et post hec S; At post hoc T   [l] et dicit add. R   [m] Ad hec AS; ad C; ac T   [n-n] Ymno uero finito A; Enimuero finito immo C; Finito hymno L; Quo finito S   [o] uuiderino A; piderino C   [p] Eadpoldo C   [q] Rumpoldum C; Rumoldum R   [r] om. AS; itaque T   [s] accipiant AS

Rumwold's supposed father is correct. Alhfrith did, however, join his father against Penda at Winwæd (HE iii. 24).

[1] The Old English form of this was 'Norþanhymbre' or 'Norþhymbre' (cf. ASC passim, and see Bosworth and Toller, s.v.). The Latin form found in Bede, HE, is generally 'Nordanhymbri' (or 'Norðanhymbri' in MS. C of HE, London, BL, Cotton Tiberius C. II, saec. viii[ex].), but 'Northanhymbri' was the most commonly-attested form in the eleventh and twelfth centuries (cf. Latham, Word-List, s.v.). The form preserved by C and originally by R seems rarer, but presumably relates to the second Old English form noted above.

[2] The reading 'excertitium' of R could have come about through a misunderstanding of the exemplar, which might have read 'Mercenorum' (the reading preserved by C), mistaken for something like 'mercenariorum', meaning 'mercenaries', and hence 'armies'. There is certainly no evidence that Penda, or any other Anglo-Saxon king, was ever accorded the honorific epithet 'King of the Armies'.

[3] Compare the account of the martyrdom of Julitta and her 3-year-old son Cyriacus, in which the child, when asked his name replies: 'christianus sum'. See p. clxxi above.

king of Northumbria,[1] with his pregnant wife, set out on the journey to his father-in-law the king of the Mercians,[2] but the labour of childbirth started, so in a pleasant field filled with lilies and roses, the servants and soldiers eagerly spread out the camp and the tents, and soon the queen gave birth to the son longed for by many, and sanctified by God. When the baby was born, he immediately cried out with a loud voice: 'I am a Christian, I am a Christian, I am a Christian!'[3] To this Widerin and Eadwald,[4] two priests, responded: 'Thanks be to God.' The child went on and said: 'I worship God the three in one, I confess and adore the Father and the Son and the Holy Spirit.' The priests and parents and all who were present marvelled, and began singing the 'Te Deum laudamus'.[5] At the end of the hymn, the child asked to be made a catechumen by the priest Widerin,[6] to be held aloft for the preliminary rite of the faith by Eadwald, and to be named Rumwold.[7]

§ 4. This rite being completed, the parents said to one another: 'Let us send for the neighbouring kings and rulers, so that they can

[4] The name 'Widerinus' is not attested elsewhere, and it is difficult to find any particularly close Anglo-Saxon (or Anglo-Norman) equivalent (see Searle, *Onomasticon*). The first element could be 'Wīd-', 'With-', or possibly 'Wiht-', or may bear some relation to the Old Norse 'Víðarr' (cf. von Feilitzen, *Pre-Conquest Personal Names*, p. 406, and 413–14), but the second element seems rather unusual. It may correspond to something like '-run', or '-rinc', or perhaps '-wine'. The only form in Searle's *Onomasticon* which comes anywhere near is 'pihtherinc' or 'pihtherincg', part of an untraced place-name in the bounds of two Anglo-Saxon charters relating to Rochester (S 165 = BCS 339, and S 514 = BCS 779). It is perhaps surprising to find a name apparently so corrupted beyond recognition, particularly since other forms, such as the place-names mentioned further on, are relatively distinguishable. By contrast, the name 'Eadwoldus' or 'Eadwaldus' is widely attested (cf. Searle). Neither of these priests is known from any other source, and it does not seem possible to trace their origin. Presumably, in the hagiographer's version of events, they were part of the Northumbrian party (or even of Penda's retinue, to stretch the fabrication), since the birth was supposed to have occurred in the middle of a field, where no settlements yet existed. Leland's account of the Life of Rumwold (see above, p. clxxx) uniquely described Widerinus as a bishop, perhaps because he was said to have been responsible for Rumwold's baptism and confirmation (Toulmin-Smith, *Itinerary*, i. 229).

[5] See p. 61 above, on the 'Te Deum'.

[6] For a discussion of the details of Rumwold's baptism, see Appendix F below.

[7] The name Rumwold (the first syllable deriving from 'rūm') is not widely attested in Anglo-Saxon England in that form, indeed the only recoverable examples are place-name elements, such as 'rumpoldes mor' (Worcs.) in the bounds of a spurious charter of Ceolwulf (875), S 216 = BCS 541 (*Place-Names of Worcestershire*, pp. 153–4); cf. 'rumboldes dene' (Glos.), S 615 = BCS 986. The form 'Rumbeald' or 'Rumweald' is hardly less rare (see Searle, *Onomasticon*). Cf. the comments on the rarity of the name in H. Kaufmann, *Altdeutsche Personennamen: Ergänzungsbuch* (Hildesheim, 1968), p. 201; see above, p. cxc, on the variation to be found in the form of the name among the manuscripts of *Vita S. Rumwoldi*.

filium karissimum^a de sacro baptismatis fonte.'¹ Hoc audiens
beatus Rumwoldus^b accersitis parentibus ait illis: 'Non quidem
decet me seruum Dei in manibus superborum ac huius mundi ^cde
regeneratione sancti baptismatis excipi diuitum,^c sed Dei ^dimitari
exemplum^d qui humilis factus^e pro nobis carnem suscipiendo
humanam² ex almo uirginis utero conceptus de spiritu sancto
noluit baptizari in fluentis Iordanicis a potentibus caduci eui, sed a
precursore sue natiuitatis;³ qui pilis ^fcameli indutus,^f degebat in
heremo, cuius esca erat^g mel siluestre atque locusta,⁴ factus inter
homines pauper uenerandus propheta precursor atque baptista.
Nam ab^h angelo nunciatus,⁵ a patre sacerdote genitus, merito
sanctum baptizauit sanctorum, regemque omnium seculorum,
sacerdotemque eternum, dans cunctis in se credentibus baptismum salutis in remissionem omnium peccatorum,⁶ quoniam in illo
nulla macula extitit uitiorum. Hinc ergo rogo me a sacerdote
Widerinoⁱ qui me presignauit baptizari atque ab Eadwaldo^j
suscipi,⁷ quia in illorum manibus per Dei uirtutem^k atque misterium cupio christianus effici.'^l

§ 5. Et hec dicens beatus Rumwoldus diuina prodente^m gratia
ⁿostendit indiceⁿ concauum lapidem haud procul iacentem in
quodam tugurio^o humide adiacentis uallicule, iubetque circumstantibus domesticis, ut illum festinanter afferant, ^pnitidaque
limpha^p impleant.⁸ Cumque illi iissent^q et exquirentes lapidem
ut Christi famulus dixerat inuenissent, nequeunt illum de loco
in quo iacebat mouere neque aliquo ingenio ^ra terra^r extra-
here. Tunc reuertentes dixerunt se incassum laborasse, atque

^a Erasure of two or three letters between kar- and -um in C   ^b Rumoldus R
^{c–c} diuitum de regeneratione sancti baptismatis excipi RT   ^{d–d} exemplum imitari
RT   ^e est add. AS   ^{f–f} indutus cameli C   ^g fuit RT   ^h om. A
ⁱ Vuiderino A   ^j Eadpoldo C   ^k uirtute C   ^l fieri AS
^m prouidente A; protegente S   ^{n–n} indice ostendit RT   ^o tugurrio R
^{p–p} undaque munda R   ^q issent AL; eissent C   ^{r–r} iter C

¹ On Rumwold's choice of godparent, see Appendix F below.
² Cf. Phil. 2: 7–8 ('semetipsum exinaniuit formam serui accipiens, in similitudinem
hominum factus, et habitu inuentus ut homo. Humiliauit semetipsum').
³ Matt. 3: 13; Mark 1: 9; Luke 3: 21; John 1: 32. The term 'precursor' is not explicitly
applied to John the Baptist in the Latin of the Vulgate (although cf. Exod. 33: 2 and Heb.
6: 20), but 'precursor altissimi' (scil. John) seems to have been the reading of the Vetus
Latina in Luke 1: 17; cf. Augustine, Tractatus in Iohannem iv. 6, ed. R. Willems, CCSL
xxxvi (1954), p. 33.
⁴ Matt. 3: 4 ('habebat uestimentum de pilis camelorum ... esca autem eius erat
locustae, et mel siluestre'); Mark 1: 6 ('erat Ioannes uestitus pilis cameli ... et locustas

receive our dearest son from the holy water of baptism [i.e. be his sponsors].'[1] When he heard this, the blessed Rumwold summoned his parents and said to them: 'It is not right for me, a servant of God, to be received from the rebirth of holy baptism into the hands of the proud and the rich of this world, but I must imitate the example of God. He, having humbled Himself for our sake, by taking on human flesh,[2] and having been conceived by the Holy Spirit in the cherishing womb of a virgin, did not choose to be baptized in the waters of the Jordan by the powerful men of a fallen age, but by the forerunner of his nativity.[3] This man [i.e. John the Baptist], clothed in camel-hair, dwelt in the desert and ate wild honey and locusts,[4] and was caused to be poor among men, but we should venerate him as a prophet, forerunner and baptist. For he was heralded by an angel,[5] born the son of a priestly father, and deservedly baptized the Holy of Holies, the King of all ages, the everlasting Priest, Who grants to all who believe in Him the baptism of salvation for the remission of all sins,[6] since in him was no blemish of vice. Hence, therefore, I require to be baptized by the priest Widerin, who anointed me, and to be received by Eadwald,[7] because in their hands, through the power and mystery of God, I desire to be made a Christian.'

§ 5. Saying this, the Blessed Rumwold, instructed by the grace of God, pointed with his finger to a hollow stone lying not far off in a certain hut in the marshy valley near by and ordered the servants who were standing around to bring it quickly and fill it with clean water.[8] When they went to look for the stone and found it as the servant of Christ had said, they were unable to move it from the place where it lay or to extract it from the ground by any contrivance. Then they returned and said that they had laboured in vain, but

---

et mel siluestre edebat'). 'Locusta' may here be taken as a collective singular, the form which is found several times in the Vulgate (for example, Exod. 10: 4, 'ego inducam ... locustam in fines tuos'). Indeed a variant reading in Matt. 3: 4, is 'locusta', in witness Z (London, BL, Harley 1775, saec. vi[in].; *CLA* ii. 197). The hagiographer presumably preferred 'locusta' because of the rhyme with 'baptista'.

[5] Cf. Luke 1: 11.

[6] Cf. Mark 1: 4, Luke 3: 3 ('praedicans baptismum paenitentiae in remissionem peccatorum').

[7] See note on c. 3, p. 99.

[8] 'Lympha' is a poeticism used frequently by Aldhelm, cf. for example, *Aenigmata*, xix. 1; xxxviii. 2; xlviii. 8 (Ehwald, pp. 401, 423, 435). The collocation 'nitidaque limpha' has the ring of a poetic tag borrowed from elsewhere, but no obvious source has hitherto been detected. The word may be taken as symptomatic of the hagiographer's stylistic ambition—see p. clxiv above.

[a]nichil om⟨n⟩ino[a] silicem perferre posse. Quibus precipiens [b]Penda rex[b] dixit ut afferrent uelociter[c] urnam siue cadum ut Christi tyro baptismum in eo acciperet.[1] At illi [d]ducentes plenumque aqua in medio constituto loco[d] ponerent,[2] sanctus Rumwoldus extimplo intuens ait: 'Cur non adtulistis lapidem?' Cui respondent famuli aientes minime ualuisse eos pro impossibilitate [e]illius iussum[e] exhibere. Tunc beatissimus Rumwoldus conuocat Widerinum[f] et Eadwaldum[g] presbyteros, illisque iubet ut in nomine Domini Nostri Iesu Christi ac[h] sancte trinitatis soli sine aliis pergant, saxumque indubii accipiant sine hesitatione, in summo omnium confidentes auctore.[3] Qui protinus euntes ad Christi futuri tyronis iussum, inuocato nomine omnipotentis Dei magni ponderis lapidem mox leuiter a [i]terre solo[i] eleuant atque sine mora ducentes, ante sanctum Rumwoldum deponunt.[4]

§ 6. Igitur sanctificatur in eo fons sancti baptismatis ab eisdem sacerdotibus predictis, sicque baptizatur beatus infans[j] Rumwoldus a Widerino[k] presbytero ac suscipitur ab Eadwaldo.[l] Baptizatus autem postulat celebrari sibi missam, darique sibi[m] Christi corpus et sanguinem, ut cuius susceperat[n] baptismum ipsius assumeret[o] sacramentum.[5] In eodem enim[p] prato in quo sanctus[q] baptizatus est[r] Rumwoldus numquam deficit [s]gratissimus odor[s] neque ibi pallescunt herbe uel[t] siccantur, sed semper in uiriditate permanent atque magna suauitate nectaris redolent. Vocatur autem locus ille nunc ab incolis prouincie illius regionis Suthtunus,[u] in quo etiam pagus situs est regie dignitati[v] subministrans debita decreto tempore obsequia.[6]

[a-a] nullatenus *ASW*; nihil omnimodis *C*; nichilomino *R*; nullo modo *T*   [b-b] rex Penda *R*   [c] *om. R*   [d-d] euntes cum plenum aqua in medio constituto loco cadum *AW*; eum ducentes plenumque aqua cum in medio *R*; eum ducentes plenum aqua cum in medio *T*   [e-e] iussum illius *RT*   [f] Vuiderinum *C*   [g] Eadwoldum *R*   [h] ad *C*   [i-i] terra *ALSW*; solo terre *T*   [j] *om. R*   [k] Vuiderino *AC*; *W resumes in full with* Widerino   [l] Eadpoldo *C*   [m] *om. CR*   [n] susceperit *W*   [o] sumeret *ASW*   [p] autem *ASW*   [q] *om. ALW*   [r] seruus Dei *add. A*   [s-s] odor gratissimus *R*   [t] nec *R*   [u] Suithunus *C*; Sutthone *L*; Suttunus *R*; Sutthunus *T*   [v] dignitate *C*

---

[1] On the use of small, portable vessels as fonts, see F. Bond, *Fonts and Font Covers* (Oxford, 1908; repr. London, 1985), pp. 123, 271–2; cf. also S. Foot, '"By water in the Spirit": the administration of baptism in early Anglo-Saxon England', in *Pastoral Care Before the Parish*, ed. J. Blair and R. Sharpe (Leicester, 1992), pp. 171–92, at 183.

[2] See p. clxv on the syntactical confusion here.

[3] It is striking that Rumwold is described as being so particular about the hollow stone to be used as his font, rejecting the 'urnam siue cadum' produced as a substitute. Possibly an inference is to be made concerning the actual mode of baptism preferred,

could not carry the stone at all. King Penda ordered them to fetch an urn or jar so that the new recruit of Christ might be baptized in it.[1] They brought this to him and when they placed it in the middle, full of water, in the place arranged,[2] St Rumwold saw it and said: 'Why have you not brought the stone?' The servants replied that they were unable to carry out his order because it was impossible. So the blessed Rumwold called together Widerin and Eadwald the priests, and commanded them to set out alone, in the name of our Lord Jesus Christ and the Holy Trinity, and confidently take up the rock without hesitation, trusting in the high Creator of all.[3] They set out immediately at the command of the future recruit of Christ and, invoking the name of Almighty God, they soon lifted the weighty stone easily from the ground, took it without delay and put it down in front of St Rumwold.[4]

§ 6. And so the water of holy baptism was blessed in it by those same two priests, and thus the blessed infant Rumwold was baptized by Widerin the priest and received by Eadwald. After the baptism, he demanded that a mass be celebrated for him, and that he should be given the body and blood of Christ, so that he might take up the sacrament of Him Whose baptism he had received.[5] In that same meadow where St Rumwold was baptized, there never ceases to be the loveliest fragrance, and the grasses neither fade nor wither but remain always green and are redolent of sweet nectar. The inhabitants of that region of the kingdom now call that place Sutton, in which also the district is situated which gives due service to the king at the decreed time.[6]

namely total immersion or affusion, rather than aspersion (cf. Foot, p. 183). Very few fonts have survived which can confidently be assigned to the Anglo-Saxon period—see H. M. Taylor and J. Taylor, *Anglo-Saxon Architecture*, 3 vols. (Cambridge, 1965–78), iii. 1064–5. There are, however, many Norman examples still in existence (Bond, *Fonts*, pp. 144–205). Possibly the point of the story was to give credence to a locally-known hollow stone, on which legend fixed St Rumwold's baptism, although it is perhaps surprising that the hagiographer did not, in that case, make explicit reference to the stone, with some phrase such as 'which may still be seen today' (cf. *Vita et Miracula S. Kenelmi* c. 6, on Kenelm's ash).

[4] There are several examples of miracles involving weight-lifting (cf. Loomis, *White Magic*, p. 49); e.g. *Vita S. Arnulphi*, cc. 24–5 (*MGH*, SRM, ii. 432–46, at p. 443); and *Miracula S. Verene* (BHL 8542) c. 10 (*ActaS*, Sept. i. 168–73, p. 170); but none seems to bear much relation to the present instance.

[5] See Appendix F.

[6] 'Suthtunus' is, of the many places called Sutton, most likely to be King's Sutton, Northamptonshire, by reason of geographical proximity to Brackley and Buckingham. King's Sutton occurs in Domesday Book as 'Sudtone', or 'Sutone' (*DB, Northants.*, 1. 8; fo. 219c), as 'Suttunes' in the Geld Roll of 1084, and 'Sutton(e)' in a Pipe Roll of 1155; see

§ 7. Itaque post finita missarum sollemnia alloquitur sanctus Rumwoldus genitorem suum atque genitricem sacerdotesque predictos, docens illos de catholica fide ᵃdeque ueraᵃ religione necnon de omni ᵇhonestate bonitatisᵇ et de ᶜpreceptis diuine legisᶜ et maxime de ᵈdilectione Deiᵉ et proximi.ᵈ¹ Post exortationem uero multorum sermonum ᶠdixit omnibus clara uoce:ᶠ 'Audite queso, cuncti hic astantes, uerba que ego loquor ᵍhodie uestris in auribus,ᵍ quoniam sapientia que os mutum aperit, linguasque infantium disertas esse facit,² per me sua misteria uobis uestrisque sequacibus pandit, quo uos gnari sitis eiusʰ agnitionis³ ⁱet intelligatis gloriam eiusdem remunerationis.ⁱ Nam hec est illa sapientia in qua Deus fundauit terram, celosque stabiliuit,⁴ queʲ sola girum celi circuiuitᵏ et in fluctibusˡ maris ambulauit, superborumque acᵐ sublimium colla propria uirtute calcauit.⁵ Hec etenim clamitat in plateis⁶ uocatque ⁿse diligentesⁿ ut ad illam declinent quiᵒ eamᵖ inuenient et eam cum inuenerint,⁷ beati suntᑫ si ʳtenuerint eam.ʳ Hecˢ quippe sua uirtute loqui me iubet, quia sapienter uniuersa creauit, meque inᵗ hoc euo nasci uoluit spiritumque uite in homine inspirauit.⁸ Non ergo mirum uobis uideatur quod contra morem nature mihi scientia uel ᵘpossibilitas data est fandiᵘ a Deo, quia ᵛinscrutabilia sunt iuditia eius,⁹ et inuestigabilesᵛ uie illius.ʷ

ᵃ⁻ᵃ ueraque *ASW*; de ueraque *T*   ᵇ⁻ᵇ bonitatis honestate *RT*   ᶜ⁻ᶜ diuine legis preceptis *RT*   ᵈ⁻ᵈ Dei et proximi dilectione *RT*   ᵉ uidelicet *add. A*   ᶠ⁻ᶠ beatus Rumuuoldus dixit omnibus clara uoce *A*; clara uoce dixit omnibus *RT*; omnibus clara uoce dixit *S*   ᵍ⁻ᵍ in uestris auribus *R*; in auribus uestris *T*   ʰ *om.* *ATW*   ⁱ⁻ⁱ *om. AW, perhaps by homoeoteleuton*   ʲ qui *C*   ᵏ circumiuit *A*   ˡ fluentibus *W*   ᵐ et *ASW*   ⁿ⁻ⁿ diligentes se *R*   ᵒ quia *ASW*   ᵖ *W ends after* inueni-   ᑫ sint *C*   ʳ⁻ʳ tenuerint illam *A*; eam tenuerint *R*   ˢ Hecque *A*   ᵗ *om. C*   ᵘ⁻ᵘ potestas fandi data est *R*   ᵛ⁻ᵛ uestigabiles *C (the rest omitted, by eye-skip)*   ʷ eius *AS*

J. E. B. Gover, A. Mawer and F. M. Stenton, *The Place-Names of Northamptonshire*, EPNS, x (1933), p. 58. The form of the name preserved in **A** may point to an exemplar earlier than *DB*, still showing the '-th' which is found in early attestations of the place-name Sutton elsewhere in the country, for example, Sutton near Peterborough, which appears in 948 as 'Suðtun' (S 533 = BCS 871). Cf. E. Ekwall, *The Concise Oxford English Dictionary of Place-Names*, 4th edition (Oxford, 1987), s.v. For further discussion of King's Sutton, see pp. cxliv–cxlvi. The phrase 'uocatur autem locus ille *nunc* ab incolis . . .' is similar to remarks made in c. 12—see commentary below.

¹ Cf. Matt. 22: 37–9; Mark 12: 30–1; Luke 10: 27.
² Wisd. 10: 21 ('Quoniam sapientia aperuit os mutuorum, et linguas infantium fecit disertas'). It is noticeable that Rumwold is made to dwell much upon 'sapientia' in his sermon, and perhaps the explanation lies in this biblical quotation, an apt text for an infant preacher, as it were. The heavenly wisdom which deigns to give infants the power to speak eloquently would be a fitting subject for the homily of just such a prodigy (cf. Ps. 8: 3, 'ex ore infantium et lactentium perfecisti laudem propter inimicos tuos').

§ 7. Therefore when the celebration of the mass was over, St Rumwold addressed his father and mother and the aforementioned priests, teaching them about the Catholic faith, about the true religion and also every grace of goodness, about the precepts of divine law and especially about love of God and one's neighbour.[1] After exhorting them with many words, he said in a loud voice to everyone: 'Listen, I pray, all of you standing here, to the words which I am saying to you, because the wisdom which opens the dumb mouth, and causes the tongues of infants to be eloquent,[2] is spreading forth His mysteries to you and to your successors through me, so that you can have knowledge of Him[3] and understand the glory of His reward. For this is the same wisdom in which God laid the foundations of the earth and established the heavens,[4] which alone has travelled around the course of the sky, walked in the floods of the ocean, and trampled upon the necks of the proud and lofty with her own might.[5] She cries out in the streets[6] and summons all who love her, so that they who find her may turn to her, and when they do find her are blessed if they hold on to her.[7] Indeed, she bids me speak by her power, because God created the universe wisely, and wished me to be born in this age, and breathed the breath of life into man.[8] So it should not seem surprising to you that God, contrary to the laws of nature, has granted me knowledge or power of speech, because His judgements are inscrutable and His ways untraceable.[9]

Furthermore, part of the ceremony of baptismal initiation (see Appendix F) was that the catechumen should receive salt on his tongue, which was intended to signify, amongst other things, the seasoning of wisdom—the administering priest is to say 'Accipe salem sapientiae propitiatus in uitam aeternam' (Warren, *Leofric Missal*, p. 235). Reflection on the rite of baptism may have put the topic of wisdom uppermost in the hagiographer's mind while composing Rumwold's sermon.

[3] Cf. Col. 2: 2 ('in agnitionem mysterii Dei Patris et Christi Iesu'); Heb. 10: 35 ('Nolite itaque amittere confidentiam uestram, quae magnam habet remunerationem'); and Heb. 11: 26 ('aspiciebat enim in remunerationem').

[4] Prov. 3: 19 ('Dominus sapientia fundauit terram, stabiliuit caelos prudentia').

[5] Ecclus. 24: 8 ('Gyrum caeli circuiui sola . . . in fluctibus maris ambulaui'); 24: 11 ('Et omnium excellentium et humilium corda uirtute calcaui').

[6] Prov. 1: 20 ('Sapientia foris praedicat; in plateis dat uocem suam').

[7] Cf. Prov. 3: 13 ('Beatus homo qui inuenit sapientiam'), and 3: 18 ('Lignum uitae est his qui apprehenderint eam, et qui tenuerit eam beatus'). Also Ecclus. 4: 14 ('Qui tenuerint illam uitam haereditabunt').

[8] Cf. Gen. 2: 7 ('Formauit igitur Dominus Deus hominem . . . et inspirauit in faciem eius spiraculum uitae'); and Ecclus. 4: 12 ('sapientia filiis suis uitam inspirauit').

[9] Rom. 11: 33 ('quam incomprehensibilia sunt iudicia eius, et inuestigabiles uiae eius!'). The variant 'inscrutabilia' for 'incomprehensibilia' occurs in the Vetus Latina version, and Rom. 11: 33 was cited in that form by numerous patristic authors (see the examples listed in *TLL*, s.v.).

§ 8. 'Deus enim ᵃsapientia uera summaque estᵃ qui mundum ex nihilo condiditᵇ celíque machinam[1] cum ᶜsyderum inenarrabili pulchritudineᶜ fabricauit,[2] cuius ᵈsedes celum est,[3] et scabellum pedum eius terra est.ᵈ Sicutᵉ Ididiasᶠ testatur in persona illius[4] dicens, "Ego in altissimis habito et tronus meus in columna nubis."[5] Est namque ipse sapientia quiaᵍ ut ait psalmista, "in sapientia fecit omnia."[6] Ideoque illi ʰflectiturⁱ omne genu[7] et confitetur omnis lingua.ʰ Est quidem et conditor omnium rerum, quia que creauit in potentia, ordinauit constituendo in magnificentia,[8] si suam discunt scientiam cum cordis corporisque innocentia. Est et principium atque initium,ʲ quia in principio (hoc est in filio) creauit uniuersa ipseque ait: "Ego sum alpha et o,ᵏ initium et finis, qui ante mundi principium uiuo in eternum."[9] Vnde et filius qui cum patre et spiritu sancto unus ˡDeus estˡ interrogantibus illum quis esset respondit: "Ego",ᵐ inquiens, "principium qui et loquor uobis."[10] Ab eo ⁿenim estⁿ omne principium et quod per initium factum est,[11] quoniam ipse est omniumᵒ creaturarum exordium et finis atque redemptio mundi. Sicut enim Deus in sapientia cuncta creauit, sic etiam suum plasma[12] perditum in sapientia redemit.

ᵃ⁻ᵃ sapientia fundauit terram, sed sapientia uera summaque est *AS*; uera summaque sapientia est *R* ᵇ creauit *R* ᶜ⁻ᶜ inenarrabili syderum pulchritudine *R* ᵈ⁻ᵈ celum sedes est, et scabellum pedum eius terra est *AS*; sedes celum est, et terra scabellum pedum eius *R* ᵉ om. *R* ᶠ *a single letter has been erased between* Idid- *and* -as *in A*; Ididias *R* ᵍ qui *AS* ʰ⁻ʰ omne genu flectitur et omnis lingua confitetur *R*; flectitur omne genu et omnis lingua confitetur *S* ⁱ om. *C* ʲ finis *RS* ᵏ ω *R* ˡ est Deus *RS* ᵐ sum *add. R* ⁿ est enim *AS* ᵒ om. *AS*

---

[1] Cf. Statius, *Thebaid* vii. 812 and viii. 310 ('machina caeli'); and Martianus Capella ii. 201 ('caeli molem machinamque'); but also Isidore, *Etym.* xiv. 8. 17 ('propter altitudinem suam quasi caeli machinam atque astra sustentare uidetur'), which might perhaps be more likely to be the hagiographer's source.

[2] Cf. Isidore, *Etym.* xiii. 1. 2 ('diuersitatem elementorum et pulchritudinem siderum'); and Augustine, *Enarrationes in Psalmos* xli. 7 ('caelum suspicio et pulchritudinem siderum'), ed. Dekkers, *CCSL* xxxviii, 464.

[3] Isa. 66: 1 ('Caelum sedes mea, terra autem scabellum pedum meorum').

[4] 'Ididias' is somewhat obscure. The name apparently refers to the writer of Ecclesiasticus, Jesus Ben Sirach. There seems to have been some confusion with one of the names given to Solomon—'Ididia' (Jedidiah) in 2 Kgs. (2 Sam.) 12: 24–5, 'genuit filium, et uocauit nomen eius Salomon, et Dominus dilexit eum . . . et uocauit nomen eius, Amabilis Domino [Hebr. Yedhidhyah], eo quod diligeret eum Dominus' (cf. 4 Kgs. (2 Kgs.) 22: 1). Cf. Jerome, *Liber Interpretationis Hebraeorum Nominum* xxxix. 4/5, ed. P. de Lagarde, *CCSL* lxxii (1959), p. 107, 'Ididia amabilis Domino'—see M. Thiel, *Grundlage und Gestalt der Hebräischkenntnisse des frühen Mittelalters* (Spoleto, 1973), p. 324. Since much of the other wisdom material in the Bible is associated with Solomon, it is possible that a statement from Ecclesiasticus, which also deals largely with wisdom, was

§ 8. 'God, the true and highest Wisdom, created the world from nothing and built the sky's fabric[1] along with the unspeakable beauty of the stars;[2] His seat is the heavens, and His footstool is the earth.[3] Thus Ididias testifies to His person,[4] saying: "My dwelling place is in the Highest, and my throne is in a pillar of cloud."[5] He is wisdom Himself, because, as the psalmist says, "In wisdom did He make them all."[6] And so every knee bows to Him and every tongue confesses.[7] He is also the founder of all things, because those things which He created in power, He has put in order by setting them up in grandeur,[8] so long as they learn His knowledge with innocence of mind and body. He is also the beginning and the origin, since in the beginning, that is, in the Son, He created the universe, and He Himself said, "I am alpha and omega, beginning and end, I, Who am from before the beginning of the world unto eternity."[9] Whence also the Son, Who with the Father and the Holy Spirit is one God, replied to those who asked Him who He was: "I am the beginning, even I who speak to you."[10] From Him is all beginning, and all that was created in the beginning,[11] since He is the start and the finish of every creation, and the redemption of the world. For just as God created everything in wisdom, so too He redeemed His lost creation in wisdom.[12]

here mistakenly attributed to him. Isidore described precisely that error: 'Librum autem Ecclesiasticum certissime Iesus filius Sirach ... composuit, qui liber apud Latinos propter eloquii similitudinem Salomonis titulo praenotatur' (*Etym.* vi. 2. 31). Compare the anonymous *Passio S. Athelberti regis et martiris*, preserved only in CCCC 308 (saec. xii), printed by James, 'Two Lives', pp. 236–44, where John, the beloved disciple, is called 'idida' (p. 238). The use of the name in *Vita S. Rumwoldi* is a further sign of the hagiographer's effort to write in what he regarded as an erudite style, albeit also an example of the dangers of 'a little learning'.

[5] Ecclus. 24: 7 ('ego in altissimis habitaui, et thronus meus in columna nubis').

[6] Ps. 103(104): 24 ('omnia in sapientia fecisti').

[7] Rom. 14: 11 ('mihi flectetur omne genu: et omnis lingua confitebitur Deo'); cf. Phil. 2: 10.

[8] Cf. 1 Chron. 29: 11 ('Tua est Domine magnificentia, et potentia, et tibi laus: cuncta enim quae in caelo sunt, et in terra, tua sunt').

[9] Rev. 21: 6 ('ego sum alpha et omega, initium et finis, dicit Dominus Deus'); cf. Rev. 1: 8; and Gen. 1: 1 ('In principio creauit Deus caelum et terram'). Cf. also John 1: 1 ('In principio erat Verbum . . .') and Isa. 43: 12–13 ('Et ego Deus. Et ab initio ego ipse').

[10] John 8: 25 ('Dicebant ergo ei: Tu quis es? Dixit eis Iesus: Principium, qui et loquor uobis').

[11] Cf. John 1: 3 ('Omnia per ipsum facta sunt: et sine ipso factum est nihil, quod factum est').

[12] The Grecism 'plasma' was frequently used in ecclesiastical Latin to refer to God's creation, man (cf. Prudentius, *Cathemerina* vii. 184), and here provided the author with a fine alliterating epithet.

§ 9. 'Sapientia[a] quidem patris [b]filius est.[b] Ergo pater [c]in filio est[c] et filius in patre[1] et spiritus sanctus, per quem[d] omnes renascuntur[e] fideles,[f] in utrisque. Et ex hoc intelligi sine dubio oportet quia idem [g]Deus est[g] pater, idem et filius, idem Deus est et spiritus sanctus.[h] Quamuis autem alia sit persona patris, alia filii, alia spiritus sancti, una est substantia, eadem est equalitas, una est maiestas atque potestas, una eternitas et perfectio, dignitas, honor, decus, [i]unum est et imperium[i] et beatitudo, una immensitas et gloria, atque immortalitas. Ita[j] itaque est credenda hec trinitas ut indubitanter confiteatur una deitas unaque esse essentia. Hanc quippe [k]mecum una[k] confitemini, quoniam hec confessio uita est cunctorum eam confitentium.'[2]

§ 10. Cumque omnes lacrimabili uoce dicerent, 'credimus, confitemur, adoramus, laudamus, benedicimus', extimplo sanctus Rumwoldus hylari uultu ac sonora uoce ait illis: 'Audistis, fratres in Christo atque consanguinei, qualiter sanctam trinitatem confiteri debetis, qualiterque ipsius unitatem firmiter in uestri cordis pectore oportet retinere et in ea credulitate, qua pater et filius et spiritus sanctus unus [l]Deus est,[l] fideliter perseuerare.[3] Nunc[m] igitur[n] doceam quomodo[o] fructus agere debetis[p] dignos penitentie[4] et si aliquod crimen in uobis est, quo[q] possitis emundari ab eius uulnere celesti medicamine. Deus enim non uult mortem peccatoris sed ut conuertatur et uiuat.[5] Ideo namque [r]unicuique peccatori dicitur[r] per prophetam: "Declina a malo et fac bonum, inquire pacem et sequere[s] eam."[6] Et iterum: "Peccasti, quiesce."[7] Penitentiam quippe agere est,[8] peccatum perpetratum demittere,

[a] Sapienti C   [b–b] est filius R   [c–c] est in filio RT   [d] ut add. AS   [e] renascantur AS   [f] est add. AS   [g–g] est Deus A   [h] om. C   [i–i] et unum imperium AS   [j] om. C   [k–k] una mecum RT   [l–l] est Deus RT   [m] Hunc C   [n] uos add. AS   [o] quos RT   [p] debeatis AS   [q] quomodo AST   [r–r] unicuique peccatori C; dictum est peccatori RT   [s] persequere RT

---

[1] Cf. John 10: 38 ('et credatis quia Pater in me est, et ego in Patre') and also John 14: 10–11.

[2] This paragraph is reminiscent of the so-called Athanasian creed or 'Quicunque Vult', generally thought to have been composed in about the 5th cent., somewhere in Gaul, and, by the end of the 10th cent., universally incorporated into the office for daily recitation at prime—see *Oxford Dictionary of the Christian Church*, ed. Cross and Livingstone, s.v. 'Quicunque Vult'; and Tolhurst, *Monastic Breviary*, vi. 50. Cf. 'neque confundentes personas, neque substantiam separantes. Alia est enim persona Patris, alia Filii, alia Spiritus Sancti. Sed Patris et Filii et Spiritus Sancti una est diuinitas, aequalis gloria, coaeterna maiestas ... Immensus Pater, immensus Filius, immensus Spiritus

§ 9. 'The wisdom of the Father is the Son. So the Father is in the Son and the Son in the Father,[1] and the Holy Spirit, through Whom all the faithful are born again, is in both. From this we ought to understand without doubt that the same God is Father, Son and also Holy Spirit. But although the character of the Father is one thing, the character of the Son a second, and that of the Holy Spirit a third, their substance is one—one equality, one majesty and power, one eternity and perfection, dignity, honour, glory, and also one rule and blessedness, one immensity and glory, and immortality. Thus, therefore, we must believe in this Trinity, in such a way that we may unhesitatingly confess that there is one deity, one essence. Indeed, confess this with me, because this confession is life to all who make it.'[2]

§ 10. And when they all said with tearful voices, 'We believe, we confess, we adore, we praise, we bless,' straightaway St Rumwold with a happy face and ringing voice said, 'Kindred and brothers in Christ, you have heard in what manner you should confess the Trinity, and how you ought to keep its oneness firmly in your hearts and to persevere faithfully in this belief, namely that Father and Son and Holy Spirit are one God.[3] And so now I shall teach you how you should bear fruits which are worthy of penitence,[4] and, if there be any sin in you, by what heavenly healing you can be purified of its wound. For God does not desire the death of a sinner but rather that he should be converted and live.[5] Therefore, through the prophet he says to each sinner, "Flee from evil and do the thing that is good; seek peace and follow it."[6] And again: "You have sinned, be at peace."[7] To be sure, you must repent;[8] put aside the sins which you

sancti. Aeternus Pater, aeternus Filius, aeternus Spiritus sanctus ... haec est fides catholica; quam nisi quisque fideliter firmiterque crediderit, saluus esse non poterit.'

[3] With 'firmiter ... fideliter', compare the penultimate phrase of the portion of the 'Quicunque Vult' cited above.

[4] Luke 3: 8 ('Facite ergo fructus dignos poenitentiae') and cf. Matt. 3: 8.

[5] Ezek. 18: 32 ('Quia nolo mortem morientis, dicit Dominus Deus; reuertimini, et uiuite'); Ezek. 33: 11 ('nolo mortem impii, sed ut conuertatur impius a uia sua, et uiuat').

[6] Ps. 36(37): 27 and Ps. 33(34): 15; thus 'per prophetam' ought to be 'per psalmistam'.

[7] 'Peccasti, quiesce' is the reading in the Vetus Latina version of Gen. 4: 7; see B. Fischer, ed., *Vetus Latina. Die Reste der altlateinischen Bibel. Nach Petrus Sabatier neu gesammelt und herausgegeben von der Erzabtei Beuron*, 2, *Genesis* (Freiburg, 1951–4), pp. 82–3. It is possible that the author of *Vita S. Rumwoldi* had encountered the phrase in some exegetical work, since the Vetus Latina version of Gen. 4: 7 was cited by a good many patristic sources (see Fischer's list).

[8] The syntax of this clause is weak, since, unless there has been an omission, preserved in every witness, 'est' is required to take on the sense 'it is necessary' or 'it is fitting'. Alternatively, 'agere' should be emended to the gerundive 'agendam'. The

bonisque operibus semper inherere et ueram pacem dilectionis Dei et proximi[1] inquirere, eamque sequendo[a] totis nisibus exercere. Parum etenim proderit peccatori [b]a peccato[b] cessare, nisi studeat ieiuniis et orationibus elemosinisque commissum deflere, et[c] sicut [d]exstiterat operator[d] malicie, ita quoque efficiatur post[e] penitentiam[f] cultor iustitie. Alioquin quod si aliquis non delinquit,[g] tamen debet exhibere mandata atque iustificationes Christi[2] propter sacramentum fidei quod in baptismate promisit, quia diues[h] qui purpura et bysso induebatur et cotidie splendide[i] epulabatur[3] non pro reatu damnatur criminis, sed propterea quod in paupere non exhibuit officium caritatis.[4]

§ 11. 'Iccirco, fratres, satagite[5] utrumque agere, hoc est ad fontem sapientie[6] accedere et ex eo potando immunditiam [j]uestri cordis[j] abluere, Christum Deum et Dominum misericordem animarum corporumque medicum indesinenter[k] expetere,[7] illique uestra colla cum humili ac nitida conscientia[l] eius precepta seruando subicere,[8] ipsumque ex toto corde[m] tota uirtute diligere[9] et ad ipsius ecclesiam omni tempore concurrere, preces ad illum pro uestris excessibus effundere, oblationes uestras sine dolo illi offerre et sacerdotes honorare et doctrinam euangeliorum que per eos manifestantur[n] gratuita ac[o] hylari deuotione excipere. Omnes christianos quemadmodum uosmetipsos amare, et unusquisque uestrum studeat alterum honore preuenire,[10] non occidere,[11] non maledicere,[12] non aliquem accusare, non uicino[p] detrahere,[13] non insidias uel laqueos ad decipiendum alicui[q] opponere,[14] non furari[r]

[a] sequentibus *RT*   [b-b] appeccato *C*   [c] ut *AS*   [d-d] exuterat operatur *C*   [e] om. *C*   [f] peccatum *AS*   [g] delinquid *C*; deliquit *RST*   [h] diuues *C*   [i] splendi *C*   [j-j] cordis uestri *RST*   [k] indesinent *C*   [l] scientia *AS*   [m] et add. *AS*   [n] manifestatur *R*; manifestata *T*   [o] etiam add. *AS*   [p] uicinum *CR*   [q] alicubi *A*   [r] furtum *RT*

error, if such it is, seems quite likely to be authorial, considering that the principal weakness of the hagiographer's Latin style was his grasp of syntax—see pp. clxv–clxvi above.

[1] See note on c. 7, p. 104.
[2] Cf. Luke 1: 6 ('incedentes in omnibus mandatis et iustificationibus Domini').
[3] Cf. Luke 16: 19.
[4] The statement that the rich man was not punished for a sin of commission so much as for one of omission was a standard element in the traditional exegesis of this text. Compare, for example, Jerome, *Homilia in Lucam Euangelistam de Lazaro et Diuite*, ed. G. Morin, *Sancti Hieronymi Presbyteri Opera Homiletica*, *CCSL* lxxviii (1958), pp. 507–16, at 507–8, lines 25–30: 'Diues iste purpuratus et splendidus non accusatur quod auarus fuerit, non quia res alienas tulerit, non quia adulter fuerit, non quia aliquid mali fecerit: sola in illo condemnatur superbia. Infelicissime hominum, partem corporis tui uides

have committed, and keep always to good works; seek the true peace of love for God and your neighbour[1] with every effort. Truly, it little benefits a sinner to cease from sin, unless he takes pains to lament the crime with fastings, supplications, and almsgiving; so, just as he had been a doer of malice, thus also he is turned into a lover of justice after his penitence. Moreover, it may be that some-one is not sinning actively, but ought to carry out the commands and justifications of Christ[2] because of the sacrament of faith, which He promised in baptism; because the rich man, who wore purple and fine linen, and dined splendidly every day,[3] is not con-demned as guilty because of that, but for the reason that he did not show due charity towards the poor man.[4]

§ 11. 'Therefore brothers, take pains to do all of these things,[5] that is, draw near to the fountainhead of wisdom[6] and, by drink-ing from it, cleanse the impurity of your heart; seek unceasingly after Christ our God and Lord, the merciful physician of souls and bodies,[7] and bow your neck in subjection to Him with a humble and pure conscience, keeping His commandments,[8] and loving Him with all your heart and all your strength;[9] hasten together to his Church on every occasion, pour out prayers to him for your transgressions, offer your oblations to Him without guile, honour priests and accept with free and happy devotion the teaching of the gospels, which are made plain by them. Love every one of your fellow Christians as yourselves, and each of you strive to surpass the other in honour.[10] Do not kill,[11] do not curse,[12] do not accuse anyone, do not disparage your neighbour,[13] do not lay ambushes or snares to deceive anyone,[14] do not steal

iacere ante ianuam, et non misereris?' Cf. also Gregory the Great, *Homiliarum .xl. in Euangelia Libri ii*, xl. 3, 'hic autem diues iste non abstulisse aliena reprehenditur sed propria non dedisse, nec dicitur quia unum quempiam oppressit sed quia in acceptis rebus se extulit' (*PL* lxxvi. 1304–5), cited verbatim by Bede, *In Lucae Evangelium Exposi-tio*, ed. D. Hurst, *CCSL* cxx (1960), p. 302.

[5] 2 Peter 1: 10 ('quapropter fratres magis satagite').

[6] Ecclus. 1: 5 ('fons sapientiae uerbum Dei') and cf. Prov. 18: 4.

[7] Cf. Augustine, *Tractatus in Iohannem*, xvii. 1 ('cum esset medicus et animarum et corporum'), ed. Willems, *CCSL* xxxvi. 170.

[8] Cf. Ecclus. 51: 34 ('et collum uestrum subiicite iugo').

[9] Cf. Deut. 6: 5 ('diliges Dominum Deum tuum ex toto corde tuo, et ex tota anima tua, et ex tota fortitudine tua').

[10] Cf. Rom. 12: 10 ('honore inuicem praeuenientes').

[11] Cf. Exod. 20: 13 ('non occides') and Deut. 5: 17; Rom. 13: 9.

[12] Cf. Rom. 12: 14 ('nolite maledicere').

[13] Cf. James 4: 11 ('nolite detrahere alterutrum fratres').

[14] Cf. Ps. 63(64): 6 ('narrauerunt ut absconderunt laqueos').

neque periurium[a] facere,[1] non blasphemare uel simplices deridere;[2] sed in omnibus bonis operibus perseuerare, Deumque omnipotentem siue in prosperitate uel aduersitate omni tempore laudare.'

§ 12. Hec itaque omnia cum dixisset sanctus Rumwoldus, cuncti[b] qui aderant gratias Deo inde referebant, eo quod [c]in tam[c] paruulo infante gratia superna inspirante tanta uirtus esset eloquentie. Tunc iterum ait beatus Rumwoldus: 'Ecce ego ingredior uiam uniuerse[d] carnis,[3] quoniam [e]non est mihi fas[e] uiuendi in hoc mortali corpore ab[f] hora qua natus sum. Post transitum autem meum uolo esse in loco in[g] quo ortus sum per unius anni spatium; postmodum uero in Braccalea[h] constitui esse per biennium,[4] finitis autem his tribus annis proposui ut [i]mea ossa[i] requiescant in loco qui uocabitur quandoque Buccingaham[j] omni tempore.'[5] Istorum autem locorum nomina non erant eo tempore nota,[k] sed post multorum temporum curricula[l] [m]inuenta uel cognita sunt.[m] Sunt quoque nunc uille in illis locis site, fertiles segetibus, iugerum multorum habentes copiam, atque dense hominum habitatione.[6] Vocatur autem locus in quo natus est Suthtunus,[n] alius uero Braccalea,[o] tertius quoque[p] Buccingaham.[q]

§ 13. Finita itaque tertia die, sicut predixerat sanctus Rumwoldus emisit Deo [r]gratissimum spiritum,[r] tertio[s] nonas Nouembris, in[t] manibus susceptus angelorum.[7] Post transitum denique eius

[a] periuriam *C (and A before correction by erasure of the suspension mark over the* a*)*; periuria *S* [b] cucti *C* [c–c] uitam *C* [d] *fragment E begins with* uniuerse [e–e] mihi fas non est *AES* [f] ab hac *R* [g] *om. AES* [h] Bracalea *AE* [i–i] ossa mea *RT* [j] Bucchingaham *R* [k] notata *AE*; uocata *S* [l] curriculam *E (and A before erasure of the* m*)* [m–m] inuenta sunt uel cognita *R*; inuenta sunt et cognita *T* [n] Suthunus *C*; Suttunus *R* [o] Bracalea *AE* [p] uero *RT* [q] Bucchingaham *R* [r–r] spiritum gratissimum *R* [s] tertia *C* [t] *om. AES*

---

[1] Cf. Rom. 13: 9 ('non furaberis: non falsum testimonium dices'); Exod. 20: 15 ('non furtum facies'). The presence of the form 'periuriam' in **C**, and formerly in **A**, suggests confusion over the declension of 'periurium' (accusative plural 'periuria'), possibly on the part of the author, in which case 'periuriam' should arguably be the preferred reading.

[2] Cf. Job 12: 4 ('deridetur enim iusti simplicitas').

[3] Cf. Josh. 23: 14 ('En ego hodie ingredior uiam uniuersae terrae'); and 3 Kgs. (1 Kgs.) 2: 2 ('Ego ingredior uiam uniuersae terrae'), and cf. Gen. 6: 13 ('Finis uniuersae carnis uenit coram me'). The present phrase seems to have been a very widely current conflation of the two ideas (cf. the translation in the Douai Bible). For example, see, *Encomium Emmae Reginae*, ed. Campbell, i. 5 (p. 14), and a charter of *c.*900 (S 359 = BCS 594), 'Quando Ælfred rex . . . uiam uniuerse carnis adiit'.

[4] Probably present-day Brackley, Northamptonshire, attested at 1086 as 'Brachelai' (*DB, Northants.* 21. 1–2; fo. 224b), and, in the later 12th cent., variously as 'Braccalea', 'Brachkelea' and 'Bracchelea' (see *Place-Names of Northamptonshire*, p. 49). For an earlier

or tell lies,[1] do not blaspheme or mock the simple-minded,[2] but persevere in all good works and praise Almighty God at all times, whether in prosperity or in adversity.'

§ 12. When St Rumwold had said all these things, everyone present gave thanks to God, that such power of eloquence should be inspired by heavenly grace in so tiny a child. Then the Blessed Rumwold spoke again: 'Behold, I am entering upon the way of all flesh,[3] since it is not permitted for me to live in this mortal body beyond the hour of my birth. But, after my death, I desire to remain in the place where I was born, for the space of a year; and then I have resolved to be in Brackley for two years.[4] When, however, these three years are over, I intend that my bones should rest for all time in the place which will sometime be known as Buckingham.'[5] The names of those places were not known at that time, but after the passage of many years, they have been discovered or recognized. Now also there are towns sited in these places, which are rich in crops, have many acres of land, and are densely populated by men.[6] The place in which he was born is called (King's) Sutton, the second place is called Brackley, and the third Buckingham.

§ 13. At the end of the third day, just as he had foretold, St Rumwold gave up his spirit dear to God, on the third of November, taken up in the hands of angels.[7] Then, after his death, he was

---

form of the same name, cf. Brackley, Hants., in a charter of Edgar, dated 967 (S 754 = BCS 1200), 'Braceleah'.

[5] This town appears as 'Buccingahamme' (dative) in *ASC* 915 D (cf. *ASC* 918 *A*); as 'Buccyngaham' or 'Buccingaham' in *Secgan*, the late 10th- and early 11th-cent. list of resting-places (Liebermann, *Heiligen*, p. 13); and as 'Bochingheham' in *DB, Bucks.* (e.g. fo. 143a). Cf. A. Mawer and F. M. Stenton, *Place-Names of Buckinghamshire*, EPNS ii (1925), p. 60. Thus three of the direct witnesses to *Vita S. Rumwoldi* seem accurately to have preserved the form current in the first half of the 11th cent.

[6] These intriguing sentences are similar to what was said of King's Sutton, 'Vocatur autem locus ille nunc ab incolis ...' (c. 6); and of Buckingham, 'qui uocabitur quandoque ...' (c. 12). The intention seems to have been to imply that, at the time of Rumwold's birth, none of these places existed as settlements, or at least, that none of them had the name which it had in the author's own day. In the case of King's Sutton, we are twice told the difference between 'then' and 'now' (cf. c. 6). Possibly this was a genuinely-held, though naïve, belief on the hagiographer's part. This third statement is the most ambiguous, and should perhaps be interpreted as an attempt to suggest that the holy sites of Rumwold's resting lay undiscovered for some time, until an 'inuentio' revealed not only the place where the body lay, but also those in which it had lain previously (cf. the 'inuentio' of Ivo, as described by Goscelin, *Vita S. Yuonis*, c. 5; *PL* clv. 84). The impression is almost that these places were believed (or at least claimed) only to have taken on significance as a result of the connection with Rumwold, and certainly to have derived their subsequent fertility and prosperity from it.

[7] The year in which Rumwold is supposed to have lived and died cannot be

sepultus est in eodem loco, sicut idem sanctus iusserat, demumque defuncto Eadwaldo[a] translatus est in alium prelibatum[b] locum ab Widerino[c] presbytero; atque finitis tribus annis delatus est in tercium locum qui nuncupatur (sicut sepe dictum est) Buccingaham;[d] ibique[e] requiescit. Ibi enim[f] et in multis locis inuocatus Sanctus Rumwoldus prestat beneficia se petentibus, dans[g] cecis uisum, claudis gressum, egris diuersis languoribus grauatis sospitatis munus, annuente Domino nostro Iesu Christo, qui in unitate trinitatis [h]ac in trinitate unitatis[h] uiuit et gloriatur[i] Deus, [j]cum genitore omnipotente unus et almo flamine[j1] per infinita[k] secula seculorum. AMEN.[l]

[a] Eadwoldo *C*   [b] prelibanum *C*   [c] Vuiderino *A*   [d] Bucchingaham *R*   [e] ubi nunc *A*; ubi *E*; ubi usque hodie *S*   [f] etenim *R*   [g] *om. AES*   [h–h] *om. RT*   [i] regnat *RT*   [j–j] *om. RT*   [k] omnia *RT*   [l] EXPLICIT VITA SANCTI RVMWOLDI CONFESSORIS *add. AE*

determined for certain, but was evidently regarded as being before 655, the date of Penda's death.

buried in that same place, as he had bidden, and at length, following the death of Eadwald, he was translated to the second pre-ordained place by the priest Widerin; and after three years were past he was taken to the third place, which, as has already been said several times, is called Buckingham; and there he rests. There and in many places, when invoked, St Rumwold bestows favours upon those who ask, giving sight to the blind, making the lame to walk, and granting deliverance to the sick weighed down by various ailments, with the consent of our Lord Jesus Christ Who, in the unity of the Trinity and in the Trinity of unity, lives and is glorified as God, one with the omnipotent Father and the Holy Spirit,[1] throughout infinite ages, AMEN.

[1] Compare Frithegod, *Breuiloquium*, 491, 'in Patris et Nati necnon et Flaminis almi | nomine'; and Byrhtferth, *Vita S. Ecgwini*, iv. 11: 'conregnante Saluatori nostro cum paterna maiestate et Almi flaminis societate'. See *DMLBS*, s.v. 'flamen'.

APPENDIX A

The following is a list of all the portions of more than ten words, which were omitted from *Vita S. Birini* by the two unprinted abbreviations **B** and **F**.

B

c. 1, futurus ... c. 2, ingenuus puer
c. 2, qui quanto se ... c. 3, fortiter inquirebat
c. 3, Electus enim ... spiritum operantem
c. 3, ordinem suscepit ... euectus est
c. 4, longe lateque ... luce letentur
c. 4, Cognouit in eo ... c. 5, scientie qualitatem
c. 5, Imperat illum ... c. 6, inire promittit
c. 6, Romanus ciuis ... c. 8, prestare preualuit
c. 9, Opponit sibi ... humiliter expectabat
c. 9, Insistunt naute ... c. 10, sudore nautarum
c. 10, Notandum est ... agnoscere preualerent
c. 11, Nec desperatione ... inquiritur uacuatur
c. 11, naturam terre experitur ... habens non metuis
c. 11, Ecce quod ... de uirtute humana
c. 12, Stabat autem ... esse potentiam
c. 12, Deus enim qui ... illibatus incederet
c. 12, Mirantur quia ... c. 13, salutis et uite
c. 13, nec potuit naufragium ... ecclesiam spiritualiter
c. 14, Merito etiam dies ... opere predicabat
c. 14, Vacuantur ... c. 15, operari dignatus est
c. 15, iam per multum ... percussa
c. 15, Inimicus ... ministrauit
c. 15, precibus inmurmurat ... aures officiunt
c. 16, Transit senex ... audire iam potest
c. 16, Stupebant ... c. 17, Beda refert
c. 17, ex uerbo apostoli ... Ephesi
c. 17, Procedit aduersum ... uota concordant
c. 17, et salutarem anime ... misterium quidem
c. 18, Vicit qui non ... uictoria coronatur
c. 18, Humiliatur sub manu ... religionem amplexans
c. 18, ac sic pulcherrimo ... in filium
c. 19, uetus homo ... et eius familia

c. 19, Videre erat . . . tendunt ad uitam
c. 20, Legit homines . . . cantare leteris
c. 21, In eadem autem ciuitate . . . in secula seculorum. Amen

F

c. 1, Oritur autem Rome . . . ubique portare
c. 2, Erat omnibus uirtutis . . . c. 3, in spiritum operantem
c. 4, Inuitatur . . . melioris antecedere
c. 6, Romanus ciuis . . . c. 8, prestare preualuit
c. 9, Opponit sibi . . . humiliter expectabat
c. 9, quo ascendente . . . tumultuante succutitur
c. 9, illum uultu . . . contendunt
c. 10, Notandum est . . . agnoscere preualerent
c. 11, timet experiri . . . inquiritur uacuatur
c. 11, Natura maris se . . . erat in celum
c. 11, In naui sedens . . . incedis
c. 11, Petrus fidei . . . uirtute humana
c. 12, Stabat autem . . . armamenta laborant
c. 12, Mirantur uentos . . . esse potentiam
c. 13, Iam iam deos . . . salutis et uite
c. 14, Bene autem per . . . opere predicabat
c. 14, Vacuantur . . . deuote querentes
c. 14, Letatur quia . . . messis excrescit
c. 15, Inimicus . . . ministrauit
c. 15, Sistitur optutibus . . . aures officiunt
c. 16, Transit senex . . . curatorem suum
c. 16, et que deprecando . . . moderatus incessit
c. 16, Stupebant . . . spiritualiter
c. 16, Manus illius . . . non operatorem
c. 17, Procedit aduersum . . . euentum uentum est
c. 17, Dicebat regi . . . c. 18, uictoria coronatur
c. 19, succedente nouitate . . . uniuersa prouincia
c. 19, Sterilis . . . tendunt ad uitam
c. 20, Legit homines . . . oculus esse non potest
c. 20, His et aliis . . . cantare leteris

APPENDIX B

The sermon for the feast of St Birinus in Oxford, Bodleian Library, Digby 39, fos. 52^r–56^r

SEQVITVR OMELIA IN EIVS SANCTA FESTIVITATE SOL-LEMPNITER RECITANTA.[1] Gaudete in Domino, dilectissimi fratres, qui ad sanctissimi patris et protectoris nostri, sancti scilicet Birini sollempnia conuenistis, et spiritali iocunditate letamini, et ex intimo cordis affectu clementiam Domini nostri Iesu Christi conlaudate qui nostram istam (hoc est Occidæntalium Saxonum) prouinciam ab idolatrie erroribus ad agnitionem sui sanctissimi nominis | (fo. 52^v) per huius sancti sacerdotis predicationem perducere dignatus est. Sequamur ergo unanimiter tam sancti doctoris uestigia. Non simus tanti patris degeneres filii, sed sanctitatem uite illius morum nobilitate quantum possumus imitemur. Abiciamus a nobis, iuxta illud beati apostoli, opera tenebrarum et induamus nos arma lucis, sicut in die honeste ambulemus.[2] Quia nox ignorantie recessit et uere scientie nobis lumen illuxit, idcirco filii lucis in omni castitate et pietate ambulemus.[3] Non sint aliicuius[4] nequitie uel malitie occulta in cordibus nostris semina, quia homo uidet in facie, Deus autem corda considerat,[5] nec aliquid illius omnipotentie oculis occultari potest. Preparemus nos in omni bonitate ut preclarus pontifex et pius predicator noster iste Birinus, cuius hodie natalicia deuote celebremus, gaudens nos ante tribunal summi iudicis in die ultimo deducat, quatinus ex numerositate tantorum filiorum illius cumulatur gloria et nos cum illo desiderabilem audire mereamur sententiam, 'Venite benedicti patris mei percipite regnum quod uobis paratum est ab o-| (fo. 53^r) -rigine mundi.'[6] Ille de celesti patria piis orationibus nostrum cotidie agonem adiuuare non desistit, desiderans suos carissimos filios, quos paterna pietate genuit in Christo, ad gloriam perpetue peruenire beatitudinis. Quapropter, fratres karissimi, unusquisque in suo ordine secundum uirium facultatem, fortiter diabolicis resistat suggestionibus ut eternam triumphi

---

[1] *recte* recitanda.

[2] Rom. 13: 12 ('Abiiciamus ergo opera tenebrarum, et induamur arma lucis').

[3] Cf. Eph. 5: 8 ('ut filii lucis ambulate').

[4] *recte* alicuius.

[5] Cf. 1 Kgs. (1 Sam.) 16: 7 ('homo enim uidet ea quae parent, Dominus autem intuetur cor').

[6] Matt. 25: 34 ('Venite benedicti patris mei, possidete paratum uobis regnum a constitutione mundi').

coronam cum pio parente nostro accipere dignus efficiatur. 'Non sunt enim condigne', ut ait apostolus, 'passiones huius temporis, ad superuenturam gloriam que reuelabitur in nobis.'[7] Igitur breue laboris tempus diuina nobis uoluit esse pietas, ad agonis nostri retributionem esse perpetuam, et pro temporali tribulatione permanentis glorie mercede gaudere. Audiuimus itaque cum Deo dilecti sacerdotis gesta licet breuiter legerentur, quantam in omni bonitate habuit deuotionem; audiuimus quoque magnam et mirabilem et uere laudabilem cordis eius in Domino constantiam quando cum beatus Doruernensis ecclesie archipresul Agustinus, sicut in gestis huius patrie legatur,[8] rogatu simul et ortatu beati pape Gregorii, Cantuariorum prouinciam idolatrie quidem eatenus | (fo. 53ᵛ) mancipatam, sed aliquatenus mitiorem cum multis fidei christiane doctoribus adierit, iste cum beati papae Honorii consilio[9] sponte hanc illis temporibus paganissimam intrepidus gentem cum diabolo pugnaturus intrauerat, et quod ille plurimorum amminiculo doctorum, iste ut ita dicam solus, sed non solus quia cum eo Deus uerbum diuinitatis amministrauerit. Hoc quoque ad ipsius augmentum preconii diuine pietati addendum placuisse pie intellegentibus patet quod cum prefate Cantuariorum nationis rex uerbum uite a doctoribus suis audisset, ut uerbis historici loquar, respondisse perhibetur, 'Pulchra quidem sunt uerba et promissa que adsertis,[10] sed quia noua sunt et incerta, non his possum assensum tribuere, relictis eis que tanto tempore cum omni Anglorum gente seruaui.'[11] Haec idcirco dixerim, quia licet beatus idem prenotatus rex, toto corde postmodum in Dominum nostrum Iesum Christum crediderit aliqua tamen refragatione, ac mentis dubietate in ipso predicationis initio caligauerit. Hocque doctoribus aliquantulum laboriosius extiterit, hic uero summus et dilectus noster tantam tamque celerem Christo opitulante in ipso | (fo. 54ʳ) sui sermonis exordio promeruit gratiam, ut nihil refragationis, nihil contrarie dubitationis audierit, nihil asperitatis senserit, sed euangelizante illo in prouincia rex ipse Cynegils absque mora catecizatus, fonte baptismi cum sua gente ablutus est, et ut omnibus se ex toto corde credidisse innotesceret ciuitatem pontificatui aptam regeneratori suo cum omni mentis alacritate concessit. Quam ille dedicatis adornans ecclesi⟨i⟩s Christianis pio labore augmentauit populis,[12] ipse postmodum superno se remuneratore largiente coronam uite percepturus in eadem quidem ecclesia corpore multorum curriculo temporum tumulatus, sed in istam post Dei prouidente gratia translatus urbem; nobis non nostris meritis sed gratuita sola

---

[7] Rom. 8: 18 ('passiones huius temporis, ad futuram gloriam . . .').
[8] Presumably meaning Bede's *Historia Ecclesiastica*.
[9] Bede, *HE* iii. 7 ('cum consilio papae Honorii').
[10] *recte* adfertis.   [11] Bede, *HE* i. 25.
[12] Bede, *HE* iii. 7 ('factis dedicatisque ecclesiis, multisque ad Dominum pio eius labore populis aduocatis').

diuina precedente clementia, ad patrocinium et solatium donatus atque concessus est. Verum ne tante gratie uideamur ingrati, ne tanti patris presentia iudicemur indigni, incedamus cum omni alacritate mentis et tota uir⟨i⟩um facultate illius uite uestigia, ut beatitudinis in qua regnat cum Christo consortes effici mereamur. Nulla carnalis concupiscentia, nulla | (fo. 54ᵛ) secularis ambitio impediat iter nostrum. Curramus per opera pietatis ad celestis patrie portas. Expectant nos ciues aeterne ciuitatis, rex ipse qui uult omnes homines saluos fieri nostram cum sanctis suis uehementer desiderat salutem. Decet enim nos illius esse cooperatores in salute nostra, qui nos in tantum dilexit, ut proprio filio suo non pepercit, sed pro nobis omnibus tradidit illum. Diligamus eum quia ille prior dilexit nos. Faciamus illius uoluntatem, quia uoluntas illius felicitas est nostra. Habeamus semper in mente, quod ipsa ueritas cuidam diuiti respondit in euangelio, 'Si uis uitam ingredi, serua mandata.'[13] 'Que sunt mandata?' 'Nisi caritas Dei et dilectio proximi, in his duobus preceptis tota lex pendet et prophete.'[14] Dilectio itaque proximi in operibus misericordie conprobatur. Qui uero seculi habet substantiam, auxilietur non habenti, qui doctrine habet scientia, corrigat errantem, dicente apostolo Iacobo, 'Qui conuerterit peccatorem ab errore uie sue, saluabit animam eius a morte, et operit multitudinem peccatorum suorum.'[15] Scire debemus, karissimi fratres, quod quantas animas [16]quisque lucratus fuerit Deo, tantas[16] accepturus erit mercedes a Deo. Quantam | (fo. 55ʳ) gloriam habere putatis Sanctum Birinum in celesti regno cum Christo qui tam innumerabilem populum sedula predicatione Christo in terris adquisiuit? Vel quanta sit gloria anime illius super astra inter angelos, dum tantum honorem habet corpus illius inter homines? Vel quid non potest pietatis precibus impetrare in celis, qui tantis in mundo claruit miraculis? Sed omnibus miraculis maior est euangelice predicationis instantia, et sancte claritatis in corde flagrantia. Valde enim uiriliter accepta dominice pecunie talenta multiplicare studuit, ideo feliciter sibi Dominum audiet dicentem, 'Euge serue bone et fidelis, quia supra pauca fuisti fidelis, supra multa te constituam, intra in gaudium Domini tui.'[17] Parua sunt presentis uite bona, in conparatione futurorum bonorum. Sed qui in his fideliter laborat, in illis feliciter requiescet. Iste sanctus, ad cuius concurrere festa uoluistis, pro multorum laborauit salute, ideo plurimorum premia in die iudicii suscepturus erit. Seipsum per abstinentie macerauit

---

[13] Matt. 19: 17 ('Si uis autem ad uitam ingredi, serua mandata').

[14] Matt. 22: 40 ('In his duobus mandatis uniuersa lex pendet, et prophetae').

[15] Jas. 5: 20 ('qui conuerti fecerit peccatorem ab errore uiae suae, saluabit animam eius a morte, et operiet multitudinem peccatorum').

[16-16] This phrase was omitted by the original scribe of the text, and has been added in the margin, probably during official correction; the same occurs a little further on. Both portions may have been omitted by homoeoteleuton, and would thus perhaps correspond to a single line of text in the exemplar.

[17] Matt. 25: 21, 23.

rigorem, aliis per predicationis profuit sedulitatem, ideo laudabilis omnibus extat, iuxta uocem sapientissimi Salomonis, | (fo. 55ᵛ) 'memoria iusti cum laudibus et nomen impiorum putrescet.'[18] Dum uita iustorum laudabitur, iniquitas impiorum quasi stercus detestatur ab omnibus. Quid est felicius ⟨quam⟩ in bona conuersatione a Deo perpetue promereri beatitudinis gloriam, et omnium ore laudari? Cogitemus cotidie qua fiducia ueniamus ante tribunal summi iudicis, quid boni operis nobiscum deferamus. Equitas illius nullius accipiet personam sed unicuique reddet secundum opera sua,[19] et qui plus laborat in opere Dei, plus mercedis accipiet in regno Dei. Vnusquisque in qua uocatione uocatus est,[20] in ea uiriliter suam operetur salutem. Omnibus celestis regni ianua patescit, sed meritorum qualitas alium introducit, alium expellit. Quam miserum est hominem a gloria excludi sanctorum, et eternis cum diabolo deputari flammis, peccatorum sarcina animam submergi in tartara! Iustitie abundantia ad celestem euehit gloriam. Frequentemus sepius ecclesiam Christi, audiamus in ea diligentius uerba Dei, et quod aure percipimus, hoc corde retineamus [21]ut boni operis fructum feramus[21] in patientia, et fraterno amore unusquisque alium adiuuare studeat. Habeamus pre-| (fo. 56ʳ) -clara sanctissimi Byrini patris nostri abundanter exempla, in omni caritatis officio, in fidei feruore, in spei longanimitate, et perseuerantia totius bonitatis. Illius quem tanta celebramus laude et tanto diligimus amore tota mentis intentione in omni conuersatione sancta sequamur uestigia, quatinus uiam uite illius currentes, aeterne beatitudinis cum illo gloriam accipere mereamur, auxiliante nos rege aeterno Domino nostro Iesu Christo qui cum patre et spiritu sancto uiuit et regnat Deus, per omnia secula seculorum, Amen.

Noli, queso pater, munuscula spernere nostra.
Paruula si uideas magna hec dilectio mittit.

---

[18] Prov. 10: 7.
[19] Rom. 2: 6 ('qui reddet unicuique secundum opera eius').
[20] Eph. 4: 1 ('digne ambuletis uocatione qua uocati estis').
[21-21] See n. 16 above.

APPENDIX C

The following material is found only in Oxford, Bodleian Library, Douce 368 (fo. 83ᵛ), as a slightly later addition to *Vita et miracula S. Kenelmi*. A very similar version of the fire may be found in one of the documents contained in the Winchcombe *Landboc*:[1]

Veruntamen, quum, processu temporis, diebus regis Stephani, hostilitate nimium ingruente, propter predonum incursiones ecclesie nostre septa pauperum casulis uallabantur, et quia eorundem indisciplinata actio actibus suis, ut decuit, preuidere non nouerat, prius tuguria, hinc ecclesie culmina uorax flamma consumpsit. Monasterio, itaque, cum scriniis, uestementis, libris, et cartis, ac edificiis omnibus, in cinerem redactis, suprascripta cartula (Willelmi de Solers de capella de Potteslep) eodem incendio conflagrauit.

Of interest is the extra list of what was lost in the fire, in the *Landboc* account, namely 'scrinia, uestementa, libri, cartae'—the last two items being of especial significance, and presumably included in the *Landboc* version because the loss of the pre-existing grant of a chapel at Postlip had to be explained.[2] A similar example of a fund-raising trip is to be found amongst the miracles of St Ecgwine recorded by Dominic. After the church at Evesham had been destroyed by fire, and no funds were available with which to rebuild, Abbot Walter decreed that two monks should set out 'cum reliquiis sancti patris nostri Ecgwini ... per Angliam'.[3]

Latin Text (Douce 386, fo. 83ᵛ)

⟨E⟩t[4] quia recentia non minus quam uetera Dei miracula ueritatis amatores letantibus hauriunt animis, quod recenter contigit scripto tamen traditum audiant et intelligant, scientes quod cum homine uox preterit, scriptum uero posteros illuminat. Anno itaque millesimo centesimo quadragesimo nono, temporis ingruentia, hostilitatis imminentia ecclesie beati martiris septa pauperum casulis uallabantur. Et quia eorundem indisciplinata actio actibus suis preuidere ut decuit non nouerat, ignis predonum nocentissimus ut qui parcere non nouit, prius

---

[1] Ed. Royce, i. 83.

[2] See the discussion of this material by Gee, 'A miracle of Saint Kenelm'.

[3] Macray, *Chronicon de Evesham*, p. 55.

[4] The first letter of this word has been omitted—a space has been left for a coloured initial, which was never added.

tuguria, hinc ecclesie fastigia lambere cepit. Monasterio denique in cinerem redacto cum edificiis omnibus, uel ex hostis humani inuidia, uel meritorum ibidem commorantium exigentia, uel ut deinceps beati Kenelmi martyris excellentia propter hoc infortunium ignotis manifestaretur prouinciis, de beati martyris ecclesia reedificanda uicini eiusdem loci fratres consuluerunt episcopos et abbates et reliquos prudentes. Verebantur etenim ad prememorate ecclesie reedificationem populorum emendicare suffragia, uerentes ob actuum eorum exigentiam horrendum illud incendium contigisse, precipue cum scriptum legatur 'bonarum mentium esse ibi suas culpas agnoscere, ubi non sunt.' Placuit denique prelatis de ecclesie eiusdem negotio pertractantibus ut eiusdem loci monachi religiosi duo uel tres cum corpore beati Kenelmi per eandem et continentes proficiscerentur prouincias, episcopi Wigornensis scripto et comprouincialium abbatum testimonio, ecclesie beati martyris incumbentem necessitatem referentibus. Preparato itaque fratrum itinere et sancti martyris peregrinatione inchoata aliquod peregrinationis hospicium Legrecestrie corpus susceperit sacratissimum. Vbi mirabilis Deus in sanctis suis ad martyris sui inuocationem languentium medelam mirabiliter est operatus. Inter quos iuuencula quedam, que pre infirmitatis nimietate in extremam (ut astantes aiebant) deciderat necessitatem, gustata aqua benedicta in qua reliquie abluebantur, quod animi deuotione petiit, celeriter recepit, largiente Domino nostro Iesu Christo qui suam misericordiam et puelle orationem non amouit a se.

⟨T⟩am[5] prospero itaque successu et iocundo miraculo excitati monachi quibus ducibus patriam beatus mar . . .[6]

English Translation

And since lovers of truth joyfully drink in the recent miracles of God no less than the old ones, let them read and understand that which has happened recently, handed on in writing, knowing that the voice passes away with the man, but writing illuminates those who come after. Therefore, in the year one thousand one hundred and forty-nine, because of the dangerous nature of the time, and the imminent threat of hostility, the walls of the church of the blessed martyr were surrounded by the huts of the poor. And because the undisciplined behaviour of these people knew not how to foresee the consequences of its own actions as it ought, fire, that most wicked of plunderers, since it does not know when enough is enough, began to play first round the huts, and from there the gables of the church. The end of it was that the monastery and all its buildings were reduced to ashes, either through the ill-will of a human enemy, or by the

[5] As above, the first letter of this word has been omitted although space was left for the initial.

[6] The text breaks off here at the bottom of fo. 83ᵛ, where the quire ends.

desert of those living there,[7] or so that afterwards, as a consequence of this misfortune, the excellence of the blessed martyr Kenelm might be made known to provinces as yet unaware of him. The brothers in the neighbourhood consulted the bishops and abbots and other wise persons about the rebuilding of the church of the holy martyr. For they were afraid to go begging for help from the people to rebuild the aforesaid church, fearing that the horrendous fire had come about as a consequence of their own deeds [i.e. their sinfulness], especially since it is written: 'it is the mark of good minds that they acknowledge their sins even where there are none.' At length the prelates who were dealing with the affairs of that church, ordained that two or three devout monks from there should set out with the body of St Kenelm to travel through that and the neighbouring provinces, carrying a deed from the bishop of Worcester and a testimony from the abbots of the province, explaining the necessity weighing upon the church of the holy martyr. Therefore when the brothers' journey had been arranged and the peregrination of the holy martyr begun, the most holy body was put up at a hospice in Leicester. There God, miraculous in His saints, wondrously provided healing to the sick upon the invocation of his martyr. Amongst these, a little girl, through excessive illness, collapsed (as those standing by reported), on the point of death. Taking a draught from the holy water in which the relics had been washed, she swiftly received that which she had prayed for with devotion of mind, through the generosity of Our Lord Jesus Christ, who did not put away from Him His mercy and the prayers of the girl.

Now, therefore, spurred on by such a favourable success and a delightful miracle, the monks, in whose care the martyr . . .

[7] Literally, the phrase 'ex . . . meritorum . . . exigentia' seems to mean 'by the requirement of the deserts/deserving'; cf. *DMLBS* s.v. 'exigentia', 2.

APPENDIX D. *VITA BREVIOR S. KENELMI*

The following is a transcript of the lections which make up *Vita brevior*, preserved only in CCCC 367, part ii, fos. 45ʳ–48ʳ.[1] One folio of the manuscript is now lost, so that the text begins part-way through the second lection. Those sections of the text which closely parallel *Vita et miracula S. Kenelmi* are printed in italics.[2] As noted above, p. cxxii, a brief account of the Life of Kenelm, apparently derived from *Vita brevior*, was included in the Annals of Winchcombe, in the twelfth-century manuscript London, BL, Cotton Tiberius E. IV (at fo. 15ʳ), and correspondences are reported in the footnotes. Furthermore, certain phrases of *Vita brevior* seem to be echoed in the antiphons and responses for the Office of the feast of St Kenelm as preserved uniquely in the mid-twelfth-century breviary, Valenciennes, Bibliothèque Municipale, 116, fos. 208ʳ–210ᵛ,[3] and these parallels have also been signalled in the footnotes, for the sake of comparison.

[. . .] *forma, perfusus diuina dilectione et gratia, Deo et hominibus amabilis erat aetatula.* Gaudebat in Christo pater super hoc unicum lumen oculorum, sicut Abraham super Isaac, et in eo sancta exultatione paternum affectum dilatabat, et in eo spem et salutem populi sui ponebat, quem de fructu uentris sui sedere super sedem suam si modo regi celorum placuisset, patria pietate preoptabat. Sed in beneplacito aeterni regis de terra in celum eius gloria translata est, et de corruptibili regno ad inmortalia sceptra Kenelmus raptus est. Raptus est ne malicia mutaret intellectum illius, aut ne fictio deciperet animam illius,[4] propter hoc properauit Dominus educere eum de medio iniquitatum,[5] quoniam gratia Dei et misericordia est in sanctos eius et respectus in electos illius.[6] .III.
Sed adhuc pia infantia florentem successorem paterni regni *pretendebat eum amor populi sui,* sed magis preelegit eum gratia Christi et dedit ei regale sceptrum martyrii, et regiam coronam glorie regni sempiterni.[7] At illum uenerabilis pater condecenter sibi heredem coram patribus et optimatibus terre designat, et maxime ipsi parricidali |(fo. 45ᵛ) nutritio eius

---

[1] See the description on pp. cxxi–cxxii above.

[2] Cf. the commentary above.

[3] See p. cxxx above, and Appendix E.

[4] Wisd. 4: 11. Compare Gerald of Wales, *Vita Ethelberti regis et martyris*, ed. James, 'Two Lives', p. 228, where this same biblical citation is applied to the death of Æthelberht.

[5] Wisd. 4: 14.   [6] Ibid. 4: 15.

[7] Cf. Valenciennes 116, fo. 208ᵛ (respond of Lesson III).

Ascheberto omni fide innocentiae commendat. Sic, sancte Kenulfe, fideliter committis causam tuam nescius infideli; sed fidelissimus Christus mira dispensatione per ipsum infidelem suscipiet fidele depositum tuum. Per ipsum infidelem et regis ac domini sui interemptorem optimus regum faciet sibi regium martyrem et dabit eum populo suo perpetuum principem, et nomen ac memoriale eius in generationem et generationem.[8] .IIII.

Igitur glorioso rege Kenulfo de terreno *ad sidereum* solium Dauitico iure assumpto regnum digno successu dignoque populi sui fauore censetur Kenelmo. Sed quia septennis fere adhuc puericia nondum preualebat, Quendrytha soror maior natu serpentina astutia regia iura preripiebat. Inde uero spem crudelem trahebat, quod si unicus germanus de medio ablatus foret nichil iam eius uoluntati et imperio resisteret. Cesset mala emulatio; nulla eius innocentiam *regnandi* temptat *ambitio*. Ille debetur precelsiori regno; ad sublimius solium iam euocatur. Cito crescat, cito mortalis eui torrentem per Mare Rubrum transeat, iam mittet in eum Dominus falcem, | (fo. 46ʳ) iam metet, iam uindemiabit eum sibi.[9] Veni martyr ad Libanum, ueni, uenies et transibis ad montes Seyr et Hermon, a cubilibus leonum, a montibus leopardorum,[10] regius lapis sanctuarii Dei, de capite platearum[11] ibis in thesaurum Domini, ut luceas in diademate regis altissimi. Veni, inuitat te mater uera Syon. O Soror, o mater pulchre dilectionis Syon: recipe fratrem, refoue pignus amabile in spiritu dulcedinis tue, illa altera soror quae eum crudeliter mittit tibi, facta est ei amarissima, tu sis ei in Christo dulcissima. In iocunditate letitie tue amplectere in gremium pacis tue eius innocentiam loetali passione decoctam, quia torrentem et salsuginem mortalitatis pertransiuit anima eius,[12] et anima eius sicut passer erepta est de laqueo uenantium,[13] superest ut requiescat et exultet in regno Christi coronatus.[14] .V.

Angebatur ergo animi *emula soror* Kenelmi,[15] nec poterat eum rectis oculis respicere nec pacifice alloqui, sicut nec Ioseph fratres sui, nec Saul Dauid. Nichil odiosius erat ei *fraterna felicitate*, nichil inportunius eius uita et salute. Sepe eius | (fo. 46ᵛ) mortem cruenta mente uersabat, sed immanitate sceleris repercussa est. Sed tandem dira cupido regnandi, seuam conscientiam ausu crudelitatis armauit.[16] Omni ergo intentione *insidiabatur* eius sanguini sic*ut Herodias Iohanni*,[17] *uel sicut Iezabel Helie, et sicut Cain* extincto *Abel* regnum querebat *fraterno sanguine*. Omnia

---

[8] Ex. 3: 15.　　　　　　[9] Rev. 14: 19.　　　　　　[10] S. of S. 4: 8.
[11] Lament. 4: 1.　　　　　　　　　　　　　　　　　　[12] Ps. 123(124): 5.
[13] Ps. 123(124): 7. Cf. Valenciennes 116, fo. 208ʳ (sixth psalm antiphon of Nocturn I).
[14] Cf. Valenciennes 116, fo. 209ʳ (respond of Lesson IV).
[15] Cf. ibid. fo. 209ᵛ (respond of Lesson V).
[16] Cf. Tiberius, E. ɪᴠ, fo. 15ʳ, 'cuius seuam conscientiam dira cupido regnandi armarat ausu crudelitatis . . .'.
[17] See n. 15 above.

temptauit, omnia fecit, in omnibus se misit, ut indolem Kenelmi absumeret. .VI.

Videns ergo Quendrytha *quia non est perniciosior pestis* ad nocendum *quam familiaris inimicus*, magistrum ac nutritorem pueri cruentissimum[18] scilicet sui furoris exsequutorem, ita Eue serpente dictante aggreditur. 'Vides', inquit, 'O Ascheberte, quia tuo labore educatum tuaque diligentia seruatum, iam omnium oculi dominum et regem huc ambiunt,[19] tibi uero nullum nomen nulla gratia tantorum beneficiorum assignatur. Ne ergo te longius morer, patet nobis regnum Merciorum, patent lati fines Anglorum, tantum modo auferatur de medio nostri unius obstaculum. Magnum scilicet mereberis talis iuguli premium[20] dum me fraterni sanguinis precio[21] emeris cum imperio Anglorum.' *Tali modo sepe consiliati absconderunt laqueos,* | (fo. 47[r]) *intenderunt arcum, parauerunt sagittas suas in pharetra ut sagittent in obscuro rectum corde.* .VII.

Ea tempestate uidit dormiens pre*claram uisionem*[22] Christi *hostia Kenelmus, quam cum* altis *suspiriis* et sancta simplicitate *referebat nutrici suae* sacrate. '*Visum est mihi', inquit, 'in somnis, O mater karissima, quod ante cubiculum meum arbor staret altissima usque ad sidera; me uero uidebam stare in eius* altissimo *uertice; unde late poteram omnia conspicere. Erat autem arbor pulcherrima; et late effusis ramis spaciosa,* uidebaturque *ab imo* usque *ad summum omnibus floribus refertissima.* Tum uero *uidebam* innumerabilibus *lampadibus et luminaribus* arborem *totam ardere,* totamque terram late hoc splendore clarescere, *michi uero regni regiones et populos cum suis opibus prona curuari deuotione. Cum ergo de tanta specula mirarer uisionem quidam meorum* hominum *subter irruentes succiderunt arborem, et illa cecidit ingenti ruina, ego uero candida* mox *efficiebar auicula, et libero uolatu* me recepi in *aethera'. Vix eloquutus erat* puer *uisionem, cum nutrix tundens pectus, 'heu me', inquit, 'fili mi dulcissime, ergone insidie tuorum ergone maligna* | (fo. 47[v]) *consilia sororis ac* procuratoris *tui preualebunt aduersum te? Heu quam timeo arborem illam succisam* pie *indolis tue presignare iacturam.* Sed credimus quia recipiet te clementia Dei celi in eternam requiem et gloriam suam, quia si uera reuelatio est passionis tue, consequenter uera creditur et coronae'. .VIII.

Tandem ergo *Aschebertus* peracturus impietatem, surgit mane uelox ad effundendum sanguinem, puerumque *abducit* secum *in siluam quasi* ad *uenandi oblect*ationem. Pergit ergo Kenelmus quasi *agnus* et quasi Isaac ad immolandum, ipsum redemptionis suae sequens agnum.[23] Ventum est in uastam siluam;[24] querit seductor ubi eum immolet. Cum ita duceretur *ad*

---

[18] Cf. Tiberius, E. IV, fo. 15[r], 'nutritore suo cruentissimo'.
[19] Cf. Valenciennes 116, fo. 208[r] (fifth psalm antiphon of Nocturn I).
[20] Cf. ibid. fo. 209[v] (respond of Lesson VI).
[21] Cf. ibid. fo. 209[r] (third psalm antiphon of Nocturn II).
[22] Cf. ibid. fo. 209[r] (first psalm antiphon of Nocturn II).
[23] Cf. ibid. fo. 209[r] (second psalm antiphon of Nocturn II).
[24] Cf. Tiberius, E. IV, fo. 15[r], 'in uasta syluaque nemorosa'.

uictimam agniculus Christi, sic arguebat *cruentum* animum *proditoris* sui, 'Nouit Deus quid in me penses; *quod facis fac citius*'.[25] Tandem ergo inuento quodam subulco iussit insontem *sub arbore spinea*[26] ubi aptior locus celandi sceleris uidebatur trucidari, et mox terra ab humanis oculis et notitia defodi. Sed qui solo *teste celo* est iugulatus, *celo teste* per *columpnam lucis* ex diuina bonitate postmodum est reuelatus.[27] *Abscisum* est igitur *caput Kenelmi* natalis et in-| (fo. 48ʳ) -nocentiae candore *lacteum*, unde *lactea columba aureis pennis* euolauit in celum,[28] dum *ipse* propriis *palmulis extensis* reciperet caput abscisum, *ut* appareret *preciosa in conspectu Domini mors sancti sui*.[29] Vbi ergo martyr occubuit sanguine purpuratus, ibi nunc est oratorium et uirtutum Dei locus,[30] ibi *fons sacer* emanauit, *qui* adhuc fideli populo et potum et *salutem inpendit*.[31] Ibi etiam sicut et ubi nunc in Christo requiescit exuberante gratia Dei liberantur uarii infirmi, soluuntur ferro aut debilitate uinculati,[32] multaque diuinorum miracula beneficiorum, commendant ⟨martyrem suum⟩.[33]

---

[25] Cf. Valenciennes 116, fo. 209ᵛ (respond of Lesson VII).

[26] Cf. Tiberius, E. IV, fo. 15ʳ, 'sub arbore spinosa'. Cf. Valenciennes 116, fo. 210ʳ (respond of Lesson IX).

[27] Cf. Valenciennes 116, fo. 211ʳ (first antiphon of Lauds).

[28] Cf. Tiberius, E. IV, fo. 15ʳ, 'uerum qui solo teste celo . . . euolat in celum'.

[29] Cf. Valenciennes 116, fo. 210ʳ (respond of Lesson VIII).

[30] Cf. ibid. fo. 210ʳ (respond of Lesson IX).

[31] Cf. ibid. fo. 210ᵛ (respond of Lesson X).

[32] Cf. ibid. fo. 210ʳ (antiphon to canticles of Nocturn III).

[33] See n. 30 above.

APPENDIX E

The office for the feast of St Kenelm from Valenciennes, Bibliothèque Municipale 116 (109), fos. 208ʳ–211ʳ.[1]

In Natalicio Sancti Kenelmi
Ant. Aue martir
Capitulum. Beatus uir qui suffert[2]
Resp. Miles Christi
In Evangelio.
Ant. Alme puer Kenelme inter natos regum preclare bene agno Christo sicut Abel mactatus est agnicule et bibisti calicem uiuum bethleemitarum innocentium et inter illa lactentia agmina sequeris agnum agnorum et cantas canticum nouum, alleluia.
Ps. Magnificat
Oratio. Presta quesumus
Commune unius martiris
Collecta. Omnipotens et misericors Deus qui nobis preclaram huius diei leticiam pro beati Kenelmi martyris tui solennitate tribuisti, intende serenus uota fidelis populi, et concede ut cuius hodie gesta percolimus, eius semper meritis et precibus sulleuemur.
Per Inuitatorium. Quo regnant reges regi Christo iubilemus. Qui dat martyrio regnum brauiumque Kenelmo. **Ps**. Venite

In I. Nocturno
Ant. Sanctus pater et rex Kenulfus sanctum et regalem florem germinauit Kenelmum et Dominus nouit uiam iustorum.
Ps. Beatus uir[3]
Ant. Hunc heredem patris querebat soror extinguere et regnare et quare meditati sunt mania aduersus Christum Domini.
Ant. Almis Kenelmi profectibus deteriorabatur soror eius more impiorum ut mirificaret Dominus sanctum suum.
Ant. Defensorem pueri compellat insidiatrix uoce Caiphe linguis enim suis dolose agebant sed tu Domine bene dices iusto.
Ant. Vides inquit soror pueri quia omnium oculi dominum et regem hunc ambiunt aufer eum de medio terre destrue Domine inimicum et defensorem quia ex ore infantium perfecisti laudem.

---

[1] The twelve lections are drawn verbatim from *Vita et miracula S. Kenelmi* and have therefore not been reproduced here.
[2] Jas. 1: 12.
[3] Ps. 111(112).

Ant. Intendit arcum obseruator paruuli Kenelmi eamus inquit in siluam ad delicias uenabulorum quomodo dicitis anime mee transmigra in montem sicut passer.
Vers. Gloria et honor

| (fo. 208ᵛ) **Lectio .I.** Kenulfus gloriosissimus . . . diuine adoptionis.[4]
Resp. Filius sanctorum puer Kenelmus sancti Kenulfi regis filius sanctus de sanctis parentibus est ortus.
Vers. Filius lucis et filius gratie Dei. Sanctus

Lectio .II. Hunc euo paruulum . . . in obscuro rectum corde.[5]
Resp. Puer Kenelmus Anglorum puerorum decus coheres angelorum et flos inter flores martirum.
Vers. Et sidus est inter sidera regium. Et flos

Lectio .III. Tandem Ascebertus ut ille . . . malorum totus soporatur.[6]
Resp. Successorem paterni regni pretendebat eum amor populi sui sed preelegit eum gratia Christi.
Vers. Et regio martyri dedit coronam glorie regni sempiterni. Gratia

Lectio .IIII. Cruentissimus nutricius . . . | (fo. 209ʳ) celebris habetur.[7]
Resp. Leta mater Syon amplectere in gremium pacis tue passam innocentiam Kenelmi quia torrentem pertransiuit anima eius exultet in regno Christi coronatus.
Vers. De torrente in uia bibit propterea exaltabit caput. In regno

In II. Nocturno
Ant. Preuiderat se glorificandum uisione preclara stare se in summitate arboris ad sidera et late sibi curuari omnia et arbor in singulis ramis erat luminarium et florum plena requiescet in monte sancto tuo Domine sine macula.
Ps. Domine quis[8]
Ant. Ibat quasi agnus et ut Ysaac ad immolandum sequens agnum redemptionis sue Domine in uirtute tua letabitur rex.
Ant. Accepto precio sanguinis tradidit Kenelmum ille alter Scarioth dominum suum sic decollatus martyr introiuit portas regis glorie.
Ant. Annuntiemus opera Dei sanctos mirificantis quia ignotum funus martyris candida bos seruabat inseparabilis.
Ant. Sepultus martyr in Anglica sua traditur celitus reuelatus in mundi specula Roma ut celestem filiolum celebraret summa mater ecclesia quam magnificata sunt Domine opera tua.
Ant. Vt rea ualde soror dixit fantasma uidetur mox a fronte cadens oculorum defuit usus.

---

[4] *Vita et miracula* c. 1.
[5] c. 2.   [6] c. 5.
[7] c. 6.   [8] Ps. 14(15).

Lectio .V. Hinc seuissimus carnifex . . . mors sancti sui commendetur.[9] |
(fo. 209ᵛ)
Resp. Emula soror martiris Kenelmi insidiabatur eius sanguini sicut
Herodias Iohanni.
Vers. Et prebet gladium innocentis capiti. Sicut Herodias

Lectio .VI. Asseritur etiam quod . . . pecualis diligentia.[10]
Resp. Dixit Quendrida procuratori fratris sui occide michi puerum
Kenelmum et accipe magnum fraterni iuguli premium.
Vers. Et morte coheredis heredem me facies regni Merciorum. Et accipe

Lectio .VII. Candida bos . . . appellari consueuit.[11]
Resp. Cum duceretur ad uictimam agniculus Christi sic arguebat
cruentum animum perditoris sui.
Vers. Videt Deus quid in me penses quod facis fac citius. Sic

Lectio .VIII. At Quendrida empto . . . | (fo. 210ʳ) sublata disparuit.[12]
Resp. Abscisum est igitur caput Kenelmi lacteum ipse propriis palmulis
recepit caput abscisum.
Vers. Vt appareret preciosa in conspectu Domini mors sancti sui. Ipse
propriis

⟨**In III. Nocturno**⟩
Ad Cantica Ant. Vbi Kenelmus occubuit et ubi nunc in Christo requiescit ibi exuberante gratia Dei liberantur uarii infirmi et ferro uinculati;
nomine eterno hereditauit Dominus martyrem.
Ps. Beatus uir

Lectio .IX. Igitur sacer apostolicus . . . eum uisa exposuere.[13]
Resp. Sub arbore spinea martirizatus est puer Kenelmus ubi nunc est
oratorium et uirtutum Dei locus.
Vers. Et miracula Dei beneficiorum commendant martirem suum. Vbi

Lectio .X. Dehinc memoratus papa . . . | (fo. 210ᵛ) muro cinctum.[14]
Resp. In loco martirii sancti fons sacer emanauit qui adhuc fideli populo
et potum et salutem impendit.
Vers. Et alibi ubi sancti feretrum requieuit alius fons sitientibus emersit.
Qui adhuc

Lectio .XI. In assumptione autem . . . Wigornense auferrent.[15]
Resp. O dilectam Deo animam Kenelmi cuius corpusculum reuelauit
fulgida columpna celestis radii.
Vers. Visa est index celestis thesauri. Fulgida

Lectio .XII. Altercantibus autem . . . in amnem decurrit.[16]

---

⁹ c. 7.   ¹⁰ c. 8.   ¹¹ c. 9.   ¹² c. 10.
¹³ c. 11.   ¹⁴ c. 12.   ¹⁵ cc. 13–14.   ¹⁶ cc. 14–15.

Resp. Flos regalis aue puer atque patrone Ke-| (fo. 211ʳ) -nelme. Te soror innocuum ceu Cain sustulit Abel. Cuius martirium tot celica signa locuntur.

⟨**Vers.**⟩ Multis multa salus fulges tibi fulget olimphus. Cuius martirium. In illo tempore. Nisi granum.[17] Euangelium.

⟨**Coll.**⟩ Omnipotens et misericors Deus

Ad laudes. Celo teste martirizatus Kenelmus celo teste est declaratus per columpnam lucis testimonia tua domine credibilia facta sunt nimis.

Ant. Sorori fratricidii magistre ceciderunt oculi a fronte ne uideret fratrem extinctum quem uidere non passa est uiuum.

Ant. A facie sancti feretri ceciderunt oculi insidiatricis super uersum quem legebat testem perditionis hoc inquit opus eorum qui locuntur mala aduersus animam meam.

Ant. Diuinitus inuentum martiris corpus ferebat ad ecclesiam populus suus regem suum plangentes sed pro martire Dominum benedicentes.

Ant. Martyris glebam comitante populo eduxit Dominus fontem sitienti-bus de terra sicut quondam de petra aque que super celos sunt et omnes abissi laudent nomen Domini.

Capitulum. Beatus uir qui suffert[18]
Resp. Sic Kenelme martyr
Vers. Et impetra
Ymnus. Martir Dei qui uincit

In Euangelio.
Ant. Sicut agnus ductus sum ut occiderer et nesciebam inimicus insidi-ator factus est michi sicut leo in siluam tradidit me quem diligebam et plaga crudeli percussit. Agne Dei suscipe in pace animam seruuli tui Kenelmi.
Ps. Beatus
Oratio. Omnipotens et misericors
Ad primam: Ant. Celo teste
Ad tertiam: Ant. Vbi Kenelmus
Ad sextam: ⟨**Ant.**⟩ Sorori fratricidii
Ad nonam: Ant. Diuinitus
Ad Vesperas: Ant. Dilecte Deo, Kenelme Deus qui iustificat per te preces nostra suscipiat nec sit qui Deo iustificante condempnet.
Ps. Dixit Dominus[19]
Ant. Vt rea ualde
Ps. Beatus uir[20]
Ant. O beate martir Kenelme pium dominum ibidem pro iniquitatibus nostris deposce.

---

[17] John 12: 24.   [18] Jas. 1: 12.
[19] Ps. 109(110).   [20] Ps. 111(112).

Ps. Laudate pueri[21]

Ant. Testis es Domine meritorum sancti tui Kenelmi quem ineffabili gratia assumpsisti. Fac eum nobis intercessorem quem tot signis fecisti uenerabilem.

Ps. Credidi[22]

Capitulum: Beatus qui suffert

Resp. Iustus germinabit sicut lilium.

Vers. Et florebit in eternum ante Dominum. Gloria

In Euangelio. Martir magne Dei puer alme Kenelme superni. Deuotis famulis tua festa colentibus assis. Virgo sequens agnum pie laudans immaculatum. Cernere quem tecum fac nos sine fine per euum Alleluia. Suscepit Dominus puerum suum Kenelmum et in sede regni eterni exaltauit eum o sancte martyr respice tuam plebem tuum patrocinium pio amore in Christo complectentem aufer omnem cladem et da nobis tecum perpetuam mansionem.

Ps. Magnificat

Coll. Omnipotens et misericors

---

[21] Ps. 112(113).   [22] Ps. 115(116).

APPENDIX F. The baptism of St Rumwold

The instructions given by the infant saint concerning the various stages of his own formal initiation into the Christian faith are fairly explicit. Indeed, *Vita S. Rumwoldi* is apparently unique among saints' Lives for the detail in which the baptism is described. Quite frequently, a saint's baptism was not mentioned at all, as is the case with the majority of Merovingian Lives edited in *MGH*, SRM, ii–vii, and in many Anglo-Latin Lives the baptism is dismissed in a single stock phrase. In order to establish the extent to which the ceremony described here conforms with what is already known about baptism in late Anglo-Saxon England, it seems best to set out precisely the import of Rumwold's stipulations. The baptism is to be that of an infant (in danger of an early death), administered in several stages, beginning with the admission to the catechumenate (during which the child's name will be used for the first time), then blessing of the baptismal water and aspersion/immersion in an *ad hoc* stone font (in the middle of a field), to be followed immediately by holy communion, apparently in both kinds. The rites are to be executed by one priest, while another priest is to act as sponsor or godparent, for both the admission to the catechumenate, and the baptism itself. The parents of the infant are virtually excluded from the ceremony, although present. It is likely that the rites described here reflect something of tenth- or eleventh-century practice in England, that is, of the time when *Vita S. Rumwoldi* was written, rather than of the seventh century, when the infant is purported to have lived.

Infant baptism, the biblical authorities for which have been hotly contested, was practised throughout Christendom as a matter of course, from at least the sixth century.[1] The missionaries sent from Rome to Britain in the sixth and seventh centuries brought with them traditions and liturgical books from home. Although at the time of the conversion, mass baptisms of adults occurred, such as were described by Bede, it is fairly clear that the practice of infant baptism (regardless of whether the child was sickly or not) was also instituted, if not already carried out, by the Celtic Church, following the Gallican rite of baptism. The various testimonies to this fact have been assembled elsewhere and do not need to be

---

[1] See J. D. C. Fisher, *Christian Initiation: Baptism in the Medieval West*, Alcuin Club Collections, xlvii (London, 1965), pp. 3–7, and J. Lynch, *Godparents and Kinship in Early Medieval Europe* (Princeton, NJ, 1986), pp. 117–22, and 334.

repeated here.[2] Hence there is nothing out of the ordinary about the baptism of the infant Rumwold.

The early Church developed a complicated rite of Christian initiation, involving several weeks of religious instruction and ritual cleansings (exorcism) for the candidates, or catechumens, leading up to the actual baptism ceremony at Easter or Pentecost (except *in extremis*). Probably the oldest known description of the baptismal liturgy as used in the West is *Ordo romanus XI*,[3] composed possibly in late sixth- or seventh-century Rome to accompany the rite contained in the Gelasian sacramentary, and certainly in use in Francia in the eighth and ninth centuries.[4] The gradual reduction of this lengthy rite to more practical proportions occurred in response to various social and other conditions, in particular the universal practice of infant baptism (which required the ceremony to be carried out all year round rather than simply at the canonical seasons). So, for example, between about 801 and 804, it is thought that Alcuin may have included among the additions he composed to the Gregorian sacramentary sent by Pope Hadrian to Charlemagne in about 785, a continuous rite which passed through the stages of the catechumenate and baptism at a single stroke.[5] Such a rite was probably also used in Anglo-Saxon England. For example, the sacramentary known as the Leofric missal, written on the Continent, with additions made *c.*970 at Glastonbury, and in the mid-eleventh century at Exeter, contains a rite which begins with the order 'ad catechuminum faciendum' and continues straight on to the blessing of the font and the baptism (fos. 312^v–319^r).[6]

The essential elements of the rites as found in the last two named liturgical books are as follows: admission of the candidate to the catechumenate, the exorcism and blessing of salt, which is then placed in the catechumen's mouth, the blessing of the water in the font, the pouring of chrism-oil into the water in the sign of the cross, sprinkling the water over those present, then the triple renunciation of Satan, his works and pomps, preceded by an inquiry as to the catechumen's name, exsufflation and the signing of the cross on the forehead and chest, a further administration of salt, touching the nose and ears with spittle, anointing of the chest and back with consecrated oil, a triple confession of faith again preceded by a

---

[2] Cf. Fisher, *Initiation*, p. 82, and Foot, '"By water in the Spirit"', pp. 171–92.

[3] Ed. M. Andrieu, *Les Ordines Romani du haut moyen âge*, 5 vols., Spicilegium sacrum lovaniense, Études et documents, xi, xxiii, xxiv, xxviii, xxix (Louvain, 1931–61), ii. 365–447.

[4] Lynch, *Godparents*, pp. 289–90.

[5] The Carolingian developments from *Ordo Romanus xi* onwards are described succinctly by Lynch, pp. 288–304.

[6] Compare also the order found in the 'Missal of Robert of Jumièges', Rouen, Bibl. mun. 274 (Y. 6), written probably in the early 11th cent., at Ely, Peterborough, or Winchester (ed. Wilson, pp. 93–100).

request to be told the name of the candidate, and baptism 'sub trina mersione, sanctam trinitatem semel inuocando'. As the candidates rise from the font, the priest makes the sign of the cross on their forehead with chrism, anoints their head with chrism and gives the candidate a white chrismal garment, and finally administers the communion.

Many of the details of Rumwold's own baptism are not described, such as the exorcism and administering of salt, the renunciation of Satan and so on. It should also be noted that there is no explicit reference to confirmation. Strictly speaking, this, unlike baptism, could only be administered by a bishop. Originally, the laying-on of hands had immediately followed baptism, but increasingly, as baptism was administered by priests to infants and adults throughout the year, the presence of a bishop became a physical impossibility, especially in rural areas, and confirmation had to be postponed.[7] Presumably, then, it is to be understood that since neither Widerin nor Eadwald was competent to carry out the ceremony, Rumwold remained unconfirmed. Despite the separation of confirmation from baptism, the holy communion continued to be administered to those newly baptized (usually in only one kind) until the twelfth century, when the theological developments of the time called the practice into question.[8] The naming of children was only formally linked with baptism in the tenth century.[9]

It is noteworthy that Rumwold's strictures are made to extend even to the question of godparents. The role of the baptismal sponsor was originally developed in the third century as the formal means by which an already baptized member of the church could provide a testimony to the good character and earnest intentions of the candidate for baptism. Since at about the same time, infant baptism was on the increase, the further function of the sponsor was to respond on behalf of the child during the scrutinies and tests involved in the baptismal rite.[10] As the rite of initiation developed, so the duties of the baptismal sponsor increased, until the natural parents of the infant were almost totally excluded from the ceremony.[11]

Baptismal sponsorship took on a social significance, in that it set up a whole new set of relationships extending beyond those of blood-kinship. A kinship was formed not only between the baptized and the godparent, but also between the godparent and the natural parents, or coparents.[12] A. Angenendt has made a lengthy examination of the political significance baptism took on during the conversion of Anglo-Saxon England.[13] Such

---

[7] Fisher, *Initiation*, pp. 80–2, 87; and Lynch, pp. 210–11.
[8] Fisher, *Initiation*, pp. 101–8.
[9] Lynch, *Godparents*, p. 172.
[10] Ibid., pp. 333–4.   [11] Ibid., pp. 288–305.
[12] See ibid. 163–204, on the spiritual family in Frankish society.
[13] *Kaiserherrschaft und Königstaufe* (Berlin, 1984), pp. 176–86.

was the context for the supposed desire of Rumwold's parents to invite 'conuicinos reges ac duces' to be the infant's godparents, with which one might compare, for example, Bede's account of the baptism of Cynegils, at which Oswald acted as godparent.[14] It was, however, not unknown for priests to become baptismal sponsors.[15]

[14] *HE* iii. 7.

[15] E.g. *ASC* s.a. 639 records that Birinus baptized Cuthred at Dorchester, and received him as a godson. Cf. Angenendt, p. 127; Lynch, *Godparents*, pp. 167–9.

INDEX OF MANUSCRIPTS

INDEX OF CITATIONS AND ALLUSIONS

A. BIBLICAL ALLUSIONS

B: SOURCES AND PARALLELS IN CLASSICAL, PATRISTIC, AND MEDIEVAL TEXTS

C: PARALLELS IN HAGIOGRAPHICAL SOURCES

GENERAL INDEX

Matthew Paris, monk of St Albans
   cxxxviif.
Maurice, bishop of London xliii, 53n.
Merefin, St clxxii
Minster Lovell, Oxon., church dedicated
   to St Kenelm cxx
Minster-in-Thanet 54n.
miracles: of St Birinus liif., 20–5, 30–3
   of St Kenelm xci, 72–89
   of St Rumwold 102–3
   of St Swithun liv–lx
missals lxiii, cxv, cxlii

Naunton, Glos. 74–5
night office, *see* lections for the night
   office

Oda, archbishop of Canterbury 93n.
   feast added to Canterbury calendar
   xxvi; see also *Vitae*
Odo, cardinal bishop of Ostia, author of
   Miracula S. Mildburge xlivn.
Old English Martyrologist, use of
   legendary by xvi
Oliver Sutton, bishop of Lincoln cxlviii
Osbern, monk of Christ Church, Can-
   terbury, hagiographer xxv, xlvf., c,
   77n.
Osbert of Clare, monk of Westminster
   52n.
Osgot Clapa 74n.
Osgot 'Digera', punished in miracle of St
   Kenelm 72–3, 75n.
Osmund, bishop of Salisbury xli
Oswald, bishop of Worcester, arch-
   bishop of York cxi, 50, 57n.
Oswald, king of Northumbria 38–9

Pailton, Warwicks., miracle at 76
passionals, *see* legendaries
passiones, see *Vitae, passiones*
Paulton, Somerset 76n.
Penda, king of Mercia xlviii, clxiif., 94–
   5, 96–7, 98, 102, 114n.
Pentridge, Dorset, church dedicated to
   St Rumwold cliii
Perryford, Glos., struggle over St
   Kenelm's relics at 68–9
Pershore, abbey of cxx
Peter and Paul, SS, homily for feast of
   liii, 2–3
Peter des Roches, bishop of Winchester
   lxxiv

Pilton, Somerset 76n.
puer senex topos clxix

Ramsey, Hunts.: abbey of xxxv, xliv,
   xlvii, xcvi, cxii, cxvif., cxxiif.
   abbots of, *see* Ælfwine; Herbert
   Losinga; Wythman
Ranulph Higden, author of *Polychronicon*
   cxxxviii
Reading, abbey of cxxviii
relics xliii, xlvin.
   of St Birinus lxi, lxxin., lxxii–lxxiv
   of St Kenelm cxivn.
   of St Rumwold cxliiif.
Remigius, bishop of Dorchester and
   Lincoln cl
rhyming prose l, xcif., clxvi
Richard of Cirencester cxxxviiif., 52n.
Rochester, priory of xxv, clviiif.,
   clxxviif.
Roger of Wendover, monk of St Albans
   cxxxviif.
Romaldkirk, N. Yorks., church dedicated
   to St Romald cliv
Rombaut/Rumold, St, of Mechlin cxliv,
   clif., cliv, clvi, clviii
Rome 2–3, 64, 86
Romsey, Wilts., abbey of lxxxii, clxxix
Romsley, Glos., well of St Kenelm 63n.,
   68n.
Rood of Grace, at Boxley abbey clvi–
   clviii
Roscarrock, Nicholas clxxx
royal martyrs xlii, cxiii
Rumboldswyke, Sussex cliii
Rumold, St, *see* Rombaut
Rumwold, St: baptism of clxx, 100–3,
   135–8
   churches dedicated to cli–cliv
   in liturgy cxl–cxlii
   popular cult cxliv–cxlvi, cxlvii–cl,
   cliv–clvi, clix
   holy wells cxlvi, clxviii, clxi
   identity of his parents clxii–clxiv
   image of clvi–clviii
   origin of name 99n.
   sermon preached by 104–12

Sackett, John, vicar of Folkestone clv
sacramentaries: Gelasian sacramentary
   4n.
   'Missal' of Robert of Jumièges lxiiif.,
   36–7n.